SIGMUND FREUD'S
CHRISTIAN
UNCONSCIOUS

Sigmund Freud's Christian Unconscious

PAUL C. VITZ

WILLIAM B. EERDMANS PUBLISHING COMPANY
GRAND RAPIDS, MICHIGAN

Gracewing. LEOMINSTER, ENGLAND

This paperback edition published 1993 in the United States by
Wm. B. Eerdmans Publishing Co.,
255 Jefferson Ave. SE, Grand Rapids, Michigan 49503,
and in the U.K. by Gracewing,
2 Southern Avenue, Leominster, HR6 0QF.

Printed in the United States of America

Library of Congress Cataloging-in-Publication Data

Vitz, Paul C., 1935–
    Sigmund Freud's Christian unconscious / Paul C. Vitz.
        p.   cm.
    Originally published: New York: Guilford Press, c1988.
    Includes bibliographical references and index.
    ISBN 0-8028-0690-2 (pbk.)
    1. Freud, Sigmund, 1856–1939 — Religion. 2. Freud, Sigmund,
1856–1939 — Psychology. 3. Freud, Sigmund, 1856–1939 —
Childhood and youth. 4. Psychoanalysis and religion.
5. Catholic Church — Influence. I. Title.
[BF173.F85V57   1993]
150.19′52′092 — dc20
[B]   92-38838
                                                          CIP

Gracewing ISBN 0 85244 232 7

In memory of my father
CARL VITZ
1883–1981

ACKNOWLEDGMENTS

This book, more than anything else that I have worked on, is deeply indebted to the scholarly contributions of others. It is a pleasure to acknowledge these debts as best I can.

My first obligation is to the memory of the psychoanalyst Gregory Zilboorg, whose book *Psychoanalysis and Religion* (1962) started me thinking about Freud and Christianity in early 1976. It was Zilboorg's writings that gave me the first glimpse of the importance of the present topic, and suggested there was much more to discover. I also acknowledge Professor Philip Rieff's *Freud: The Mind of the Moralist* (1979). This work was a major influence for it allowed me to understand Freud primarily as a great "negational symbolist."

My single greatest debt is to Peter Swales, a self-trained historian and Freud scholar extraordinaire. Swales is a kind of Sherlock Holmes whose relentlessly collected historical evidence, combined with historically based arguments, is in the process of changing the basic understanding of Freud's personal life and its relevance to his theory. When I first spoke with Swales, in 1980, he had already understood the importance of literature for a basic grasp of Freud's thought, and he facilitated my appreciation of this important influence on Freud. Also, it was Swales who informed me of the probable significance of *Walpurgisnacht* and especially of cocaine for understanding Freud's "pact" with the Devil. In short, my discussion of these two ideas derives from Swales's earlier insights. (My perspective on and interpretation of these events are, however, quite different from those to be proposed by Swales.)

The various articles in which Swales's own viewpoints are developed are essential for anyone interested in the broader context of this book, and I highly recommend them. Unfortunately, most of these articles are not widely available; however, some of his work will be accessible in his forthcoming book, *Wilhelm Fliess: Freud's Other*. He is presently working on another book, focused on Freud, Rome, Minna Bernays, and the Anti-Christ; when published, this will bring his research on the connections of these important subjects to a wider audience.

An additional debt to Swales is that he has always been generous with his detailed scholarly expertise. There is nothing more frustrating, at least for me, than the problem of the lost footnote. Nine times out of ten when I asked him, he knew what I was looking for or where to find it. Even when I had to continue my search, Peter's friendly reception of my inquiry was greatly appreciated.

There are others to whom I owe much. Here in the Psychology Department at New York University, Professor Robert Holt has read and commented on my work at various stages. I have benefited often from his insightful comments. I am especially grateful to Professor Harry Bober who in his usual gracious and scholarly manner first filled me in on the cultural significance of *Walpurgisnacht* and on a number of art history issues raised in the course of this work.

Dr. Marianne Krüll's book *Freud und sein Vater* (1979; recently published in English as *Freud and His Father*, 1986) has been of great help. In addition, she has generously given her own personal comments on my final draft. The Dutch psychologist Dr. G. J. M. van den Aardweg read Chapters 4 and 5, and I appreciate his remarks on Freud's relationship to the Devil. I would also like to acknowledge the helpful and stimulating comments of a young clinical psychologist and former student of mine, John Gartner.

Two Czech scholars have been quite helpful—for, as the reader might imagine, getting information about daily life in mid-19th-century Moravia (in Czechoslovakia) is not easy. Here most of what I know has come from two native-born Czechs who were always gracious and generous with their time: Professor Jindrich Zezula of New York University, and Professor Sidney Rutar of St. Francis College, Brooklyn. In addition, I would like to acknowledge a student of mine, Fred Drobin, now a psychotherapist, whose thesis on Freud, written under my direction, was very helpful. Others, colleagues and friends, who have contributed helpful comments and suggestions are James Blight, Professor Armand M. Nicholi, Jr., and Professor Robert Sollod.

A positive personal source of support was Dr. Karl Menninger. Though we have never met, his reading of drafts of this book, his suggestions, and his encouraging letters have been greatly appreciated. Professor Paul Roazen has also been helpful, and his book *Freud and His Followers* (1975) has been indispensable.

I would like to list other scholars and their books that have proved of special relevance for me. I only hope I do them justice in the text and footnotes. These are, in alphabetical order: David Bakan, *Sigmund Freud and the Jewish Mystical Tradition* (1958); John Bowlby's trilogy,

ACKNOWLEDGMENTS

Attachment and Loss (1969, 1973, 1980); Robert Byck (Ed.), *Cocaine Papers by Sigmund Freud* (1974); Ernst Freud, Lucie Freud, and Ilse Grubrich-Simitis (Eds.), *Sigmund Freud: His Life in Pictures and Words* (1978); John E. Gedo and George H. Pollock (Eds.), *Freud: The Fusion of Science and Humanism* (1976); Alexander Grinstein, *Sigmund Freud's Dreams* (1980); Ernest Jones's three-volume *The Life and Work of Sigmund Freud* (1953, 1955, 1957); Mark Kanzer and Jules Glenn (Eds.), *Freud and His Self-Analysis* (1979); Dennis B. Klein, *Jewish Origins of the Psychoanalytic Movement* (1981); Mortimer Ostow (Ed.), *Judaism and Psychoanalysis* (1982); Théo Pfrimmer, *Freud, Lecteur de la Bible* (1982); Carl E. Schorske, *Fin-de-Siècle Vienna* (1980); Max Schur, *Freud: Living and Dying* (1972); Jack J. Spector, *The Aesthetics of Freud* (1972); Frank J. Sulloway, *Freud, Biologist of the Mind* (1979); and Gaston Vandendriessche, *The Parapraxis in the Haizmann Case of Sigmund Freud* (1965).

I would also like to thank Madeleine Tress and Ellen Paritz at NYU who have helped appreciably in the preparation of the manuscript. In addition it is a pleasure to acknowledge my editors at Guilford Press, Seymour Weingarten and Maxine Berzok, who have been a steady and very professional source of support for this project.

A last and most important acknowledgment is to my wife, Timmie, and our six children. I believe it was Daniel, some years ago, who first asked, "Mommy, why does Daddy always talk about Freud?" I hope this book both answers that question and will allow family life to move on to new and (at least from their point of view) more interesting topics.

PREFACE

This book is an extended biographical essay on Sigmund Freud's little-known, life-long, deep involvement with religion, primarily Christianity and in particular Roman Catholicism. This topic should be of serious interest to at least two major groups of readers. First, there are those people, among whom I often count myself, who have an interest in or more typically a fascination with Freud's life and thought. Such people may love him or hate him—in true Freudian fashion, they usually do a good deal of both—but they find that in their attempts to understand and cope with the modern period, there is no denying his centrality, complexity, and greatness. Such readers, being generally familiar with the large literature on Freud, need an explanation of why this new book is worthy of their attention. My reply is that there is at present no other systematic, biographical treatment of Freud's relationship with Christianity, in spite of its importance. Beyond that, all I can do is promise that much of the material and most of the interpretive framework presented here is new and, I hope, challenging.

The other group of potential readers consists of those, among whom I always count myself, who are interested in psychology and religion and in the great conflict that has raged between them for the last 100 years and more. In this struggle, Freud's critique of religion certainly has been the best known and the most widely influential. Hence, it is no surprise these days to hear the comment, as I did recently, "Didn't Freud disprove religion?" However overstated and oversimplified, such a remark captures the general impact of Freud's thought for countless educated people today.

But how can a biographically focused treatment of Freud be addressed to readers concerned with the larger issue of the conflict between psychology and religion? Here it is necessary to recall that Freud's critique was a psychological one. That is, he argued that religion is untrustworthy because it is based on a person's childish needs and wishes. These desires, mostly of an unconscious kind, are in turn heavily influenced by early neurotic experience. In making such claims Freud was arguing *ad hominem*, or, if you will, *ad "biographicam"*; his attack was not aimed at the reasonableness of the beliefs themselves, but was instead an exposé of the unreasonableness of the presumed motives behind them. Thus Freud established the central relevance of a person's early life for an understanding of his later religious beliefs.

What I attempt to do here is to show how Freud's *anti*-religious beliefs and theories are to be understood as an expression of his own unconscious needs and traumatic childhood experiences. This explanation of Freud's rejection of religion is not an interpretation restricted only to him; the analysis is general enough to have applicability to the motives of many who reject God today.

So I urge the reader who is not otherwise directly interested in Freud's life to weigh carefully, nonetheless, the biographical evidence that constitutes the major part of the book. This biographical material, presented in Chapters One through Six, contains relatively little reference to the question of Freud's theories of religion. This procedure allows these chapters oriented toward Freud's life to be developed in depth and detail, and to stand on their own with respect to their claims. It is only in the Epilogue (Chapter Seven), where the theoretical significance of the biographical evidence is drawn out, that Freud's critique of religion is addressed directly. Thus, the purpose of this book is more than just to fill out the life history of Freud (however interesting it may be in its own right); rather, it is to show how the curious and sometimes traumatic events in the life of one small Jewish boy growing up in Central Europe over 100 years ago have cast a very long shadow over the religious life of the modern West.

CONTENTS

CONTENTS

CONTENTS

Chapter One

The First Three Years

THE STANDARD interpretation of Sigmund Freud is that he was a thorough enemy of religion, in particular of Christianity, and there is much well-known evidence that shows Freud in this light. After all, Freud did write that religion is a universal obsessional neurosis.[1] He said, too, that religious doctrines, psychologically considered, are illusions—that is, projections of infantile needs that comfort people unable to face suffering, uncertainty, and death.[2] Furthermore, Freud often developed his critical interpretations in major works in which he presented new psychological theories with which he attempted to justify his conclusions about religion.

Certainly Freud publicly proclaimed his religious skepticism, and all his biographers agree that he was an atheist or agnostic. For example, Ernest Jones, in his three-volume biography, has written that Freud "went through life from beginning to end as a natural atheist. . . . One who saw no reason for believing in the existence of any supernatural Being and who felt no emotional need for such a belief."[3] Freud's daughter Anna declared only a few years ago that her father was a "lifelong agnostic."[4]

The preceding picture is brought into further focus by the fact that Freud affirmed his ethnic and cultural Jewishness while living in an Austro-German culture during a time when anti-Semitism waxed and waned—but mostly waxed, and to the point of paroxysm. This anti-Semitism eventually forced Freud to leave Vienna toward the end of his life, after National Socialism (Naziism) rose to power. In short, Freud is commonly viewed as a secularized Jew who accepted his Jewish ethnic identity but rejected all things religious, including and especially Christianity; he is seen as a pessimistic free-thinker, an unrepentant atheist, a scientist–humanist, a skeptical realist.

The Thesis: Freud's Pro-Christian (and Anti-Christian) Unconscious

But in a state of curious coexistence with this standard image of Freud the atheist (and anti-Christian), there is another side of Freud. Many of his biographers, including Jones, have noted, at least in passing, a substantial number of pro-religious comments, concerns, and relationships scattered throughout Freud's life. Freud was, after all (for many years—indeed, until his death), very preoccupied with religious issues, as his important writings on religious topics make clear. He persistently, and in many ways obsessively, returned over and over to religion. For example, at the end of his *Moses and Monotheism* (1939), he came back to the same set of closely related issues he had treated much earlier in *Totem and Taboo* (1913).

Paul Roazen, biographer and Freud scholar, implies that Freud's feelings about religion were deeper and more ambivalent than he ever acknowledged. "Whenever Freud sounds intolerant, it is likely that something in him was threatened and he may have been more involved with the problem of religion than he cared to know."[5]

To the extent that Freud's involvement with religion was with Judaism, this issue has been extensively treated by several authors.[6] What primarily concerns us at present, however, is Freud's personal, often positive, relationship with Christianity. This topic has not been systematically addressed before.[7] The neglect is apparently due in part to an almost reflexive acceptance of the standard interpretation of Freud as anti-religious, and in part to the fact that many of Freud's letters and other biographical material have only recently become available. But it must be said that it is also due in part to the common lack of knowledge about and at times antipathy toward things Christian within contemporary psychological scholarship.

Despite this neglect, I think that even before beginning this discussion, the reader reasonably familiar with Freud's life and thought will grant upon reflection that Freud's relationship to religion—in particular Christianity—was not one of simple, uncomplicated rejection. He was a public atheist, but he was certainly not a simple, "natural atheist." In any case, it is the present thesis that Freud was deeply ambivalent about Christianity; such ambivalence requires at least two strong opposing psychological forces. Since much of the anti-religious character of Freud's life and thought is now well established and documented, the emphasis in this book is usually on the other side of the coin. Indeed, I develop the claim here that Freud had a strong, life-long, positive identification with and attraction to Christianity. I hasten to add, however, that an important secondary emphasis of this book is on Freud's little-known, unconscious hostility to Christianity, which is reflected in his curious preoccupation with the Devil, Hell, and related topics such as that of the Anti-Christ. All of this very substantial Christian (and anti-Christian) part of Freud should provide an understanding of his ambivalence about religion. It should also furnish a new framework for understanding major aspects of Freud's personality, and allow us (as already mentioned) to re-evaluate Freud's psychology of religion.

His Catholic Nanny: General Importance

Young Sigmund had a Catholic nanny or nursemaid at least until he was two years and eight months old: "I even retain an obscure conscious memory of her."[8] We will return shortly to the central importance of this woman, but first we need some background information.

Freud was born on May 6, 1856, in the small town of Freiberg in Moravia—a town that is now part of Czechoslovakia and called by its Czech name, Příbor[9] (see Figure 1-1). The town is 150 miles northwest of Vienna and about 12 miles from the border of present-day Poland.[10] At the time, Moravia was an especially devout Catholic region; devotion to the Virgin Mary was so pervasive that Moravia became known as a "Marian Garden."[11] It was famous for its pilgrimages and shrine churches devoted to the Virgin (and, to a lesser degree, to St. Anne, mother of the Virgin). Nemec reports that even today Moravia still has about 250 Marian churches, chapels, and outdoor shrines.[12] That is, Moravia is still Catholic in many respects, in spite of "fierce state repression"[13] by the Communist authorities.

Sigmund lived in this small Moravian town until he was three years old.[14] Sometime in 1859, probably in late spring or early summer, his family moved to Leipzig briefly, and then went on to Vienna in 1860, where Freud lived all but the last 15 months of his life. The town of Freiberg had a population of about 4500, over 90% of whom were Roman Catholic. About 3% of the Freibergians were Jewish, and a like number were Protestant.[15] The statistics for Vienna were similar, although there Catholics did not so fully outnumber other groups. As a result, Freud spent almost his entire life as a Jew in a society dominated by Roman Catholic culture. Any understanding of Freud and religion must always take into consideration this general situation.

During Sigmund's years in Freiberg, the Freud family lived on the second floor of a two-story house that was owned by the Zajic family.[16] The living arrangements are in part observable in Figure 1-2, which shows the house in which Freud was born and lived during this period. The Zajics, who had lived in the town for generations, ran a locksmith business out of a workshop on the first floor; the upper floor, consisting of two large rooms (one on each side), was used for living quarters.

Figure 1-1. Freiberg (Příbor) in Moravia, Czechoslovakia, Freud's birthplace. Town is shown from a distance. (Mary Evans/Sigmund Freud Copyrights)

Figure 1-2. The house in Freiberg where Sigmund Freud was born and where he lived until the age of three. The Freud family lived in the upstairs room on the right. (Mary Evans/Sigmund Freud Copyrights)

Jakob, Sigmund's father, Amalia, his mother, and the children lived in one of the rooms, and the Zajics lived on the other side.[17]

The fact that the Freuds lived in one room obviously means that they were far from well-to-do. It does not, however, imply real poverty either; after all, they had a nanny, and (as we will see) Amalia was able to travel with the nanny to a spa. The most accurate words to characterize the family's financial situation are "lower-middle-class" and "struggling." As we will see, there is no doubt that for many years Sigmund was acutely aware of his relative poverty. His friends, colleagues, fellow students, and mentors were almost always much better off than he. The absence of money would be a constant frustration to his aspirations as a young man.[18]

The name of the nanny is of interest. There is documentary evidence that her name was Resi Wittek—namely, an old record of a registration at the spa town of Roznau.[19] The registration, in German, is dated June 5, 1857, and it reads in translation: "Amalia Freud, wool trader's wife (spouse) with the child Sigmund and female servant Resi Wittek from Freiberg."[20] "Resi" is a common Czech short form of "Theresa," which was a reliably Catholic first name of the time and place.[21] Roznau, about

45 kilometers from Freiberg, was (and is) a place where people took the "cure," the "waters," for various ailments. Jones notes that Amalia, because of a tubercular condition, occasionally visited Roznau.[22]

It is also significant that the Emanuel and Maria Freud family lived about three or four blocks away[23]; as we will see, Sigmund often played with Emanuel and Maria's children, who were roughly his age. Emanuel Freud was Sigmund's much older half-brother; he was in his mid-20s and was the eldest son of Freud's father by an earlier marriage.[24] (Jakob Freud's first wife had apparently died.[25]) Philipp, another half-brother who was a year or two younger than Emanuel and was unmarried, lived even closer, in a house right across the street.[26]

Exactly when the Czech woman, Resi, began to function as young Sigmund's nanny is not certain, but her involvement clearly began quite early in his life. Freud wrote that he was in his nurse's charge from some time "during my earliest infancy."[27] Besides the presence of Resi in June 1857, when Sigmund was just over a year old, inferences based on other historical facts support Freud's statement. In particular, Sigmund had a younger brother, Julius, who was born when Freud was about a year and five months old.[28] This child became sickly and died on April 15, 1858, when Freud was not quite two.[29] It is likely that Freud's mother would, of necessity, have been preoccupied with this second child, and that the nanny would have assumed a major maternal role for Sigmund by this time—probably earlier.

Freud's biographers agree that it is of significance that as an adult Freud recalled the psychological importance for him of the birth of this baby brother, Julius, and of his death[30]: "I welcomed my one-year younger brother (who died within a few months) with ill wishes and real infantile jealousy . . . his death left the germ of guilt in me."[31] Certainly this report suggests a situation in which Sigmund felt he was losing some of his mother's and possibly even some of his nanny's previously available attention. To make matters worse, the death of Julius was followed only seven and a half months later by the birth of a sister, Anna, on December 31, 1858.[32] And, of course, Amalia would have attended to the new child and nursed it, at least for some weeks afterwards. If we put all of this together, it becomes clear that Freud must have found his mother, Amalia, relatively unavailable to him from the time he was a little under a year old until he was close to three years old. After all, his mother was busy with two pregnancies and two births, and had a sick child who died during this time, while Sigmund was put in the charge of his nanny. There is no evidence that there was anyone else available to help the mother out. Freud's father, Jakob, worked elsewhere in the town and often traveled in the surrounding area buying wool.[33] There is, then, every reason to believe that the nanny filled the maternal vacuum during this important period, and that Freud experienced her as a second mother—or even (as we shall see) as his primary mother.

It is not clear where Julius was born, since there is no record of his birth in Freiberg. Since the births of the other Freud children were recorded in Freiberg, it is reasonable to assume that Julius was born elsewhere[34]—perhaps Roznau, or perhaps Vienna, the home of Amalia's family. It is relevant that Amalia had a brother named Julius, only a year or two younger than she, who lived in Vienna. However, he died of tuberculosis on March 15, 1858, one month before the baby Julius died.[35] Swales has suggested that, knowing her brother was ill, she went to visit him in Vienna while she was pregnant, and thus had baby Julius in Vienna. If so, she might easily have left young Sigmund with his nanny.[36] In any case, the death of her slightly younger brother and her baby, both named Julius, within a short time of each other must have been deeply disturbing for Amalia.

During the first 32 months of Sigmund's life (i.e., until Anna's birth), his mother was pregnant a total of 18 months. During pregnancy a mother's milk supply diminishes. Furthermore, the fact that his mother became pregnant so soon after Sigmund's birth (about five months afterward), and also soon after Julius's birth, strongly implies that she did not breast-feed or at least did not fully breast-feed very long after her children's births. It is rare for a woman to get pregnant while nursing her baby regularly during the first six months after giving birth.[37] In any case, it is unlikely that Sigmund was nursed by his mother for more than a brief period.

It is not entirely clear in the relevant texts whether the nanny was a wet nurse. She is sometimes described as "old," but she may have been only in her late 30s or early 40s (i.e., "old" relative to Freud's 21-year-old mother). There is no reference to any other wet nurse. Freud did describe her with the word "*Amme*," the German word for a nurse for very young children[38]; Mahony notes that *Amme* means "wet nurse,"[39] as does McGuire.[40] Therefore, it is likely that Resi was Sigmund's wet nurse.

Schur, in his biography of Freud, using the information of Sajner, has written that the Freud women frequently worked together in some kind of "garment district" warehouse, while the children were cared for by a maid.[41] (The maid was presumably the Czech nanny.) This also suggests that Freud's mother was often out of the home when not directly pre-empted by her pregnancies, and again underlines the importance of the nanny as a mother-figure. If so, Sigmund would have been almost exclusively with the nanny for many weeks during his earliest years.[42]

Freud himself directly acknowledged the foundational significance of the nanny for his character, in his letters to his friend Wilhelm Fliess— letters written when Freud was in his 40s, during his personal psychoanalysis. Insights from this self-analysis, which was the first psychoanalysis, formed the basis of Freud's great work *The Interpretation of Dreams*, published in 1900. About his nanny, Freud wrote in 1897 to Fliess:

My "primary originator" (of neurosis) was an ugly, elderly but clever woman who told me a great deal about God and hell, and gave me a high opinion of my own capacities. . . . If . . . I succeed in resolving my hysteria I shall have to thank the memory of the old woman who provided me at such an early age with the means of living and surviving. You see how the old liking breaks though again.[43]

Later, in *The Interpretation of Dreams*, he wrote (as noted earlier) that he even had a vague conscious memory of her. He added that "it is reasonable to suppose that the child [Freud] loved the old woman."[44] Additional evidence of the nanny's great importance is provided by another letter, in which Freud was commenting upon a recent dream: "The real meaning is that the old woman, the nanny, stood for me, and that the doctor's mother was my mother."[45]

These are most significant admissions, for if Freud's nanny did provide the basis of his early self-confidence and his first "means of living and surviving," she was his functional mother and therefore much more than just the origin of his neurosis (even though the "neurotic" properties of Freud's personality are extremely important for an understanding of him and of the origin and nature of psychoanalysis). His awareness of his love for her breaking through, and his comment that in the dream the nanny stood for himself, underscore the positive contribution of this old woman to Freud's personality with particular clarity: In a fundamental sense, she was a parent (an originator), a mother, to him. It is the basic positive significance of the nurse that other commentators have neglected. Furthermore, it should be kept in mind that Freud nowhere made such claims about the *early* importance of his own mother. Indeed, this lack of evidence further supports the present view that the nanny was the primary mother.

His Nanny: Importance for Religion

What we must look at is whether this woman influenced Freud's understanding of religion, and, if so, how. Here again, the letters of Freud provide direct evidence. As quoted above, Freud noted that his nanny "told me a great deal about God and hell. . . ." A short time later, in the next letter, Freud picked up the same theme again, and wrote as follows:

I asked my mother whether she remembered my nurse. "Of course," she said, "an elderly woman, very shrewd indeed. She was always taking you to church [*in alle Kirche*—in all the churches; Freiberg, though small, had at least three

Catholic churches]. When you came home you used to preach, and tell us all about how God [*der liebe Gott*—the loving God] conducted His affairs." [German from the original letter.][46]

That the two- or three-year old Freud was always being taken to church would have been unusual even in most Christian homes at the time, although for a pious woman attendance at Mass several times a week would not have been unusual. For this to have occurred in a Jewish home, however liberal or secular, would have been quite striking. On such church visits, Freud almost certainly received an introduction to Christianity, a sort of elementary catechesis. How else to account for his ability to come home and preach sermons to his family?

Young Freud would have frequently experienced the special atmosphere of the Catholic Mass (see Figure 1-3). He would have seen paintings and statues of the Madonna and of the Madonna and Child, images of saints, and the like. He would have heard Latin; he would have watched the distribution of Holy Communion. He would have been taken to Mass during the seasons of Advent and Lent, with their penitential overtones and distinctive violet (or purple) colors in the robes of the priests and in the shroud over the cross in Lent. He would have experienced the Christmas season, and most especially he would have been taken to church for the two major holidays, Easter and Pentecost. These were by far the two greatest feasts of the Christian year in 19th-century Europe. In a small, devout Catholic town, these two celebrations would have involved the entire community.[47]

It would have been in church that Freud would most probably first have heard music: bells, organ, and instrumental music, as well as choirs and chants. (This was of course long before radio or any other modern technology of sound.) Music would have been an important part of the service. Czechoslovakia was renowned in the 18th and 19th centuries as the most musical country in Europe, and the regions of Moravia and Bohemia were especially known for their folk and church music.[48] The main church at Freiberg was famous, in its region, for its chimes. (The church had been renovated just a few years earlier.)[49]

In church he would have been in a large, dimly lit, and arching space (any church would seem large to a young child). The church would have flickered with the lights of candles, which were (and still are) commonly lit for the souls of the dead, or as prayers. It is very possible that Sigmund or his nanny may have lit a candle for the soul of his recently dead baby brother. It is almost certain that Freud and his nanny would have talked about the religious meaning of death. Zilboorg concurs in this by saying that she "consoled him, that his little brother who died would live again."[50] Certainly Heaven and Hell would have been natural topics. Ernest Jones apparently accepts this understanding of the situation, since

Figure 1-3. The main church in Freiberg, Mariae Geburt (The Nativity of Our Lady). (Lee Miller, Philadelphia)

he comments, "She [the nanny] implanted in him the ideas of Heaven and Hell and probably those of salvation and resurrection."[51] Jones says very little about Freud and Heaven and Hell, and he never documents or pursues further Freud's relation to salvation and resurrection. But, as is shown below, Freud indeed did have a lifelong involvement with all these very Christian ideas.

It should also be noted that there was no synagogue in Freiburg, and hence Freud was not exposed in these early years to any equivalent Jewish religious experience.[52] Nor is there any evidence that the Freuds celebrated the Jewish holidays, had regular Friday Sabbath meals, or kept the Jewish dietary laws in the Freiberg days. There is no reason to believe that Freud's mother gave him religious instruction; she is known to have been uninterested in religion. There is no certain support for it, but Jakob Freud probably said his prayers on Friday, thus providing some Jewish presence in the home.[53]

In any case, the nanny, this functional mother, this primitive Czech woman who was the "primary originator" of Freud, was his first instructor in religion. These first lessons were of a simple, no doubt often simple-minded, Catholic Christianity.[54]

What would the elements of this simple religious education have been? The basic components can be gathered from Freud's own words, from Jones's comments, and (as I indicate throughout the rest of this work) by certain Christian themes and actions that occurred throughout Freud's life. The basic concepts in Freud's religious unconscious were the following: God, *der liebe Gott* (this, of course, is in common with Judaism); Heaven and Hell and the Devil (all related to the notion of judgment); and also salvation and resurrection. These last two themes, it will be shown, were associated by Freud with Easter, the celebration of the resurrection of Christ, and with Pentecost or Whitsun, the celebration of the receiving of the Holy Spirit. For Freud, as in standard Christian doctrine, salvation and Heaven would have meant being saved from damnation and from Hell.

In addition, this very basic Christianity would have had a heavily Catholic character. Freud's experience of Christianity was in the distinctive environment of 19th-century Catholic piety. This would also have meant a heavily feminine Christianity for Freud, the female aspect being represented in his life by his devout nanny and also by the Marian emphasis so common at the time. Freiberg's main church was named after Mary's birth.[55] In the center of the town square was a statue of Mary[56]; such statues are very common throughout Austria and much of Czechoslovakia.[57] The cult of St. Anne (or Anna), the mother of Mary, was also extremely popular in Moravia. Anna was a common name, and many churches throughout the region were named after St. Anne.[58] No doubt Freud saw priests and heard occasional references to the Pope, but the strong masculine characteristics of Catholic Christianity would not have been an important part of Freud's childhood experience. In short, Freud's early religious experience had a basic Christian core, situated within a Catholic and feminine context.

For some reason, Jones denies that Freud's experience with his nanny contributed to Freud's neurotic attitude toward religion:

Much has been made of this nannie [sic] by writers who are eager to discover a neurotic origin for Freud's negative attitude towards religion. It is of course easy to weave conjectures and speculations on a theme of this sort, but I am not aware of any evidence that might justify one in attributing any lasting influence to the nannie's theological beliefs, and in any event the contact ceased at the age of two and a half. [Actually, the contact lasted longer; see below.][59]

This is a most curious statement, for what Jones is saying is that early childhood experience is insignificant in relation to adult behavior and personality.[60] Surely this is an amazing position for a psychoanalyst of the classical type to take. Jones's "unwillingness to weave conjectures" is all the stranger,[61] since Freud himself stated (as quoted earlier) that his nanny was essential to his neuroses. Indeed, even Jones declares in Volume 1 of his biography, "Freud has taught us that the essential foundations of character are laid down by the age of three and that later events can modify but not alter the traits then established."[62] One does not have to consider that this theory of character is universally true to accept that it was most certainly true for its originator.

One thing to keep in mind about Freud as a child is that he was attractive and precocious. Sajner reports that Johann Zajic, the landlord, years later recalled Sigmund in his Freiberg days "as a lively youngster who liked to play in the workshops and to make small toys out of metal scraps."[63] His genius for language has been remarked on by many (his German style is outstanding and is part of the power of his work), and apparently this gift was apparent from Freud's earliest childhood. Certainly a child who could give even some semblance of a sermon when aged only two and a half or so was already giving signs of very early conceptual ability and unusual verbal talent. As an adult, Freud was fluent in English and French. He was also moderately familiar with Spanish, Italian, Latin, and Greek.[64]

Freud also mentioned that he was able, during the period of his own psychoanalysis, to recover some of his memory for the Czech language, which he had not used since he left Freiberg roughly 40 years earlier.[65] (This would exclude a few short visits to Freiberg by Freud in his teens. At these times, he visited Jewish friends and spoke mostly German.[66]) For Sigmund, the world of the nanny would have been based on Czech (to some extent associated with Church Latin), while with his parents the language was German (and Yiddish). Language would have differentiated these two worlds rather sharply.

The Nanny: How Long Was She with Sigmund?

The nanny disappeared suddenly from Freud's life. She was dismissed, sometime after December 31, 1858, but before the family left Freiberg. The first thing to establish, then, is when the family of Jakob Freud left

Freiberg. According to a document describing him as a man of good standing, Jakob Freud was still in Freiberg on March 23, 1859.[67] Certainly for a family to migrate to a new city in winter or early spring just after the wife had had a new baby would seem most ill advised and unlikely.[68] It was a dismal time of year; the journey would have required a 12-mile trip by cart to the nearest train station, in Stauding (Studenka)[69]; and the family had had a baby die about a year earlier. It is therefore probable that they did not leave until somewhat later than March.

There is also a record of Amalia Freud already in Leipzig requesting a passport extension; this record is dated August 11, 1859.[70] Thus the Jakob Freuds clearly left Freiberg for Leipzig sometime between March 23 and August 11, and probably not until late spring or summer. Freud himself wrote in his *curriculum vitae* in 1885 that he was three years old when he left with his parents for Leipzig and then Vienna.[71] Also, he noted in 1899 in an autobiographical writing (*Screen Memories*) that he left his birthplace when he was a *"full* three years of age" [*"von voll drei Jahren habe ich nämlich meinen kleinen Geburtsort verlassen"*].[72] Both of these comments would mean that he left after May 6, his birthday. Krüll assumes that one of Freud's famous memories took place in Freiberg in middle to late spring of 1859, and this would imply that they were still there in May or early June of 1859.[73] I take all this to mean that the Jakob Freuds were in Freiberg until sometime between late May and late July at the latest. Evidence is given below to suggest an early June departure from Freiberg.

The next question to ask is this: When was the nanny dismissed? The standard answer, first proposed by Jones and uncritically accepted since then, is some time shortly after December 31, 1858. At this time (i.e., by January 6), Sigmund was already two years and eight months old, not two and a half, as Jones claims.

But I now propose a different and later date for the nanny's sudden removal from Freud's life. There are grounds for a psychological interpretation, presented later, involving Freud's emotional associations with Easter and especially Pentecost (Whitsun); these imply that the nanny vanished on or shortly after one of these important holidays, presumably in the spring of that year. In 1859, Easter was unusually late, occurring on April 24; Pentecost would have fallen seven weeks later, on June 12.[74] (Pentecost is 50 days after Easter, specifically seven Sundays after, and it usually falls in late May.) That Freud had his nanny until late May or early June, when he would have been just over three years old, is consistent with Freud's own comments and with Krüll's proposal that the family left Freiberg in the late spring or early summer of 1859.

The major piece of evidence used to date when the nanny was fired is the letter written by Freud to his colleague, Wilhelm Fliess, in October 1897 (part of which has been cited earlier):

I asked my mother whether she remembered my nurse. "Of course," she said, "an elderly woman, very shrewd indeed. She was always taking you to church. When you came home you used to preach, and tell us all about how God conducted His affairs. At the time I was in bed when Anna was being born" (Anna is two-and-a-half years younger) "she turned out to be a thief, and all the shiny Kreuzers and Zehners and toys that had been given you were found among her things. Your brother Philipp went himself to fetch the policeman, and she got ten months."[75]

This passage tells us why the nanny was dismissed, but not exactly when it happened. Read carefully, it can mean that when Amalia was home in bed with the newborn Anna, Sigmund would come home and preach. This was Christmas time—December 25 through January 6—and there would have been much in the church services to interest a child at this season. Then the letter says, "she turned out to be a thief." The expression is ambiguous and implies that at some unspecified later date, she turned out or was discovered to be a thief. It certainly does *not* necessarily mean that she was so discovered on or about December 31.

Another thing to remark about this passage's seeming to link December 31, 1858, with the nanny's dismissal is that although Freud was putting it in quotes, he was of course recalling a conversation with his mother. Thus the whole passage was a reconstruction of the original conversation. This conversation could easily have covered two separate ideas, the first being young Sigmund's coming home to preach to his mother (who was, for the time being, regularly at home in the week or two after Anna's birth), the second being "she turned out to be a thief." It would be natural in a reconstruction to have put these two ideas together, or even to have misunderstood that the mention of the discovery of the nanny's stealing right after the mention of his coming home to preach implied that the two events occurred at the same time.

It is relevant to note in this case that Amalia Freud was in her early 60s and recalling things that had happened almost 40 years before.[76]

There is also some good psychological evidence, based on one of Freud's memories, that places the nanny's dismissal in the late spring or early summer of 1859. It is now well established that Siegfried Bernfeld has conclusively proved that Freud's *Screen Memories* essay was an autobiographical report.[77] In this paper, Freud described the following scene:

I see a rectangular, rather steeply sloping piece of meadowland, green and thickly grown, in the green there are a great number of yellow flowers. . . . At the top end of the meadow there is a cottage and in front of the cottage door two women are standing : . . a peasant-woman with a handkerchief on her head and a nursemaid. Three children are playing in the grass. One of them is myself (between the age of two and three); the two others are my boy cousin, who is somewhat older, and his sister, who is almost exactly the same age as I am. We are picking the yellow flowers. . . . The little girl has the best bunch; and, as though by mutual agreement, we—the two boys—fall on her and snatch away her flowers. She runs up the meadow in tears and as a consolation the peasant-woman gives her a piece of black bread. . . . (We) hurry to the cottage and ask to be given some bread too. And we are in fact given some; the peasant-woman cuts the loaf with a long knife.[78]

From this description, first, it is fairly certain that a nanny was present (a "peasant-woman" or nursemaid); second, given that we consider this to be the report of an authentic memory, it is clear that it occurred in the late spring or in the summer. It is understood that the two other children are Freud's "cousins" (actually, his half-nephew and half-niece) John and Pauline. John was about a year older than Sigmund, while Pauline was younger than Freud. Krüll places this very important memory in the spring of 1859, and hence Freud was somewhat older than he remembered, as were the other two children.[79]

Thus, if the discovery of the thieving took place in May 1859 or a little later, Freud would have had his nanny until the age of three or so, and Freud's claim of her great importance thus makes more sense. Furthermore, the evidence described throughout much of the rest of this study of the emotional significance for Freud of Easter and Pentecost is also much more understandable if these holidays were associated by him with the loss of the nanny. (For example, the *Screen Memories* paper was itself written the week before Pentecost.) In short, if the nanny was suddenly dismissed in late May (or early June), the event would have provided a basis in experience for what I call Freud's "Easter–Pentecost complex." (For much more on this, see Chapter Three.)

Finally, it is clear that Freud connected the loss of his nanny with train travel and his leaving Freiberg, and thus it is likely that she disappeared only shortly before the family left Freiberg.

There are still other reasons to think that the dismissal occurred later than Christmas of 1858–1859. One is that there is no mention of another nanny during 1859, who, under the circumstances of the new baby, would most definitely have been needed. Another point to keep in mind is that early memories are often inexact with respect to dates. The order of old events is usually recalled correctly, but the "blank" intervals of time between events are frequently dropped out, thus collapsing important occurrences into a shorter time period. Indeed, this kind of error occurred in the immediately preceding letter to Fliess, dated October 3, 1897 (just 12 days before the letter under discussion). There Freud wrote as follows: ". . . later (between the ages of two and two-and-a-half) libido towards *matrem* was aroused; the occasion must have been the journey with her from Leipzig to Vienna, during which we spent a night together and I must have had the opportunity of seeing her *nudam* . . ."[80] This passage occurs right after the sentences quoted earlier about the nanny being his (Freud's) "primary originator," and it contains an error with respect to time. Specifically, the train journey from Leipzig to Vienna is known to have occurred when Freud was about three and a half, since the family moved to Vienna in late 1859 or 1860 after several months in Leipzig. At this time, Sigmund was three and a half or slightly older. This error, commonly noted by Freud's biographers,[81] is one of placing an event too early.

In summary, then, I believe there are excellent reasons to think that the nanny was dismissed some months after December 31, 1858, and that late May (or early June) is the most plausible time. (More evidence for the late May or early June time is given below in connection with Freud's associations to Pentecost.) And I also believe that the family left Freiberg shortly thereafter. Again, more evidence for this time of year is given in the later sections dealing with Easter and Pentecost.

Was His Nanny a Thief?

In fact, the entire episode of the nanny's alleged theft is strange. First, why would a woman acknowledged as shrewd be so foolish as to leave stolen coins in a readily discovered place or among her possessions? Did she hide them in the Freuds' one room? On her person? Then how account for the toys? Why not spend the coins quickly or at least hide them in a safe place? Also unusual is that Freud's mother said the nurse stole the toys, since these were also found among the coins. She might steal toys for members of her family,[82] but why keep several of them together with stolen money? All this is most odd, especially given the extreme likelihood that Freud's mother must have looked on the nanny with increasing jealousy and dismay. Here was this peasant woman who was in many ways taking over the role of a mother in the life of her lively and attractive first-born son. Not only was the nanny coming to be extremely important to her son's affections, but she was also taking him to church and instructing him in Christianity. Amalia Freud was never very serious about her own Judaism; still, there is certainly no reason to think she was benevolently disposed toward Christianity. Possibly, her young son's early training in Christianity aroused real concern. If so, this was a reason why the Freuds, in particular Amalia, would have wished to get rid of the nanny.

In addition, the issue of proving theft involving a nanny and her charge would have been immediately understood as difficult. Two- and three-year-old children have no concept of money, and frequently give coins to those they like. During the writing of this book, I often noticed that my own three-year-old son would ask occasionally for coins, especially shiny ones, and that just as often he would give coins to me. He also did the same with some of his caretakers. Thus, should a nanny be found with a bunch of coins, one might suspect her of theft, but making a legal case against her would be most difficult. A strong suspicion of theft might lead to a dismissal, but not to a jail term.

There is still another problem with the story of the nanny's theft and jailing. The Freuds were part of a very small number of Jews in Freiberg, most of whom were relatively recent immigrants from further East. To have publicly brought charges of stealing money against a local woman would have risked alienating the local population and stirring anti-Semitism.[83] Unless there were other issues involved, why create all this trouble and risk?

What is one to make of all this? One plausible interpretation is that the situation was something as follows: Amalia or Philipp did find a cache or collection of coins and toys, which led to a suspicion of the nanny and to her abrupt dismissal. It is also possible that Philipp went to the police or other authorities and discussed the matter. It is even possible that a penalty of ten months in jail came up when they talked things over. However, under the circumstances, there are reasons (discussed below) to doubt that the nanny was actually jailed for such a term. (The Freuds would not have been in Freiberg to verify it, since, at the very earliest, the nanny would have completed her ten months in November of that year, after they had left.) I suspect that the expression "ten months" became in Amalia's mind or in family tradition a reality instead of a hypothetical or maximum penalty.

On the other hand, it has been suggested that the whole story is fabricated or that the real situation has been very seriously distorted. It is clear that Amalia's memory was emotionally charged, and the facts as reported seem quite odd. It is possible that Amalia's anxiety over the religious impact of the nanny might have been enough to make her want the nanny dismissed on whatever charge she could find. There is, however, yet another completely different explanation of the nanny's dismissal, which derives from a recent thesis of Krüll. This possibility is not directly germane to our present focus on the nanny's religious significance, and hence it is postponed to the next chapter.

Was Freud Secretly Baptized?

Upon hearing about the clearly pious nature of the nanny, a number of people with whom I have spoken have raised an interesting question: Did the nanny secretly baptize Sigmund? (These have been people—Catholic priests, etc.—familiar with the mentality of devout Catholic women who care for children.) Many readers may not be aware that anyone who has reached the age of reason can baptize any unbaptized person, using any water that is at hand. This fact, however, was (and is) commonly known by devout Catholics.[84] The ritual need not be performed in church and can be done in five to ten seconds. Usually such informal or covert baptism is advised only in extreme circumstances, such as when death is imminent.

Several factors would have strongly predisposed Freud's nanny toward baptizing him. The death of Freud's younger brother Julius would have raised the issue in most concrete terms. For a devout Catholic woman of the time, the death of an unbaptized child who was close to her would have been a most disturbing tragedy. Czech culture has several familiar folk tales in which this occurs and the child's soul goes to Hell or leads an unpleasant life in a kind of limbo.[85] Either the nanny baptized the sickly and obviously dying Julius, thus establishing a precedent for her baptizing Sigmund, or she failed to baptize him, which would have aroused her fears. A Czech custom may have encouraged her as well. In Czech churches, it was traditional for baptismal water always to be present and visible in the baptismal bowl or font throughout the year. This water was commonly blessed on Holy Saturday (the Saturday before Easter).[86] In the dimly lit churches of the time, it would have the appearance of black or dark water. Such a possible covert baptism, in church or otherwise, may have had a lasting effect on Freud's memory; if the nanny had talked about the meaning of baptism, it would have left permanent traces. In any case, Freud in his attendance at services would most probably have witnessed and discussed the baptism of others.[87]

Whether Freud was covertly baptized must on the basis of present information remain unknown, but that this nanny was consciously trying to influence Sigmund with respect to becoming a Christian is virtually certain. Why else take the child so often to church? Why else instruct him so as to enable him to preach rudimentary sermons? The nanny could easily have felt that she had no greater gift to give her beloved charge than baptism.

To exemplify and underline something of the psychology of Freud's nanny, I relate a story told to me by a Roman Catholic priest of the New York diocese when I mentioned Freud's nanny to him. (This priest was one of the people who spontaneously raised the issue of a possible baptism.) The story is about the priest's own mother, who is still living but quite elderly. She arrived in New York City in the 1920s, a young girl fresh off the boat from Ireland. She was and still is a very devout Catholic. Her first job was as governess or nanny for a Jewish couple living in Greenwich Village. This couple had one child, a boy aged about three, when she started her job. Although her employers were of a Jewish background, they were then serious and active Communists, recently back from a trip to Russia. (The nanny recalls a visit to the home by Dorothy Day when she was still a Communist.) As such, the parents were strong atheists, and no religious instruction or environment was provided for the child. (The absence in Freiberg of any serious Judaism in Freud's home would have been a similar situation.) This young Irish nanny grew to love the boy very much, and because of this she could think of no better gift than to baptize him. She did this at home without the boy's being aware of it. The child, now grown up to be a prominent New York professional, presumably doesn't know to this day that he was baptized years ago. Just prior to the baptism, the family had had a dangerous automobile accident while traveling in New England with the nanny. No one had been injured, but the accident had raised the issue of the boy's possible death. This event, analogous to the death of Julius Freud, precipitated the concern on the nanny's part and resulted in her baptizing the child.

There is some interesting and relevant material bearing on this issue. Martin Freud (Sigmund's oldest son), in his autobiography, *Glory Reflected* (1957), a book that gives much information about the Freud home, has mentioned that his younger sister Anna had a nanny. This was in Vienna just at the turn of the century. Martin Freud, writing 60 years later, recalled her very well; even though this was his sister's nanny, he wrote, "Still, that nanny, Josefine, had great influence over me."[88] He continued:

My father [Sigmund] described his own nurse as an old and ugly woman, a Catholic, who used to take him to her church services in Freiberg, possibly with the idea of laying the early foundations of a conversion. I do not think for one moment that Josefine had any thoughts of this kind, but one day when I was with her alone, the other children being left at home for some reason I have forgotten, she took me into the nearby Votivkirche to a service. The church was crowded; the ceremonial was magnificent and colourful, and I was greatly impressed by the preacher: but I suspect Josefine's object was merely to sit down, not to impress a little Jewish boy with the splendor and dignity of a Catholic service. Possibly she needed spiritual food, and as she could not, or dared not, dump me anywhere, she towed me in behind her.[89]

Several comments are salient here. The expression, "possibly with the idea of laying the early foundations of a conversion," sounds very much as if the family, at least in retrospect, was suspicious about this with respect to Freud's nanny. In addition, rather surprisingly, the Sigmund Freuds had a serious Catholic nanny for their children, just as Freud had had himself. (Josefine was probably at Mass because it was a holy day of obligation.) Also noteworthy is that after 60 years, even this one visit to a Catholic service was still memorable for Martin Freud.

Apparently it was rather common for a nanny to have lasting effects on the life of the child in her charge. Sencourt, a friend and biographer of

T. S. Eliot, has made this point with regard to Eliot's Irish nanny, who "frequently talked to him about God."[90] Also, she often took the young future poet to Catholic services. This was in St. Louis, Missouri, where Eliot was born and grew up in an otherwise liberal environment of Unitarianism. Sencourt suggests that Eliot's later rejection of his family's religion and his conversion to the Church of England, with its then very strong Anglo-Catholic character, was in part determined by the effect of these early Catholic experiences on the impressionable young Eliot.[91]

Washed in the Blood of the Lamb

Those stimulating letters from Freud to Fliess contain a number of extremely curious comments, but perhaps none so strange as those he made in a letter of October 3–4, 1897. Here Freud wrote:

Last night's dream produced the following under the most remarkable disguises:
  . . . I saw the skull of a small animal which I thought of as a "pig" in the dream, though it was associated in the dream with your wish of two years ago that I might find a skull on the Lido to enlighten me, as Goethe once did. But I did not find it. Thus it was "a little Schafskopf." (literally a little "sheep's head;" figuratively, "blockhead") The whole dream was full of the most wounding references to my present uselessness as a therapist. Perhaps the origin of my tendency to believe in the incurability of hysteria should be sought here. Also *she* (the nanny) *washed me in reddish water in which she had previously washed herself* [emphasis added] (not very difficult to interpret; I find nothing of the kind in my chain of memories, and so I take it for a genuine rediscovery). A severe critic might say that all of this was phantasy projected into the past instead of being determined by the past. The *experimenta crucis* would decide the matter against him. The reddish water seems a point of this kind. Where do all patients derive the horrible perverse details which are often as alien to their experience as to their knowledge?[92]

What is one to make of these most unusual references? Apparently Freud's biographers have remained largely silent because of the obscurity of the passage, despite Freud's frustrating aside, "not very difficult to interpret." Confused silence was certainly my initial response. However, after reading a draft of the present text, a colleague and scholar of Freudian theory, Professor Robert R. Holt, has proposed a religious interpretation with which I agree.[93]

First, Holt makes the important observation that nowhere in the letter did Freud claim that he had recovered direct memories of actual early events. Instead, he was giving constructions or hypotheses, which, if true, would explain his dreams. But he was not giving the exact texts of the dreams themselves. Notice that he wrote, "Last night's dream produced the following under the most remarkable of disguises."

Holt focuses on the comment that the nanny washed young Sigmund in reddish water. Most people, when asked about this remark, interpret it to mean that Freud was somehow washed in water that had been colored by the nanny's menstrual blood; in other words, that this was literally water in which she had previously washed herself. Such an interpretation, however, opens up much more of a mystery than it solves. For, as Holt observes, why on earth would she have done such a thing? If one judges by contemporary attitudes of women somewhat comparable to this Moravian peasant, such an action seems extremely unlikely. It seems improbable that a pious Catholic woman, whose personal habits recommended her for a job of child care, would have allowed a little boy to get "contaminated" by her menstrual blood; menstrual blood is commonly considered unclean by simple people, and taboo for males.

Instead, Holt proposes that what Freud was reporting was a conflation of two sets of associations to blood: menstrual blood, and baptism as being "washed in the blood of the Lamb." Freud may indeed have had memories of seeing reddish water in which his nanny had washed herself. Remember that this was in the days before sanitary napkins, when the problem of menstruation for women was a far messier one than it is today: Rags were used, washed out, and reused. Generally they were left to soak in the bathroom in containers of cold water. All this may well have aroused intense curiousity in little Sigmund.

But Freud might also have another set of memories—of having been secretly baptized. And part of the explanation would have been that he was told that he had been "washed in the blood of the Lamb," as the nanny had been herself. They had been washed in the same water, which was also the blood of the Lamb.[94]

Freud's associations in this letter add support to this view. Just prior to his remark about the reddish water, he referred to the skull of a "little sheep"; a little sheep, of course, is a lamb. A skull is also often associated with the crucifixion of Christ, since it took place on Golgotha, which means "the place of a skull."[95] Many paintings of the crucifixion represent this with a skull somewhere on the ground near the foot of the cross.

A few sentences later, Freud used the expression *experimenta crucis*—that is, "the test of the cross"—to suggest that the memory of the reddish water was not a fantasy, but, rather, derived from an actual early experience. All of this implies that when he wrote that his nanny washed him in "water in which she had previously washed herself," Freud was referring to his covert baptism.[96]

It is worth pointing out, with respect to this interpretation, two things: First, the idea that Christ is "the Lamb of God who washes away the sins of the world" is a basic concept in Christian thought, repeated daily in the liturgy of the Mass. Second, and more specifically, a great deal of popular piety in the 19th century was deeply preoccupied with blood.

Almost every village in a devout area such as Moravia would have had at least one large public crucifix, almost always with Jesus shown bleeding from his head, hands, feet, and side. Thus, the blood of Christ, and Christ as the Lamb of God, would have been familiar to Freud as a child.

Freud's Response to the Loss of His Nanny

Whatever the reason, Freud's nanny was dismissed. She suddenly disappeared, and there is no question that Freud felt abandoned by his nanny. The threat of abandonment was the theme of his "casket" or "cupboard" memory, in discussing which he related the function of "screen memories." ("Screen memories" are consciously retrievable memories from childhood that rather frequently come to mind, and that cover, block, or screen a traumatic experience that occurred at the same time or slightly earlier.)

If the woman disappeared so suddenly . . . some impression of the event must have been left inside me. Where is it now? Then a scene occurred to me which for the last twenty-nine years had been turning up from time to time in my conscious memory without my understanding it. I was crying my heart out, because my mother was nowhere to be found. My brother Philipp . . . opened a cupboard for me, and when I found that my mother was not there either I cried still more, until she came through the door, looking slim and beautiful. What can that mean? Why should my brother open the cupboard for me when he knew that my mother was not inside it and that opening it therefore could not quiet me? Now I suddenly understand. I must have begged him to open the cupboard. When I could not find my mother, I feared she must have vanished, like my nurse not long before. I must have heard that the old woman had been locked, or rather "boxed" up.[97]

Obviously, he was anxious and fearful over his nanny's disappearance, a disappearance that he did not understand (he was, after all, only three years old). Even if he had understood, it would have made little difference to his feeling of great loss.

Thus, the nanny, Freud's functional mother during his crucial first three years—this woman who provided him with his "means of living and surviving" (or what Freud and many of his followers would call "ego-strength"); who gave him his first lessons in religion; whom he loved as only a young child can love; and to whom he may have given his money and toys—suddenly abandoned him at a most impressionable age. He heard that she had been locked up, but only much later did he understand that it was for stealing from him. In short, Freud's earliest, most basic experience of religion was connected to his earliest emotional attachment: It was traumatic; it was Catholic; and, as we shall see, it was the source of great ambivalence.

Freud and Separation Anxiety

The disappearance of the nanny would have precipitated a now widely acknowledged elementary and powerful anxiety known as "separation anxiety." In my discussion of separation anxiety, I depend heavily on the work of John Bowlby and his conceptualization of the origin and consequences of this anxiety. I use Bowlby because his trilogy, *Attachment and Loss*, is already recognized as the classic statement on separation anxiety, and as a significant contribution to the psychology of childhood in general. It is equally helpful that Bowlby writes out of a psychoanalytic background, in which he ties his concept of separation anxiety into Freud's theoretical writing on anxiety.[98]

Before proceeding, perhaps I should make it clear that I do not intend to argue that Freud suffered from anything like a debilitating case of separation anxiety. I do believe, however, that Freud had a moderate and significant degree of separation anxiety. But let us first take up Bowlby's definition of this condition.

The prototypical separation anxiety is the intense anxiety generated in the child by separation from its mother or mother-figure. The loss may be temporary, as when the mother leaves for a few weeks, or permanent, as when brought on by her death. A crucial period during which such separation can have most profound and enduring effects is in early childhood—which for Bowlby, as for Freud, means the first four or five years.[99] Freud, of course, attached a similar importance to this period; in particular, Freud wrote that "the periods between the ages of two and four seem to be the most important."[100]

When a child is separated from its mother, the anxiety response goes through three stages, only the first of which is properly called separation anxiety, although all three reactions are closely related to each other. The first phase, "protest," is found to raise the problem of anxiety; the next, "despair," raises the issues of grief and mourning; and the last, "detachment," raises the issue of defense.[101]

The first phase of protest is probably familiar to anyone who has observed and reflected upon the vigorous way in which children so often protest when their mothers leave them, or when they are left in a new place (such as a hospital or even a nursery school). Bowlby's research and writings powerfully document the frequently long-term effects of such separations when they are permanent or repeated throughout childhood. One case cited by Bowlby is especially relevant: a 1919 report by Helene Deutsch on a little boy who was brought up by nannies because his mother was working.

When he was just two years old his first nurse left and was replaced by a second. Despite the fact that he remained at home and that his mother was there every evening, the behavior he showed after his familiar nurse's departure conforms to pattern. On the night of her going he cried a great deal, was sleepless, and insisted on his mother remaining with him. Next day he refused to let the new nurse feed him, and he reverted to being wet and dirty. During each of the subsequent four nights his mother had to stay with him and to assure him of her love, and his daytime behavior continued disturbed. Not until the sixth day did much of his behavior return to normal and not until the ninth day did he appear to be himself again. Although there was clear evidence that he was missing his familiar nurse, he never once again mentioned her by name and seemed reluctant in any way to refer to her absence.[102]

Bowlby very effectively establishes the importance of separation anxiety as a major factor in childhood and adult pathology, and he also shows that Freud himself eventually came to a very similar interpretation of the origin of our most basic anxiety. Bowlby summarizes his case[103] by noting that Freud first linked separation and anxiety in a very brief discussion in *Three Essays on the Theory of Sexuality* (1905). Here Freud gave the topic only one paragraph, and he wrote: "Anxiety in children is originally nothing other than an expression of the fact that they are feeling the loss of the person they love."[104] In 1917, in his *Introductory Lectures on Psycho-Analysis*, he again linked anxiety (in this case, infantile anxiety) with separation, in a three-page development. As Bowlby summarizes it, "a child missing 'The sight of a familiar and beloved figure— ultimately his mother' [is] the 'situation which is the prototype of the anxiety of children.'"[105]

But it was not until his major late work *Inhibitions, Symptoms and Anxiety* (1926) that Freud accorded separation the central place in what was to be his final theory of anxiety. Freud concluded then: "Missing someone who is loved and longed for . . . [is] the key to an understanding of anxiety."[106] Although earlier he had often postulated links between sexuality and anxiety, Freud ended up focusing on separation as the prototypical anxiety experience. (It is interesting to note, in this connection, that in his discussions of separation Freud tended to hedge the use of the actual word "mother," using vaguer terms—e.g., "beloved figure," "the person they love.")

Let us take it as established that separation anxiety is extremely important to the understanding of personality and that it is caused by separation, primarily in childhood, from the mother or mother-figure. What concrete evidence is there that Freud suffered from any degree of anxiety of this sort? Let us go back over some things we have looked at earlier: First, Freud described his nanny as the originator of his neuroses; second, his nanny, his "loved one," disappeared suddenly; third, he uncovered this in his own psychoanalysis—in particular, he remembered a scene (the "casket scene") in which he was "crying my heart out."[107] There is already, then, substantial evidence for the nanny's being linked to the emergence of a separation anxiety in Freud. There are other examples as well.

Freud's Travel "Phobia" and Separation Anxiety

Biographers have commonly referred to Freud's so-called travel phobia. At the time, travel was generally by train, and thus Freud's fear was centered on an irrational avoidance of train travel. This fear (*Reisefieber*) was especially active, according to Jones, in the years 1887–1899, a period that included Freud's own difficult self-analysis.[108] Freud directly connected his travel fear with his suddenly leaving Freiberg, traveling by train to Leipzig, and then shortly afterward moving to Vienna.[109]

Jones, paraphrasing Freud, writes: "On the trip from Freiberg the train passed through Breslau, where Freud saw gas jets for the first time; they made him think of souls burning in hell!"[110] The visual appearance of such gas lights in the city or in a dimly lit train station would have been very similar to the experience in a church of candles lit for the souls of the dead. The religious comment and imagistic associations for Hell (and, implicitly, of death and judgment) are obviously Christian, and are hard to account for on any other basis but the nanny. (This is also the conclusion of Suzanne Bernfeld and of Grigg.[111])

Now Freud's fear of train travel was not a true phobia, as evidenced by the fact that once Freud actually got on a train and began to travel, the fear became markedly less or disappeared entirely. In fact, Freud liked to travel and spent much time doing it and enjoying it. (A true phobia becomes *more* intense as a person comes closer to the feared object or situation.) Instead, Freud's anxiety was much like the standard separation anxiety shown by many children in their fear of going to school.

Bowlby and others have made it clear that such fears are frequently an expression of the child's fear of separation from the mother or mother-figure.[112] It is not school or the like that is feared, but separation. In this case, obviously, what Freud feared was separation from the nanny who had suddenly disappeared. Little Sigmund may well have expected to see her again; even if she was indeed locked up, she would eventually be let out. But the Freud family left Freiberg shortly afterward, and this would have killed Freud's hopes of being reunited with his nanny. And indeed he never did see her again.

The actual reasons for the departure of the Freud family from Freiberg are not known. It has been suggested that because of investment losses in South Africa, prospects did not look good in this small town.[113] This is possible, but even if so it does not explain why the Freuds left Freiberg or why the family split up. In general it was, in fact, a good time for business, and the Jewish friends of the Freuds, all of whom stayed, did quite well.[114] Jones has implied that anti-Semitism was a factor, but this suggestion has been rebutted thoroughly by several authors.[115] An explanation for the departure is presented in the next chapter.

It should always be kept in mind that, in addition to sorrow and mourning, part of the psychological response to separation is great anger at the mother-figure for leaving. Thus anger and mourning, along with his attachment and love, would have become part of Freud's association to the nanny and all she stood for. Bowlby gives many examples of the anger set up by separation experiences and the subsequent anxiety.[116] Perhaps the most dramatic and poignant are cases such as that of an adolescent boy who murdered his mother and afterward exclaimed, "I decided she would never leave me again."[117]

The importance of this separation experience for Freud is summarized by Suzanne Bernfeld in her essay on Freud's early life, when she writes about the move from Freiberg that "this simple geographic change was a catastrophe for Freud and he spent the next forty years of his life trying to undo it."[118] The material presented below shows that Freud never did undo it, and that his nanny and his early Freiberg days would haunt him not just for the next 40 years, but for the rest of his life.[119]

The Theme of the Two Mothers

Freud's biographers have noticed many things about him, but with rare exceptions they have overlooked Freud's lifelong preoccupation with great figures who had two mothers. (An exception is Gedo, who in one article does draw attention to the "two mothers" theme in Freud's life[120]; another who notes this is Spector, who brings up the issue of two mothers with specific reference to Freud's interpretation of Leonardo da Vinci.[121])

Certainly, one famous figure with two mothers is Oedipus, whose story served as the basis for Freud's most distinctive and best-known contribution to personality theory, the Oedipus complex. The interesting point, for us, is that Oedipus has two mothers: his biological mother, Jocasta, and his functional mother, Merope. Jocasta, informed of the prediction that her newborn son would one day kill his father, has the baby Oedipus taken by a servant to be exposed in the nearby mountains. Instead of leaving the baby to die of exposure, the servant takes pity on him and gives him to a peasant, who in turn, takes the child to his master, Polybos, the King of Corinth. He is brought up in Corinth at the court by the King and the Queen, Merope. The tragedy *Oedipus Rex* itself focuses emphatically on the ambiguous parentage of Oedipus. Indeed, the powerful lines of the seer, addressed to Oedipus in Scene One, haunt the entire play: "Who are your mother and father?: Can you tell me?" And these questions are posed by Oedipus himself a few lines later: "My parents again! Wait: who are my parents?"[122]

Another great personality who never ceased to attract and intrigue Freud was Moses. It is agreed by Freud's biographers that in many respects Freud identified with this great Old Testament figure.[123] Freud was particularly fascinated by Michelangelo's statue of Moses, which Freud acknowledged as the work of art that most powerfully affected him; he studied it extensively, and finally discussed it in his now famous essay, *The Moses of Michelangelo* (1914a). Freud had a life-long interest in Moses, and, of course, his last great work, *Moses and Monotheism* (1939), was a book-length treatment of this great figure.

According to the Old Testament account, young Moses was the son of a Hebrew couple who was taken care of by his natural mother for three months until it was no longer safe to do so: The Pharaoh had decreed that all male Hebrew babies were to be killed. The baby was then put in a basket and set in the river where it was found, at its edge, by the Pharaoh's daughter, who kept and raised him. Through a ruse, Moses's natural mother nursed him for some time afterwards. But the eventual outcome was that his natural mother "brought him to Pharaoh's daughter, and he became her son; and she named him Moses."[124] In short, Moses had two mothers: a biological mother, who was a Hebrew, and a functional mother, who was Egyptian.

Thus, the two most important "theoretical" characters for Freud, throughout his life, were both deeply involved in situations of ambiguous parentage. Both had two mothers, one primarily biological and one functional, just as he had.

The "two mothers" theme becomes all the more interesting when we consider Freud's treatment of still another great historical character in his essay *Leonardo da Vinci and a Memory of His Childhood* (1910a). In this work, Freud presented the world's first psychoanalytic interpretation of a painting. The painting in question is Leonardo's *The Virgin and Child with St. Anne* (see Figure 1-4). As its title indicates, this well-known work contains the three figures St. Anne (Anna), the Virgin Mary (Maria), and the baby Jesus, who is holding a lamb. The problem that this painting raised for Freud is that the two women are both painted as young. Why should St. Anne be represented as young when, as Jesus's grandmother, she clearly had to be older then her daughter, Mary? (Also, Christian tradition holds that Anne was quite old when she conceived Mary.) Freud answered this question as follows:

The picture contains the synthesis of the history of his childhood. The details of which are explainable by the most intimate impressions in Leonardo's life. . . .

Figure 1-4. Leonardo da Vinci, *The Virgin and Child with St. Anne.* (Alinari/Art Resource, NY)

Leonardo's childhood was precisely as remarkable as this picture. He has had two mothers, first, his true mother, Caterina, from whom he was torn away when he was between three and five, and then a young and tender stepmother, Donna Albiera, his father's wife.[125]

Clearly, Freud's interpretation of Leonardo fits perfectly with his own childhood. Caterina, a peasant woman, was the older and "his *true* mother," from whom he was "torn" shortly after he was three years old in order to be placed with the young and more aristocratic stepmother,

Donna Albiera, the wife of the much older Piero da Vinci (who represents Jakob, in Freud's projected interpretation).

In support of this understanding, Spector identifies the very subjective, personal involvement of Freud in his Leonardo interpretation.[126] Working from Jones[127] (who also notices that Freud had a clear autobiographical involvement with this painting), and from the art historian Schapiro,[128] Spector notes that Freud minimized the importance of Leonardo's father and made the abandoned older mother the decisive influence.[129] Spector shows that Freud did this in spite of good evidence, *of which Freud was aware*, that Leonardo's father was, in fact, probably a very early and important presence in the artist's life.[130] Spector links Freud's nanny to the theme of the two mothers and suggests that the St. Anne figure is a symbol for the nanny. Spector's analysis also implies that for Freud, his own father was somehow not that important in the Freiberg years, being instead rather distant or "out of the picture," as Freud supposed Leonardo's father had been.[131] One remaining point: Freud's autobiographical identification with this painting also very definitely means that in some sense he viewed himself as the baby Jesus. After all, from Freud's viewpoint, Jesus also had an ambiguous paternity and (in the painting) two mothers.

Reviewing these three examples of "two mothers," we see that in the story of Oedipus, the biological mother is the one who is enmeshed in her son's painful fate; that is, the biological mother is the "problem" mother. In *Moses and Monotheism*, Freud's central thesis was that Moses was an Egyptian and not a Jew. Since Freud on occasion spoke of himself as Moses, and all agree he often identified with Moses, a most straightforward interpretation of this identification is that in it Freud was denying his own Jewishness (at least his religious Jewishness) and identifying with Egypt. In any case, Freud was again viewing the biological mother as the problem; he also implicitly was endorsing the functional (non-Jewish) mother as the true mother. Finally, in Leonardo's case, there was a direct preference for the older peasant mother, Caterina, over the "young tender stepmother, Donna Albiera," a representation of Amalia. In short, "see how the old liking breaks through."[132]

Freud's First "Anna," or What Was the Nanny Called?

The name of the nanny, as already mentioned, was Resi (Theresa) Wittek. This name is *not* how she would have been referred to by young Freud or by members of his family, however. It is safe to assume that she was called "*Amme*" by the members of Sigmund's family, since this is the common German name for a such a woman in the home, and since this was the name Freud himself once gave her.[133] In this connection, it is important to note that Freud's mother's name, Amalia, is phonetically very similar to "*Amme*"; certainly she must have been called "mama" often, and "*Amme*" and "mama" are quite close.

But this peasant woman would have spoken Czech exclusively, and this would have been the language used with the children. The customary Czech name for such a woman is "Nana," which is one of the most frequent variants of the name "Anna."[134] That is, "Nana" is both the popular Czech equivalent for "Nanny," and also one of the popular nicknames for Anna. Therefore, "Anna" and "Nana" are in the case of a nanny inextricably connected. This use of "Nana" is documented as especially typical of Moravia.[135] "Nana" is obviously an analogue to the English "Nanny," which is itself a variant of the name "Anne." Apparently Anne or Anna, the grandmother of Jesus, became a widely used word for a mother substitute. If the actual grandmother had been the nanny, she would probably have been called "Nana"; otherwise she may have been called "Anna."[136] Both words are very close in sound, and even if "Anna" was not used, "Nana" is quite similar.

No wonder Freud was drawn to Leonardo's painting of Anne (Anna), Mary (Maria), and Jesus! Even the name of the older, preferred second mother in the painting was the same as that of his own older second mother. To make the analysis of Leonardo's painting even more over determined, "Maria" has sound similarity to "Amalia." (And it should be recalled that Maria Freud, the young wife of Emanuel, was also part of Freud's Freiberg years.[137]

One might also wonder whether Freud knew in an earlier version of the painting, Leonardo also included young John the Baptist, thus bringing Freud's half-nephew ("cousin") John into the "associative picture."[138] Freud's biographers have often noted the life-long influence of John on Freud's life. In the final version, as shown in Figure 1-4, a lamb was substituted for John. Some of the possible associations to "lamb" have already been noted.

One concluding remark about the name "Anna" is in order. It should be noted that Freud declared that the names of his own six children were "chosen, not according to the fashion of the moment, but in memory of people I have been fond of. Their names made the children into revenants."[139] With the word "revenant," Freud was referring to his belief that a name results in the recreation (almost the reincarnation) of the previous person with the name. The only child of Sigmund Freud who received a decidedly Christian name was his daughter Anna, who was also Freud's favorite child. By one of those ironies of life, it was his daughter Anna who was to become Freud's nurse—his "Nana-Anna"—in the long illness of his later years.

Chapter Two

Childhood and Student Days: 1860–1882

R ELATIVELY LESS is known about this period than about others in Freud's life. Nevertheless, we do know about a number of quite important events and pieces of information bearing directly on Freud's relation to religion.

Vienna Childhood: 1860–1872

Freud described the first years in Vienna as "hard times and not worth remembering."[1] No doubt he missed the open fields and woods, his playmates—and, as we have seen, most especially his "*Amme*-Anna" of the Freiberg years.[2]

The psychological difference between the two worlds of Freiberg and Vienna was described by Freud:

When I was three years old, I left the small town of my birth and moved to a large city. All my memories occur in the town in which I was born. In other words they fall in the second and third year. They are mostly short scenes [as we have seen], but they are well preserved and possess clear details of all senses . . . after my third year the recollections are fewer and less distinct.[3]

Jones also mentions that Freud's continuous memories began at the age of seven. In other words, Freud's early Viennese experience, from ages four to seven, was one of few memories; what memories there were, as Jones and others have noted, were "evidently unpleasant."[4]

As far as separation anxiety goes, the early years in this period would have encompassed grief and mourning, followed by detachment and defense building.[5] Here, Freud's formula for the development of the ego is particularly relevant: "The ego is a precipitate of abandoned object-cathexes."[6] Certainly, the first, and in many respects the *only*, abandoned cathected person (lost object of love) for Freud was his nanny, and thus the earliest development of his own ego would have come out of this experience—coping with his grief over the loss of his functional mother, and of the surrounding Freiberg environment. Bowlby's evidence shows that such childhood sorrow can often have life-long consequences, and that defensive processes are a regular response to mourning at all ages: "In infants and children, it appears, defensive processes once set in motion are apt to stabilize and persist."[7]

Ricoeur well characterizes the Freudian notion of the ego as the result of the psychological work of mourning. That is, as Freud saw it, mourning or sorrow is the underlying emotion of the ego, and the ego itself is developed through the need to adapt to the loss of the objects (primarily people) that have been loved. Ricoeur expands on this further by pointing out that Freud's theory "brings absence into the very make-up of the ego," and that "it is impossible to separate the ego's coherence and structural autonomy from the work of mourning without also abandoning the peculiar field of speech in which psychoanalysis operates."[8]

One of the essential characteristics of Freud that is elaborated throughout Chapter Three is his underlying mood of sorrow—his pervasive pessimism and lack of joy. This feeling originated in the loss of his nanny and the lost "Eden" of Freiberg; because of the nanny's religious significance, Freud's sorrow, bitterness, and longing were all intermixed with Christianity.

The religious situation in Vienna, according to Jones, was that Freud's parents were "secular Jews" who maintained little Jewish observance in the home. "It is certain that in practice they were free-thinking people."[9] This interpretation is something of an overstatement. For example, one of Jakob's grandchildren has reported:

It was not a pious household but I do remember one Seder at which I, as the youngest at the table, had to make the responses to the reading of the song about the sacrifice of the kid: I was greatly impressed by the way grandfather recited the ritual, and the fact that he knew it by heart amazed me.[10]

Hence, the Passover Seder was certainly celebrated in Jakob Freud's household, at least some of the time.[11] Reuben Rainey reports.

There is no information concerning the family's synagogue attendance or Sabbath observance in the home. . . . Rosh Hashona, Yom Kippur, Pasach and Purim were observed in the household as late as 1874, when Freud was in his second year of medical studies.[12]

Jones writes that the Freud family did not observe the Jewish dietary laws, and there is no reason to think otherwise.[13]

However, the religious atmosphere in the Freuds' home was consistent with the liberal or Reform Judaism of 19th-century Vienna. Jakob and Amalia were married by Isaac Noah Mannheimer, a leading rabbi of the Reform Movement.[14] In addition, the Philippson Bible (Old Testament) (see Figure 2-1) that Jakob inscribed for his son on the occasion of Sigmund's 35th birthday was translated and edited by a leading scholar of the Reform Movement, Ludwig Philippson. (Freud became familiar with this Bible very early, and its great importance is discussed later.) Jakob inscribed this Bible as follows (in Hebrew, even though Sigmund was unable to read that language)[15]:

My dear Son,
   It was in the seventh year of your age that the spirit of God began to move you to learning. I would say the spirit of God speaketh to you: "Read in my Book; there will be opened to thee sources of knowledge and of the intellect." It is the Book of Books; it is the well that wise men have digged and from which lawgivers have drawn the waters of their knowledge.

Figure 2-1. Moses; from the Philippson Bible frontispiece.

Thou hast seen in this Book the vision of the Almighty, thou hast heard willingly, thou hast done and hast tried to fly high upon the wings of the Holy Spirit. Since then I have preserved the same Bible. Now, on your thirty-fifth birthday I have brought it out from its retirement and I send it to you as a token of love from your old father.[16]

Certainly this passage suggests that Freud's upbringing was far from totally devoid of religious influence, in particular, it contained a belief in God and a respect for the Bible. However, as Bergmann points out, this passage shows Jakob Freud's "enlightment" or liberal form of Jewishness: "No orthodox Jew would speak lightly of the Spirit of God speaking to a seven-year-old. Nor would any religious Jew see the Bible as belonging to mankind as a whole."[17] (It is also possible that Jakob's belief in God was stronger in his old age when he wrote this inscription than it had been 30 years earlier when he and his young son had read the Bible together.)

A piece of correspondence from Freud's very early years shows at least nominal religious influence. In this short letter, written when he was about seven years old to his brother Emanuel, Freud wrote, "I and my dear parents and sisters are, thank God well."[18]

Most importantly, Freud himself acknowledged in *An Autobiographical Study*: "My deep engrossment in the Bible story (almost as soon as I had learnt the art of reading) had, as I recognized much later, an enduring effect upon the direction of my interest."[19] In fact, the reading of the Bible with his father was in many respects the single most important intellectual experience for Freud. Théo Pfrimmer, in his book *Freud, Lecteur de la Bible*, has given a remarkably detailed, almost 500-page scholarly summary of the impact of the Bible on Freud. For example, Pfrimmer has identified 488 different Biblical references found in Freud's writings and letters (and more are apt to come to light in the future).[20] Many of these references have already been spotted by various scholars, but others seem to have been first observed by Pfrimmer. Above all, what Pfrimmer shows is the profound impact on Freud of his early Biblical reading. It was the Bible as literature, as psychology, as cultural history, and as religion that formed the mind of Freud. In contrast, there is little evidence that *young* Freud had any real interest in physical or biological science.

Freud scholars single out Samuel Hammerschlag as a significant religious influence during Freud's adolescence.[21] Hammerschlag was responsible for Freud's liberal Jewish instruction during his "high school" years in the Gymnasium, and Freud always had fond memories of him, as evidenced by his remarks in a letter to his fiancée years later. He wrote Martha Bernays:

The old professor . . . informed me that . . . a rich man had given him a sum of money for a worthy person in need, that he had mentioned my name and he was herewith handing it to me. . . . It is not the first time the old man has helped me in this way. . . . I do not know any people kinder, more humane, further removed from any ignoble motive than they [the Hammerschlags] . . . quite apart from the deep-seated sympathy which has existed between myself and the dear old Jewish teacher ever since my school days.[22]

Thus, throughout this period of schooling prior to his going to college at the University of Vienna, Freud did receive a modest but positive introduction to the Hebrew concept of God through his father and his religion teacher, and above all he was thoroughly grounded in the rationalistic and liberal Philippson Bible (Old Testament).

Certain important experiences, however, were totally lacking during this time. First, there is no evidence that Freud's mother had any religious impact on her son. Amalia Freud, as mentioned in Chapter One, was decidedly less religious than Jakob. Support for this view comes from the fact that after Jakob's death in 1896 the modest celebration of Jewish festivals came to an end, for "Amalia ignored Jewish feasts."[23]

Second, there are no data to suggest that Freud was instructed in any specifically Jewish literature, as distinct from the Old Testament, which is common to both Judaism and Christianity. The psychoanalyst Trosman, writing on Freud's cultural background, notes that "nowhere do we see any real familiarity with the Talmud nor are there citations from it [in Freud's writings]"; he further notes that "specific Jewish sources for his thought are not striking."[24] The absence of any known direct Talmudic influence is a glaring one for those seeking Jewish *religious* influence on Freud's thought. There is simply no evidence that Freud ever read the Talmud, although there was some indirect influence through the occasional Talmudic scholars cited by Philippson in his remarks and discussions about the Biblical text.[25] This is, of course, not to deny the great effect on Freud of Jewish stylistic, cultural, and ethnic factors.

Finally, in this period of Freud's life, there were no figures within his family or among close acquaintances who were deeply and impressively religious; that is, there were no believers strong in their religious convictions and in their personality. Jakob's liberal Judaism is never described as impressive, or it would have been reliably identified by the many Freud scholars that have investigated the question. For Freud, therefore, Jewish religion was associated with his father and his teacher, Hammerschlag. Both of these men were admirable, but neither of them was strong or forceful in thought or action. I stress this point, since it is well known that strength and courage were extremely important qualities to Freud.

Freud's Rejection of His Father

In very fundamental ways, Freud rejected his father; indeed, the central psychoanalytic concept of the Oedipus complex is one powerful expression of this rejection. Of special relevance to the present topic is the fact that Freud's expression of his rejection is often—indeed, typically—found in a religious context. The attempt to understand this rejection takes us rather far afield of our topic, but it is necessary to go into this in order to grasp much of Freud's attitude toward God, and in particular his motives for the rejection of Jewish religiousness.[26]

Jakob Freud (pictured with young Sigmund in Figure 2-2) is regularly described as a happy man with considerable wisdom who was apparently rather content with life.[27] Jones comments that Freud's father had a gentle disposition and that he was loved by all his family.[28] We see the other side of this type of character in Freud's description of his father in Micawber-like terms as being "always hopefully expecting something to turn up."[29] People reliably speak of Jakob as having a good sense of humor, which was frequently expressed in Jewish anecdotes—a trait noticeable in his son as well.[30] There seems to have been nothing in Jakob of the stern father or disciplinarian so common at the time in German culture. Instead, he comes across as a kindly, permissive, somewhat nurturant grandfather figure. We may recall that he was much older than Amalia and actually became a grandfather at about the time of his marriage to her. (Jakob's first grandson was Emanuel's son, John, who was born one month after Jakob and Amalia's marriage.[31]) At least in Vienna, Jakob was far from a business success. The poverty of Freud's early years left a life-long mark on him. Apparently, Jakob lacked real energy and focused drive, since these characteristics did not show in his business (or elsewhere, for that matter).[32]

That Jakob was not a strong and manly figure was one of the great disappointments of Sigmund's life. The following incident, frequently commented upon, shows how painfully Freud responded to what he perceived as his father's weakness:

I may have been ten or twelve years old, when my father began to take me with him on his walks. . . . on one such occasion he told me a story to show me how much better things are now than they had been in his days. "When I was a young man," he said, "I went for a walk one Saturday in the streets of your birthplace; I was well dressed, and had a new fur cap on my head. A Christian came up to me and with a single blow knocked off my cap into the mud and shouted: 'Jew! get off the pavement!'" "And what did you do?" I asked. "I went into the roadway and picked up my cap," was his quiet reply. This struck me as unheroic on the part of the big, strong man who was holding the little boy by the hand.[33]

Figure 2-2. Sigmund Freud, about eight years old, and his father, Jakob. (Mary Evans/Sigmund Freud Copyrights)

Much has been made of this passage as a source of Freud's ambivalence toward his father. It certainly is ideal for the precipitating of Oedipal motivation. But other, equally disturbing, and much earlier experiences would have had similar but probably more powerful effects on Freud's relation to his father, and would especially have fueled Freud's Oedipal motivation.

Krüll persuasively argues that the change in family life between Freiberg and Vienna must have been rather shocking for young Sigmund. First, they moved from a small country town dominated by native Czechs to a relatively urban Jewish neighborhood (Leopoldstadt).[34] But the change in Freud's parents, at least from his perspective, must have been the real change. In Freiberg the father, however distant and with his frequent travels, was very clearly the patriarch. He was the oldest, and was the head of a family which included his two elder sons, Emanuel and Philipp (and Emanuel's family), plus, of course, his own wife and children. In Freiberg Jakob was the head of his own business, and was on a par with other Jewish businessmen (e.g., Ignaz Fluss) who were also in the emerging and profitable textile and garment business there.[35] In Vienna, the situation was quite different. Here Jakob Freud was without any family except his brother Joseph, and Jakob was no longer an independent businessman. Instead, he apparently worked for others in the garment business; he never paid taxes, and the source of the family income is ambiguous. What is clear is that he was not very successful; his large family probably received considerable financial help from his wife's family, who lived in Vienna, and from his sons Emanuel and Philipp, who had left Freiberg to settle permanently in Manchester, England. He also appears to have ceased traveling and was at home much more. Thus, for Sigmund, his father would have sunk from the status of a distant but impressive patriarch to that of a petitioner.[36]

To make matters worse, the Uncle Joseph mentioned above was arrested in Vienna in 1865 for passing counterfeit Russian bank notes. In 1866 he was sentenced to ten years in prison (he was apparently released after serving only four years). This incident was common public knowledge at the time, as it was carried in the Viennese newspapers.[37] It must have further weakened the status of the father's family in the eyes of Sigmund. The whole affair covered the period from Freud's ninth until about his 14th year. The authorities never did find out who the printer of the bank notes was; however, there is evidence to suggest that they strongly suspected Emanuel and Philipp, who were in England.[38] Freud referred to this chapter of his family's story only in the most veiled and ambiguous of terms, thus suggesting his embarrassment at the incident and his reluctance to be candid about it.[39]

But there is evidence of another, far deeper insult to Jakob Freud's power and legitimacy in the eyes of his son. The thesis that I summarize here is a major contribution of Krüll.

The Alleged Affair of Amalia and Philipp

Essentially, what Marianne Krüll argues is that there was a sexual affair going on in Freiberg between Amalia and her stepson Philipp, and that Sigmund was a witness to it. Krüll postulates that this affair was taking place during the year or so before the family left Freiberg.[40] Now there is considerable evidence for the opportunity for such an involvement. We may recall that Philipp, who was the same age as Amalia (perhaps a few months older), was unmarried and living in the house directly across the street. We should remember, too, that Jakob was frequently away on long trips of a week or more in connection with his business as a wool trader. There were very few other Jews in Freiberg, the total number being a little over 100. Thus, there easily could have been no other attractive young Jewish women to provide more suitable involvements for Philipp.

Krüll has also suggested that the marriage of Amalia and Jakob was something of a mismatch: Jakob was both much older than Amalia (he was, as mentioned above, about to become a grandfather when they married) and not very wealthy. He seems to have been doing satisfactorily in Freiberg, but a one-room flat is no great luxury; in view of the later descriptions of Jakob, it is quite possible that Amalia realized shortly after the marriage that she had married what we might call today a "nice guy but a loser"—a man who would not be successful and able to support her at the level of her own family. Amalia herself is described as quite attractive and strong-willed.[41] In any case, if the marriage was a mismatch—if there was in it some discrepancy in expectations—Amalia may well have been disappointed in her new husband, and would hence have been vulnerable to an affair.

But opportunity and motivation aside, let us now turn to some of the evidence of this affair. As Krüll notes,[42] there are dreams and memories from Freud's childhood in Freiberg in which Amalia and Philipp appear together, and from which it is clear that the precocious little Sigmund felt that the two were not indifferent to each other. One such early memory I have already quoted in part:

I was crying my heart out, because my mother was nowhere to be found. My brother Philipp . . . opened a cupboard for me, and when I found that my mother was not there either I cried still more, until she came through the door, looking slim and beautiful.[43]

Freud interpreted this scene as fear of the loss of the mother, whom he thought had been locked up or "shut up" as his nanny had recently been after her arrest. Freud's further associations are especially important for Krüll's hypothesis. Freud wrote about the child (himself):

The wardrobe or cupboard was symbol for him of his mother's inside. So he insisted on looking into this cupboard, and turned for this to his big brother (Philipp), who . . . had taken *his father's* place as the child's rival. . . . there was a . . . suspicion against him—namely that he had in some way introduced the recently *born baby* into his mother's inside [Krüll's emphasis].[44]

In short, little Freud suspected his half-brother Philipp of having made with his mother the recently born baby! The rival who took away his mother and was responsible for producing new babies was not his father but his stepbrother! In line with this, Jones suggests that in the eyes of young Freud, it would have been natural to pair off the older Jakob with the nanny, and his mother Amalia with Philipp, who were of the same age.[45]

In a different work, Freud gave his associations to a most interesting dream, which he had when he was in Vienna at the age of about nine. First, the dream:

I saw *my beloved mother, with a peculiarly peaceful, sleeping expression on her features, being carried into the room by two (or three) people with bird's beaks and laid upon the bed.* [Freud's emphasis]. I awoke in tears and screaming, and interrupted my parents' sleep.[46]

Freud's associations to the dream were that the image was based on a picture or pictures (see Figure 2-3) from the Philippson Bible, which we already know he read assiduously, and which he acknowledged as important. Thus, the first association was to a Bible that featured on the title page the name "Philipp-son"—a Bible commonly called by this name.

The next association Freud provided was that at the time of the dream he had heard for the first time, from a playmate by the name of Philipp, the vulgar word for "coitus" in German—"*vögeln*," which is very much like the word for bird ("*vogel*"). Jones himself was surprised that Freud did not associate the name of the playmate with his half-brother Philipp.[47]

Krüll argues that in Freiberg Freud had surprised his mother in sexual intercourse with Philipp, and that this image had appeared to him in a dream, perhaps disguised somewhat by the Egyptian bird- (*vogel-*) headed figures. Krüll finds an important support for her interpretation in the work of Grinstein.[48] Grinstein has carefully examined all the many illustrations in the Philippson Bible to find those that might fit Freud's description. There are only two possible images, and Grinstein identifies the Biblical texts that these images are paired with. The first text is the part of 2 Samuel containing the story of David and Abner. This section is summarized by Grinstein as presenting "the elements of death and

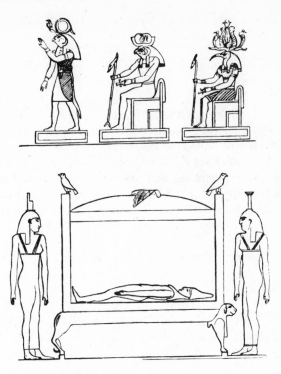

Figure 2-3. Illustrations from the Philippson Bible showing images like those reported by Freud in his childhood dreams. See text for a complete explanation of their significance.

castration (smiting in the groin) combined with the themes of murder and the possession of a forbidden woman."[49] The other and more likely text is connected with the story of David and Absalom (David's third son). This chapter of 2 Samuel tells a well-known story, which Grinstein nicely summarizes:

The Biblical account reported above portrays a tragic father–son relationship. Absalom is angry with his older brother Amnon for his incestuous relationship with Tamar. Later, he himself desires to be king and to depose his father. Flagrantly, and in the presence of all Israel, he has relations with his father's concubines. As a consequence of his actions, he is finally killed by his father's men. The sadness of the story lies in the bitter grief which King David feels over his son's murder even though his son would have killed him. No clearer presentation of the father–son conflict can be imagined.[50]

Krüll very naturally stresses the importance of these dream images, for they strongly suggest that Sigmund was aware of the incestuous relationship between Amalia and Philipp, and of the father–son conflict that it involved.

All of this means that Freud's Oedipus complex would have been derived from a very important core of his own childhood experience. It would have been his older half-brother Philipp—not some remote aborigine—who "first" had the idea of sexually possessing the mother, and by implication of killing the father. And it is Philipp's behavior that would have raised the Oedipal issue, not Freud's unprimed unconscious of its own volition. Freud's introduction to the primal group of sons hostile to the father (as in *Totem and Taboo*) would have been in his own family, when he was about three years old. For much of his life, Freud would have to struggle to come to terms with this experience and its deeply disturbing implications.

The Meaning of the Name "Sigismund"

It is relevant here to mention the story behind Freud's name, "Sigismund," and its German equivalent, "Sigmund," which he consistently used after his early youth. (His Hebrew name was "Schlomo.") It has been suggested that he was named after Sigismund I, a famous king of Poland, who defended the religious rights of the Jews in Lithuania, a country then under Polish domination.[51] This is possible, but another, more likely meaning of the name "Sigismund" is Czech and Catholic. At the time (as in most Catholic cultures), the first or Christian names given to children were typically saints' names. St. Sigismund was a patron saint of Bohemia, which borders on Moravia; his relics are in Prague, and his saint's day, May 1, is noted in Czech Catholic missals.[52] Thus "Sigismund" had both Catholic and Czech significance; Freud's parents could easily have picked it because they wanted a name with positive connotations for the surrounding culture, and because his feast day, coming just before Freud's birth on May 6, had suggested it to them.

The deeper and psychological meaning of the name, however, comes from the strange story of St. Sigismund himself in a story well known in Czechoslovakia.[53] The original Sigismund was a Burgundian King of the Franks in the sixth century. His first wife, by whom he had a son, Sigeric, died, and the king remarried. The new queen had a falling-out with Sigeric, her stepson, and she moved against Sigeric by telling King Sigismund that his son plotted to kill him to usurp the kingdom.

The king, incited by the queen, had his son killed: The youth was throttled while he slept. When the deed was done, King Sigismund showed great remorse. He spent many days in weeping and fasting. Apparently because of his deep repentance and the holy life he led after having his son killed, he was considered, by popular judgment, to be a saint. In short, an Oedipal drama (one involving a strong father, an unreliable second wife, and a potentially parricidal son) surrounded Freud's very name. It is likely, in view of the importance of names for Freud, that at some time he heard the story. The following remark certainly implies as much: ". . . not even a first name can occur arbitrarily to the mind, without having been determined by some powerful ideational complex."[54] And Freud once wrote, "A man's name is a principal component of his personality, perhaps even a portion of his soul."[55]

But let us return to Krüll's thesis about Philipp and Amalia, for there are other pieces of evidence not mentioned by Krüll that make it clearer still that Sigmund suspected Philipp of having sexual relations with his mother—and, as a natural corollary, that he had doubts about who his own actual father was. Jones reports an anecdote about how the youngest child of Jakob and Amalia was named. This child was a boy, ten years younger than Sigmund. Jones writes:

An example [of a "Family Council"] was the choice of a name for a younger son. It was Sigmund's vote for the name Alexander that was accepted, his selection being based on Alexander the Great's generosity and military prowess; to support his choice he recited the whole story of the Macedonian's triumphs.[56]

The very fact that Freud recalled the incident and thought it important enough to relate it to Jones many years later is interesting. (Freud was about 52 years old when Jones first met him.[57]) But second, and more importantly, who was Alexander the Great if not the powerful and successful son of a powerful king in his own right, Philip of Macedonia— a king who prepared the military and political conditions for Alexander's own great conquests? Almost all biographies of Alexander begin with Philip and feature him rather extensively. To tell (as Freud did) the "whole story" is to tell of Alexander *and* of Philip. Hence, by insisting on the name Alexander, the ten-year-old Sigmund was indirectly claiming that his own brother was fathered by his half-brother Philipp, and implying (perhaps hoping?) that he too was the son of Philipp. It is also relevant that in successfully pushing for the right to name his own brother, Sigmund was challenging his father. To name a child, especially a son, is to take over the father's role.

Another piece of evidence for the Amalia–Philipp affair was brought to my attention by Peter Swales, who pointed out that there is no record that Philipp ever visited the Freud family once he left for England.[58] Emanuel visited a few times; in 1883 Philipp did come to Germany, where he visited Sigmund in Leipzig—a visit Freud wrote about to his fiancée.[59] But there is no record of Philipp's ever visiting Jakob and Amalia in Austria. There seems, in short, to have been some real estrangement. When, years later, Freud was finally promoted to a full professorship at the University of Vienna Medical School, Philipp wrote a card to congratulate Sigmund. (Incidentally, he referred to Sigmund as "Sigismund," suggesting that the family still sometimes used the older form.) The card was sent to Freud's sister Mitzi in Berlin; Philipp was already *en route* back to Manchester (presumably from Berlin) at the time. Philipp wrote (the card was dated March 12, 1901): ". . . the good news of our beloved brother Sigismund. I would be grateful if you would inform me more about the promotion at Manchester."[60] It was as though Philipp was not to contact Freud or Amalia directly, or literally to see Amalia again.

In conclusion, although none of Krüll's or other evidence for the Amalia–Philipp affair is conclusive, the evidence taken together is very strong that the "affair" was at least *psychologically* real for young Freud; that is, the affair was a significant part of Freud's psychology. It certainly helps to explain Freud's persistent interest in sexuality in childhood, in great figures of ambiguous parentage, and in sexual conflict between father and son, as well as to shed light on Freud's rejection of his father.

The Religious and Other Significance of the Amalia–Philipp Affair

Krüll's thesis is important not merely because of its intrinsic importance for understanding the life and psychology of Freud, but also because it is centrally connected to Freud's relationship to religion. The Amalia–Philipp affair explains why Freud would place Oedipal conflicts (i.e., conflicts between father and son over the mother) at the center of his theory of the origin of religion. After all, the Bible had provided Freud's first theoretical framework for interpreting his own family situation. It was in the Bible that such conflicts (such as that between David and Absalom) were first discussed.

Furthermore, this incident may provide the explanation for why the Jakob Freud family left Freiberg so suddenly. In leaving Freiberg, Jakob also left behind his two elder sons, never to live near them again; the move established a permanent split in the family, since shortly after Jakob left, his sons emigrated to Manchester, England. There were occasional later visits, but the father and sons lived henceforth many hundreds of miles apart—and, as noted, Philipp never visited the Jakob Freud household. I strongly agree with Krüll's additional proposal that the reason for the move from Freiberg was that Jakob learned of or began to suspect the affair between Amalia and Philipp. The move was thus motivated to a significant extent by the desire to put a stop to this liaison. Such a motivation would explain why Amalia and Jakob left even though social and economic conditions were favorable; why they left rather suddenly;

and why there was apparently no family tradition for why the move occurred. Finally, it would explain why the Jakob Freud family split up permanently.

The existence of this (probable) affair at the heart of the family also allows another interpretation of why the nanny was so suddenly fired, and why she obviously aroused so much emotion and somewhat confused testimony from Amalia. The one adult most likely to know about this affair would have been Freud's "Anna." Her normal duties would have made her privy to such a situation, and young Sigmund could easily have raised questions directly with the nanny as well. If the nanny knew of this situation, she would have been a most threatening presence. Any public notice of such an incestuous relationship would have had grave repercussions for the reputations of all involved. Getting rid of the nanny would almost have been a necessity. We may recall that in Amalia's story, it was Philipp who was present and who went to the police. It is very strange that such an official action was not handled by the older Jakob, the husband and Philipp's father. If Jakob had been at home, this would have been most unusual indeed. One must assume that he was out of town at the time. Jakob's absence would almost have been necessary in order to arrange the whole thing with a minimum of danger from the nanny.

Of course, they could not just dismiss her; to do so would invite her to retaliate by talking about the Philipp–Amalia affair. A charge of thievery would thus protect them from her talking, for then if she should talk, that could be discounted as motivated by revenge. (It is even possible that she was paid to leave Freiberg for a few months, until the Freuds left.)

The Hannibal Complex: Freud's Siding with Rome

We return to Freud's more direct relationship to Christianity. Throughout his life, Freud was drawn to admire and to identify with strong, successful historical figures. His biographers have mentioned that his heroes in his teenage years, most of whom were military figures, included Napoleon and Napoleon's general Massena, commonly believed to be a Jew.[61] Other examples of such positively viewed figures were Oliver Cromwell,[62] after whom he named one of his sons, and the just-discussed Alexander the Great.

The most frequently mentioned and emphasized of these militaristic heroes with whom Freud identified was Hannibal, the great Carthaginian general. Hannibal's relationship with his father, Hamilcar Barca, provides another example of a strong, positive father–son relationship like that between Philip and Alexander the Great. In *The Interpretation of Dreams* (1900), Freud wrote of this identification:

Hannibal . . . had been the favorite hero of my later school days. Like so many boys of my age, I had sympathized in the Punic Wars not with the Romans but with the Carthaginians. And when in the higher classes I began to understand for the first time what it meant to belong to an alien race, and anti-semitic feelings among the other boys warned me that I must take up a definite position, the figure of the semitic general rose still higher in my esteem. To my youthful mind Hannibal and Rome symbolized the conflict between the tenacity of Jewry and the organization of the Catholic Church.[63]

This passage is a favorite of Freud's biographers, because it provides one of the major pieces of support for the standard interpretation of Freud as an enemy of Christianity in general and of Catholicism in particular. In some respects, of course, it is a useful quotation for them. But is it really as advantageous as has been argued? Let us look at the situation a little more carefully.

To begin with, one might recall that Hannibal was ultimately not an especially successful general: He was finally thoroughly defeated by the Roman general Scipio Africanus, who avenged his own father's earlier defeat at the hands of the Carthaginians. In the end, Hannibal committed suicide, and Roman power was greatly increased.[64] Freud was certainly familiar with this outcome, which makes of Hannibal a far from strong choice as an anti-Roman hero. As the psychoanalysts Gedo and Wolf, to whom I owe this insight, have put it: "It is all very well to admire good losers, but adolescents need to identify with bigger battalions."[65]

Gedo and Wolf quote Freud's letters to show that as a young man he quite consciously identified with the very man who defeated Hannibal— Scipio himself!

We [Freud and a fellow student, Edward Silberstein] became friends at a time when one doesn't look upon friendship as a sport or an asset, but when one needs a friend with whom to share things. We used to be together literally every hour of the day . . . We learned Spanish together, had our own methodology and secret names, which we took from the dialogues of the great Cervantes. . . . in writing as well as in conversation he was known as Berganza! I as Cipio. How often I have written: *Querido Berganza!* and signed myself *Tu fidel Cipio.*[66]

Gedo and Wolf come to a conclusion that overturns the standard view of Freud's "Hannibal complex":

"Freud's choice of the secret pseudonym Cipion for himself betrays that his openly declared identification with Hannibal . . . was ambivalent at best and more probably stood as a thin screen hiding his partisanship for Rome."[67]

This issue of a strong, hidded partisanship for Rome will surface again and again as we look closely at other biographical material.

Don Quixote

There are still other significant connections between Freud, in his adolescent preuniversity days, and religion. The appeal of *Don Quixote*—what Gedo and Wolf call its "deep personal significance"[68]—was not just due to Cervantes's psychological insights and humor, but must also have derived from the religious atmosphere that suffuses the narrative. This is no modern tale debunking religious belief or ideals, nor is it notably hostile to the Church. In spite of its comic representation of chivalry and of chivalric ideals, at the heart of the work is a great reverence for Don Quixote and for the ideals that he embodies.

There was obviously something of the knight-errant in the young Freud's self-image, and (as Gedo and Wolf point out) his frequent references to his fiancée as "princess" had their origin in *Don Quixote*.[69] No doubt the ambivalent way in which Cervantes treated knight-errantry made it attractive to Freud; as in all things religious, ambivalence was Freud's dominant attitude. Freud remarked about *Don Quixote*:

Don't you find it very touching to read how a great person, himself an idealist, makes fun of his ideals? . . . [once] we were all noble knights passing through the world caught in a dream, misinterpreting the simplest things, magnifying commonplaces into something noble and rare, and thereby cutting a sad figure. . . . we men always read with respect about what we once were and in part still remain.[70]

Silberstein and Fluss Letters

There are surprisingly numerous references to things religious in Freud's rather lengthy correspondences with Edward Silberstein and Emil Fluss, written when Freud was 16 and 17. Silberstein was a schoolmate and pen pal; Fluss was a young friend living in Freud's boyhood town, Freiberg, with whom he corresponded between 1872 and 1874. Gedo and Wolf, in another article "The 'Ich' Letters", brought these still mostly unpublished letters to my attention.[71]

For example, Freud referred in the Silberstein letters to his reading of Ludwig Feuerbach's *The Essence of Christianity* (1841/1957), a well-known and influential critique of Christianity.[72] In this work, Feuerbach (1804–1872), a left-wing Hegelian, wrote as follows:

[T]he historical progress of religion consists in this: that which during an earlier stage of religion was regarded as something objective is now recognized as something subjective, so that which was formerly viewed and worshipped as God is now recognized as something human. . . . God is merely the projected essence of Man.[73]

This kind of interpretation of religion served to solidify Freud's well-known conscious and rational rejection of Christianity. In fact, the Feuerbachian analysis is the origin of much of Freud's critique that religion is a projection of human needs. A work like *The Future of an Illusion*, written many decades later, is essentially an elaboration of Feuerbach.[74] (See Chapter Seven.)

But, as always, Freud's ambivalence was also present at this time. In Gedo and Wolf's summary of short excerpts of the Fluss letters they note (among other things) the following Old Testament or religious references in these letters, all made from September 1872 through June 1873: "the cup runneth over," "the inscrutable workings of a divine power," and "with fear and trembling."[75] Gedo and Wolf do not mention, however, the fact that "with fear and trembling" also occurs four times in the New Testament Pauline Epistles, as in to "work out your own salvation with fear and trembling."[76] Other references noted by Gedo and Wolf include "an angel with a fiery sword," "a Tower of Babel," and "find . . . favor in my eyes."[77] Finally, there is a very Catholic (and surprising) quotation, which Freud picked up somehow from the Mass of the Dead: "There comes the day, the longest day, when. . . ."[78]

University Years: 1873–1882

In choosing to go into medicine, Freud made the decision to move toward science, and (professionally at least) to allow his literary interests and talents to be put largely aside. He began his studies at the University of Vienna in the fall of 1873. He finished his course work in four years, but did not officially complete his degree until 1881.[79] Much of the latter four years (1877–1881) was spent in extensive laboratory study and research. During this time Freud thoroughly immersed himself in the world of medical research—in particular, in physiology and anatomy.[80]

The period of Freud's academic studies was very much under the general influence of such world-famous scientists as Helmholtz, Darwin, Fechner, and (in Vienna) the renowned Ernst Brücke.[81] It was a time of great enthusiasm for science—and enthusiasm permeated by an ideological commitment to materialism, rationalism, and determinism. (This ideological kind of science is known as "scientism.") As a student and young scientist, Freud imbibed much of this attitude, and it was one that in important respects remained with him all his life. He would often discard or ignore important aspects of this "philosophy" when it came to developing his own theories, but he kept a 19th-century scientific world view as a general position that he hoped or assumed would someday be found to underlie psychoanalysis. This heavily materialistic and deterministic theory is now quite dated and very hard to defend, but during Freud's lifetime it wielded enormous influence. Such a scientific position left no place, of course, for religious beliefs or genuine religious experience; indeed, both were aggressively attacked in the course of the 19th century, and their divine or supernatural legitimacy was denied by the proponents of this sort of view. Thus, in *The Future of an Illusion* Freud attacked religion (especially Christianity) as an illusion, and he contrasted religion with this kind of science, which Freud believed was no illusion.

Professor Robert Holt has identified in some detail the specific intellectual sources for Freud's materialist philosophy.[82] In addition to Ludwig Feuerback (mentioned above; see also Chapter Seven), Freud was influenced by W. E. H. Lecky's (1838–1903) *History of the Rise and Influence of the Spirit of Rationalism in Europe* (1865/1955) and Ludwig Büchner's (1824–1899) very popular *Force and Matter* (1855/1924). The latter book mixed a kind of hardline materialism and reductionism with hostility to religion. (As Holt points out, it also had its own curious kind of abstract, metaphysical cosmology.) Büchner often quoted Feuerbach and also David Friedrich Strauss (1808–1874), another modernist theologian well known for his attacks on the historicity of Jesus and on supernatural religion. Ernst Renan, a favorite of Breuer, was also part of this 19th-century secular humanistic "theology."[83] I certainly do not deny the skeptical and atheist aspect of Freud's thought, which is a very legitimate part of the standard interpretation. My goal is to show that alongside of this commonly articulated attitude was another position, in many respects equally powerful but largely unconscious.

Even in this period of his life, when Freud (like so many college students) was actively developing his modernist, "no-nonsense" materialistic training and preparing for his career, he showed signs of real ambivalence. For example, in *The Interpretation of Dreams*, Freud recalled:

The . . . scene . . . dated from my early student days. There was a discussion in a *German* students' club [Freud's emphasis, here and throughout] on the relation of philosophy to the natural sciences. I was a green youngster, full of materialistic theories, and thrust myself forward to give expression to an extremely one-sided point of view. Thereupon someone who was my senior and my superior, someone who has since then shown his ability as a leader . . . stood up and gave us a good talking-to: he too, he told us, had fed swine in his youth and returned repentant to his father's house. I *fired up* (as I did in the dream) and replied boorishly . . . that since I now knew that he had fed *swine* in his youth I was no longer *surprised* at the tone of his speeches. (In the dream I was *surprised* at my German nationalist attitude.) There was a general uproar and I was called upon from many sides to withdraw my remarks, but I refused to do so. The man I had insulted was too sensible to look upon the incident as a *challenge*, and let the affair drop.[84]

This anecdote is dominated by imagery from one of the most famous of New Testament stories: that of the prodigal son.[85] The anecdote reveals that by the time of the dream, when Freud was in his 40s, he could look back and see the unbalanced quality of his own early enthusiasm for materialism. There is even the strong hint that part of Freud's oversensitivity was precipitated by his opponent's references to Scripture. It all brings to mind the comment by Roazen (quoted in Chapter One) that whenever Freud's remarks seem intolerant, something in him was threatened, and that this was likely to have been the case with respect to religion.

The Influence of Franz Brentano

There was one other major expression of Freud's attraction to Christianity during this period, and that was Freud's involvement with the prominent Austrian philosopher Franz Brentano.[86]

Franz Brentano (1838–1917; see Figure 2-4) was until recently an ignored figure in the history of philosophy, but is now accepted as a major thinker whose work did much to initiate phenomenology. (As noted below, he is also linked to the origin of Gestalt psychology—a kind of phenomenology of perception—and to Freud and psychoanalysis. Thus, for psychology, Brentano appears to be one of the most influential of modern philosophers.) He came from a distinguished literary family, and early in life decided to pursue a vocation in the Catholic priesthood. He was ordained in 1864, but after a personal religious crisis he left the Church in 1873—a crisis that might have been augmented by his disagreement with the church over the First Vatican Council's declaration of papal infallibility.[87] Not only did he retain his belief in God, but he remained a simple Christian believer[88] and spoke of Catholicism with great respect,[89] and his belief in the immortality of the soul was important to his theorizing.[90]

Brentano began teaching at the University of Vienna in 1874, the academic year that Freud started his studies.[91] Brentano became a prominent and popular teacher, numbering among his pupils Edmund Husserl, philosopher; Thomas Masaryk, founder of the Czechoslavakian Republic; Franz Kafka, author; Christian von Ehrenfels, considered by many (e.g., Max Wertheimer) to be the father of Gestalt psychology; Carl Stumpf, Alexius Meinong, Franz Hillebrand and Kazimir Twardowski, important psychologists; and also Sigmund Freud.[92] Concerning the last-mentioned association, Jones remarks, "Freud had . . . attended Brentano's lectures, as indeed had half of Vienna, since he was a very gifted lecturer. . . ."[93] Jones is implying that Freud was one of a large number of the curious who occasionally attended the philosopher's lectures, and

Figure 2-4. Franz Brentano. (Mary Evans/Sigmund Freud Copyrights)

that the connection between them was of minimal significance. Here again, there are serious reasons to disagree with Jones.

First, Freud was far from being a mere casual attender of Brentano's public lectures. Merlan has discovered, in the University of Vienna archives, that Freud enrolled in *five* different philosophy courses taught by Brentano.[94] These courses were the only philosophy courses that Freud took in his eight semesters of medical study; they were, indeed, the only nonmedical courses that Freud ever took as a university student. These courses were all free electives. One was on Aristotle; one was on logic; and the other three had the rather general title of "Readings of Philosophic Writings."[95] It is virtually certain that courses such as the last three would have contained much of Brentano's own thought. Brentano's greatest work, *Psychology from an Empirical Standpoint* (1874/1973), had just been published, and no doubt the distinctive ideas in it would have influenced his lectures substantially.[96]

While taking these courses, Freud wrote to his friend Silberstein: "One of the courses—lo and behold—just listen, you will be surprised—deals with the existence of God, and Professor Brentano, who lectures on it, is a marvelous person. Scientist and philosopher though he is, he deems it necessary to support with his expositions this airy existence of a divinity."[97] Freud continued in a later letter: "This peculiar, and in many respects ideal man, a believer in God, a teleologist, a Darwinist and altogether a darned clever fellow, a genius in fact. For the moment I will say only this: that under Brentano's influence I have decided to take my Ph.D. in philosophy and zoology."[98]

Philosophically, Brentano stood firmly in the Catholic, Aristotelian–Thomistic tradition.[99] He absorbed Aristotle through his teachers, and St. Thomas Aquinas and the Scholastic tradition were standard fare in seminary.[100] (He would also have learned much Aristotle as filtered through Aquinas.) Brentano's Aristotelian position is clear in his work.[101] As Brentano said in a letter to Oskar Kraus (quoted by Srzednicki), "In these times of woeful downfall of philosophy I could find none better than the old Aristotle. Aquinas had to serve as a guide to the understanding of a text that wasn't always easy to follow."[102] Brentano was also for a time in the Dominican order, the community to which St. Thomas belonged and the one that has sustained Thomism in the Catholic world.[103]

Brentano's very distinctive philosophy was a psychological phenomenalism. His purpose was to construct a "scientific philosophy" without categories or forms, in reaction to German idealism, with its emphasis on abstract ideas and the dialectical and historical movement of ideas. The empirical focus of his philosophy was a close, descriptive concern with mental life as it was experienced, in contrast to idealistic philosophies, with their involvement in hypothesized historical forces, or abstract categories of thought, all of which are far removed from the "empirical" world of natural mental life. Essential to his psychology was the notion that all mental acts are "intentional" and related to objects.[104] Brentano, thus, put the motivational character of psychology at the center of his theory; this is one reason for Brentano's being classified as the founder of what is called "act" psychology.[105] James R. Barclay elaborates on this:

The doctrine of the intentional existence is the core of Brentano's own theory of intentionality . . . *In essence the basic tenet is that the soul is the dynamic intending force behind psychic activities which actively structures and confers meaning in the act of perception* [emphasis in original].[106]

What must be kept in mind is how radically different this type of psychology-philosophy was from the German idealist philosophy of historical forces (Hegel) or abstract categories of mind (Kant), or from the English emphasis of the time on logic, on sensory experience as the basis of all knowledge, and on utilitarian theories of value. These approaches generally dominated the 19th-century understanding of the mind.

In emphasizing intentionality and the soul as its origin, Brentano was reviving a Scholastic (especially a Thomist) notion that sensory stimulation is organized and given meaning in consciousness through the efficient causality of the mind or soul.[107] Barclay traces Brentano's teaching on "intentionality" back to St. Thomas.[108]

Now this all has an important similarity to some of the concepts of Freud, who used the idea of intentionality in both his early and his later stages of theorizing. For instance, Freud wrote that it is the intentional character of dreams that makes them "psychical phenomena of complete validity—fulfilments of wishes."[109] Vergote (quoted by Ricoeur) has observed, "[T]his . . . contains the whole of Freud's discovery: 'the psychical is defined as meaning, and this meaning is dynamic and historical.' Husserl and Freud are seen as heirs of Brentano, who had them both as students."[110]

More recently, the strong similarity between Brentano and Freud has been persuasively presented by Raymond E. Fancher, who compares Brentano's *Psychology from an Empirical Standpoint* with Freud's early metapsychology, especially as expressed in his *Project for a Scientific Psychology*.[111] Fancher finds the following major similarities, some of which I have already alluded to:

In psychological theory, both men stressed the motivated nature of thought and a conception of a "psychological reality" that is superior to "material reality." (Here in his own theorizing Freud breaks with the standard scientific materialism of his day.) Both saw consciousness of one's own mental activity as arising retrospectively and having a calming effect on emotions. Both emphasized a process of "judgement" or reality testing made possible only by the presence of a strong unity of consciousness or ego. Methodologically, both agreed that the retrospective analysis of subjective experience is the principal tool of psychology. Freud eventually agreed with Brentano that psychology proceeds best when separated from physiology.[112]

These are all foundational similarities, and, again, similarities that contrast markedly with the other approaches to the mind popular at the time. But there are still further connections between Brentano and Freud. Both believed that thought—cognitive structure—was permeated by and in many respects directed by emotionality.[113] It is also of importance that in his 1874 book Brentano discussed the issue of the unconscious mind in a serious way. He came to a negative conclusion concerning its existence. However, his answer followed largely from his definitions of consciousness and unconsciousness, and the evidence subsequently available to Freud did not, of course, figure in Brentano's thought.[114] In any case, Freud very likely first heard a serious discussion of the unconscious from his professor Brentano. No wonder Fancher concludes that there was some important Brentanian influence on Freud.

It is an intriguing fact that, in introducing the concept of the unconscious in *Psychology from an Empirical Standpoint*, Brentano stated, "One of the first men who taught that there is an unconscious consciousness was Thomas Aquinas."[115] In other words, Brentano came to an anti-Thomist conclusion, while Freud would later, perhaps unknowingly, side with Aquinas on this central matter. There appear to be many important similarities between Freudian psychoanalysis and Thomism, not the least of which is St. Thomas's frequent use of the word and concept "libido"— sometimes in a more specific sense than Freud, but always in a manner in agreement with the Freudian use.[116] This is not the place to go into an analysis of the Thomist–Aristotelian nature of Freud, or the "Freudian" aspects of Aquinas's thought. Suffice it to say that a number of thoughtful writers aware of the two systems have noticed important resemblances. As far as I have been able to discover, no one really grounded in both systems has attempted a thorough comparison or synthesis.[117]

There are other, less easily documentable reasons for assuming an influence of Brentano on Freud—less documentable, but not necessarily less likely. Throughout his life Freud was apt to identify very strongly with impressive male figures who were older and obviously accomplished. Brentano had certain qualities that would have had a special appeal to Freud, besides his brilliant reputation. These factors undoubtedly account for the great number of historically important students known to have been attracted to him; they also do much to explain why Freud, while a student, would have visited Brentano at his home.

Some hint of the influence of Brentano on Freud can be found in an unpublished letter from Freud to his friend Edward Silberstein on March 27, 1875. Peter Swales brought this letter to my attention.[118] Freud declared that he was under the influence of various arguments put to him personally by Brentano and was afraid that one day he might succumb to belief in the alleged scientific proofs of "spritualism, homeopathy, Louise Lateau, and so on."[119] Louise Lateau was a Belgian mystic who attracted worldwide attention from 1868 until her death in 1883 for having the stigmata.[120]

Brentano's religious situation would most probably have struck a sympathetic chord in Freud. Brentano, in leaving the Church and in rejecting papal infallibility, had become an outsider—someone like Hannibal who had done battle with Rome and lost, and yet maintained his honor and professional stature. Moreover (if the present thesis is correct), the fact that this defeated outsider still kept much of his faith would have attracted Freud as well. A still further positive ingredient was the illustrious literary family from which Brentano came—a family with many close personal connections with Freud's favorite author, Goethe.[121]

We do know that Freud, during his university days, was quite capable of being influenced in ways that would not show up until he left medical science and developed his own system of ideas. Freud described one of these very early intellectual influences much later, in a letter written in 1913 to Elise Gomperz, the recent widow of Theodor Gomperz. Gomperz was an important figure in •Freud's life from 1879 until about 1900.[122] He was an assimilated Jew, part of the wealthy Jewish establishment, who had been a professor of classical philology at the University of Vienna and a widely acknowledged great scholar.[123] This letter to Elise Gomperz included the following:

The little notebook containing the handwriting of your unforgotten husband reminded me of that time lying so far behind us, when I, young and timid, was allowed for the first time to exchange a few words with one of the great men in the realm of thought. It was soon after this that I heard from him the remarks about the role played by dreams in the psychic life of primitive men—something that has preoccupied me so extensively ever since.[124]

Merlan reports that Freud translated a volume of John Stuart Mill's philosophy for Gomperz.[125] (Gomperz was the editor of the complete works of John Stuart Mill, which were being translated into German under his direction.[126]) A natural question is this: How did Gomperz hear about the young Freud and know that he was capable of such a translation task? The son of Gomperz wrote Freud in 1932 and inquired about this. Freud wrote back:

I know I was recommended to your father by Franz Brentano. Your father, at a party . . . mentioned that he was looking for a translator, and Brentano, *whose student I then was or had been at a still earlier time*, named my name [emphasis in the original quote from Merlan].[127]

It is not surprising that Gomperz's son, after noting the two theorists' mutual emphasis on the psychic apparatus operating in a way more or less independent of the physical apparatus, goes on to suggest an influence of Brentano on Freud.[128]

There are other little-recognized associations between Brentano and Freud, which derive from the fact that both men were part of the same group or network of people in Vienna. This network had much to do with social connections and with political views. Both Freud and Brentano were part of a group that was politically liberal in outlook, usually quite educated, interested in ideas and the arts, and generally very well off economically. Indeed, many were quite wealthy. Freud became a member of this class of society after going into private practice on Easter Sunday of 1886 and getting married later that year. Freud belonged to this class on the basis of his education and his friends; his financial condition was much better than in his youth, but he was never what would be called affluent. On the other hand, most of his patients were wealthy, influential, and from the established, rather assimilated, older Jewish families.[129]

This group of people, a kind of "Our Crowd" in turn-of-the-century Vienna of which Freud was a part, was also primarily Jewish; one should add that in spite of anti-Semitism, its members were very active and influential in the cultural, social, and political life of Vienna.[130] That Freud was part of this group is generally known, although the consequences of the fact that his patients were largely upper-class assimilated Jews and often related to the families of his friends, colleagues, and associates definitely have not been fully investigated.

What is less known is that Brentano was also a very real part of this same group. This resulted from his university connections and from his politically liberal views, but it was also a consequence of his having married in 1880[131] Ida Lieben, who came from a very wealthy and influential Jewish family that was closely allied with the liberal Jewish circles in the city.[132] (Puglisi and Rancurello both report that Ida was a Catholic, thus implying that she had converted.[133]) Sulloway reports that Brentano and Breuer corresponded extensively with each other from about 1885 to 1895, and, of course, Freud was a close colleague and friend of Breuer[134]; Kraus notes that Breuer was Brentano's personal physician.[135] Furthermore, Anna Lieben, the niece of Theodore Gomperz and a member of Ida Lieben's family, was a patient first of Breuer and later of Freud.[136] What this means is that Brentano was not just an important university influence who was left behind after graduation, but that he must have remained a presence in Freud's social and intellectual environment in the 1880s and much of the 1890s as well. This would have been in a time when Brentano was a prominent and respected figure, and when Freud, years before the founding of psychoanalysis, was still anxiously concerned with making his mark.

Conclusion

In this survey of Freud's youthful years, we have examined a variety of subjects, ranging from the proposed Amalia–Philipp affair and Freud's rejection of his father, through the major impact of the Philippson Bible and his view of himself as the faithful Scipio, to the influence of Franz Brentano. And I think we can safely say that whatever the young Freud was, he was far indeed from being a "natural atheist."

Chapter Three

Young Manhood and Early Maturity: 1882–1900

W E NOW TAKE UP what will prove for our topic to be the most important years in Freud's life: his late 20s, his 30s, and his early 40s. These were his adult years before his major ideas were published and before he became a public figure. At the end of this period he was engaged in founding psychoanalysis, but throughout this time Freud was an ambitious but unknown physician–scientist struggling to make a name.

Engagement Letters: Easter, Pentecost, and Other Christian Themes

Freud and Martha Bernays (pictured together in Figure 3-1) became engaged in June 1882 and were married when Freud was 30 and his wife 25, in September 1886.[1] Schur comments in his biography on this four-year engagement (a period that ended when Freud was in a financial position to support a family): "To the dismay of the lovers, but to the delight of future biographers and critics, Freud and his beloved were separated most of the time. Freud wrote to her practically every day."[2]

These letters tell us much about Freud's attitude toward religion when, in his late 20s, he was preoccupied with his fiancée and with furthering his scientific research career. Eissler calls this time of Freud's engagement a *"Sturm und Drang"* period.[3] The immediately preceding years at the University found Freud "vacillating in his interests, doubtful about his place in the world and mildly hypochondriacal,"[4] though under no great psychological tension. But Freud during his engagement is well described by Eissler as "passionately ambitious, acutely rivalrous, and

Figure 3-1. Martha Bernays and Sigmund Freud at the time of their engagement. (Mary Evans/Sigmund Freud Copyrights)

suffering from spells of short-lasting, almost pathological jealousy."[5] It was also a time in which Freud was frequently depressed and hopeless almost to the point of despair. Elements of these reactions can be seen in the correspondence quoted below.

A major contributor to these reactions, especially to the jealousy and depression, was almost certainly Freud's separation anxiety. This old anxiety would have been reactivated by the fact that his assiduously courted fiancée left Vienna the day after their engagement and returned with her mother for a 12-week stay at Wandsbek near Hamburg in northern Germany. Later, in June of the next year, the Bernays moved back to Wandsbek.[6] (The Bernays were Orthodox Jews who had rather recently moved from Hamburg to Vienna, and the mother always preferred the northern city. It is, moreover, likely that Freud's future mother-in-law was unenthusiastic about Sigmund. After all, he was a poor man; a free-thinker who rejected Jewish practices; and a man who brooked no rivals for Martha's allegiance.[7])

The woman to whom he wrote the letters is of great relevance, and I pause here to provide some information about her background and character. Martha Bernays was a petite, attractive girl who came from a culturally distinguished Jewish family. Her grandfather, Isaac Bernays, had been the chief Rabbi of Hamburg, and had fought actively in the 1840s against the Jewish Reform movement, which had been especially strong at the time.[8] Grandfather Bernays was a friend of the great writer Heinrich Heine, and the Bernays were related to Heine through marriage.[9] Two of Isaac's sons, Martha's uncles, went into academic life; one, Michael Bernays, became a professor at the University of Munich. He reached this rank in part because he converted to Christianity.[10] Some such conversions were deeply religious, while others involved only modest religious elements, but commonly they were primarily motivated by personal expedience. Because of official barriers to them, many Jews whose faith was not strong converted to remove hindrances to their advancement. Heine himself converted, and apparently his conversion was of the type that involved some small amount of genuine religious motivation.[11] The other Bernays brother and Martha's father both remained true to their Jewish heritage.[12]

Martha's father Berman, who had died prior to Freud's meeting Martha,[13] had been a merchant, and his family was decidedly Jewish; the parents have been described as adhering to the strict rules of Orthodox Judaism.[14] (Martin Freud has also described Emmeline Bernays, Martha's mother, as Orthodox.[15]) The Jewish Sabbath and holidays were regularly observed in the Bernays home.[16] Martha herself does not appear to have been strongly religious in any intellectual sense, but she had a deep family loyalty, was observant, and had almost certainly a respect and love for the traditional observances. Although Martha was quite capable of standing up to Freud, she nevertheless went along with the rejection of religious observances in family life.[17] In the Sigmund Freud household there were no Jewish observances. Martha acquiesced in this with a reluctance that remained throughout their long and in many ways successful marriage. On this issue, Roazen writes:

In 1938 Martha and Freud were still carrying on a long-standing humorous (and yet serious) argument over the issue of lighting candles on Friday evening; Martha joked at Freud's monstrous stubbornness which prevented her from performing the ritual, while he firmly maintained that the practice was foolish and superstitious.[18]

Jones makes it clear that over Jewish practices there was some real conflict between Freud and Martha's family.[19] In going against such practices, Freud was taking risks with respect to his relationship with Martha and her mother, Emmeline: He was jeopardizing his marriage plans, for Martha was a seriously practicing Jew.

It is important for the reader to keep several points in mind as we examine these letters. They were, of course, Freud's love letters to his fiancée. But they were far more than simple expressions of affection. They were interesting, disturbing, often moving expressions of Freud's character and philosophy of life. In these letters, he was implicitly introducing himself to his future wife, letting her know what kind of man he was, telling her about his emotions, his values, his aspirations. At times we find hints that he was trying to look unrealistically good, but, considering the tendency for all lovers to misrepresent themselves in this way, Freud's letters were models of frankness; they were (and are), in addition, impressive examples of literary expression.

We may begin by noting a general—and striking—religious quality to the correspondence. All told, there are 94 published letters from Freud to Martha (some 1500 love letters were written and saved; only this group of 94 has been published),[20] and one is struck by the surprising number of references to God or to the Bible that are scattered throughout. For a "natural atheist," Freud certainly referred to what he did not believe in rather often. Here are a number of examples[21]:

May God punish him for it. (Letter 4)
. . . as I have always expected Christian Fürchtegott [fear of God] Gellert to look. (Letter 6)
. . . as if . . . they . . . lived in fear of God. (Letter 6)
. . . fear of God . . . love of God . . . love of God . . . Joy of God . . . (Letter 7)
[and also other references to God, all in an explicitly positive Jewish context] the Almighty. (Letter 8)
the Bible. (Letter 16)
. . . he is a miserable devil living by the grace of God's patience. (Letter 31) [in this statement, "he" and "a miserable devil" referred to Freud.]
They are, thank God . . . (Letter 40)
May we never have another like it. Amen. (Letter 50)
. . . the privilege of the Almighty that to Him . . . (Letter 52, to Minna Bernays, Martha's sister)

God only knows what I owe him already! (Letter 65) ["Him" was a friend—or was it God?]

I am quite calm and very curious about how the dear Lord is going to bring us together again.[22] [In this letter of March 1885, Freud was in an atypical confident mood.]

. . . and God was on their side. (Letter 85) ["Their" refers to the Biblical patriarchs.]

Thank God it's over. (Letter 94)

These references to God, even if just "figures of speech," were typically made in contexts where they were far from required by the sense of the topic. In addition, these expressions almost always conveyed considerable affect. Only in a pre-Freudian mentality can they be considered as "unimportant"; it was Freud himself who taught us to take such things seriously.

It is the specifically Christian nature of Freud's interests and preoccupations that is of the greatest relevance to us. Let us begin by looking at Freud's references to Whitsunday, or Pentecost.[23] At the end of a lengthy letter, written on May 29, 1884, he concluded as follows:

Fond Pentecost greetings, darling. What memories this season brings back—precious, lovely ones, and some bitter ones as well. If only you had stayed here! Your leaving will cost me part of my life. I shall be with you for your birthday, after all.

Once more, a fond Pentecost greeting from
Your
Sigmund[24]

The holiday of Pentecost, usually occurring in May, is of course distinctly Christian, and is seldom referred to outside of its religious significance. (Pentecost is the day that marks the descent of the Holy Spirit to the early Christian community—the Apostles, Mary, and the faithful—50 days after Easter.) In Catholic Moravia, Pentecost was a most important holiday, in some respects rivaling Easter.[25] Since Pentecost was also celebrated throughout the Austrian Empire, it inevitably became a fact of life for everyone, Christian or not. But Freud's reference here was far from a simple factual one; instead, it was quite emotional and fervent. Twice, he explicitly extended "fond Pentecost greetings" to Martha. For a secular Jew to have written this to his decidedly Jewish fiancée is most peculiar indeed. One also notes in the passage in question that Freud referred to memories in such a way as to suggest a more distant time than merely the two years during which Freud had been engaged to Martha. (Freud presumably experienced Pentecost with his Czech nanny.) The concern with separation, combined with "precious, lovely . . . and some bitter" memories, can, I believe, be best understood as a redintegration of Freud's association of the season of Pentecost with the loss of his nanny as described in Chapter One brought on by the present separation from his fiancée. Freud's reaction to Martha's absence is so peculiar that its link to his early separation trauma seems certain. He writes:

a frightful yearning—frightful yearning is hardly the right word, better would be uncanny, monstrous, ghastly, gigantic; in short, an indescribable longing for you.[26]

The theme of Pentecost appeared many times throughout Freud's life. All through his various correspondences, he referred to this feast often, generally to suggest a time of year for a meeting or reunion. (In his letters, it was always Freud who initiated the use of the word "Pentecost"; very occasionally, his correspondent would *then* use it once or twice as well.) In a letter to Martha a year later at Pentecost (May 26, 1885), Freud again brought up the subject:

My precious darling,
It would seem that as a result of the sympathy existing between us, your Pentecost has been no better than mine; that would be bad. Did you never wonder when you left Vienna how we should ever meet? Don't you remember how pleased I was when you promised to remain here?[27]

Again, there was no *a priori* reason for Freud to raise the topic of Pentecost, except that it was indeed that time of year; again, he brought it up in the context of an underlying melancholy over separation. Also worthy of note is his special pleasure when Martha had promised "to remain." But (like his nanny) she was unable to keep the promise, having had to leave Vienna for family reasons and go to live in Wandsbek.[28]

One of the important pieces of psychological evidence that Freud's nanny was dismissed at the time of Pentecost is the curious fact that years later in 1899 Freud used "the week before Pentecost to write the essay on 'Screen Memories'. . . "[29] In view of the biographical nature of this essay, such an anniversary reaction would reinforce the link among the nanny, separation anxiety, and the time of Pentecost.

There are other, curiously Christian accents in the Freud–Martha correspondence. In one of his first letters to Martha, written June 27, 1882, Freud listed some great places in the world that Martha would enjoy visiting: "the Alps, the waterways of Venice and the splendors of St. Peter's in Rome."[30] Since Freud had not yet seen any of these places himself, the list suggested more his own desires than anything else. As to his listing St. Peter's—the very center of Catholic Christendom—as one of the three places that his Jewish fiancée would most enjoy, it seems perhaps somewhat tactless; it was certainly odd.

During this same period, Freud made clear his rejection of the Jewish marriage ceremony. In October 1883, Freud's sister Anna married Eli Bernays, Martha's older brother. Freud did not attend the wedding of his sister and future brother-in-law.[31] (The reason for his absence is not clear.) In any case, from hearsay descriptions of the ceremonies, Freud labeled them "simply loathsome."[32] In 1884, he did attend the marriage of his friend Joseph Paneth, and in reaction wrote a 16-page letter to Martha expressing his horror at the odious scene, which he described in "a spirit of malign mocking" throughout the course of the long letter.[33]

If we grant, as Jones documents, that Freud wanted Martha to give up her "religious prejudices," how are we to account for the various pro-Christian comments made to her by Freud? A year later in 1885, Freud wrote, "What does it matter about the cross? We are not superstitious or piously orthodox."[34] The remark about the cross has been footnoted, "A jocular reference to Martha's remark that she ought to 'go to the cross'—i.e., humble herself."[35] Again, the language in the correspondence is suggestive of a Christian preoccupation. Unfortunately Martha's letter and the context of her remark have not been published, for possibly a "jocular" exchange was not all that was going on. Freud's comment that the cross did not matter because he was "not superstitious" sounds rather unconvincing when one reads a few letters later: "Do you believe in omens?" and "Since meeting you I have actually become quite superstitious."[36]

In October 1885, Freud visited Paris for several months in order to meet and study with the great medical scientist Charcot, then particularly known for his contributions to the study of hypnotism and psychopathology. This was Freud's first visit to Paris, and it was an important event in his life.[37] (He was able to afford the trip in large part because he had been awarded a fellowship for this specific purpose.[38])

Aside from his meeting Charcot, the experience with the greatest impact on Freud appears to have been his visits to the Cathedral of Notre Dame de Paris. He described his first visit:

> You are right, my darling, in saying that I have even more to tell you than before, and usually there is something I even forget to tell you, for instance my visit to Notre Dame de Paris on Sunday. My first impression on entering was a sensation I have never had before: "This is a church." . . . I have never seen anything so movingly serious and somber, quite unadorned and very narrow. . . .[39]

Besides the obvious significance of the experience for Freud, it should be mentioned that this visit was on a Sunday, when it is almost certain that Mass was being celebrated at least somewhere in the cathedral. In *The Interpretation of Dreams*, published 15 years later, Freud wrote: "The platform of Notre Dame was my favorite resort in Paris; every free afternoon I used to clamber about there on the towers of the church between the monsters and the devils."[40] The very name "Dame" would have resonated with his "*Amme*." To visit here—to be in the cathedral during Mass—would have been a partial recovery of his Czech "Dame," lost so long ago. Jones reports that "Freud's choice of a souvenir of Paris was a photograph of Notre Dame."[41] Again, all of this constituted a surprising communication to a Jewish fiancée who irritated Freud by her observance of the dietary laws in her house and by her refusal to write letters on the Sabbath. Both rules, after pressure, Freud got Martha to abandon.[42]

Charcot, whom Freud admired greatly, was somehow associated for him with Notre Dame. In a letter written a few days after the letter about Notre Dame, Freud wrote to Martha that he was being deeply affected by his stay in Paris, especially by Charcot, about whom he said:

Charcot, who is one of the greatest physicians and a man whose common sense borders on genius, is simply wrecking all my aims and opinions. I sometimes come out of his lectures as from Notre Dame, with an entirely new idea about perfection.[43]

The link between Charcot and Notre Dame—and Catholicism—was further developed in another letter, in which Freud described Charcot as "like a worldly priest."[44] Charcot did have a profound impact on Freud, for as a result of his exposure to Charcot's discussions and observation of hysteria and hypnosis, Freud's attachment to physiological and anatomical types of science weakened, and his interest in psychopathological phenomena increased markedly. Throughout his life Freud kept his admiration for Charcot, and it was for him that he named his eldest son Jean-Martin.[45]

Other religiously "loaded" expressions were used in Freud's Paris letters. For example, in correspondence anticipating the Paris trip, he wrote optimistically of going to Paris, where he would become a great scholar and "then come back to Vienna with a huge enormous halo"[46]— the halo, implying sanctity, being of course a strictly Christian iconographical symbol. In another letter he speaks of Paris and the Parisians as "uncanny" and of the whole visit as representing a pleasant, confused dream.[47] (More is said about this confused dream-like quality of the Paris visit in Chapter Four, in the section on Hugo's *Notre Dame de Paris*.) Near the end of his stay, he exclaimed: "[W]hat an ass I am to be leaving Paris now that spring is coming, Notre Dame looking so beautiful in the sunlight. . . . "[48] In short, the Paris episode was positive, exciting, dreamlike, uncanny; at its center were Notre Dame (*Amme*) and the priestlike Charcot, with their suggestion of "an entirely new idea about perfection."

It is an interesting detail—and presumably a reflection of the mind set we have just been discussing—that just before the trip to Paris, Freud asked Martha to embroider what Jones calls two "votive panels," which Freud wished to hang over his desk in his hospital room.[49] One of the inscriptions came from Voltaire's *Candide*, the other from St. Augustine

("When in doubt, abstain"). A third, which Martha embroidered three years later, was a favorite saying of Charcot: "One must have faith."[50]

Still another (and especially important) involvement of Freud with Christian themes was expressed in these engagement letters to Martha Bernays. In a letter written rather early in the engagement, on December 20, 1883, Freud recounted a visit that he made with his half-brother Philipp to the city of Dresden: "Right next to the castle we discovered a wonderful cathedral, then a theater, and finally a spacious building . . . it was the so-called Zwinger which houses all of Dresden's museums and art treasures."[51] Freud admired and wrote movingly of three paintings he saw there. The first was Holbein's *Madonna* (see Figure 3-2):

The Madonna holds the boy in her arms and gazes down on the worshippers with such a holy expression. . . . The Madonna herself is not exactly beautiful— the eyes protrude, the nose is long and narrow—but she is a true queen of heaven such as the pious German mind dreams of.[52]

Freud then described the second painting, Raphael's *Madonna* (see Figure 3-3):

Now I happened to know that there was also a Madonna by Raphael there and I found her at last in an equally chapel-like room and a crowd of people in silent devotion in front of her. You are sure to know her, the Sistina. . . . The painting emanates a magic beauty that is inescapable, and yet I have a serious objection to raise against the Madonna herself. Holbein's Madonna is neither a woman nor a girl, her exultation and sacred humility silence any question concerning her specific designation. Raphael's Madonna, on the other hand, is a girl, say sixteen years old; she gazes out on the world with such a fresh and innocent expression, half against my will she suggested to me a charming, sympathetic nursemaid, not from the celestial world but from ours.[53]

As for the third and final painting, Titian's *Maundy Money* (see Figure 3-4), Freud wrote:

But the picture that really captivated me was the "Maundy Money" by Titian. . . . This head of Christ, my darling, is the only one that enables even people like ourselves to imagine that such a person did exist. Indeed, it seemed that I was compelled to believe in the eminence of this man because the figure is so convincingly presented. And nothing divine about it, just a noble human countenance, far from beautiful yet full of seriousness, intensity, profound thought and deep inner passion. . . . I would love to have gone away with it, but there were too many people about, . . . so I went away with a full heart.[54]

Freud's heart was filled almost certainly from springs that went back to his Freiberg days and to the nanny whom he loved and who took him to so many churches. All the cues were right. He was with his half-brother Philipp, whom he had rarely seen after leaving Freiberg—the brother involved with his nanny's arrest and sudden disappearance. He was

Figure 3-2. After Hans Holbein, *Madonna of Bürgermeister Meyer of Basel*. (Staatliche Kunstsammlungen Dresden)

Figure 3-3. Raphael, *The Sistine Madonna.* (Staatliche Kunstsammlungen Dresden)

Figure 3-4. Titian, *The Tribute Money*; called "The Maundy Money" by Freud. (Staatliche Kunstsammlungen Dresden)

visiting a new city, Dresden, which is situated north of Vienna, not too far from Breslau in eastern Germany, and which is reached via train by traveling through Czechoslovakia, including Moravia.[55] After stopping at a "wonderful cathedral," Freud spent his time before paintings either of the Madonna and Child or of Christ. His comments indicate a previous knowledge of one of these paintings (Raphael's *Madonna*) and a special interest in the age of the Madonna—an issue that made him think of a nursemaid. The chapel-like atmosphere of reverence would also have supported reveries and associations from the past. The visit occurred during the Christmas season, a time associated with the nanny. The entire discussion prefigured Freud's analysis, 25 years later, of Leonardo's *Virgin and Child with St. Anne* (1910a). Furthermore, in Freud's autobiographical response to all these paintings, there was an implicit identification of himself with Jesus as an infant (and, in the last painting, with Christ at the time of his betrayal). Then, too, strong sound similarities would have linked his two mothers with these paintings: "Amalia" and "Mama" all easily connect to "*Amme*," to "Dame," and then to "Anna" and "Nana"—all summed up in "Madonna."[56]

Above all, Freud's remarks were not about the style or form of these works. His reactions were not those of the art historian or aesthete. Freud was a man who always responded to a work in terms of its psychological content; he reliably ignored purely historical and stylistic issues (sometimes at his peril, as, for example, Meyer Schapiro has shown).[57] It is also worth noting that aside from the *Mona Lisa*, the only paintings that Freud wrote about were explicitly Christian paintings, almost always centered on one or more members of the Holy Family: Mary, Anne, or Jesus. Freud may have personally collected and admired pre-Christian antiquities, but the art that moved him deeply enough for him to write about it was essentially religious and typically Christian. Even Michelangelo's *Moses*, to be discussed later, belongs in a Christian context: The work is, of course, by one of the greatest Christian artists; it is part of a tomb in Rome honoring a great Pope; and Freud observed it from inside a small Christian church.[58]

The Fliess "Roman" Letters: 1887–1902

After his marriage, Freud settled into family life and began concentrating fully on his career as a practicing physician, specializing more and more in the psychopathologies. By this time Freud had turned away from a research career at the University of Vienna, where he worked in the laboratory of great scientists, such as Ernst Brücke. One important reason for leaving the university research setting was that Freud's relative poverty and to some degree his Jewishness were real barriers to advancement. I would argue that Freud was also beginning to suspect that his basic intellectual motivation and interest lay not in physiology and anatomy, but in the direction of psychology; he could study the latter just as well through his own practice, and in association with a hospital. This does not mean that Freud abandoned his youthful ambitions of a university research career without painful regrets. But abandon them he did.[59]

During his 30s—that is, roughly from the time he was married at age 30 until his 40th birthday in 1896—Freud's intellectual life was in transition. From his training in medicine, neurology, anatomy, and related topics, he moved to an increasing involvement with what had been his earlier predilections for psychology, literature, cultural history, mythology and anthropology. It was, if you will, a midlife crisis, in which Freud was finding out that his essential and natural motivation lay with ideas quite far removed from his prior university training. During this decade, he became familiar with the technique of hypnosis; he began to appreciate the importance of sex in the etiology of neurotic problems; and he first began to understand the significance of fantasies and dreams. His "monomaniacal" study of the neuroses[60] brought him some notoriety because of the unusual character of the conditions he was studying, as well as a modest reputation as an authority on certain neurotic conditions, such as hysteria.[61] He was appointed as a lecturer at the University of Vienna, but it was not a time of success.[62] Freud was still deeply discontented—both financially, for his practice was small and his family large, and in a deeper sense, for he was still searching for the center of his intellectual and emotional life. He was at the threshold of what is now known as psychoanalysis, and indeed of the entire psychological mentality so prevalent today. But this threshold was not crossed until Freud went through his own personal psychoanalysis.

Before we come to this systematic "self-analysis," a few more words are in order about the shift from the university world to private practice. Freud's career as a young scientist at the University of Vienna was dominated by non-Jewish figures. The major model for Freud was Professor Ernst Brücke, head of the research institute in which Freud was studying. Freud expressed this directly and at length:

[I]n Ernst Brücke's physiological laboratory, I found rest and satisfaction—and men, too, whom I could respect and take as my models: the great Brücke himself, and his assistants Sigmund Exner and Ernst von Fleischl-Marxow. With the last of these, a brilliant man, I was privileged to be upon terms of friendship.[63]

The other men, Exner and Fleischl (the "von" and Marxow are usually omitted from Fleischl's name) were the assistants in Brücke's lab and directly superior to Freud in rank. Exner was in the process of becoming a world-famous physiologist. He, like Fleischl, was from a wealthy and socially prominent Viennese family.[64]

Thus, in this university-based, scientific period of Freud's life, his most influential models were, first, Brentano; then Charcot (for whom he named his eldest son, as noted above); also, in limited respects, Meynert[65]; and finally Brücke (for whom he named his son Ernst),[66] Exner, and Fleischl. All were Gentiles except the last: Fleischl was an assimilated Jew.[67] Because of Fleischl's illness—to which I return later—he was the least scientifically prominent of the group, but he was Freud's best friend at the lab. By contrast, the world into which Freud was moving—the world of private practice and informal intellectual networks that would culminate in the group of psychoanalysts centered around Freud himself—was primarily Jewish, and would remain so throughout Freud's life.

At the end of this decade of change from the university–science–biology world into his specialization in psychopathology, Freud was to start on his self-analysis, which took place roughly from 1896 to 1899. The death of Freud's father on October 23, 1896, was a most important event that apparently accelerated this analysis, for (among other things), it brought back the meaning of his father to him as a child. It also freed Freud to face his own attitudes toward his father in a way that would not have been possible if Jakob had still been living.

Whatever one may think of psychoanalysis, it is important to recognize the courage that this first analysis required—the toughness to investigate alone early hatreds and sexual desires, mostly directed at members of one's immediate family. Freud received real help and encouragement during this time from Wilhelm Fliess. This aid was mostly from a distance, through the exchange of letters, although the two men did have very important occasional visits together.

Fliess was a friend of Freud's; he was also a doctor and secular Jew, with interests similar to Freud's.[68] He lived in Berlin, and the two carried on a lengthy correspondence, which was fascinating and brilliant, but often bizarre. Fliess was, at the time of the friendship, a rather prominent physician and intellectual; certainly he was much better known than Freud. Sulloway, in a major biographical treatment of Freud, has shown that many fundamental "Freudian" concepts had their origin with Fliess. Among these concepts were infantile sexuality, latency, sublimation, reaction formation, bisexuality, and others.[69] (Fliess also had other ideas, which by today's standards are quite strange—e.g., that the nose is closely connected to the origin of both physical and psychological illness.[70]) Sulloway convincingly demonstrates the essential intellectual importance of Fliess for Freud, and he dispels the earlier myth of Fliess as an obvious intellectual "kook" who apparently appealed to Freud only because of obscure personal reasons and because he gave Freud a sympathetic, noncritical hearing of his ideas when others were rejecting them.[71]

As a person, Fliess is described as a man of considerable personal charm and charisma to whom many were attracted.[72] Eventually he and Freud quarreled bitterly. The relationship began to deteriorate in 1898, and it was over by 1902.[73] Part of the quarrel, as Sulloway makes clear, was fueled by Fliess's anger that some of his ideas about bisexuality had been passed on by Freud to people in Vienna, who subsequently published on the topic without acknowledging Fliess.[74] (Academics will understand this rage.) Sulloway has also shown that Freud's intense rivalry with Fliess underlay his failure to acknowledge the many contributions of his friend and colleague from Berlin.[75]

But Sulloway's primary contribution is to document thoroughly the particular scientific sources of much of Freud's philosophy and general scientific attitude. Freud's rationalism, his determinism, and his assumption that the mind is ultimately physical (or, rather, physiological) came from such great scientific theorists as Darwin, Romanes, Helmholtz, Brücke, Fechner, and others.[76] We should never lose sight of the fact that Freud was operating in a medical environment, where biological science, Darwinian theory, and good medical practice were the common models from which one approached an understanding of the mental life. (The other and, I argue, even *more* fundamental source of influence on Freud's ideas and "philosophy" was, in fact, literature. This argument is taken up in Chapter Four.)

The correspondence between Fliess and Freud—particularly the letters of Freud—is well known as being of great historical importance for the origin of psychoanalysis; in a somewhat censored form, the letters have been available for years.[77] They have already been frequently cited here, as they constitute the primary source on Freud's childhood memories. In the letters, he discussed his recovery of the memory of his nanny, of his baby brother's death, and of various other topics already examined. A major new theme occurred in the critical last five years of the correspondence, 1897–1902. This theme—or pair of linked themes—was that of Rome and Easter.

Freud first wrote of Rome to Fliess on December 3, 1897: "I dreamt I was in Rome . . . the Rome of my dreams was really Prague . . . the dream had fulfilled my wish to meet you in Rome rather than in Prague."[78] Here we see the connection between Rome and Prague; both of these were associated with Freud's Czech *Amme*, whose memory he had recovered earlier that year.[79]

Freud was aware that his repeated mention of Rome, and his dreams about it, indicated an underlying conflict. In the same letter, he noted: "Incidentally, my longing for Rome is deeply neurotic. It is connected with my schoolboy hero-worship of the Semitic Hannibal, and in fact this year I have no more reached Rome than he did from Lake Trasimene."[80] But almost everything deeply neurotic about Freud went back (as he himself asserted) to his first three years in Freiberg. And we have already seen how Freud's identification with Hannibal was at least in part a screen for his partisanship with Scipio and Rome.

At this time in his life, as Freud commented about Hannibal's failure to reach Rome, he had not yet been able to overcome his block to visiting

Rome, though he had traveled in Italy. It would be four more years before he could overcome his inhibitions and finally make the visit he had long dreamed of. Returning to the Fliess letters, we find this ambivalence stated again in October 1898: "In any case I am not in a state to do anything else, except study the topography of Rome, my longing for which becomes more and more acute."[81]

On February 6 of the next year, Freud brought the topic of Easter into his Roman preoccupation:

The secret dossier is getting thicker and thicker [presumably—though one cannot be certain—this refers to the "dream book" Freud was working on, which was soon published as "*The Interpretation of Dreams*], as if it were really looking forward to being *opened at Easter. I am curious myself about when Easter in Rome will be possible* [emphasis added].[82]

Then two or three weeks later he wrote: "I cannot wait for Easter to show you in detail one of the principal features—that of wish fulfillment and the coupling of opposites."[83] Later in the same letter, we find: "Rome is still far away; you know my Roman dreams." In the same letter, Freud went on: "Sunday is still a fine institution, though Martin thinks that Sundays are getting fewer and farther between. Easter really is no longer so distant. Are your plans fixed yet? I am already itching to be off." And finally, near the end of this letter:

Also I have a secondary motive; the realization of a secret wish which might mature at about the same time as Rome, so, when Rome becomes possible, perhaps I shall throw up the lectureship. But, as I have said, we are not in Rome yet.

What the secret wish may have been is not clear, though Velikovsky has one plausible interpretation (see below). Whatever this wish was, it apparently involved leaving Vienna, possibly to settle in Rome—something Freud spoke openly of later.

The next Roman reference was made in August 1899:

What would you think of ten days in Rome at Easter (the two of us of course) if all goes well, if I can afford it and have not been locked up, lynched or boycotted on account of the Egyptian dream book? I have looked forward to it for so long. Learning the eternal laws of life in the Eternal City would be no bad combination.[84]

Finally, in his letter of April 16, 1900, Freud wrote in the last paragraph: "If I closed with 'Next Easter in Rome,' I would feel like a pious Jew."[85] (For a pious Jew, the expression is, in fact, "Next year in Jerusalem"!)

I think it is simply impossible to avoid the conclusion that Freud was deeply attracted to Christian Rome. How else is one to account for his preoccupation with Easter, with its theme of rebirth or resurrection, and with Rome, the symbolic locus of the Christian (specifically, Catholic) faith? Now, as I have said several times, I do not wish to deny Freud's strong, consciously articulated hostility to Rome and Christianity, but his well-known anti-religious statements cannot be allowed to blind us to the obviously pro-Christian aspects of the passages quoted from his letters to Fliess. In them, he spoke repeatedly of Rome, and above all of being there on Easter![86] He described his emotion as one of acute longing, a phrase strongly implying a personal longing for someone—in this case, almost certainly his nanny. It is as though, somehow, even after 40 years, Freud dreamed of being reunited with his Anna "in Rome" (in all the deep symbolic sense of that word); of discovering rebirth and salvation; of being made whole with her.

Why should he associate missing his nanny with Rome and Easter? There are several possible reasons. Obviously, his nanny was Catholic and often took him to Mass, but why Rome? I have discovered by asking those familiar with Moravian Catholic customs that not only was Easter a major and drawn-out holiday in which the entire village would have participated; but there was also a strong tradition that every good Catholic should try to visit Rome at least once in his lifetime. Above all, the desire was to be in Rome on Easter.[87] This desire to make a pilgrimage to Rome for Easter could easily have been communicated to Sigmund by his nanny.

There is also a most interesting story that was told to little Czech children at Easter. On Good Friday in Czechoslovakia, the bells of every church were silent in honor of Christ's suffering on the cross. Since church bells were an important part of any town's atmosphere, the children would naturally ask about their silence, their "absence." They were told that on that day, Good Friday, all the bells had flown to Rome to be rejuvenated; they then flew back on Holy Saturday, ready to ring out noisily in honor of the Resurrection on Sunday morning.[88] This simple story was (and is) apparently as commonplace in Czechoslovakia as the more complicated Santa Claus story is here in America.

At this late date, it is probably impossible to find any documentable evidence for this Czech cultural influence on Freud, but it is obvious that the nanny and Rome were strongly associated in his mind (some additional evidence is given below).[89] Furthermore, it must be emphasized that Rome and Easter, linked together, very definitely signify resurrection, salvation, or rebirth. This is the meaning of Easter. For Freud to speak enthusiastically about Easter in Rome—where St. Peter's Square would be crowded with people celebrating the resurrection; where the whole city would be affected by the Easter atmosphere—was quite simply for Freud to reveal his hidden partisanship for Christian Rome. We may recall his reference to a "secret wish," to his desire possibly to start a new life in Rome "learning the eternal secrets." Of course, he referred as well to his identification with Hannibal, and there can be no doubt about his conscious hostility to Rome; however, we should also recall that his just-proposed principle of wish-fulfillment includes the "coupling of opposites."

We have looked at some of the major references to Easter and Pentecost, but what is also striking is the sheer *number* of references to these Christian holidays, coupled with the absence of any mention of any Jewish holidays. In the 1954 edition of the letters to Fliess, there are 23 references to Easter; the complete edition of 1985 provides 12 additional references to Easter in the period 1897-1902. References to Pentecost (Whitsunday), with its association to spiritual rebirth, occur in six letters of the 1954 edition and eight more letters of the 1985 edition.[90] In a clearly Christian reference, Freud described his young son Ernst in one letter as being as "full of wounds as Lazarus"[91]; the reference is unmistakably to the beggar mentioned in Luke 16:20 ff. (See the discussion of Heine's *Lazarus* poems in Chapter Six.)

Freud referred to God occasionally in the correspondence, and not in any obviously negative way—though sometimes with a certain sarcasm, as here: "Now in this case the Almighty was kind enough to remove the father by death before the child was eleven months old."[92] In any case, in this series of 150 letters, I could not find a single reference to any strictly Jewish religious idea.

After Freud had completed and published *The Interpretation of Dreams*, he finally overcame his inhibitions and visited Rome. However, Freud never did visit Rome at Easter, which was his greatest desire. Some inhibition permanently held him back from that. Instead, his visits were almost always in September—the worst time of year with respect to weather, and the least likely to have any Christian liturgical significance.[93] Be all that as it may, his first visit was a most important event, about which he wrote to Fliess as follows:

I ought to write to you about Rome, but it is difficult. It was an overwhelming experience for me, and, as you know, the fulfillment of a long-cherished wish. It was slightly disappointing, as all such fulfillments are when one has waited for them too long, but it was a high-spot in my life all the same. But, while I contemplated ancient Rome undisturbed (I could have worshipped the humble and mutilated remnant of the Temple of Minerva near the forum of Nerva), I found I could not freely enjoy the second Rome; I was disturbed by its meaning, and, being incapable of putting out of my mind my own misery and all the other misery which I know to exist, I found almost intolerable the lie of the salvation of mankind which rears its head so proudly to heaven.[94]

Statements such as this one have been used (e.g., by Jones) to portray Freud's attachment to Rome as based only on his attraction to ancient and modern Rome; the image is of a Freud who rejected medieval and Renaissance Rome.[95] Nothing could be farther from the truth, and (oddly enough) the evidence for the erroneousness of such an interpretation is abundantly provided by Jones himself. First, there is the ambivalence expressed in the statement "I could not freely enjoy the second Rome": Freud did not say he could not enjoy Catholic Rome, only that he could not enjoy it *freely*. Moreover, Freud found *intolerable* the "lie of salvation." With this curiously strident tone, what Freud was communicating was his anger that salvation does not exist; there is here a clear sense of disappointment. It is as though something that Freud had hoped for did not happen—or, one might say, that someone he had hoped to meet was not there.

Certainly another difficulty with the Jones thesis is that, at the time of Freud's visits at the turn of the century, Rome had a very strong, profoundly Catholic atmosphere—much more so than is the case today. In those days, modernism had not yet affected the city in all its frenetic, secularist, and materialistic ways as it has today. It was a time when churches and church bells, Christian pilgrims, and religious processions were an essential part of Rome's outward (and inward) character. Catholic religious figures (priests and monsignors, monks, nuns) in clerical dress were omnipresent. In short, anyone who was seriously disturbed by Christianity—in particular, by Roman Catholicism—would have had real difficulty in developing a strong liking for the Rome of 80 years ago.

Evidence indeed shows that Freud was positively drawn by many things Christian in Rome and elsewhere in Italy. One need merely look at the sorts of things Freud visited and described in Rome and in other Italian locales. In 1898, before he had yet been able to bring himself to go to Rome, he was already speaking of "our lovely Italy," on the basis of his travels in the northern part of the country.[96] In a visit to the town of Aquileia, he wrote that "several hundred of the prettiest Friulian girls had gathered in the Cathedral for High Mass. [It was, in fact, Easter Mass, though this is not always indicated.[97]] The splendor of the old Romanesque Basilica was comforting in the midst of the modern poverty."[98]

Once Freud broke the ice with Rome, he went as often as he could and constantly praised Rome and its effect on his emotional life.[99] As mentioned earlier, he even suggested once that he would like to settle there permanently with his wife.[100] (This wish is reminiscent of his peculiar suggestion—made once, rather in passing, to Martha in their correspondence—that he might set up practice in Silesia or Moravia, thus, near Freiberg.[101])

Also in northern Italy, he much enjoyed his visit to Venice (mentioned in a letter to Martha), in which he went up the tower at St. Mark's; visited a church and the Scuola San Rocco; and enjoyed a plethora of

Tintorettos, Titians, and Canovas.[102] He visited Assisi; in Milan he went to see the *Last Supper*, and spoke favorably of it.[103] At another time he spoke of "comparing memories, the view from the fortress reminded us of Florence, the Fortrezza itself of S. Pietro in Verona."[104] I find it hard to imagine someone more devoted to Italy and Rome than Freud; it must also be said that Freud hardly attempted to avoid Christian art in Italy (if he had, it would have been hard to succeed). In any case, his frequent expressions of appreciation for Christian art would indicate a tolerance for Christianity, if not outright admiration for it.

But Freud's ambivalence remained. One particular example bears this out in an intriguing manner. Gregory Zilboorg, whose succinct analysis I quote, has identified and commented on this detail:

Freud in *The Psychopathology of Everyday Life*, reports how he remembers relating to a fellow train passenger his profound impression of the frescoes in the Duomo [cathedral] of Orvieto. To his amazement, Freud was unable to tell at the moment either the subject matter of the frescoes or the name of the artist. By way of a series of free associations, he finally recalled the name of the master painter, Signorelli. By way of careful self-analysis, he concluded that he had repressed the name because of its first half, *Signor*, to which he arrived via a number of associations, one of them being the German word *Herr*.

It was a remarkable piece of self-analysis on the part of Freud. Yet what appears not less remarkable is that that piece of psychoanalysis done in 1898 . . . lacked the recognition of what now appears so obvious: *Signor* is the Italian equivalent of *Lord* in Church language, as is the German word *Herr*. Freud saw mainly the formal connections in his associations; he failed to see some of the deeper content of the repressed. It is, for instance, of particular interest that the subject matter of Signorelli's frescoes in the Orvieto Duomo is *The Last Judgment*.[105]

In short, Freud repressed God but admired His paintings. It should also be mentioned that God, who was denied access to Freud's conscious mind in this incident, occurred here in the very Christian context of a painting of the Last Judgment by a Christian artist in Italy, and that Freud was deeply moved by this fresco.

Another instance of Freud's "slipping" with respect to God, again in a decidedly Christian context, has been cited rather often. In a letter to Fliess in February 1899 (a letter in which he immediately afterward spoke of wanting to be in Rome for Easter), Freud wrote:

The art of deceiving patients is certainly not very desirable. What has the individual come to, how slight must be the influence of the science of religion, which is supposed to have replaced the old religion, if one no longer dare disclose that it is this man's or that man's turn to die. . . . The Christian at least has the last sacraments administered a few hours in advance. Shakespeare says: "Thou owest Nature a death."[106]

Here is the slip: The quotation from Shakespeare should have read, "Thou owest *God* a death." This was not just an example of forgetfulness, because Freud was very accurate in general when it came to quoting Shakespeare. Moreover, the line as "rewritten" does not scan properly. (Freud made the same error later in *The Interpretation of Dreams.*[107]

To return to Freud's Christian activities, here is a passage by Jones, in which he describes Freud on a visit to Rome in 1907. Jones writes:

Rome was as heavenly as possible. If only we could live there. On the last day he climbed the Castle S. Angelo for a view of Rome, visited the Sistine Chapel once more and revelled in the wonderful antiquities of the Vatican Museum.[108]

Later in the same volume, Jones mentions receiving a postcard from Freud in 1912, in which he stated that "Rome had worked its old magic."[109] A few days later Jones received a letter from Rome in which Freud wrote of a bout with ill health that had begun before his arrival in Rome, but that was now improving: "I feel strengthened and relieved by the air and the impressions of this divine town. In fact, I have been more happy than healthy at Rome, but my forces are coming back."[110] While in Rome, Freud reported visiting the catacombs and enjoying the Vatican galleries; he commented about the city, "These brief visits leave one with an unappeased longing."[111]

We must not forget Freud's famous visits to study the *Moses* statue by Michaelangelo (see Figure 3-5)—visits that would result in Freud's famous essay on the work. In 1912, Freud visited the statue every day for a week or more.[112] To examine the piece, by the world's best-known Christian sculptor, he sat in the Church of San Pietro in Vincoli (St. Peter in Chains), where the statue adorns the tomb of Pope Julius II. (This Pope had the same name as Freud's brother Julius, whose death "planted the seeds of guilt.") Here, as Freud returned day after day to look at the Old Testament prophet (and father figure) set in a New Testament environment, he spent many moving hours.[113]

A letter written by Freud to Karl Abraham in 1913 perhaps best captures not only how Freud loved Rome, but also how much Rome did for him emotionally. It certainly makes clear that Freud's love was not for a churchless Rome: "I have quickly recovered my spirits and zest for work in the incomparably beautiful Rome, and in the free hours between visits to museums, churches and the Campagna I have managed to write. . . ."[114] It cannot be overemphasized that in the voluminous correspondence of Freud (and he wrote a staggering number of letters), almost the only times that he expressed happiness and joy, the times in which he escaped his baseline mood of melancholy and even sorrow, were when he was in Rome or speaking about it. Only in Rome did the sun seem to break into his life. Perhaps it was only in Rome that he was able to

Figure 3-5. Michelangelo, *Moses*, Chapel of St. Peter in Chains. (Alinari/Art Resource, NY)

recapture the presence of his *Amme*–Anna. Certainly much of his pleasure here went back to his childhood.

Some very specific support for this interpretation comes from a comment Freud made about the women of Rome: "The women in the crowd are very beautiful, so far as they are Roman. Roman women are, strange to say, even beautiful when they are ugly, but not many of them are that."[115]

One is reminded here of Bowlby's discussion of the reactions of people to the death of a loved one. For example, Bowlby describes one major phase of mourning as involving "yearning and searching for the lost figure lasting . . . sometimes for years."[116] Bowlby speaks of visits made by grieving persons to old haunts associated with their dead loved ones as they continue to search for them. It is into this pattern that Freud's visits to Rome, Notre Dame, and various other churches can be integrated, and in this context they make sense.

Freud was explicit about the source of happiness: "Happiness is the subsequent fulfillment of a prehistoric wish. That is why wealth brings so little happiness: money was not a wish in childhood."[117] What was Freud's childhood wish, if not reunion with his nanny? Possibly Freud had also through her learned to want to be in Rome, especially at Easter. Perhaps there was just a general association in his mind between his nanny and churches in general. Perhaps the refreshment of Rome was even more childlike and simple: If the bells flew to Rome to be rejuvenated, then so might he. Of course, Freud's wish to be in Rome at Easter may in fact have been a wish for some kind of salvation, and it is to that possibility that we turn next.

The Desire for Baptism: Velikovsky's Thesis and Freud's Dreams

In 1941, Emmanuel Velikovsky published an article analyzing the dreams of Freud as found in *The Interpretation of Dreams*. Velikovsky has proposed that these dreams showed that at the time of his self-analysis, Freud was struggling with the possibility of converting to Christianity— specifically, to Roman Catholicism. Enough material suggesting or at least consistent with such a possibility has already been presented in the present book to make Velikovsky's suggestion seem far from preposterous, and its out-of-hand rejection by Jones[118] is attended to later. But first Velikovsky's argument needs to be summarized.

According to Velikovsky, a major driving motivation for Freud at this period in his early 40s was professional advancement, and Freud was quite aware that his Jewishness was a serious obstacle to his desired goal of a professorship at the University of Vienna. Velikovsky claims that Freud's "inner struggle for unhampered advancement" meant that "he would have to conclude a Faust-pact; he would have to sell his soul to the Church."[119] Though he is unsure on this point, Velikovsky conjectures that Freud was unconscious of this desire.[120]

A Faust pact *with* the Church—a pact involving baptism—is a contradiction in terms; the Faust legend is part of the Christian tradition, and thus can hardly see baptism as diabolical. Velikovsky's notion that as part of his Faust pact Freud would "sell his soul to the Church" cannot, then, be accepted. (There is, however, a possibility that Freud was considering an insincere conversion. Freud might even have considered converting for the purpose of undermining the Church, but more is said on this question in the next section.)

Velikovsky begins his case by quoting (or quoting from and paraphrasing) a number of Freud's dreams. After each dream, he quotes (or quotes from and paraphrases) Freud's own interpretation of the dream, and then he gives his own interpretation. What I do here is to quote extensively from Velikovsky's presentation of Freud's dreams, Freud's interpretations, and his own interpretations; I then add my own commentaries. Because the amount of Velikovsky's material is considerable, and because much of it in my judgment is somewhat unconvincing, I cite only those portions of his argument that I consider to furnish the clearest case. (The curious reader is invited to read Velikovsky's entire article.)

I should say in advance that while I think it is virtually certain that Freud was both unconsciously and consciously tempted to convert, I do not believe that actual conversion was likely. There is a great deal of evidence of Freud's pride in his ethnic Jewishness, as well as evidence of his powerful rational skepticism about religion. These factors would, I believe, have served as a virtually insurmountable barrier to such a calculated conversion.

There is, however, ample reason to think that Freud was tempted to convert—really, to assimilate—for reasons of ambition and self-interest. Freud knew many who had been baptized at least in part for purposes of career advancement—for example, the much admired Heine, as well as his uncle-in-law Michael Bernays, the Goethe scholar. There was also the case of the well-known Austrian composer Gustav Mahler, who was baptized in Vienna during Freud's personal crisis in February 1897, and who then experienced a dramatic and immediate advancement in the Vienna music world.[121] (Mahler, like Freud, was Jewish and spent his early years in Moravia.[122])

But, in general, the reader is urged to view this dream interpretation material as supporting the thesis that Freud had a powerful unconscious attraction to Christianity, derived from his nanny and connected to the hope of her return and also to the hope of salvation; that this attraction would naturally be found in Freud's dreams; and that it would express itself in part through a veiled concern with conversion.

FREUD'S DREAM OF THE BOTANICAL MONOGRAPH

I have written a monograph on a certain plant. The book lies before me: I am just turning over a folded colored plate. A dried specimen of the plant as though from a herbarium is bound up with every copy.[123]

FREUD'S ANALYSIS AS PRESENTED BY VELIKOVSKY

Associations and Day-residues. In the morning he had seen in a book-seller's window a volume entitled The Genus Cyclamen, obviously a monograph on this plant. The cyclamen is his wife's favorite flower. He forgets to bring her flowers. . . . A memory from the time he went to high school (Gymnasium) is connected with the herbarium. The principal instructed the pupils to clean a herbarium in which there were small bookworms. On the pages (taken from the herbarium) were *crucifers* [emphasis Velikovsky's]. Preliminary examination in botany (again *crucifers*) [emphasis Velikovsky's] and weakness in this subject. Then "Crucifers suggest composites. The artichoke too is really a composite, and in actual fact one which I might call my favorite flower.[124]

VELIKOVSKY'S INTERPRETATION

The associations regarding crucifers (crucifers were mentioned three times by Freud in his associations) should not have led only to composites and artichokes but also to crucifix and crux. *Crucifer* means one who carries a cross (crux), hence a baptized person.

Herbarium suggests the sound association to Hebrew. A herbarium which contains a crux would be a baptized Hebrew. A herbarium which is a book (or contains pages from a book) containing a "crucifer" is the Bible, or Gospel. A monograph would be the writings on monothesism. To page through also means to turn the pages (*umschlagen*), to convert. Cyclamen contains the word "Amen."[125]

MY INTERPRETATION AND COMMENT

Freud's failure to associate the Christian significance of "cross" and "cross-bearer" to "crucifers" was indeed a telling omission. Freud himself seemed to sense his blockage here when he commented in his analysis on his weakness in botany, as evidenced in his failure to identify crucifers in his preliminary examination. He referred several times to cyclamens and artichokes as "favorites." A plausible word-play interpretation of cyclamen is "repeated (cycle)-amens." (In this context, it is worth noting another of Velikovsky's observations: "Trimethylamin remained a riddle for Freud in another dream. Tri—three; amin—Amen: hence belief in the Trinity, and baptism."[126])

FREUD'S DREAMS OF ROME

Before giving the next dream Freud states: "I note the fact that although the wish which excites the dream is a contemporary wish, nevertheless it is greatly reinforced by memories of childhood. [Was Freud here consciously referring to conscious and unconscious bases of conversion temptation? The "wish which excites the dream" is never identified—Vitz.] I refer to a series of dreams which are based on the longing to go to Rome. For a long time to come I shall probably have to satisfy this longing by means of dreams." Two dreams about Rome are briefly mentioned but not told. In regard to the second one it is stated: "The motive to see the promised land from afar is here easily recognizable."

The third dream about Rome: "I am at last in Rome as the dream tells me. To my disappointment the scenery is anything but urban: it consists of a little stream of dark water on one side of which are black rocks, while on the other are meadows with large white flowers. I notice a certain Herr Zucker (with whom I am superficially acquainted), and resolve to ask him to show me the way into the city."[127]

FREUD'S INTERPRETATION AS PRESENTED BY VELIKOVSKY

"It is obvious that I am trying in vain to see in my dream a city which I have never seen in my waking life." The scenery reminds him of Ravenna where he saw beautiful water-lilies in black water. Further the narcissi of Aussee. The dark rock recalls the valley of the Tepe at Karlsbad. The name Karlsbad reminds him of several Jewish anecdotes. One concerns a Jew who because he has no railroad ticket is put off the train repeatedly and who, upon being asked at one of the stations of his martyrdom where he is going replies: "If my constitution holds out—to Karlsbad." The memory of Karlsbad explains the peculiar circumstance that "I ask Mr. Zucker (*Zucker*—sugar) to show me the way." We usually send our patients with the constitutional disease, diabetes [*Zuckerkrankheit*] to Karlsbad. "Asking the way" is a direct allusion to Rome, for we all know "all roads lead to Rome." "The occasion for this dream was the proposal of my Berlin friend that we should meet in Prague at Easter. A further association with sugar and diabetes might be found in the matters which I had to discuss with him."

"During my last Italian journey I considered the plan of traveling in the following year to Naples via Rome." "I myself had walked in Hannibal's footsteps; as little as he was I destined to see Rome, and he too had gone to Campagna when all were expecting him in Rome. Hannibal, with whom I had achieved this point of similarity had been my favorite hero during my years at the "gymnasium" . . .

Freud continues: "Hannibal and Rome symbolized, in my youthful eyes, the contrast between the tenacity of Jùdaism and the organization of the Catholic Church. The significance for our emotional life which the anti-semitic movement has since assumed helped to fix the thoughts and impressions of those earlier days. Thus the desire to go to Rome has in my dream-life become the mask and symbol for a number of warmly cherished wishes, for whose realization one had to work with the tenacity and single-mindedness of the Punic soldier, though their fulfillment at times seemed as remote as Hannibal's life-long wish to enter Rome. And now, for the first time, I happened upon the youthful experience which even today still expresses its power in all these emotions and dreams."[128]

Freud then recited the incident of his father and the Christian who knocked off his hat and insulted him for being a Jew (this is mentioned in

Chapter Two). He also thought of Hamilcar, who made his son swear vengeance on the Romans.[129]

VELIKOVSKY'S INTERPRETATION

It is Rome, not however the scenery of a town but "a small stream with black water." Thus Rome is not the city but the Roman-Catholic Church which Freud had also mentioned in associations. . . . Rome is for him the symbol "of the cherished wishes, for whose realization one would like to work with the tenacity of the Punic soldier."

"Dark water" is the water of baptism. "On one side of the dark water, black rock"—Judaism, the sad life of the children of the Jewish people, "on the other, meadows with large white flowers"—Christianity, the happy life of those who are not persecuted.

It is characteristic that Freud in his associations twice arrived at the word "constitution." We shall interpret it in the civic–legal sense. According to the constitution the Jew does not have equal rights. In the anecdote too the Jew does not have equal rights. In the anecdote too the Jew is put off the train again and again "because he has no ticket." Under this constitution he cannot get on. The anecdote deals really with himself. To be a Jew is a "constitutional disease."

This road to Rome would not be Hannibal's road. For Hannibal Rome was no "promised land." But it might be for a Mr. Zucker who knows the roads. Not to submit, but to gain a victory the semitic general led his army towards Rome. But for a Jew the promised land was Jerusalem. The small stream of black water, a border like the Rubicon, signifies temptation and the anguish of the lonely wanderer from that dispersed people of whom he knew that it had stubbornly resisted powerful Rome for a thousand years.[130]

MY INTERPRETATION AND COMMENTS

The associations to this dream are obviously heavily involved with Freud's Jewishness, and as Velikovsky and I would both argue, with Roman Catholic Christianity. (Baptismal water was customarily left in the baptismal font year-round in Czech churches; such water would have appeared dark in the dimly lit churches of the 19th century.)

But let us go back to Freud's remarks in *The Interpretation of Dreams* just before he reported this dream. He said, in reference to an earlier Roman dream,

I dreamt once that I was looking out of a railway-carriage window at the Tiber and the Ponte Sant'Angelo. The train began to move off, and it occurred to me that I had not so much as set foot in the city. The view that I had seen in my dream was taken from a well-known engraving which I had caught sight of in the sitting-room of one of my patients.[131]

This quotation makes it clear that although Freud had not yet been to Rome, he could nonetheless dream of it as an urban environment if that was what his unconscious wanted. Hence, Velikovsky's claim that this was a symbolic dream involving the Catholic Church is, I think, very strong. It is significant that a few lines after the passage quoted above, Freud wrote about a Roman dream as follows: "There is more in the content of this dream than I feel prepared to detail; but the theme of 'the promised land from afar' was obvious in it."[132] We therefore have reason to believe that some of the religious aspects of these Roman dreams were censored by Freud in his commentary. Unlike Velikovsky, though, I think that for Freud Rome, not Jerusalem, was clearly "the promised land." After all, that desire would have gone back as far as his nanny (whom Velikovsky did not know about). We may also recall that Freud wrote to Fliess, "Next Easter in Rome" instead of "Next year in Jerusalem," which is the common Jewish expression of a religious hope.

We must also ask further about Karlsbad. The name means "Karl's baths or waters"—certainly another possible illusion to baptism (i.e., taking the waters). Underlying Karlsbad could also be Freud's unconscious memories of being bathed by his nanny; if so, such warm and intimate moments would further reinforce the baptism association. In any case, Strachey mentions that both "Rome and Karlsbad came to be identified as symbols of unattainable aims."[133] Karlsbad is in Czechoslovakia (Bohemia), and thus like Prague and Rome can be understood as a nanny symbol.[134]

We should remember, too, that Freud's allegiance to Hannibal hid his strong (or stronger) identification with Rome, so with respect to his opposition to Rome, perhaps "he doth protest too much."

But let us look at some new material. Just before Freud brought up the subject of Hannibal as an association to one of his Roman dreams, he wrote:

I was in the act of making a plan to bypass Rome next year and travel to Naples, when a sentence occurred to me which I must have read in one of our classical authors: "Which of the two, it may be debated, walked up and down in his study with the greater impatience after he had formed his plan of going to Rome—Winckelmann, the Vice-Principal, or Hannibal the Commander-in-Chief?"[135]

This unnamed "classical author" (whom Strachey identifies in a footnote as "Jean Paul"[136]) was alluding to Joachim Winckelmann (1717–1768), a well-known historical figure, considered by many to have been the founder of classical archeology. This archeologist and art historian came from a poor German Lutheran background, and for a time was a medical student in Vienna; however, in part for financial reasons, he moved into other occupations. He became very interested in and knowledgeable about ancient Roman art and architecture. Through this interest he met influential art connoisseurs among the Roman clergy. After several years of crisis in his 30s over conversion, he did convert to Catholicism. He moved to Rome, where he became librarian to Cardinal Passionei. After his conversion, Winckelmann went on to become a famous scholar who was received in Vienna with great honor by the Empress Maria Theresa of Austria. On the way back to Rome after receiving these honors, he was murdered under strange circumstances by a fellow traveler.[137]

There are obvious similarities between Winckelmann and Freud: a poor background; the study of medicine in Vienna; great interest in the past, especially in Roman archeology; and, if Velikovsky is correct, a concern with conversion, based at least in part on the desire for professional advancement. (One wonders whether Freud's acquaintance Herr Zucker, who was to show him the way to Karlsbad, was also associated with conversion. I have been unable to unearth any relevant information on this issue.[138])

Grigg, to whom I am indebted for bringing the importance of Winckelmann to my attention, has also very decisively connected Rome and the old nanny in Freud's Roman dreams.[139] Thus, Grigg further reinforces the Catholic meaning of Rome for Freud. Grigg is concerned to show how the nanny is part of Freud's Oedipus complex; he argues that Freud's travel phobia and his tendency to avoid Rome were part of unresolved Oedipal anxieties. It is possible that Oedipal anxiety was a factor in causing Freud's travel fears, over and above separation anxiety. But, in fact, I am not impressed by a proposed Oedipal basis for travel fear; separation anxiety provides a stronger basis. Still, both could conceivably operate together. An evaluation of Grigg's position is not necessary here, since his primary purpose is to emphasize the negative emotions of Freud associated with the nanny. I certainly do not wish to deny the existence of such negative feelings; however, Grigg, like the rest of the psychoanalytic authors, passes over the positive importance of this woman for Freud, though Freud himself directly testified to it (as we have seen).

Grigg brings up in passing another Christian component in this dream of Freud's. First, Grigg notes the similarity between the traveling Winckelmann and the traveling impecunious Jew (Freud, in his dream) who stowed away without a ticket. The problem of the nonexistent ticket is a symbol that Freud would have connected to his admired Heine, who was well known for saying that baptism is "the admission ticket to European civilization."[140]

He was caught, and each time tickets were inspected he was taken out of the train and treated more severely. At one of the stations on his *via dolorosa* he met an acquaintance who asked him where he was traveling to. "To Karlsbad" was his reply, "if my constitution can stand it."[141]

But this term of Freud's—"*via dolorosa*," or "way of sorrows"—is a Christian expression, since it refers to Christ's sorrowful journey to the crucifixion. This "way" is commonly commemorated in Catholic churches, especially on Good Friday. The commemoration involves what are called the "Stations of the Cross," in which the sufferings of Jesus (an "impecunious Jew") on Good Friday are remembered and identified with. Here Freud was expressing an unconscious identification with Jesus, as he was, in his dream, thrown out at a succession of "stations." This was one of the very few instances of Freud's identifying with Jesus, or any "suffering servant." Freud vastly preferred more clearly successful figures.

The historian Carl Schorske proposes the same significance for the "*via dolorosa*" in his discussion of the Rome dreams. He comments, "The lofty vision of Moses-Freud seeing Israel-Rome 'from afar' had its lowly analogue in the picture of the little-Jew-Christ-Freud reaching Carlsbad-Rome on a *via dolorosa*."[142] Schorske claims that all the Rome dreams "suggest, in one form or another, redemption or fulfillment that is never achieved . . . a longing for an assimilation to the gentile world that his strong waking conscience—and even his dream censor—would deny him."[143]

I want now to bring in a dream and its interpretation that Velikovsky overlooks, but whose anti-Jewish and implicitly pro-Christian aspects have been spotted by the psychoanalyst Oehlschlegel[144] and by Schorske.[145] The dream concerned Freud's uncle with the yellow beard.[146] I introduce it here to exemplify the concept of wish-fulfillment. The particular concern of Freud was to show that in the dream "we find the child and the child's impulses still living on."[147] Thus he was proposing that this dream showed his own childhood impulses. Freud's interpretation was that the impulses behind the dream content were derived from his intense ambition to be promoted to full professor. The dream expressed his rivalry with two of his colleagues who were Jewish and also up for promotion. Freud admitted that (in the dream) he maltreated his worthy colleagues merely because they were Jewish; One he represented as a simpleton, the other as a criminal. Freud concluded his analysis by mentioning that he had behaved as if he were the government minister in charge of making the promotions: "I had put myself in the Minister's place."[148] Oehlschlegel claims that in this dream Freud was revealing his rejection of his Jewishness and an identification with the Gentile minister. Jones pooh-poohs Oehlschlegel, but without providing any serious rebuttal of her position.[149] Oddly enough, despite Freud's repeated references to his strong desires for promotion (desires that have been termed "pathological"[150]), Jones, in rejecting Oehlschlegel, makes the unsupportable claim that "worldly advancement meant very little to him."[151] There Oehlschlegel's neglected interpretation might have remained, were it not that recently the same conclusion has been independently reached by the more prominent Schorske, who concludes that the "uncle" dream "revealed a disguised wish either not to be Jewish, or to have the power to eliminate Jewish rivals."[152]

Before we leave the Roman dreams, a last remark by Freud seems appropriate—a remark, made in a footnote, about his desire to go to Rome: "I discovered long since that it only needs a little courage to fulfill wishes which till then have been regarded as unattainable; and therefore became a constant *pilgrim* to Rome [emphasis added]."[153] Thus, one of Freud's childhood wishes—that of becoming a pilgrim and not a mere tourist or casual visitor to Rome—had been accomplished, and with it the hoped-for pleasure and psychic renewal.

FREUD'S DREAM ABOUT RIDING TO A CHAPEL

I am riding a gray horse, at first timidly and awkwardly, as though I were merely leaning on it. Then I meet a colleague, P., also on horseback and dressed in rough frieze (tweed); he is sitting high on his horse. He calls my attention to something (probably to the fact that I have a very bad seat). Now I begin to feel more and more at ease on the back of my highly intelligent horse; I sit more comfortably, and I find that I am quite at home up here. My saddle is sort of a pad which completely fills the space between the neck and the rump of the horse. I ride between two vans, and just manage to clear them. After riding up the street for some distance, I turn around and wish to dismount, at first in front of a little open chapel which is built facing the street. Then I do really dismount in front of a chapel which stands near the first one; the hotel is in the same street; I might let the horse go there by itself, but I prefer to lead it thither. It seems as though I should be ashamed to arrive there on horseback. In front of the hotel there stands a page-boy, who shows me a note of mine which has been found, and ridicules me on account of it. On the note is written, doubly underlined: "Nothing to eat," and then a second sentence (indistinct) something like: "No work." At the same time a hazy idea that I am in a strange city in which I do no work.[154]

FREUD'S ANALYSIS AS PRESENTED BY VELIKOVSKY

Associations: He had suffered in the night from boils and the last thing he could possibly have done was to ride. But the dream plunges him into this very activity. (He cannot ride at all.) It is the negation of suffering. The gray color of his horse corresponds to the pepper-and-salt suit in which he saw his colleague P. the last time. Highly seasoned food is considered a cause of boils. Dr. P. liked to "ride the high horse" after he had replaced Freud in the treatment of a female patient who, like the Sunday equestrian, led him where she wished. "Thus the horse comes to be the symbolic representation of a woman patient (in the dream it is highly intelligent)." "I feel 'quite at home' refers to the position which I occupied in the patient's household before I was replaced by my colleague P." It is a feat to practice psychotherapy for several hours daily while suffering from furunculosis and the dream is a dismal allusion to the situation: "Do not work and do not eat." The street in the dream is built up out of impressions of Verona and Siena, the association is Italy ("*gen Italien*" in German means to Italy) and an association to this.[155]

VELIKOVSKY'S INTERPRETATION

Riding horseback is also called to career. It is a career dream. Therefore "riding a high horse." Colleague P., as Freud mentions, is a person who is after a successful career (we suppose a Christian or a baptized Jew, not a Jew). The gray, very intelligent horse consequently is Freud's career. In the same book we read that his hair is already getting gray. One who worried about his career will frequently compare the color of his hair with the distance he has traveled and the success that did not come. He has a "bad seat."

Vans (Lastwagen) among which one rides may be symbolic of a load taken off one's conscience, but usually means a load on one's conscience (*Entlastung— Belastung*). "I turn around" means conversion (*ich kehre um-Bekehrung*). "Open chapel"—we know a psychoanalytic sexual interpretation for this, but the reader will know himself already what the open chapel means, it needs no interpretation.[156]

Velikovsky goes on to propose that the latter part of the dream refers to the explicit or implicit anti-Semitism found when traveling, since a Jew had to show his passport giving his religion when staying at a hotel.

MY COMMENTS AND INTERPRETATION

Velikovsky's suggestion that this is a career dream receives further support from information that was unavailable to him. Dr. P. was Freud's colleague Dr. Josef Paneth, who took Freud's place after Freud reluctantly left Brücke's laboratory.[157]

The dream as Freud recounted it referred to two different chapels on a street of Italian character (another example of the Catholic meaning of Italy for Freud). What is interesting is that Freud in his analysis completely omitted any comment about the significance of either chapel. Since Freud in this book was demonstrating his theory of interpretation by analyzing dreams word by word, or at least phrase by phrase, the fact that Freud skipped this obviously important part of his dream meant that it was associated with highly censored ideas. Freud hinted at a sexual meaning for the dream (e.g., riding horseback on a female patient). However, a religious meaning is certainly present, and there is, of course, no reason why both sexual and religious meanings are not possible. (This possibility is taken up in the next chapter, and it is at the center of a recent thesis by Swales.[158])

FREUD'S DREAM ABOUT "*AUF GESERES*"

On account of something that is happening in Rome it is necessary to let the children flee, and this they do. The scene is then laid before a gate, a double gate, in ancient style (the Porta Romano in Siena, as I realize while I am dreaming). I am sitting on the edge of a well and am greatly depressed; I am almost weeping. A woman—a nurse, a nun—brings out the two boys and hands them over to their father who is not myself. The elder is distinctly my eldest son, but I do not see the face of the other boy. The woman asks the elder boy for a parting kiss. She is remarkable for her red nose. The boy refuses her the kiss, but says to her, extending his hand in parting, "*Auf Geseres*," and to both of us (or to one of us) "*Auf Ungeseres*." I have the idea that this latter indicates a preference.[159]

FREUD'S INTERPRETATION

This dream is built on a tangle of thoughts induced by a play I saw at the theatre, called "Das neue Ghetto" (the new Ghetto). The Jewish question, anxiety as to the future of my children, who cannot be given a fatherland, anxiety as to educating them so that they may enjoy the privilege of citizens—all these features may be easily recognized in the accompanying dream-thoughts.

By the waters of Babylon we sat down and wept. Siena, like Rome, is famous for its beautiful fountains.

An association to a co-religionist who has to give up the position in a state asylum which he secured with great effort.

Geseres is a Hebrew word and means ordained sufferings, doom. . . . *Ungeseres* is a word I coined myself and at first I am at a loss regarding it. The brief observation at the end of the dream—that *Ungeseres* indicates an advantage over *Geseres*—opens the way to the associations and therewith to understanding. This relation holds good in the case of caviar; the unsalted kind is more highly prized than the salted. Caviar for the people—"noble passions." . . . But a connecting-link is wanting between the pair, salted and unsalted and *Geseres-Ungeseres*. This is found in *gesaeuert* and *ungesaeuret* (leavened and unleavened). In their flight-like exodus from Egypt the children of Israel had not time to allow their dough to become leavened, and in commemoration of this event they eat unleavened bread at Easter [*sic!*] to this day.[160]

VELIKOVSKY'S INTERPRETATION

Do I perform an act of grace for my children if I let them "flee," if I make bigoted people of them (double gate—bigate), Catholics ("Rome"), "refugees," choose a godfather for them ("hand them over to their father who is not myself"), let them enact the kissing ceremonials of the church? I should "not be a father anymore for my children." Do not children who grow up in the Christian faith become estranged from their Jewish father? Would my children, thus torn, not become neurotics? (red nose—nez rose—Neurose—Neurosis).

But this will not happen. The older boy already seems to show a national or Jewish-religious attitude. In the eyes of Freud this latter would be a neurosis.

The boy "refuses the kiss" and says he chooses for himself the ordained suffering and doom. He offers to his father what the father offered him in the dream: "*Auf Ungeseres*" which indicates a preference over *Geseres*.[161]

MY COMMENTS AND INTERPRETATION

Here is another dream dealing with Jewish and Catholic issues. In this case, it involved "a woman—a nurse—a nun" who "brings out the two boys and hands them over to their father who is not myself." The nun or nurse was an obvious reference to the old nanny, and yet Freud never mentioned her. (Velikovsky, we may recall, did not know about her.) She was the one with the red nose, so my interpretation is that she was the "prime originator" of his neuroses—as Freud said in a letter to Fliess, unknown to Velikovsky, written on October 3, 1897.[162]

The two words "*Geseres*" and "*Ungeseres*, were connected to "salted" and "unsalted" by Freud in a religious setting. Since salt is a primary ingredient in making food kosher, Freud's rejection of *Geseres* or "salted," and his preference for "unsalted" or *Ungeseres*, suggested a preference for non-kosher food—that is, for the "advantage" of the gentile world.

One other interesting meaning in this dream was the symbolism of Freud's sons (or even Freud himself as a child) being handed over to a new father (a priest?), in a parting involving the old nanny.

There are two important Christian themes in the dream that have been commented upon neither by Freud nor Velikovsky; both of them have, however, been noted by Grinstein. First, the association of Freud, "By the waters of Babylon we sat down and wept," was a quote from the first line of a famous poem by Swinburne—a poem itself obviously inspired in part by Psalm 137 ("By the rivers of Babylon"). Grinstein summarizes the poem as involving a comparison between the destruction of ancient Italy, and Jerusalem's destruction followed by the Babylonian exile.[163] The poem goes on to compare the rise of Italy to its ancient glory, with the rising of Christ and the growth of Christianity. There are references to Jerusalem, and specifically to Calvary, Gethesemane, and Golgotha—all places directly involved in Christ's betrayal and crucifixion.[164]

The other Christian association is the remarkable reference by Freud to the Jewish Passover as "Easter"! Grinstein suggests that "as Easter refers to the Resurrection of Christ, it fits in with the reference to the Swinburne poem," an interpretation confirmed by Freud.[165] The substitution of Easter for Passover is all the more curious, since Freud himself did not comment upon it at the time, or in any of his many later editions of *The Interpretation of Dreams* (a book to which he continually added more explanatory material). It is possible that through the years Freud never noticed this slip. (Velikovsky does not comment upon this substitution, because in his quoting of Freud he incorrectly uses the word "Passover"; why, I do not know.) In any case, the substitution can be directly interpreted as expressing Freud's unconscious preference for the Christian holiday. All this fits in with Freud's repeated emphases on Easter and resurrection themes; more on this now familiar theme in Freud's life is given below.

Still another Christian association to this dream was made by Freud right after his slip about Easter and Passover. He wrote:

I remembered how, during the previous Easter, my Berlin friend and I were walking through the streets of Breslau, a town in which we were strangers. [They were then asked directions to a street by a little girl whom they could not oblige.] Shortly afterwards, I caught sight of a door-plate bearing the words "Dr. Herodes. Consulting hours: . . . " "Let us hope," I remarked, "that our colleague does not happen to be a children's doctor."[166]

Grinstein correctly observes that this was an association to the Herod of the New Testament accounts, but although over a page of historical summary about Herod the Great and his son Herod Antipas is provided, Grinstein misses the point of Freud's remark altogether.[167] What Grinstein fails to mention is that the New Testament importance of Herod is that he ordered the killing of all baby boys in and around Bethlehem, after hearing (from the Magi) that the King of the Jews had been born there. This is, of course, a very familiar story for Christians, and it makes Herod a symbol of danger to children. Thus Freud ruefully hoped that Dr. Herodes was not a children's doctor.[168] Freud's association to Herod as a baby-killer reveals his familiarity with basic Christian references. The story of Herod's ordering all the babies to be murdered is something Freud could easily have first heard from his nanny. The Gospel account of it is commonly read during the Christmas season, especially on the Feast of the Holy Innocents (December 28).

THE COUNT THUN DREAM

This is a long dream, and, rather than give the analysis of it by Freud and Velikovsky, I merely identify very briefly the kind of Christian symbols and associations that occur in it; they are rather unequivocal. This dream refers to a Count Thun or a Count Taaffe.[169] The dream is usually known by the former name, but the name "Taaffe" is significant, since the word for baptism in German is "Taufe" and the sound similarities are considerable; Velikovsky puts some emphasis on this.[170] In the dream Freud referred to his "favorite flower," which from an earlier dream we know brings in "crucifer" and also "artichoke." The color, mentioned by Freud, of the artichoke flower is violet, and the color violet figures in this dream twice—once as the color of upholstered furniture and once as the color of some "violet-brown violets" near his buttonhole. Violet is the color of the baptismal stoles worn in the first part of a ceremony that Freud very likely saw with his nanny.[171] Violet is also a common color in Catholic churches, especially during Lent. (Roughly 60 or 70 days of the year are marked as violet or purple days in the traditional Catholic calendar.[172]) Furthermore, in this dream, one of Freud's associations to a "favorite flower" was to think "also of the rose of Jericho."[173] From a footnote by Strachey, we learn that this flower is known as the "Resurrection plant" because the effect of water (baptism) on its leaves is to rejuvenate them, to cause them to unfold.[174]

In his associations to this dream, Freud brought up an incident already mentioned, in which, in his early student days, he aggressively argued for a simple materialistic theory and was effectively rebutted by "a leader of men . . . who . . . stood up and gave us a good talking to: he, too, he told us, had fed swine in his youth and returned repentant to his father's house."[175] Freud then described how he "fired up" and replied boorishly ("*saugrob,*" literally "swinishly gross"). Thus, in this language, he equated his own position to that of the swine among which the prodigal son awoke. (This familiar story is told by Jesus in Luke 15:11–32.)

"THE THREE FATES" DREAM

Still another dream with an especially telling incident was the dream of "The Three Fates," which involved three female figures regularly interpreted by Freud and others[176] as including his mother and also a nurse or nanny figure. One of Freud's important associations to this dream was to "a drug from the dispensary which removes hunger: cocaine."[177] The German word for dispensary is "*lateinische Küche*" or "Latin kitchen."[178] If one interprets cocaine as the obvious or manifest content, then the latent meaning would be that the food that removes hunger is to be found in Rome, in a Latin kitchen—especially in the tabernacle that holds the white communion wafers.

Grigg, in his article on the role of the nursemaid in Freud's dreams, makes some important observations and draws some interesting conclusions.[179] Two of these are that Freud felt robbed ("stolen from") by the disappearance of his nurse, and that the theme of maternal abandonment (in Bowlby's terms, separation anxiety[180]) was clearly present in his dreams and associations.

THE BRIDGE DREAM

One last dream and some of its interpretation by Velikovsky are of interest. This dream was about a bridge across a chasm, or the "self-dissection" dream.[181] The dream referred at the start to old Brücke, the head of the Research Institute. Now the name "Brücke" means "bridge" in German. A bridge figured later in the dream, and Freud specifically associated the name of Brücke with its meaning as "bridge."[182] Velikovsky notes the connection of "bridge" to *"pons," "pontis,"* and *"pontificus"*—that is, the bridges of Rome and the Pope.[183] Velikovsky also points out that the word for "pelvis" (*"Becken"*), also occurring in the dream, is close to *"Taufbecken"* (Count Taffebecken?), or "baptismal bowl or font."[184] At the end of this dream, Freud was walking across two planks that "bridge the chasm which had to be crossed."[185] Velikovsky mentions that "to be crossed" in German is *"Uebertritt,"* or "conversion."[186] Freud in the dream was terrified at this point and thought that "the children were to make the crossing possible," and then woke up.[187] In short, again there was a conversion concern, in the context of the children's needs. (None of this, however, was commented on by Freud.)

ADDITIONAL EVIDENCE AND FURTHER DISCUSSION

To provide some additional evidence for the Velikovsky thesis, I would like briefly to summarize Erik Erikson's interpretation of the famous Irma dream.[188] Erikson concentrates on the manifest content, not on the latent or hidden meaning, by focusing on the form of the dream in the context of Freud's personal life, at this time in which Freud was at the threshold of a discovery of historical importance. Erikson interprets the dream as like a religious rite of conversion or confirmation. He identifies the old nanny as the source of the Catholic ritual that provided the framework of the dream. As previously mentioned, Freud would have been exposed to the ritual of the Mass many times as a child. (It must also be said that Freud "hung around" Catholic churches in Paris and Rome a great deal, and must necessarily have heard the Mass celebrated often.) Erikson, moreover, says of the nanny that she would have provided for Freud "a measure of a sense of trust."[189] Thus, at a moment of initiation or conversion in Freud's life—the beginnings of psychoanalysis—the nanny, and all that she represented for him, again recurred.

Erikson makes one other relevant point in this article—namely, that contemporary man has great difficulty admitting to being at the mercy of unconscious religious forces.[190] Indeed, religion is now the only remaining seriously threatening, even taboo, topic. The possibility of having unconscious sexual desires for one's mother, murderous hatred for one's father, homosexual desires—all these have become accepted, even expected. But as for unconscious desires for God and an unconscious desire for salvation, these possibilities are today (at least for most intellectuals) still inadmissible.

Earlier in this section, a reference is made to Jones's rejection of the Velikovsky hypothesis that Freud expressed in his dreams a conflict over conversion. In his reply, Jones first makes fun of some of the Velikovsky evidence, but he never deals with the claim within the framework of dream analysis.[191] Jones's dismissal of Velikovsky is most unimpressive. Ernest Jones is a curious biographer, for he presents an almost Victorian piece of hagiography with respect to his interpretation of Freud's character: It is as the complete secular saint that Freud is offered up to us. Nothing of a seriously religious involvement must mar the Freudian biographical cameo that has been so carefully wrought. It appears that Jones simply does not want to think about Freud's possibly having any religious desires or religious feelings.

One can plead some extenuating circumstances for Jones, however. He did not get to know Freud personally until 1908, when his subject was over 50 years old, and hence already well past his youthful crisis and his self-analysis with its Roman themes[192]; by 1908 Freud was already beginning to attract international attention. Neither was Jones's role as the younger, faithful, orthodox student, however admirable it may have been in many respects, optimal for the production of impartial biography.

And Jones does have redeeming virtues as a biographer: One is very grateful for the enormous amount of material that he provides, including raw information that does not fit in with his own interpretive theories. The information and the theories generally occur on different pages. In the present instance, only a few sentences later after testily rejecting Velikovsky's position, Jones writes: "Freud did once, it is true, for five minutes toy with this idea [of conversion], but for anti-religious reasons; a Protestant was allowed to have a civil wedding, and Freud detested religious ceremonies of any kind, Jewish as much as Christian."[193] This is certainly a strange interpretation. A man who loved and was engaged to a girl like Martha Bernays (who was from a prominent and practicing Jewish family), and who did not wish to alienate Martha's family, would not "toy" with such an idea unless he was remarkably estranged from religious Judaism, and to some degree attracted to Christianity. After all, to convert or to officially assimilate certainly involves being in another religious ceremony: baptism.[194]

This "conversion" question involved a discussion between Freud and his older Jewish colleague Breuer in 1884. At that time, Freud was revealing some positive attitudes to Christianity in his letters to Martha (discussed earlier in this chapter), and he was also influenced by the career ambitions fueled by his desire to get ahead in Brücke's lab. In this lab, as already noted, the major models for him were Gentile, especially "the honored name of Brücke."[195] It was after a talk with Brücke, in which Freud's impoverished situation and very likely his Jewishness were discussed as serious barriers to advancement, that Freud decided unhappily to leave science (i.e., research in the university setting) and to go into private practice.[196] In short, the discussion with the Jewish Breuer concerning conversion was probably precipitated by the conscious aspirations of Freud (not to mention his "Christian" unconscious desires), and conversion was probably given some serious thought.

Freud, at the time, would also have had the example of Martha's uncle to serve as a possible model. Although it was at the cost of a family estrangement, Michael Bernays—the one who became a prominent professor at the University of Munich—had converted. This uncle was best known for a major work on Goethe, Freud's most admired author.[197]

Let us pause here to take up one of the strange and unexplained relationships in Freud's life, which is the one he had with Breuer. More than ten years after the just-mentioned conversion discussion (i.e., in the late 1890s), Freud became estranged from his friend of 20 years, advisor, and colleague. Why Freud became so hostile to Breuer is a puzzle to his biographers.[198] The intensity of Freud's rejection is clear from the following story, recounted by Breuer's daughter-in-law, of an event that occurred years after their break:

Breuer's daughter-in-law remembered walking with him as an old man; suddenly she saw Freud coming straight toward him, and Breuer instinctively opened his arms. Freud passed by, pretending not to see him, which gives some idea how deeply the break must have wounded him.[199]

I would like to suggest that one of the possible bones of contention between the two could well have been Freud's discussion of conversion—a topic that must have taken longer than Jones's "five minutes," and could easily have come up several times. Perhaps Breuer once betrayed this conversation to someone Freud disliked, or perhaps there was some real unpleasantness associated with their exchanges on the topic. In any case, it is curious that the book that these two men coauthored, *Studies on Hysteria* (1893–1895), dealt extensively with another kind of "conversion." That is, in this book, the authors described how psychological symptoms, especially hysterical symptoms, represent an expression of excess psychic energy derived from aspects of the past that the patient is unable to accept; this energy is "converted" into symptoms. At the conscious level, this new term "conversion" was drawn from the physical sciences, in which energy was often "converted" from one form to another (e.g., electrical energy into mechanical). However, the German word Freud and Breuer used for psychological conversion (*"Konversion"*) also has a religious meaning (as it does in English, French, and other languages as well). Since this vocabulary emerged after Freud's greatest personal involvement with conversion, and when, moreover, he was working closely with the one man with whom he is known to have discussed religious conversion, one must wonder. Freud is, it should be noted, on record as being the one who initiated the use of the term "conversion" in the psychological sense.[200]

C. F. Meyer: Poems and Novels

I conclude this chronological treatment of the religious significance of Freud's adult life prior to 1900 by turning to his involvement in the literary culture of his time.

In 1898, Fliess drew Freud's attention to the poetry and short novels of Conrad Ferdinand Meyer (1825–1898), a Swiss–German writer who is still considered one of the more important contributors to German literature in the 19th century. Following Fliess's suggestion in 1898, Freud read a 12-line poem by Meyer, "*Am Himmelstor*" ("At the Gate of Heaven").[201] Shortly thereafter, he began reading widely in Meyer's work and became something of a Meyer fan. It is informative to describe briefly those works of Meyer in which Freud had some serious involvement.

Freud quoted most often from Meyer's lengthy 1871 poem *Huttens Letzte Tage* (*Hutten's Last Days*).[202] Set in the past, like all of Meyer's major works, the poem is centered on Ulrich von Hutten (1488–1523), an historical figure well known as a soldier who fought against Rome for German political and religious freedom.[203] This German Protestant knight, sick and outlawed, was provided by Zwingli (the famous Swiss Protestant theologian) with a peaceful retreat on an island in the Lake of Zurich. Here, Hutten spent his last days; he died in the summer of 1523, not long after his arrival. The poem is set in these last days.

On the surface, the strongest theme of *Huttens Letzte Tage* is its expression of German nationalism, but it contains many other various symbolic and ambivalent currents underneath this more obvious, or manifest, meaning. Freud probably had some modest response to German nationalism, but he never quoted these parts of the poem, and it is rather obvious that the other themes were the real basis of its appeal for him. One of these themes is the portrayal of the conflict between German Reformation values and culture and those of Catholic and Renaissance Rome. In spite of the clear preference for the German side, there is still a real appreciation of the Roman world. C. F. Meyer, like Goethe and Freud, had visited Rome, and Meyer's biographers agree that it was a decisive and positive experience for him.

Other themes in this work also have what by now we can recognize as a "Freudian" character. In the first section of the poem, Hutten arrives on the island with his pen and sword. Curiously, his host on the island is a

Catholic priest and doctor, who gives Hutten a famous Dürer engraving, *Ritter, Tod, und Teufel* (*Knight, Death and Devil*). Near the end of this first part, Hutten realizes he will soon die. He contemplates a crucifix, and also finds comfort in his encounters with St. Paul and Socrates, subtitled "*Ein christliches Sprüchlein*" and "*Ein heidnisches Sprüchlein*" ("A Christian Proverb" and "A Pagan Proverb," respectively).

The next section involves recollections of Hutten's struggle with Rome and includes scathing tirades against the Roman Catholic Church. Somewhat later, Hutten confronts his internal demons as they assail him with doubts about the validity of the causes for which he has lived and fought; he hears the Devil mocking him as a fool fighting for clouds (i.e., illusions), and his mother lamenting that he has forfeited his salvation. Next comes a forceful section on Hutten's humanity ("*Homo sum*"), in which his many internal contradictions are noted. This poem concludes with Freud's favorite lines from Meyer, "*[I]ch bin kein ausgeklügelt Buch,/ Ich bin ein Mensch mit seinem Widerspruch*" ("I am no subtle contrived book,/ I am a man with his contradictions"). In a following section, Hutten proudly confesses his attack on the Pope; there then follow sections with praise of Luther and his translation of the Bible. Later Hutten is visited by St. Ignatius Loyola, founder of the Jesuits and a representative of Catholic power. Loyola's nocturnal flagellations and deep devotion to the Virgin are described as both impressive and ominous, for Meyer's description hints at future religious conflict. Finally, at the end of the poem, there are conversations with the island's priest about science, which suggest that absolute religious pronouncements will be increasingly questionable in the future.

This brief summary makes it clear that *Huttens Letzte Tage* is a retrospective, melancholic, symbolic work, filled with hostility and bitterness toward—and also attraction to—aspects of Roman Catholicism. Hutten, like Hannibal, is an enemy of Rome, but Rome is not conquered and Hutten is dying. Many things Roman Catholic (e.g., the crucifix, St. Paul, the priest) have a positive significance, in spite of much other serious opposition to things Catholic, especially the Pope's power. And, of course, the hero Hutten is a Christian—a committed Protestant. The religious atmosphere is also strengthened by demons and the Devil who make their appearance, and by a mother-figure bemoaning her son's lost salvation.

Die Richterin (*The Female Judge*), a short novel, received serious attention from Freud in a letter to Fliess.[204] In fact, Freud's remarks on this work constituted the first psychoanalytic interpretation of a piece of literature. The story has a decidedly Christian setting: The first chapter opens in Rome, with monks chanting the Mass just after Charlemagne has been crowned Emperor by the Pope.[205] *Die Richterin*'s major importance for Freud, however, stemmed from the family situation portrayed by Meyer. Freud proposed that the story contains evidence of C. F. Meyer's defense against an incestuous relationship with his sister. (Meyer in fact did have a very close, possibly incestuous relationship with his younger sister.) In this interpretation, Freud was giving his first expression of ideas that were to bulk very large in his later theories. C. F. Meyer certainly gave Freud much to work with, since the story involves a violent passion between a stepson, Wolfrin, and his half-sister, Palma. There is also the mother (a female judge), made pregnant by another man (a priest) just before her marriage. The mother poisons her husband shortly after the marriage. The story ends with a dramatic judgment scene, interspersed with powerful quotes from the Mass. For example, Palma condemns her mother (the judge) with these words: "*Concepit in iniquitatibus me mater mea. . . .*" In short, *Die Richterin* is a family history involving ambiguous parentage, incest, murder, love, and guilt, all brought to light at the end of the story in a very Catholic context.

Freud also enjoyed Meyer's *Die Hochzeit des Mönchs* (*The Monk's Wedding*), which he considered Meyer's best novel.[206] Set in Italy of the 13th century, this is a rather ambiguous and disturbing work centered on a monk, Astorre, who renounces his vows (under extreme pressure from his father) in order to marry his brother's recent widow, Diana. Later Astorre breaks his vows to Diana. The poet Dante is an important figure, the narrator of the story. The complex relationships among Astorre, Diana, and others are the focus of the story. Again, there is an historical treatment in a Catholic setting; for example, Dante refers to Christ's great compassion for others and to Christ's wounds. Astorre's religious motivation is portrayed as deep and serious, but the meaning again focuses on personal relationships—relationships that remain dark and ambiguous. The themes of sexuality, guilt, and murder are present, but all subject to different interpretations by different literary critics.

Regarding *Gustav Adolfs Page* (a short novel), Freud commented that the idea of deferred action occurs twice in the story; then he ironically noted that in Innsbruck they actually show the chapel where the central (and, unlike Hutten, entirely fictional) character in the novel supposedly was received into the Catholic faith. Otherwise, Freud made no comment except that he found the story bewildering and implausible.[207]

Besides *Die Hochzeit*, the other Meyer novel that Freud acknowledged reading with enthusiasm was *Die Versuchung des Pescara* (*The Temptation of Pescara*).[208] The setting is Italy, this time in the Renaissance and in a complex political situation, Machiavellian in many respects. Pescara, a half-Spanish and half-Italian general, is in this work asked (or tempted) to lead an Italian conspiracy against the Spanish emperor. Again the novel's action occurs in something of a Catholic historical setting, but one where religion is usually treated skeptically and on the surface; beneath lie complex but quite ordinary human passions for power. Nevertheless,

Christian symbolism makes a major appearance. Pescara, who receives a wound in the side, is shown through his connection to an altarpiece in the Convent of the Holy Wounds to be a Christ symbol. Yet Pescara has no real religious beliefs, and the basic attitude of the story is one of doubt and skepticism. Regardless, Meyer seems deliberately to have left the Christ-figure interpretation of Pescara as a possibility. As Marianne Burkhard notes, the author seems to have been expressing his personal religious ambivalence.[209] Shortly after completing *Pescara*, Meyer wrote: "For in spite of my efforts to escape Christianity . . . I feel [myself] being led back to it . . . regardless of any critical and philosophical knowledge."[210] We have seen ample reason why the presence of such a motivation would appeal to Freud.

Freud also read Meyer's *Der Heilige* (*The Saint*), a fictionalized account of the life of St. Thomas à Becket.[211] Here the story is set in a thoroughly medieval Christian world of monks, priests, and bishops. Again, Meyer's treatment of his central figure's motivation is ambiguous: Is Becket truly a religiously motivated saint, or just a subtle seeker of revenge on the king, his former friend?

Throughout his stories, it is clear that Meyer was a master of ambiguous polarities set in a religious historical past: Renaissance versus Reformation; ancient pagan versus Christian; Catholic versus Protestant; simple piety versus complex skepticism. Meyer also often created a fusion of images and emotions from the past with those of the present—certainly another reason, no doubt, for his appeal to Freud.

In any case, Meyer's writings, with their Christian (typically, Roman Catholic) settings, are certainly more appropriate to a reader struggling with belief, or to an apostate Christian, than to a cool, secular scientist who went through life with no personal involvement in or need for religion.

Conclusion

The wealth of material cited in regard to this approximately 20-year period of Freud's early maturity reveals the deepest of religious preoccupations. Fond Pentecost greetings, longings for Rome, both conscious and unconscious desires for conversion, and enjoyment of ambiguous Christian literature were expressed by Freud time and time again. Yet these secret desires were held back from any kind of direct fulfillment. The psychological nature of Freud's unconscious religious inhibition is the next issue for consideration.

Chapter Four

Freud and the Devil: Literature and Cocaine

I N THIS AND THE NEXT chapter, we break from the chronological treatment of our subject to investigate a complex and in many ways sinister theme that makes a persistent appearance throughout Freud's life. This theme is Freud's relation to the Devil, and closely connected to it are the topics of Heaven, Hell, damnation, and the Anti-Christ. An alternate title for this and the next chapter, therefore, might be "Sigmund Freud's Anti-Christian Unconscious."

One important point before beginning is that the present concern is only with the psychological reality of the Devil for Freud. The question of the actual existence of the Evil One is a separate question, a question that properly belongs to theology and philosophy and thus is outside the scope of this book. As we will see, the psychological question, by itself, is a rich and complex one.

Freud's Pact: Part One

The idea of a Freudian "Faust pact" was initially but briefly raised by Velikovsky in 1941. Later the possibility of a Freudian pact with the Devil was given extensive biographical treatment by David Bakan in his stimulating 1958 book, *Freud and the Jewish Mystical Tradition*. I take up Bakan's thesis, which first introduced me to this topic, in more detail later, but I should say right away that I do not agree with Bakan that Freud's interest in and involvement with the Devil were primarily derived from his proposed contact with Jewish mysticism (especially the Sabbatian tradition). To begin with, the Devil does not receive much emphasis in Judaism, and typically may be entirely absent from the thought of liberal or enlightenment Jews such as Jakob Freud, who interpret Judaism primarily as a kind of ethical monotheism.[1] There is no evidence that the idea of the Devil was ever part of Freud's Jewish education. Second, and more importantly, there is not a single explicit reference by Freud to any of the writings of the Jewish mystical tradition. Bakan's case is based mostly on some similarities in preoccupations between the writings of Freud and those of the Jewish mystics—and, indeed, in large part on what he considers to be the general Jewish character of Freud's thought. That there may have been some slight connection is possible, but a major one is most unlikely. My skeptical response has apparently been that of most of Bakan's readers.[2]

There is still another reason for doubting that Judaism had anything to do with Freud's "demonic" preoccupation. As Trachtenberg[3] has documented, there was a well-established anti-Semitic tradition linking the Jews to the Devil and to magician figures like Faust. This linkage was especially strong in Germanic and Central European popular cultures, and it was used to justify all kinds of persecutions. A Jew would normally actively avoid anything connected to such a dangerous stereotype.

Now if the Devil is a fairly minor figure in the Jewish tradition, he certainly looms large in much of Christianity—as do various themes connected with him, such as damnation and Hell. Hell was a topic of very considerable concern to Protestants and Catholics alike in the 19th century, as in preceding centuries. Certainly the New Testament clearly sets out the Christian view that Heaven and Hell exist, and frequent references are made to the Devil or Satan.[4] Since Christianity does have a serious concern with the Devil, and since Freud was (as already shown) strongly influenced by Christian concepts, it is a reasonable *a priori* assumption that Freud's relationship with the Devil was also significantly conditioned by the religion of his early childhood and of the surrounding environment. Before returning to Bakan's thesis and the question of Freud's "pact" with the Devil, I examine the extensive evidence, in sources typically overlooked by his biographers, of Freud's Christian connections to the Devil.

His Nanny and the Devil

Where and when did Freud first hear of the Devil? There can be little doubt that his Catholic nanny, who taught him about Heaven and Hell, also told him about the Devil. It is almost impossible to talk about Heaven and Hell without also talking about God and the Devil; in any case, the kind of sophisticated theological discourse that can describe Hell without mentioning the Devil would have been well beyond a simple peasant woman instructing a young child. Within Christian theology, Hell only makes sense in terms of the existence of evil, and evil for the orthodox Christian is not an abstraction: There is an Evil *One*, a spiritual and personal expression of evil—in short, the Devil—to tempt others to do evil.

Again, although there is no direct evidence, one must wonder whether the nanny was anti-Semitic and made hostile remarks about Judaism. She may have laid some of the foundation for Freud's rejection of Jewish religiousness.

In any case, as the Devil is a compelling topic in himself, and as Freud first learned about him at the impressionable age of two or three from his functional mother, it should not be surprising that this topic had a permanent impact on him. As noted in Chapter One, Freud said that he had guilt feelings about the death of his younger brother Julius. Now, any death viewed in a Christian perspective raises the question of what happens to the soul of the dead person. It is clear that Julius's death, at a time when Freud was close to his nanny, must have been connected for him with Heaven and Hell (and the Devil). Freud's extraordinary association of the gas lights at Breslau with souls burning in Hell is both a primitive Christian image and one virtually certain to be connected with the notion of Satan, who is central to that iconography.

Not only did Freud get his initial grounding in the concept of Hell within the Christian tradition, but his subsequent involvement in this and related ideas was continuously maintained by his thorough and ongoing immersion in texts permeated by the Christian concept of the Devil. These texts were the most important literary influences in Freud's adult life; they were texts that he read and admired, to which he referred often, and that he frequently quoted in his letters and in his scientific works. As such, they represent an immediate, undeniable source, as well as an expression, of Freud's attraction to the idea of the Devil. There is no need to seek out remote or esoteric sources for this interest.

Freud and Literature

As Sulloway has shown, biological science certainly had an impact on Freud's theorizing; he was a physician and a research scientist.[5] But there was an even greater source of ideas for Freud, and this was literature. The foundation text of Freud's literary approach, amply documented by Pfrimmer, was the Philippson Bible so important in his childhood.[6] When he was an adult, the influence of novels, poetry, biography, and similar types of material became profound and pervasive throughout his work. It is not just that Freud was preoccupied with Biblical figures, nor yet that such concepts as the Oedipus complex have literary sources; what is most striking is the enormous frequency with which Freud cited literary texts in order to exemplify his crucial psychological insights.

Indeed, I believe it is fair to say that psychoanalysis (and with it much of modern psychology) was created by the collision and integration of literature and biology, and that literature was the dominant force in this process. Evidence of the central importance of literature to Freud comes from a number of sources, not the least of which is Freud himself. He once said in an interview:

[T]he first impulse which led to the discovery of my method came to me from my beloved Goethe. As you know, he wrote *Werther* to free himself from the morbid oppression of sorrow: for him literature was *catharsis*. And in what consists my method of curing hysteria save in making the patient tell everything to free him from obsession? I did no more than force my patients to act like Goethe. Confession is liberation and that is cure. The Catholics knew it for centuries, but Victor Hugo had taught me that the poet too is a priest; and thus I boldly substituted myself for the confessor.[7]

In short, Freud defined his method of healing as a *literary* method, one that makes of the patient a narrator; he also asserted that he learned this method from Goethe and Hugo, two major writers, to whom I return below. (The reader, no doubt, has also noted in this quotation the identification of the doctor as poet and priest and of confession as a cure. In Freud, as we will see, literature is intimately connected with religion.)

Many years before the interview quoted above, Freud commented in *Studies on Hysteria* (1893–1895): "It still strikes me as strange that the case histories I write should read like short stories and that, as one might say, they lack the serious stamp of science."[8] Here again Freud acknowledged his literary bent and style. Even a brief glance at the index of a work by Freud readily reveals the rich use he made of literary material. Unfortunately, as the literary culture of the 19th century fades, Freud's intellectual framework has become increasingly alien to the contemporary mentality.

If by a theory's fruit one shall know it, then the literary quality of Freudian theory is overwhelmingly apparent in the impact of psychoanalysis on the world of the literary arts. Not only were writers as different as D. H. Lawrence and André Breton directly influenced by Freud; so countless others have been at least indirectly influenced. And in the last few decades Freud's ideas have had really an enormous effect on literary criticism, as well as on other fields in the humanities, such as history and biography.[9]

In marked contrast, Freud's impact on the biological sciences has been minimal. If anything, the possibility of finding a biological grounding for most of Freudian theory looks more remote today than it did in the early part of the century. There was also almost a total absence in Freud's life of any youthful interest in natural science; this alone suggests a fundamentally nonscientific mentality. It is a routine observation that superior talent for natural science expresses itself very early. Certainly, by the age of 16 or 17, a future great biologist would have shown his interest in nature, physics, chemistry, or mathematics. Except for a minor interest in plants and flowers (a theme that showed up in his dreams), Freud showed none of this; in contrast, his youthful involvement in languages and literature, such as the Philippson Bible and the works of Cervantes, Goethe, and others, was already substantial. In his autobiography, Freud made his fundamental cultural and nonscientific mentality explicit:

My interest, after making a lifelong *détour* through the natural sciences, medicine, and psychotherapy, returned to the cultural problems which had fascinated me long before, when I was a youth scarcely old enough for thinking: At the very climax of my psycho-analytic work, in 1912, I had already attempted to make use of the newly discovered findings of analysis in order to investigate the origins of religion and morality.[10]

And, in fact, it has been on literature, the humanities, cultural theory, and religion that Freud has made his mark.

With this in mind, I now take up a discussion of a series of literary works that made up a large proportion of those important in Freud's life. These works give star billing to the Devil.[11]

Flaubert's *The Temptation of St. Anthony*

Along with *Don Quixote* (discussed in Chapter Two), the other book that, according to Jones, made the deepest impression on Freud in his late 20s was Gustave Flaubert's *The Temptation of St. Anthony*. He read this book in July 1883, while on his first visit to the Alps with his mentor Breuer; he was visiting with the very successful Breuer at his vacation home in Gmunden.[12]

The book is worth summarizing, for it provides a good example of Freud's immersion in a heavily "Christianized" piece of literature. But first, a description of Freud's reaction to *The Temptation* is in order. Jones quotes a letter of Freud's:

I was already deeply moved by the splendid panorama, and now on top of it all came this book which in the most condensed fashion and with unsurpassable vividness throws at one's head the whole trashy world: for it calls up not only the great problems of knowledge, but the real riddles of life, all the conflicts of feelings and impulses; and it confirms the awareness of our perplexity in the mysteriousness that reigns everywhere.[13]

Jones says about this letter: "Then comes a long and lively description of the contents of the book, which he [Freud] likens to a *Walpurgisnacht*" [Witches' Sabbath].[14]

St. Anthony is shown as a solitary monk living in a mountain hut, removed from civilization. Discouraged with prayer and the holy life, he is under constant attack by temptations, which come in the form of visions or hallucinations, the vividness of which so impressed Freud. These hallucinatory scenes often involve St. Anthony in dialogues with various figures. One of them is the Devil, who, as a black, shadowy flying figure with bat-like wings, makes an early appearance (in the second section) and brings with him the seven deadly sins. In this same section St. Anthony is confronted with sexuality and lust, embodied by the Queen of Sheba. Next comes perhaps the greatest temptation of all for him: that of knowledge, which his former disciple Hilarion offers to him. In the middle sections of the work, the hermit confronts a series of figures representing many of the great Christian heresies (the Manichaeans, the Arians, the Montanists, and others), as well as the old gods of the Mediterranean world (Apollo, Jupiter, Juno, Diana, and Isis). In the sixth and penultimate section, St. Anthony, in a lengthy dialogue, is tempted by the Devil himself. In some instances, St. Anthony gives in to the temptation, but before he has the chance to carry out his sin the hallucination suddenly vanishes. At the very end of the seventh section, after confronting Death, Luxury, and the Sphinx, St. Anthony still hopes for God's love. He lifts his face to the rising sun, which has on it, as on a great disc, the face of Christ; then, crossing himself, he returns to prayer.

Flaubert's portrayal is always ambiguous with respect to the experiences of the hermit. We can never be sure whether what is being described is an hallucination of a psychopathological kind or a true religious vision, or perhaps some mixture of the two. Freud explained the experiences depicted in part with a reference to Flaubert's epilepsy.[15] In any case, *The Temptation* is a book saturated with Christian cosmology and theology. This traditional Christian material is here in the hands of an ambivalent, early modernist writer. Flaubert portrays the experience of temptation, as when nightly this poor, wretched, and somewhat unprepossessing hermit struggles in his mind (or psyche, or soul) to resist evil, and to save his soul. There is much of *Faust* in this work, and indeed Flaubert acknowledged the influence of Goethe's classic.[16]

Goethe's *Faust*

Goethe was Freud's most admired writer, and thus in many respects it was fitting that Freud, who never received the Nobel Prize, was awarded the Goethe Prize.[17] Much of Freud's identification with Goethe is captured in the following remarks, made in an interview near the end of his life:

I am a scientist by necessity, and not by vocation. I am really by nature an artist. Ever since childhood, my secret hero has been Goethe. I would like to have become a poet, and my whole life long I've wanted to write novels.[18]

Later in the same interview, Freud referred to his "beloved Goethe." The only other literary candidate for such an influence might be Shakespeare. Freud had great admiration for the English playwright, but Goethe as a German and as a modern figure was clearly much closer to his heart, and in the case of Shakespeare Freud had almost no biographical information that could permit a strong personal "identification" with him. Goethe's *Faust* was the literary text that Freud most frequently cited and referred to; it was the piece of literature that most powerfully influenced him throughout his life.[19]

It might be well to refresh the reader's memory about this classic. The major point to keep in mind is that the central event of the work is a pact between Faust and the Devil. Now this *Faust* is one in a long line of works of the same title and on the same theme, which can be traced back to medieval times. All of these works are set up within a decidedly Christian framework.[20] This is not to imply that Goethe's *Faust* is a "Christian" work; on the contrary, if anything, it is closer to an *anti*-Christian piece. That is, its hero, who signs up with the Devil, is clearly someone with whom the readers are to identify. It is indeed the positiveness of this depiction of the Faust figure that breaks with the tradition. The work is at times explicitly hostile to the Catholic Church and the clergy, and disparaging remarks are made about theology. We should, however, note that Christ himself is not referred to negatively. And the sincere, simple faith of Margaret (or Gretchen[21]) and the villagers is portrayed with considerable sympathy. Though this kind of faith is considered impossible for the intellectual, jaded Faust, the inability to believe is presented essentially as a loss.

But let us look briefly at the story, paying special attention to those aspects of it that bear most directly on Freud's life and situation.[22]

The play begins with a short scene set in Heaven, in which God (*der Herr*) and the Devil (Mephistopheles) are in conversation: The upshot is a wager that Mephistopheles cannot get the soul of Faust. The story then begins as Faust is alone in his Gothic study–laboratory. The time is the late evening just before Easter Sunday (i.e., late Holy Saturday or Easter Eve)—incidentally, a time of year that makes of *Faust* another part, and a significant one, of Freud's already documented Easter complex. Faust is a disgruntled scholar who is depressed and sarcastic about the meager results of his years of study. He jibes at himself, at theology, and at the Church, while bragging that he is not afraid of the Devil. His glance happens to fall on a bottle filled with an extract, a poison. He decides to swallow it and escape this life by passing over into death. He raises the cup to his mouth to drink, but just as he does this, Easter morning is announced by a loud chiming of bells and choral music. The Easter music makes him pause and then decide not to drink the poison. The words of Faust that describe his reasons for not going ahead with his suicide are quite relevant.

(*Bells and Choral Songs Announce Easter*)
FAUST: Has the time come, deep bells, when you make known the Easter holiday's first holy hour? . . .

> Although I hear the message, I lack all faith or trust
> And faith's favorite child is miracle.
> For those far spheres I should not dare to strive,
> From which these tidings come to me;
> And yet these chords, which I have known since infancy:
> Call me now, too, back into life.
> Once heaven's love rushed at me as a kiss
> In the grave silence of the Sabbath day,
> The rich tones of the bells, it seemed, had much to say,
> And every prayer brought impassioned bliss.
> And unbelievable sweet yearning
> Drove me to roam through wood and lea,
> Crying, and as my eyes were burning,
> I felt a new world grow in me. . . .
>
> Now memory entices me with childlike feeling
> Back from the last, most solemn deed.
> Sound on, oh hymns of heaven, sweet and mild![23]

In these dramatic passages, there is much that would have reminded Freud of his own childhood. The most likely "Freiberg" lines would have been those referring to bells, Easter, childhood and infancy, memory, yearning, and even roaming through wood and lea.

The next part of the play is set in the Easter holiday, and there are references to the resurrection of Jesus and to the general religious atmosphere and activities. It is during this time that Faust, just as disillusioned as ever, meets (or in fact calls up) Mephistopheles, with whom he signs a pact. The agreement is that Mephistopheles is to be Faust's servant in this life; after Faust's death, the situation will be reversed. The pact is made in writing—in blood. A short time later, while traveling with Mephistopheles, Faust sees a young girl in her early teens; this is Margaret with whom he falls in love. He asks Mephistopheles for help in seducing her, which is duly provided. Faust then drinks a narcotic brew concocted by a witch; this fully seals the pact. The witch's brew gives Faust youth and virility. Shortly after taking the drink, Faust first actually meets Margaret, who is simple, beautiful, religious, and pure. Mephistopheles and Faust are, of course, more than a match for the girl, and her downfall is assured. As a result of Faust's blandishments, Margaret gives her mother a sleeping potion, so that she and Faust can spend an undisturbed night together. But the potion causes the mother to die. Then Margaret's brother is killed by Faust in a duel, with help from Mephistopheles. Later, Margaret bears Faust's child, whom she drowns. She eventually goes mad in prison from the horror and shame of her situation. At the end of Part One of the work, Margaret dies, but her soul is carried to Heaven; she is saved. It must be said in defense of Faust that Mephistopheles has kept Margaret's suffering from him by taking him off to a *Walpurgisnacht*; this is one of the most dramatic scenes in the play. *Walpurgisnacht* is, according to European tradition, a gathering of witches from all over Europe on the night of April 30, for a celebration of evil, sex with the Devil, and a general orgy. In Central Europe, *Walpurgisnacht* is especially well known, and in peasant communities it was celebrated with many local folk customs. It is something like America's Halloween, though it is not for children, and in rural areas it was dreaded by many.[24]

Part II of *Faust*, written later, shifts from the Germany of Goethe's day to an entirely different environment. In this part, which has tended to be less popular (and which Freud cited much less often), Faust travels through an imaginary world of scenes and characters taken from the myths of classical Greece and Rome. He is still traveling with Mephistopheles, but the general atmosphere of ancient myths seems, shall we say, more "Jungian," whereas Part I has a "Freudian" feel. At the end, four Grey Women approach: They are the personifications of Want, Need, Debt, and Care (Sorge). The last of these, Sorge, is a harbinger of Faust's approaching death. As she leaves Faust she breathes on him, making him blind. (This is reminiscent of the fate of Oedipus.) Shortly afterwards the blinded Faust dies, and to the deep disgust of Mephistopheles, Faust's soul is carried off to Heaven. Faust's final salvation does not seem convincing to many readers (including myself): He never shows remorse for his actions, and indeed never renounces his pact—yet saved he is!

Now there are various aspects of the play that would have spoken directly to Freud. The text is filled with references to dreams and fantasies; in fact, the whole atmosphere is dark, romantic, and dream-like. (In this respect, there are strong resemblances between *Faust* and Flaubert's *The Temptation*.) Faust himself is an academic, a scholar, whose worldly, disillusioned attitudes would have struck a strong responsive chord in Freud's pessimism and in his skepticism about any higher ideals. Faust is portrayed as a doctor, and in an early scene he expresses his awareness that many of his "cures" are not cures at all. That is, Faust is a "bad doctor," providing false cures, or cures resulting from coincidence. Of course, the central theme and meaning of the entire work is Faust's pact with the Devil—a pact portrayed by Goethe as worth making. This pact is made in spite of reservations and longings, dating from childhood memories of an "Easter faith."

The Faust–Margaret relationship has certain important structural similarities to the Freud–Martha engagement period. The two adversaries with whom Freud had real conflicts over Martha were her very Jewish mother, who was unenthusiastic about Sigmund, and Martha's brother Eli, who functioned as head of the house (the father having died several years earlier). Freud held the "heartless" mother responsible for Martha's leaving him in Vienna and going to live near Hamburg.[25] And of course, Freud, who was so conscious of name similarities, must have been struck by phonemic parallels in the names of the two couples: *Faust–Margaret* and *Freud–Martha*.

Cocaine and the Devil

We need now to develop a deeper understanding of *Faust* by showing the story's connection to Freud's use of cocaine. Freud's important, rather lengthy involvement with cocaine is now being widely recognized.[26] (Jones discusses cocaine briefly as an episode, but he plays down the subject to the point of distorting the record.[27]) Quite recently, both Swales,[28] to whom this section owes much, and Thornton[29] have made clear the pervasive effects of cocaine on Freud's thoughts, moods, and fantasies.

Freud began experimenting with the drug in 1884, when he was 28, at a time when cocaine was almost unknown in scientific circles.[30] During the period 1884–1887, Freud took cocaine frequently, sometimes in heavy doses.[31] After taking the drug himself and getting some preliminary reports from others, Freud published glowing descriptions of cocaine. Not only did Freud think at the time that the drug had antimorphine effects; he was enthusiastic as well about its contributions to mental well-being. It was an antidote to his frequent depressions, and also provided increased physical strength and sexual potency. Like Faust, Freud was enamored of the idea of a drug-induced rejuvenation. Freud's initial involvement with cocaine thoroughly captured both his emotional and intellectual interests. He enthusiastically recommended it to others, including his fiancée.[32] He administered the drug (very likely via hypodermic needle) to his friend and colleague Ernst Fleischl, who was suffering from a drawn-out, terminal nerve condition that required the use of morphine to ease his pain.[33] Freud got Fleischl to take cocaine, which he thought would cure his friend's morphine addiction and have no undesirable effects of its own. Instead, after a brief period of benefit from the drug, Fleischl became addicted to cocaine as well as to morphine, and suffered particularly from cocaine-induced hallucinations (e.g., crawling "cocaine bugs") and delirium tremens.[34] Freud later bitterly acknowledged that he might have hastened his friend's death, saying it was "the result of trying to cast out the devil with Beelzebub."[35]

In the eyes of many, Freud was soon seen as a public menace: One prominent doctor wrote of Freud as having unleashed "the third great scourge of mankind," the first two having been alcohol and opium.[36]

In Freud's defense, it should be said that at the time little was known about the drug, although he clearly displayed very poor judgment. His overenthusiasm for cocaine stemmed from three pressing personal desires, which the drug promised to satisfy. First was his intense desire to get married soon, for he was "pathologically" anxious about his separation from and lengthy open-ended engagement with Martha, who was in northern Germany. He was afraid he might lose her. He had already been separated from her for a year when he began using cocaine, although it seemed much longer to him, for he recalled it once as a two-year separation and once as lasting several years.[37] A second driving concern was career ambition.[38] A medical success, such as the discovery of positive effects from a new drug, would at once advance his career and improve his financial situation, enabling him to marry. Thus, both of these desires would be satisfied by a "cocaine" success. The third need was Freud's desire for an escape from his deeply neurotic depressions, induced to a large degree by his separation anxiety. (We may recall some of his letters to Martha, as discussed in Chapter Three.[39])

Jones summarizes Freud's motives for working on cocaine as involving the enhancement of virility, as well as promising to speed up marriage with Martha; Jones also notes that in getting involved with cocaine, Freud had "forsaken the straight and narrow path of science to seize a short cut to success."[40] His attitude toward the new "soma" was expressed in a dramatic passage from a letter to Martha on June 2, 1884, shortly after he first took it:

Woe to you, my Princess, when I come [for a planned visit]. I will kiss you quite red and feed you until you are plump. And if you are forward you shall see who is the stronger, a gentle girl who doesn't eat enough or a big wild man who has cocaine in his body. In my last severe depression I took coca again and a small dose lifed me to heights in a wonderful fashion. I am just now busy collecting the literature for a song of praise to this magical substance.[41]

Freud received some scientific acclaim for bringing cocaine to the attention of the medical world, but within a year of his official reports the negative effects of the drug were being reported. These criticisms Freud himself described as "grave reproaches,"[42] and they put him under something of a cloud. Jones admits, "It was a poor background from which to shock Viennese medical circles a few years later with his theories on the sexual etiology of the neuroses."[43]

Ironically, it was a young doctor friend of Freud—Carl Koller, an ophthalmologist—who became famous overnight by discovering that cocaine was an effective local anesthetic for the eye, thus enabling anesthetic to be given for eye operations for the first time.[44] Freud had suspected this, but had not immediately investigated the possibility; Koller did. As a result, Koller, to whom Freud had introduced the drug, reaped the career advancement and financial rewards of which Freud had dreamed.

Now the Devil comes into all this through two facts, whose importance Peter Swales has recognized and which he brought to my attention.[45] The Swalesian theory is thus the third published interpretation of a Freudian pact with the Devil.[46] Freud first took cocaine on the night of April 30, 1884—that is, *Walpurgisnacht*.[47] In doing this, Freud, who took the drug in liquid form (as a "brew"), was clearly imitating Faust in his pact with Mephistopheles.[48] The whole affair could easily have been primed by the fact that Goethe's *Faust* was the talk of Vienna in early 1884, following a series of well-publicized performances at the Old Burgtheater.[49]

The yellow smoke gets thicker when another aspect of the situation is considered: Freud obtained his cocaine, which was expensive, from the drug company of Merck in Darmstadt, Germany. He got a local chemist to contact Emanuel Merck, the head of the company. Later, Freud and Fleischl corresponded with Merck personally.[50] (An example of the Merck bottle of cocaine, and of a prescription, written by Freud to Merck for cocaine, is available. This particular prescription is from a later date, June 1893; it proves Freud's continued connection with the drug.[51]) What Swales has pointed out is that the Merck who founded the company was Goethe's model for Mephistopheles when he wrote *Faust*. Goethe, in his well-known autobiographical work *Dichtung und Wahrheit*, not only referred to Merck as a "great negator" and as a man of the world "who had the greatest influence on me"[52]; more significantly, he compared Merck to Mephistopheles at least three times.[53] Freud knew Goethe's work well, and was presumably familiar with this text. In writing to the great-grandson of the first Merck, Merck's "revenant," he was, psychologically speaking, contacting the Devil.

It is remotely possible that in 1884 Freud had not yet read Goethe's famous autobiography, in the second half of which Merck figures so prominently. Freud certainly did read *Dichtung und Wahrheit* at some time, though, since in 1917 he published an analysis of a childhood memory of Goethe cited in this work.[54] The memory in question, which Freud interpreted as an expression of sibling rivalry, was one he said he had long known but had only written about for publication when he had come to a psychoanalytic understanding of its meaning.[55]

Freud also pointed out in his review of the history of cocaine, published in July 1884, that the Spaniards, who first wrote of the use of the coca plant by South American Indians, suspected that it was the work of the Devil.[56]

In conclusion, it is clear that cocaine for Freud was thoroughly linked to the Devil, and, indeed, was connected from the beginning to some kind of pact. Thus, while Freud was still a young physician—years before the beginning of psychoanalysis, and some 10–12 years before the psychological "pact" that Bakan proposes—he was already very strongly involved with the Devil. The exact nature of the pact is still not clear, but it appears to have been modeled on Faust's pact, and it was certainly precipitated by Freud's admittedly "severe" depressions, his longing for Martha, and his "pathological ambition."[57]

Thornton's Cocaine Thesis

E. M. Thornton has very recently published an extensive discussion of the effect of Freud's cocaine use on both his personal psychology and his theories.[58] Although, for reasons given below, I think Thornton has overgeneralized the significance of cocaine for understanding Freud, she does make a number of important contributions to Freud scholarship.

To begin with, she identifies two time periods when Freud took cocaine[59]: the first from 1884 to 1887, first noted by Jones, and a second period, beginning in late 1892 and continuing into the middle or late 1890s.[60] Thornton is not especially clear on when Freud last took cocaine, but she clearly implies that he took it well after 1900, perhaps until 1912.[61] However, because of the complete and uncensored letters of Freud to Fliess, very recently published, it appears that Freud permanently ceased taking cocaine in October 1896, when he wrote to Fliess that he had put his cocaine brush aside.[62] An important consequence, in the following months, would be that Freud was often struggling with cocaine withdrawal experiences, especially depression. Thornton also points out that Freud used pure, unadulterated cocaine; he used it frequently and often in strong doses.[63] Thornton's major claim is that Freud suffered from cocaine poisoning and from powerful drug-induced psychological states.[64] In particular, she claims that Freud's psychological theory was simply the natural consequence of extensive cocaine usage.[65] It is well known that cocaine causes hallucinations, vivid dreams, and extensive fantasies in frequent users. Cocaine use can also cause sexual preoccupation to become obsessive. Other reliable psychological effects from taking too much cocaine are periods of elation, optimism, and an almost messianic belief in having discovered the great secrets of life; these intervals are followed by periods of deep depression often accompanied by paranoia and murderous impulses toward friends.[66] All of these symptoms, Thornton argues, are clearly shown in Freud's letters to Fliess—and often in Fliess's ideas as well, since Fliess was also a heavy user of cocaine. (Both suffered from severe headaches and from nasal and sinus infections during this period as well. Such symptoms are typical when cocaine is taken through the nose, as was the case during these years for both Freud and Fliess.[67])

My primary critique of Thornton is that much of Freud's psychology was clearly apparent before he took cocaine. Therefore, although the drug would have accentuated and sometimes distorted Freud's already existing psychology and intellectual interests, it would not have caused them in the first place. For example, Freud was mentioning his extreme depressive reactions to Martha's absence before he took cocaine. For example, on August 18, 1882, he wrote, "Without you I would let my arms droop for sheer lack of desire to live"[68]; on February 14, 1884, he exclaimed, "Do you realize it is two whole days since I heard from you and I am beginning to worry!"[69]

Likewise, Freud's previously discussed expressions of religious preoccupation—his lengthy letter about the Christian paintings in Dresden, his many youthful references to God, his early quotes from *Faust*, and his references to the Devil—all preceded his cocaine use. Most of his involvement with Brentano and the letters to Fluss and Silberstein that have been cited also antedate his use of cocaine, as does his attraction to Flaubert's *The Temptation of St. Anthony*, with what Freud called its wild *Walpurgisnacht* character. Finally, we can observe Freud's very early expression of extreme self-confidence in a letter written when he was 17 to his friend Emil Fluss. Freud was writing about his high grades in his school (Gymnasium) examinations. One of his professors told him that he had an outstanding writing style, and Freud remarked:

I was suitably impressed by this amazing fact and do not hesitate to disseminate the happy event, the first of its kind, as widely as possible—to you, for instance, who until now have probably remained unaware that you have been exchanging letters with a German stylist. . . . preserve them [the letters]—have them bound—take good care of them—one never knows.[70]

Another way to place Thornton's cocaine claims in perspective is to compare the very different effects of the drug on Freud and on Fliess. Both became somewhat magalomaniacal; both showed occasional signs of sloppy (probably drug-affected) thinking; both became preoccupied with sex. But the differences were even greater and can be plausibly explained by the different personal psychologies and professional backgrounds of the two men. Fliess focused on the sexual significance of the nose [71]; Freud never seriously theorized about the nose. Fliess emphasized his proposed female and male sexual periods of 28 and 23 days, respectively, while Freud turned to sexual experiences in childhood between the ages of two and four. Freud analyzed dreams and fantasies, but Fliess seems to have had no real interest in these phenomena. In short, these were very different ways to approach sexuality, and therefore I conclude that the major effect of cocaine was to accentuate or heighten Freud's pre-existing thought patterns and psychological preoccupations. At times, cocaine may have distorted his reactions; for example, it may have made his depressions darker and harder to fight. But cocaine did not create the primary content and structure of Freud's mind and thought. (The question of whether Freud's theories are correct is also one that Thornton addresses extensively. This issue, however important in its own right, is not of concern here; instead, the present discussion is focused on understanding the origin and nature of Freud's thought with respect to religion, especially Christianity. The question of the validity of Freud's theories is treated only with respect to his interpretation of religion, and then only in the last chapter of this book.)

Milton's *Paradise Lost*

In 1907, Freud received a letter in which he was asked to name "ten good books." In his response,[72] Freud noted that he was not asked to name the ten *greatest* books, in which category he would put the tragedies of Sophocles, Goethe's *Faust*, and Shakespeare's *Hamlet* and *Macbeth*. Nor was the request for *significant* books, like Darwin's *Origin of Species*. Nor again was he asked for his *favorite* books; nonetheless, he provided the titles of the two works that he termed his "favorites." (No other titles were mentioned as favorites.) These two, which presumably were those he found the most personally satisfying, were Milton's *Paradise Lost* and Heine's *Lazarus*. Let us look briefly at the former. (The *Lazarus* poems are discussed in Chapter Six.)

Paradise Lost is, of course, a Christian classic by a great English Puritan, with a theme identified in the title. It is the story, first, of the revolt of Satan and his banishment from Heaven, then of the fall of man and his expulsion from Paradise (Eden). About this work, Freud, as a young man, wrote to Martha:

I don't know how it came about, but today I was thinking that everyone ought to have someone great and powerful to be his lord and protector, to whom he could turn in dark, heavy hours. I reached out for John Milton, with his sublime enchantment that can transport me as nothing else can from the dull, unsatisfying world of daily care, so that the earth becomes like a little dot in the universe, and the vast heavens open.[73]

Aside from Milton's "sublime enchantment," there are various character-istics of this work that would have appealed to Freud—that would have spoken to his memories and to his patterns of thought. Freud's remark about himself as "the happy child from Freiberg" is relevant here as a description of his own lost Eden.[74] In another text as well, Freud evoked these memories:

> When I was seventeen . . . I returned for the first time to my birthplace for the holidays. . . . I know quite well what a wealth of impressions overwhelmed me at the time. . . . I believe now that I was never free from a longing for the beautiful woods near our home.[75]

Paradise Lost would have been, even more than the early part of *Faust*, a powerful literary redintegration and representation of Freud's own lost childhood world. (One is reminded here that while in Rome Freud particularly enjoyed staying in the Eden Hotel.[76])

The main character of *Paradise Lost* (i.e., the one given the greatest literary prominence and power) is, of course, Satan, who, after rebelling, seduces Eve by assuming the form of the serpent, and then Adam through Eve. So again we find a Freudian fascination for the literary celebration of Satanic power.

At the heart of Milton's work is the great opposition between Heaven and Hell.[77] God is in Heaven with the Messiah and the angels; Satan has "fallen into Hell," into the "great Deep," where as the poem begins he is "lying on the burning lake." He has been driven out because of his disobedience, because of his attack on God the Father—an Oedipal rebellion, if you will. Satan comes to earth at night, and enters the serpent. (Throughout the poem, Satan is associated with the night and with a lower, darker world. He is described as an evil spirit who has escaped from the deep.) The next morning Eve relates a disturbing dream to Adam, a dream anticipating her coming temptation. She is soon in fact seduced by Satan into eating the fruit of the Tree of Knowledge; Adam, rather than live without her, also eats the fruit; their joint fall is the result. Considering Freud's own intense desire for knowledge, one wonders if he didn't side with Adam and Eve—and Satan—on the fundamental question of knowledge. Relevant here is a letter written by Freud to Martha in the summer of 1883. Freud, feeling quite depressed about their separation and worried about their future, quoted from *Paradise Lost*:

> Let us consult
> What reinforcement we may gain from hope,
> If not, what resolution from despair.[78]

What Jones, who cites this letter, does not mention is that Freud was quoting Satan here. The passage in question occurs when Satan is licking his wounds after being thrown out of Heaven; he is speaking with one of his fallen helpers and planning a new attack on God.

The story continues with Adam and Eve's expulsion from Paradise, but at the end of the poem they learn that redemption will come many years in the future: It will come through the seed of Eve, and with it Paradise will be restored. (It is interesting to note that Eve learns of all this through a dream, just as she dreamed of her temptation in advance. That dreams are to be taken seriously was assumed by Milton, and by many other writers who influenced Freud as well.) The major explicit expression of this final redemptive outcome is, of course, found in Milton's sequel to this work, *Paradise Regained*. Freud does not appear to have read this poem, though, given his knowledge of literary culture, he must have known of its existence and general theme.

There is an interesting parallel between Milton's three-tiered world of Heaven (God)–Earth (man)–Hell (Satan) and the superego–ego–id of Freudian theory. Moreover, the greatest power appears to lie with the id (Satan), who is the energetic leader of rebellion, seduction, and violence. Adam and Eve, as representations of the ego, are certainly the weakest in this trio, while God, Jesus, and the loyal angels (the superego) are portrayed in Milton, but not in Freud, as the ultimate victors. But despite the eventual future victory, it is Satan who at the end of *Paradise Lost* has won the first great battle by bringing about the loss of Paradise for mankind, and it is Satan, the spirit from the deep, who comes across within this work as the true power to be reckoned with.[79]

Mozart's *Don Giovanni*

Freud expressed an unusual, and indeed most peculiar, attitude toward music. Here was a man living in perhaps the major music capital of the world, during a period of great creative musical activity—a man who, moreover, was very open to culture—but who explicitly said that he did not like music. Freud's words on the subject are revealing: "[W]ith music, I am almost incapable of obtaining any pleasure. Some rationalistic, or perhaps analytic, turn of mind in me rebels against being moved by a thing without knowing why I am thus affected and what it is that affects me."[80] In general, this self-description seems to have been quite accurate, for Freud rarely if ever went to concerts, and showed little interest in music. As I have already proposed above, I believe that this rejection of music came from Freud's early experience of church music. To hear organ, instrumental, and choral music, and also bells, would have activated painful, unconscious memories in Freud—memories of his lost nanny and her world.

And yet there were a few exceptions to Freud's categorical rejection. Freud did occasionally go to the opera, and he definitely enjoyed a few of them. Now an opera, of course, has a plot or story, and as a result Freud's penchant for rational understanding would be much less thwarted than in the case of "pure" music, so it is not difficult to understand this exception.

But what particular operas did Freud like? Jones, in discussing Freud's personal life, refers to only three operas. One was *Carmen*, an opera he seems to have enjoyed moderately[81]; the other two were operas by Mozart, who was clearly Freud's favorite composer. Two of Mozart's operas figured with some frequency in Freud's letters and other writings: *The Marriage of Figaro* and *Don Giovanni*. Without a doubt, the latter was Freud's favorite. Jones relates:

[Freud] was shocked to find that his friend . . . did not know that *Don Giovanni* was composed by Mozart, so he insisted on taking him to see it; . . . Martha and he had seen the opera in their days together in Vienna. Then . . . [Freud had] decided to complete his Mozart education by seeing the *Magic Flute*. This proved rather disappointing. "Some of the arias are wonderfully beautiful, but the whole thing rather drags . . . The action is very stupid, the libretto quite crazy, and it is simply not to be compared with *Don Giovanni*."[82]

Let us take a look at this one opera that Freud so especially liked. The opera is set in Spain, and the plot is established in Scene One.[83] Don Giovanni (Don Juan), who has spent his life successfully seducing women, is now in Seville at the palace of an elderly, dignified nobleman, the Commendatore (or commander). Don Giovanni is accompanied by his servant Leporello, who has helped Giovanni in many of his escapades. The action begins with a struggle on the stairs of the palace between Giovanni and Donna Anna, the daughter of the Commendatore. Giovanni is pressing his physical attentions on Donna Anna, who is resisting him. As they lurch down the stairs, suddenly the Commendatore appears, sees his daughter struggling with her would-be seducer, and challenges Giovanni to a duel. Don Giovanni, goaded by the old gentleman, draws his sword and swiftly kills him; Giovanni then leaves hastily with his servant. Donna Anna and her betrothed, Don Ottavio, discover the body; grief-stricken Donna Anna makes Don Ottavio swear to avenge her father's death. Together they vow vengeance in a duet that ends the scene: "Che giuramento, O Dei" ("What an oath, O Gods").

The action then portrays Donna Anna's attempt to avenge the death of her father, the Commendatore. Because she was unable to see the face of Giovanni in the earlier scene, this takes some time. Other important parts of the opera concern Giovanni's attempts to seduce other women and to avoid the consequences of similar past actions. The climax occurs in Scene Four of the second and final act. Don Giovanni is in a graveyard with Leporello; in the graveyard is a statue of the late Commendatore. Giovanni is jocularly relating his recent adventures when a deep, sepulchral voice suddenly declares that they will soon end. Don Giovanni commands Leporello to ask the statue to dinner the following evening. The statue nods acceptance; to make sure, Don Giovanni repeats the invitation; the statue replies "Yes."

The last scene is set in the banquet hall of Don Giovanni's castle. There is beautiful music and a lavish meal. Suddenly, Donna Elvira, with whom Don Giovanni has had a prior affair, appears. Don Giovanni dismisses the musicians and his other lady friends. Donna Elvira pleads desperately with her former lover to mend his evil ways; Don Giovanni finds her pleas amusing. Donna Elvira, rebuffed, rushes toward a door. She opens it, shrieks in terror, and runs out through an opposite door. Don Giovanni goes to the door, opens it, and discovers that the statue of the Commendatore has arrived. The marble statue enters, grasps Don Giovanni's arm, and orders him to repent; Don Giovanni stubbornly refuses. At this, the statue announces that the time has come; it pulls Don Giovanni along toward the door through which it entered. "Smoke and flames begin to develop Don Giovanni; a chorus of hollow demon voices summons him to hell, where worse agony awaits him. . . . Don Giovanni, with a final scream, vanishes amid hellfire and smoke."[84]

Now there are a number of what we might term "Freudian" elements in this opera. The initial killing of the Commendatore is an obvious Oedipal conflict, in which the old father is killed by a son-figure. The killing, and Giovanni's sexual crimes, lead to his final damnation. Also, this opera is another example of Freud's early preoccupation with three-layered universes: the gods above, then Earth, and Hell with damnation below.

Many of the names in Mozart's work would also have struck deep responses in Freud. The heroine's name of "Donna Anna" would have evoked his nanny, and possibly his sister (also, eventually, his daughter). "Don Giovanni" (Don Juan) would have suggested his "cousin" John. "Leporello" is the Italian for "Lipperel," the diminutive of "Philipp." It is as if Mozart chose his names precisely from the Freud "family romance." Finally, the marble man, the statue of the Commendatore, can be viewed as an expression of many of the elements that Freud found so powerfully fascinating in the statue of Moses: Both statues are, in particular, judgmental, stone father-figures.

Victor Hugo's *Notre Dame de Paris*

While Freud was in Paris for several months from the fall of 1885 to early 1886, studying with Charcot, he read Victor Hugo's *Notre Dame de Paris*. He wrote to Martha that to understand Paris "it is the novel to read, for it is the truth about Paris."[85] But he declared that one should only read the book in Paris, and if one is in a calm mood. Jones says that Freud entered into the spirit of *Notre Dame*, which he had not previously thought highly of, but which he now preferred to neuropathology, his field of study.[86]

The novel centers around the young, beautiful Esmeralda, and three men with dramatically contrasting natures who compete for her love. They are Quasimodo, the devoted hunchback; Frollo, the diabolical archdeacon; and Phebus, the handsome, somewhat superficial captain. By far, the most powerful characters are Frollo and Quasimodo. Frollo, portrayed as possessed by the Devil, is responsible for the death of Esmeralda. Once he knows that he cannot have her love (she loves Phebus), he arranges for her to be falsely accused of murder and witchcraft, which results in her being publicly hanged. As she dies on the gibbet, Frollo watches from the parapets of Notre Dame, and his Satanic laughter is a chilling expression that he is possessed and no longer really human. Quasimodo avenges his beloved by pushing Frollo off the cathedral tower to his death. The omnipresent cathedral is virtually a character in itself in the novel; it is at any rate a powerful context—a physical, almost living presence—in which the action is set.

There is much in Frollo that would have interested—even attracted—Freud. Frollo is an intellectual; what he thirsts for is knowledge ("science"). Like Faust, he first studies theology; then (among many other things) medicine. He is celibate, in love with an attractive girl; he is, moreover, hard pressed for money. In short, he is not so very unlike Freud! (Note also: *F*reud–*F*rollo–*F*aust.)

As for Quasimodo, this character is named for the first Sunday after Easter ("*Quasi modo . . .*" are the first words of the Introit of the Mass of that day). He is ugly and deformed, but in the text he is the embodiment of goodness and devotion. He is the bellringer of Notre Dame. I would like to suggest that Quasimodo was associated for Freud with his nanny, who was also ugly, devoted, and associated with church bells and Easter.

Freud's favorite part of Notre Dame was, incidentally, the platform high up on the tower, among the gargoyles and demons—the place, in fact, from which Frollo falls to his death.[87] (See Figures 4-1 and 4-2.)

The novel has many other "Freudian" properties. Esmeralda and Quasimodo do not know who their true parents are, and the theme of

---

Figure 4-1. (top) Notre Dame Cathedral, (bottom) Gargoyles; from a popular edition of Hugo's novel *Notre Dame de Paris*, illustrated by Ch. Guillaume, that was published in Paris in 1885, a few months before Freud's visit to the city. (Marpon & Flammarion edition)

Figure 4-2. Frollo falling to his death from the tower of Notre Dame. (Marpon & Flammarion edition)

ambiguous parentage is a significant one in the work. As to the bells, not only is Quasimodo (as noted) the bellringer, but Hugo devotes entire pages to bells and their powerful auditory and emotive powers; they provide an important part of the novel's atmosphere. Still more Freudian are the visual hallucinatory experiences of Frollo, which are described in great detail. These hallucinations would have been very interesting to Freud because of their similarity to dream images; because such images or visions constitute the method or mode whereby the Devil is experienced;

and because, at the time, Freud's use of cocaine would have made him especially liable to hallucinations of his own.

While Freud was in Paris, he was frequently taking cocaine. Three of the published letters from him during this stay in Paris refer to this: "a little cocaine to untie my tongue" (January 18, 1886); "I, quite calm with the help of a small dose of cocaine . . ." (January 20, 1886); and "a bit of cocaine I have just taken is making me talkative" (February 2, 1886).[88] Both Swales and Thornton have suggested that part of Freud's strange reaction to the Parisians was due to cocaine-induced moods. On December 3, 1885, he wrote Martha that "the city and its inhabitants strike me as uncanny; the people seem to me of a different species . . . they are all possessed of a thousand demons."[89] Freud also reported that in Paris he heard Martha calling his name—an auditory hallucination attributable to his cocaine use.[90]

A final note: We may recall (see quote, p. 104) that Freud said of this work that in it Hugo "taught me that the poet too is a priest; and thus I boldly substituted myself for the confessor." Here we see Freud with a literary identity as poet describing himself as both like, and as in competition with, a priest.

The Interpretation of Dreams: Rome, Malleus Maleficarum, Witchcraft, and Related Themes

Thanks to his letters to Fliess, there is considerable information available concerning Freud's personal motivations during the time, about ten years after his stay in Paris, during which he was writing the "dream book," generally considered to be his greatest contribution to psychology. (Figure 4-3 shows Freud with Fliess at about this time.) The Devil and related topics made repeated appearances in these letters as Freud worked out his ideas. Let us look through this correspondence for references to the Devil and to related Christian themes.

In the spring of 1896 came the first mention of a book that would eventually become The Interpretation of Dreams, some three and a half years later. In December 1896, Freud mentioned three chapters, and he gave the introductory quotations that would precede them. He wrote that one chapter would be preceded by these lines:

> They are exceeding all bounds, I fear a breakdown;
> God does not present the reckoning at the end of every week.[91]

The meaning of this is not entirely clear, since Freud did not identify the source, but anxiety and the fear of God's reckoning are obvious.

For another major chapter, Freud suggested a quote from Goethe (from Zahme Xenien), which translates as "Cut it short! On doomsday it

Figure 4-3. Sigmund Freud and Wilhelm Fliess in 1890. (Mary Evans/Sigmund Freud Copyrights)

won't be worth a fart."[92] Here again the theme of final judgment can be seen. With respect to this work, Walter Kaufmann writes: "The *Xenien* who 'revere Satan, our sire and singer,' were polemical verses written by Goethe and Schiller."[93]

Finally, for the chapter on symptom formation, Freud proposed a line from the *Aeneid: "Flectere si nequeo superos Acheronta movebo"* ("If I cannot bend the higher powers [the gods], I shall stir up Hell [the river Acheron]."[94] This quotation is most significant, since Freud ultimately selected it as the motto not merely for a chapter, but for the entire book. These words, Schorske points out,[95] are spoken by Juno, who hates Aeneas and struggles unsuccessfully to prevent the founding of Rome. Here is another example of Freud's Hannibal complex. Once again, then, we have a powerful literary expression of a three-tiered universe, with Freud taking the side of the lower level, Hell, against the higher powers, who are on the side of Rome (and implicitly of Christianity). Freud's ambivalence was clearly present here, in that he associated himself in this quotation with an enemy of Rome who is fated to lose: We know Juno cannot keep Aeneas from his destiny—his kingdom.

Three letters later in the correspondence (January 3, 1897), Freud was writing about his new psychology and about his optimism in the new year. First he commented (and here we can note that he was siding with the angels!): "When I am not afraid I can take on all the devils in hell. . . . "[96] The letter continued with the idea that the first three years of life are the most important for the development of a person's psychology. Freud then mentioned his hope of being with Fliess at Easter, perhaps in Prague. In the letter's final paragraph, he proposed a motto to introduce his chapter on sexuality: "from heaven through the world to hell," a quote from *Faust*. (With this, Freud was back in more familiar company.)

A short time later (January 17, 1897), Freud took up the medieval notion of possession, which he said was "identical with our theory of a foreign body and the splitting of consciousness."[97] In this important letter, Freud proposed that the Devil is a psychological experience of part of the unconscious—one that is due to a split in the person, or one that can give rise to a splitting in consciousness. One part then comes under the control or influence of the unconscious "demons" (more is said on this in Chapter Five).

In his next letter (January 24, 1897), Freud continued to note parallels between his own ideas and the medieval theory of demonic possession.[98] He mentioned that he had ordered a copy of the book *Malleus Maleficarum* (*The Witches' Hammer*), which he planned to study diligently. Since we can assume that he did this, it is useful to describe briefly something of the content of this still well-known (and infamous) treatise.

This 15th-century work was written by two Dominicans on the subject of witchcraft, and it defines witches as possessed, either consciously or unconsciously, by the Devil.[99] The Devil, demons, and evil spirits are featured in every chapter. Several chapters take up the ways in which a conscious pact or arrangement with the Devil is made; thus one section is entitled "On the Way Whereby a Formed Pact with Evil Is Made."[100] The pact may be made in a gathering of witches in a *Walpurgisnacht* setting, or alone. A clear rejection of God, Christ, the Church, and Christianity is an essential ingredient of such a pact. Although most witches (like hysterics) are women, some are men, and one important such male, possessed by the Devil, is noted in this book: He is the Anti-Christ.[101]

Now it is clear that Freud saw hysterical patients as people who in earlier centuries would have been described as witches. We should also note that Freud often thought of himself as an hysteric—as one with hysterical symptoms. Hence, Freud as a male hysteric would have been in his own eyes like a male witch. This understanding of hysterical symptoms as similar to what once was called "possession," Freud proposed as early as 1886 and 1888, when he published his earliest papers commenting on the subject of hysteria.[102]

Let us return to the January 24 letter. Freud discussed witchcraft with respect to a patient, Herr E., who as a child had had a nurse or nanny whom he deeply loved (a patient not unlike Freud himself, as is so often the case). In his fantasies, this woman's money was always turning to excrement. Apparently E. saw his nurse as a witch; this was what his associations of her money with excrement implied. Freud reported in the letter that he had just read (in the medieval accounts of these phenomena) that it is when the Devil gives money to his victims that they become witches.[103]

Later, Freud reported that he was "beginning to dream of an extremely primitive devil religion."[104] The whole issue of the similarity between the stories of alleged witches and his hysterical patients had greatly captured his imagination.[105]

The theme of the Devil next appeared with a Freiberg association, in a letter of October 27, 1897, when Freud quoted *Faust* again: "And the shades of loved ones appear, and with them, like an old, half-forgotten myth, first love and friendship"[106] (a reference to Freud's just-emerging memories of his Freiberg childhood?). Next came many of the letters speaking so powerfully of Freud's longing for Rome, especially for Rome with Fliess at Easter. In one of these letters, Freud quoted from *Faust* yet again: "The best that you know you cannot tell to the boys"[107]—a statement made by the Devil to Faust, implying the constant need for censorship, since most people are not sophisticated enough to understand. This line was one of Freud's favorites, and he quoted it often in his letters. It implies that Freud was aware that many of his central motivations and associations were artfully concealed, not only from the public but perhaps from "the boys" (his friends, perhaps even Fliess) as well. In this context, it is worth noting that Freud evaluated Goethe, his favorite writer, as "a great revealer" but also "in spite of the wealth of autobiographical hints, a careful concealer."[108]

Several letters later in the correspondence, in April 1898, Freud was recounting a visit to Italy (the letter included the description quoted in

Chapter Three of the pretty girls gathered outside a cathedral for Easter Mass). Freud described a visit to the dramatic caves of St. Canigan, which he likened to the *Inferno* as depicted by Dante.[109] Four letters later (July 7, 1898), Freud wrote again of Dante and of the secret theme of "unsatisfied revenge and inevitable punishment, represented by Dante as continuing through all eternity."[110] The theme of Easter and Rome surfaced once more in the early months of 1899, with his longing to visit Rome.[111] In July of that year, he told Fliess that he would use the line from the *Aeneid* as his motto[112] for the "Egyptian Dream Book," which was about to go to press.[113]

The correspondence continued with many Easter references, and one letter (March 23, 1900) contained the statement: "No one can help in what oppresses me, it is my cross, which I must bear, and heaven knows my back is getting noticeably bent under it. . . . "[114] All in all, this was quite a Christian definition of his situation, especially since the next sentence referred to his plan at Easter to visit Trent. The cross Freud referred to was a deep inner crisis involving depression and the collapse of intellectual or emotional illusions, the exact nature of which was unspecified.

In a letter of May 1900, Freud wrote:

[I]t will be a fitting punishment for me that none of the unexplored regions of the mind in which I have been the first to set foot will ever bear my name or submit to my laws. When breath threatened to fail me in the struggle I prayed the angel to desist, and that is what he has done since then. But I did not turn out to be the stronger, though since then I have been noticeably limping. Well, I really am forty-four now, a rather shabby old Jew . . .[115]

In this passage, Freud was comparing himself to Jacob, who wrestled with the angel of the Lord (Genesis 32), the result being a wounded thigh and a limp.

There is further evidence of Freud's concern with the Devil in a letter to Fliess, dated July 1900. *The Interpretation of Dreams* had now been out for some months, but I think that these words of Freud's (which evoke Dante's *Inferno*) very accurately describe the intellectual struggle that led to the "dream book" and that continued for some time afterwards:

The big problems are still unsettled. It is an intellectual hell, layer upon layer of it, with everything fitfully gleaming and pulsating; and the outline of Lucifer–Amor coming into sight at the darkest centre.[116]

Presumably this passage refers as well to Freud's new book, *The Psychopathology of Everyday Life* (1901), which he was working on at the time. When some time later he was told of the popular success of this book, Freud replied by quoting from *Faust*: "Not even if he had them by the scruff of the neck, I swear, would ever these people smell the devil."[117] This disturbing statement, along with the two preceding quotes, certainly implies that, in some sense, Freud saw himself as actively working against the angels of the Lord.

Conclusion

If we look back on Freud's life from the time of his late 20s up until his self-analysis, and for a few years afterward, it is apparent that the issues of Heaven and (especially) Hell, of the Devil and damnation, were deeply connected to his personal motivation. What were the works that most powerfully moved him? *The Temptation of St. Anthony, Faust, Notre Dame de Paris, Paradise Lost, Don Giovanni,* the *Malleus Maleficarum,* the *Aeneid,* the *Inferno,* and much of *Huttens Letzte Tage* all belong in this list. All these works are centrally preoccupied with the Devil or with evil; with Heaven and Hell; or with hostility to Rome as a symbol of Catholicism. When the Devil does appear in person in these works, it is invariably as a compelling and fascinating figure; God may be the ultimate and highest good (and the final victor), but the Devil and Hell are psychologically and literally dominant in this literature.

Furthermore, it was to themes that Freud was drawn in a work, and not much to an author or his style. Thus, there is no evidence that Freud read any Flaubert except *The Temptation* (he never read, for example, the much more famous *Madame Bovary*). The only Victor Hugo Freud seems to have read is *Notre Dame.* There is no evidence that Freud read *Paradise Regained* or Dante's *Purgatorio* or *Paradiso.* No doubt Freud knew of these great works and their general meaning, but he apparently never read them.

These writings constituted the core of Freud's involvement with literature, and much of this core is focused on the Devil, on the demonic. Although the material cited in earlier chapters shows Freud's positive attraction to the Christian God, the evidence cited here makes a strong case that a very important part of Freud sided with Satan against God and Heaven and Christ, and sided with the enemies of the Church.

But what is one to make of all this? Before again taking up the thesis of a pact with the Devil, and offering a new interpretation, we must take a detour into some major and almost unexplored aspects of Freud's own psychology.

Chapter Five

Freud and the Devil: Sexual Seduction and Splitting

IN THIS CHAPTER, some significant pathological characteristics of Freud's personal psychology are discussed. This is needed in order to provide an understanding of his preoccupation with the Devil; in particular, a portrayal of Freud's psychology is needed to understand his demonic pact.

Was Freud Sexually Seduced as a Child?

There are serious reasons proposed by Krüll to believe that Freud was sexually seduced or at least significantly eroticized as a child.[1] We have already seen a hint that the nanny might be associated with something of the kind, but there is evidence that points in other directions as well. In any case, it will become clear that the issue of Freud's possible childhood seduction is central to an understanding of Freud's relationship both to religion and to the Devil.

I begin by quoting a statement of Freud's (part of which has been quoted in Chapter One). Freud was writing to Fliess about his nanny, his brother Julius (who died), his half-nephew John, God, and Hell:

I still have not got to the scenes which lie at the bottom of this. *If they emerge, and I succeed in resolving my hysteria* [emphasis added], I shall have to thank the memory of the old woman who provided me at such an early age with the means for living and surviving. You see how the old liking breaks through again.[2]

In this statement, by referring to his own hysteria, Freud also implied that, whatever the cause of hysteria might be, he had experienced it himself. Now, in the mid-1890s, Freud very strongly believed that all hysteria was traceable to sexual seduction and abuse. His claim for such an origin for hysteria was first published in 1896,[3] and his commitment to this idea was strong for a number of years; indeed, to some extent, he always considered real sexual abuse as an important factor in hysteria. This theory, known as the "seduction theory," he later modified and replaced with the now well-known psychoanalytic alternative: namely, that hysteria, although sometimes due to actual childhood sexual seduction, is not always the result of such abuse. Instead, hysteria is understood as more often the result of childhood *fantasies* of sexual seduction. Freud always, however, assumed that childhood seduction could be a factor in mental pathology; that is, he never completely abandoned the seduction theory.[4]

This particular issue has quite recently received widespread attention in the writings of Jeffrey Masson, who claims that Freud abandoned the original theory, in spite of solid supporting clinical evidence, because it was so badly received by his colleagues.[5] Freud, according to Masson, essentially "chickened out" and substituted the fantasy world of incest (e.g., the Oedipus complex) for the real world of actual sexual abuse. Masson's case for this interpretation of Freud's motivation is, in fact, not very convincing. Typically, his critics have pointed out that the evidence proposed by Masson is weak and often forced.[6] In addition, Sulloway has amply documented that Freud's psychoanalytic theory was part of a long-term systematic intellectual evolution.[7] And, of course, there was evidence of sexual abuse *not* resulting in hysteria, as well as cases of hysteria without any actual sexual seduction or abuse.

Also to the point, both Peter Swales and Marianne Krüll have provided differing but mutually supportive alternative explanations of the factors behind Freud's abandonment of the original seduction theory. Thornton and Swales, besides showing the relevance of cocaine to Freud's concept of libido (sexual energy),[8] both identify cocaine as a factor in Freud's powerful fantasy life.[9]

More relevant to our present concerns is Swales's important work on the intellectual impact of the late medieval theory of witchcraft and demonic possession proposed by Johann Weier in 1563.[10] Weier proposed that the many witches who freely confessed to being such were suffering from *fantasies* of making pacts with the Devil and of committing crimes against others—fantasies often brought on by terrible "melancholy" (i.e., depression).[11] Freud acknowledged the persuasiveness of Weier's theory,[12] and in 1896 and 1897 (just prior to his rejection of the seduction theory), this medieval understanding assumed a central place in his letters to Fliess.[13] For our purposes, it is only necessary to emphasize that Freud very strongly connected hysteria to witches and to real (or more often fantasized) early sexual seduction, and that he connected all of this to a pact with the Devil.

As already stated, I do not think Masson's explanation for why Freud changed his seduction theory is correct. Nevertheless, I do believe that some of Masson's claims are both important and valid. In particular, Masson's emphasis on the frequency with which children (especially girls) suffer sexual abuse is justified, not only because sexual abuse is far more frequent than previously supposed—especially in the lives of those seeking psychological help—but also because psychoanalysis has without doubt overemphasized the fantasy world as a source of mental pathology.[14] Indeed, the essential argument of this chapter is that Freud himself suffered from a moderate degree of childhood sexual abuse, and that this experience helps us to account for some of his own psychopathology as well as his persistent intellectual interest in early sexual trauma.

It is plausible to assume that Freud's theoretical constructs were commonly derived from his response to at least a kernel of actual experience similar to that of his patients. For example, Krüll's interpretation (discussed in Chapter Two) that Freud witnessed his mother's affair with Philipp makes Freud's Oedipal theory an elaboration of an early experience, not the expression of an innate mental predisposition or structure. Likewise, if Freud suffered early sexual abuse, then his own theories can be interpreted in part as the response of a victim, and his failure to keep focused on real experiences as a way of protecting those who abused him. (For example, the basic argument of Krüll is that Freud wanted to protect his father from the charge of abusing his own children.) Masson cites moving examples of the great reluctance of children to accuse their own fathers or mothers.[15] Therefore, it is proposed that Freud's own failure to do the same with those who perpetrated abuse of him fits into this familiar pattern.

Now, if Freud was sexually seduced as a child, and his great preoccupation with the subject stemmed from this abuse, the next question is this: Who was the guilty party? To begin with, Freud noted that the most frequent perpetrators of sexual abuse are fathers. In a recently disclosed letter, he wrote, "Unfortunately, my own father was one of these perverts and is responsible for the hysteria of my brother (all of whose symptoms are identifications) and those of several younger sisters."[16] In another letter of the same period (one central to Krüll's thesis), Freud also implicated his father in respect to his own hysteria: "Then the surprise that in all cases, the *father* [emphasis in original], not excluding my own, had to be accused of being perverse . . ."[17] (The words "not excluding my own" were censored out of the original published letters.[18]) Krüll and Balmary have independently concluded from these passages that Jakob Freud was probably guilty of seducing or otherwise eroticizing, if not Sigmund, then some of the other children.[19] They both propose that Freud turned away from the original seduction theory in large part to spare his father's memory.

However, are these quotes of Freud to be given great weight, at least with respect to Freud's *own* possible childhood seduction? I think probably not. Beside the fact that a father's homosexual seduction of a son is rare, Freud never again in his voluminous writing raised the issue, nor did any of his case histories deal with such a seduction. In view of the strong autobiographical character of the case histories that he chose to write about, such a life-long silence would have been very strange. It should also be noted that Freud's comments about his own father primarily implicate Jakob with respect to Freud's siblings, not himself. Finally, Freud's own psychology had relatively little of a homosexual character; what there was was centered primarily around men his own age, not father-figures. Freud loved and hated men on a pattern that he said himself redintegrated his relationship to his half-nephew John (of Freiberg), already mentioned in connection with his screen memory.[20] Of course, it is still possible that Freud's father was the source—or at least one source—of Freud's own sexual seduction. If this was the case, such a seduction would *strongly* support much of the interpretation of Freud's relation to the Devil that is proposed below. Nevertheless, I do not think, as argued above, that Freud's father seduced young Sigmund.

Another possible candidate for this abuse is Freud's nanny. Krüll has developed such a proposition.[21] As the reader may recall, Freud made to Fliess the following curious comment: "She was my instructress in sexual matters, and chided me for being clumsy."[22] The "she" is assumed to have been Freud's nanny (although the possibility of a young servant girl is also supported by material given below). If we assume that it was the nanny, and that this was not just a fantasy,[23] what could the sexual "seduction" of a two- or three-year-old boy have consisted of, especially given the picture of the nanny as old, ugly, and rather strict?

One interpretation presented by Krüll is that the nanny would rub or stroke the boy's penis in order to soothe or quiet him.[24] Such an activity would certainly eroticize both the boy and his relationship with his nanny—and, by generalization, Freud's relationship to his mother and other mother-substitutes. This kind of behavior on the part of the nanny might appear bizarre or even perverse by contemporary standards. Yet such a thing has been common and even today is probably far from rare. Philippe Ariès, in his classic *Centuries of Childhood*, documents that events very like this occurred in the French royal household in the early 17th century. Ariès notes that the one-year-old future King of France, Louis XIII, "laughed uproariously when his nanny waggled his cock with her fingers."[25] During Louis's first three years, nobody in the household "showed any reluctance or saw any harm in jokingly touching the child's sexual parts."[26] According to Ariès, this was common in the treatment of children at this time. By the age of seven, however, the future king was expected to behave properly; others were no longer allowed to touch him, nor was he permitted to display himself to others or to be otherwise sexually explicit at court.[27]

Ariès notes that this kind of attitude is still found in certain parts of Islamic society today.[28] Perhaps it was also a part of mid-19th-century Moravian culture? There are reasons to think it may still be reasonably frequent in the West today. For example, two friends of mine mentioned to me that they knew of such practices in their own families—that is, the stroking of the penises of little boys, presumably as a way of quieting them. It would certainly be easy for such a habit to get started while a child was being bathed or having his diapers changed. Freud himself addressed the issue clearly when he remarked: "It is one of the commonest things—psychoanalyses are full of such incidents—for children's genitals to be caressed, not only in word but in deed, by fond relations, including even parents themselves."[29]

Freud also refers in the Fliess letter to being chided for his "clumsiness." This may mean only that Freud recalled being scolded for touching his genitals. (Such a scolding could easily set up a castration fear; see the discussion of the Wolf-Man case, below.) Of course, a scolding for his "clumsiness" might also have been nothing more than a criticism for soiling his pants. However, it may refer also to something explicitly sexual. The questions raised by this language require that we explore more carefully Freud's early years, using material scattered throughout his writing—material that is, as we know, highly biographical in character.

Let us first consider Freud's *Screen Memories* paper, already reliably accepted as disguised autobiography. Freud started the paper by referring to hysteria and obsessional neuroses as the kinds of pathology that provide the observational basis for his interpretation of screen memories. (Freud is also on record as referring to himself and to Oedipus as obsessive types.[30]) After emphasizing the then radical point that great pathogenic importance must be attributed to the earliest years of childhood, especially the ages of two to four,[31] he referred to a study that had just appeared; in it, V. and C. Henri had published the earliest childhood memories of 88 adults. Freud mentioned only two of the memories referred to in this study. The first memory was that of a professor who recalled a table with a basin of ice—a memory dated from between the ages of three and four. Freud interpreted this memory as a screen for the death of the child's much-loved grandmother, an event that occurred at the same time. The selection by Freud of this memory within the autobiographical context of the paper is easily interpretable as an analogue to the loss of his own loved nanny—a loss that I have proposed occurred for Freud in late May or early June 1859, when he was between the ages of three and four. The only other memory picked out by Freud was a man's early recollection of a walk during which he (as a child) broke off or pulled off the branch of a tree. (I take up Freud's interpretation of this shortly.) Then Freud launched into his own biography; of course, he made an initial attempt at disguise by saying that the man in question was 38 (five years younger than he) and in a very different field. (Bernfeld comments that, here, Freud was simply "lying."[32])

The screen memory described in detail by Freud was that of the meadow with yellow dandelions, discussed in Chapter One. The scene, we may recall, involved Freud (when he was about three years old) and his cousin John (John was actually Freud's half-nephew), who fell upon and took a bunch of flowers from Pauline, John's sister. At the top of the meadow stood a nursemaid and a peasant woman. The children rushed to the top of the meadow, where the peasant woman gave Pauline and the two boys some delicious bread; she cut the bread with a long knife. Freud gave a lengthy interpretation of the associations and psychological meaning of this recollection as representing the themes of love and hunger.

What is odd is that Freud gave no really clear trauma or decisive event as hiding behind the screen. The theme of "deflowering" the little girl by stealing her flowers and the knife as a symbol of castration anxiety were mentioned, but there was no obvious trauma for the young Sigmund. If, however, we use Freud's interpretation of and associations to the memories (taken from the Henri study), then two painful events worthy of being screened do suggest themselves. There is the obvious possibility that what the memory screened was the loss of Freud's nanny. The loss might have occurred shortly thereafter, or perhaps the nursemaid in the screen memory was a new nanny, one hired to cover the short time before the departure from Freiberg after the very recent loss of Sigmund's beloved "Nana." Another, slightly different, interpretation concerning loss is that the nursemaid in the screen memory was the nanny of John and Pauline, and that the scene remembered took place just after the dismissal of Freud's own nanny.

The other possible trauma that might have been screened is suggested by Freud's interpretation of the second memory from the Henri study that he brought up—the memory of a child pulling off a branch. Freud mentioned that the expression "to pull off" in German is a vulgar expression for masturbation. Freud then continued (about himself): "The scene would then be putting back into early childhood a seduction to masturbation—someone was helping him to do it—which, in fact, occurred at a later period."[33]

I propose, then, that Freud's screen memory covered or screened two things: the loss of his nanny, and a seduction (perhaps at a later time) to masturbate by a party unknown. A shift in time is not rare, as Freud specifically noted that screen memories may shift an event to a different place or time, and that such memories may have "merged two people into one or substituted one for the other. . . ."[34]

Let us look at more supporting evidence for the sexual abuse of Freud as a child. In 1896, Freud stated in *Heredity and the Aetiology of the Neuroses* that a passive sexual experience before puberty—usually in the age range of two to five years—is the specific cause for hysteria.[35] (Here it should be noted once again that since Freud so often wrote out of his own experience, that the presence of an autobiographical element behind his primary theoretical preoccupations should always be considered a strong likelihood.) In his next paper in the same year, *Further Remarks on the Defence Neuro-Psychoses*, Freud continued on the same subject by reiterating the childhood sexual trauma theory, and then went on to present evidence for his ideas, based on 13 cases of hysteria that he had observed in his practice. All of these people suffered from "grave sexual injuries."[36] He described the perpetrators:

Most prominent among *the people who were guilty of these abuses with all their serious consequences were nursemaids, governesses, or domestic servants*, to whose care children are all too thoughtlessly abandoned, and teachers and tutors appear regrettably often; *in seven of the thirteen cases, however, assaults were perpetrated by innocent childish assailants, mostly brothers, who had for years carried on some kind of sexual relation with somewhat younger sisters.* The course of events was probably in all cases similar to that which we were able to follow in some individual cases— namely, the boy was *first misused by a person of the female sex*, by which his libido was prematurely awakened and then a few years later he committed a sexual aggression reproducing exactly the procedure to which he himself had been subjected. [Emphasis added in all cases.][37]

Freud continued by observing that masturbation is a common pathological consequence of seduction, and that it is not a cause but rather a long-lasting symptom or expression of psychoneurosis. Just a few lines after the passage quoted above, Freud introduced a short but important case history:

[O]n one occasion I was able to observe a brother, a sister, and a somewhat older male cousin who were all ill. I learnt from the analysis which I undertook with the brother that he suffered from self-reproaches for being the cause of his sister's illness; he had been seduced by his cousin, who in his turn—as was known in the family—had himself been the victim of his nursemaid.[38]

The similarity of Freud's own family situation to this case history is striking, to the point of raising one's suspicion that this is a disguised self-description. Freud had a somewhat older half-nephew, John (the "cousin" in Freud's screen memory); he had a younger sister (several, in fact); he described himself as being an hysteric. Moreover, Freud was preoccupied with nursemaids and servants as sources of sexual trauma leading to neurosis. He was especially so preoccupied during this period of his self-analysis.

A page or so later, Freud remarked that obsessions are always reproaches related to a sexual deed performed with pleasure in childhood. This pleasure usually means masturbation, but also included is the pleasure involved in the seduction of another, such as a sister. Further on, Freud introduced a case history of an 11-year-old boy who suffered from obsessive rituals engaged in before he was able to go to bed. The explanation Freud provides is that "years before, a servant-girl, who had put the handsome boy to bed, took the opportunity of lying upon him and abusing him sexually."[39] This kind of comment makes one wonder about Freud's remark, already quoted from the autobiographical *Screen Memories* paper, that a screen memory involves "putting back into early childhood a seduction to masturbation" that had "in fact occurred at a later period."

In yet another paper of 1896, *The Aetiology of Hysteria*, Freud reiterated that every case of hysteria has its origin in early sexual experience,[40] and he listed three kinds of abuses. This list was based on his experience with now a total of 18 cases of pure hysteria or hysteria combined with obsession—6 men and 12 women. In a few of these cases, the abuser was a stranger who assaulted the child, and the primary experience of the child was terror. The most numerous cases of sexual abuse were due to "some adult attendant of the child—a maid, nurse, governess, teacher, unhappily only too often a near relation. . . ."[41] The third category involved sexual relations between two children of a different sex, and Freud added: "[W]here there had been a relation between two children I was sometimes able to prove that the boy—who played the aggressive part—had previously been seduced by a woman. . . ."[42]

Krüll proposes that Freud's famous staircase dream indicates the nanny as a source of sexual seduction.[43] This dream was first mentioned in a letter to Fliess in 1897. Freud wrote to Fliess:

. . . I dreamt that I was walking up a staircase with very few clothes on. I was walking up very briskly . . . when I noticed that a woman was coming up behind me, whereupon I found myself rooted to the spot, unable to move, overcome by that paralysis which is so common in dreams. The accompanying emotion was not anxiety but erotic excitement.[44]

Whether this was the nanny or some other woman is not clear. Freud called her a "woman" here, but a "maid-servant" later when referring to a nonsexualized, more toned-down version of the dream in *The Interpre-*

tation of Dreams (1900).[45] Relevant here is a remark Freud made just after the passage quoted above: He claimed that earlier in the night before the dream he was discussing, he had climbed the stairs from the flat below, and it had occurred to him at the time "that I might meet a neighbor."[46] One wonders whether Monika Zajic (a member of the landlord's family) or some other neighbor girl back in Freiberg was the female source of this early sexual excitement.

Let us stop here and take stock. Obviously the evidence so far does not allow a definitive answer; however, it does strongly imply that Freud was sexually seduced as a child, or at least that he was masturbated or taught to masturbate, and that this prematurely eroticized him. (That Freud had a long-term "problem" with masturbation originating in childhood has been suggested by Jones[47] and by Bernfeld,[48] and supported in some detail by Swales.[49])

In any case, it is certain that Freud's own seduction was associated by him in some way with a nursemaid or female servant. It is possible that his own nanny was the cause of this association, but in view of Freud's young age and his later connection of the nanny to strong castration anxiety, it seems more likely that she was not a true "seducer" and that some other nursemaid or servant girl was involved. A seduction experience even from the Vienna years, however, easily could have been projected back in time and associated with the nanny. Finally, the evidence also suggests that Freud was explicitly initiated into masturbation by his half-nephew John, and that this was brought on by John's being seduced earlier by his own nanny. Because we know Monika Zajic was hired by Emanuel as the nursemaid for John and Pauline, and because of the case history noted above, Monika Zajic is again suggested as a seducer for the young Sigmund. There is also the implication that young Freud "seduced" or eroticized one of his own sisters, possibly at a later date in Vienna.

A seduction by "cousin" John gives a reason for Freud's life-long ambivalence in the many later adult relationships that Freud said were patterned on his friendship with John.[50] These relationships (e.g., Freud–Fleischl, Freud–Fliess, Freud–Jung, *et al.*) combined homosexual and aggressive elements—a kind of Cain-and-Abel or Romulus-and-Remus pattern. Jones claims that this John was the most important figure for Freud's psychological development other than his parents in the Freiberg years.[51] It is of considerable interest that the one time "cousin" John visited the Freud family in Vienna, Freud and John read parts from a play. John played Caesar, and Sigmund played Brutus![52]

The point of this interpretation is to make clear that, whatever the particular facts may have been, at a minimum Freud connected a nanny figure to sexual seduction, *at least psychologically.* Such a deep and early association—even if, as seems likely, it was a fusion of two or more experiences with different people—would nevertheless have added an extra dimension to Freud's neurotic ambivalence toward his nanny and all she stood for. It would also help explain the erotic component of his Oedipus complex, since his nanny was so thoroughly part of the mother for him.

So far, I have only examined Freud's minor and brief case histories. But, in fact, *all* the major relevant case histories of Freud present substantial and curious similarities to Freud's life. The identification of these autobiographical elements reinforces the picture of Freud's childhood sexual abuse described above. (The reader should keep in mind that we are going into all this so as to better comprehend Freud's relationship to the Devil, as well as Freud's view of religion.)

Brody has identified the major or most detailed case histories of Freud; there are only 12 of these—eight female and four male patients.[53] The four major male case histories are those most relevant for understanding Freud. One of these four is the already discussed case presented in *Screen Memories* and known to be actual autobiography. Another of these four is Freud's famous "Wolf-Man" case. I now take this case up in some detail, because, besides being similar to Freud's own life, it involved important religious elements. In fact, it was the *only* major case history of Freud that dealt with religion at all,[54] and even here Freud was only giving an interpretation of the patient's childhood religious beliefs. (That is, the patient himself was an adult nonbeliever, and had been so for some years prior to entering psychotherapy.)

The Wolf-Man case[55] centered on a neurotic disturbance that began when the patient was three years old. The neurosis lasted into the tenth year, and it was analyzed retroactively by Freud, for the patient was treated when he was in his 20s. That is, Freud was thus, as usual, treating childhood memories. The disturbance began as an anxiety–hysteria (an animal phobia—fear of wolves), then changed into an obsessive neurosis with religious content. The major facts were these: The patient's father (like Jakob) was often absent, in this case at a sanitarium; the mother (like Amalia) was also not always present, as she suffered from "physical illness and as a consequence she had relatively little to do with the child."[56] Instead, "the boy as far back as he could remember was looked after by a nurse (nanny), an uneducated woman of peasant birth with a deep affection for the boy."[57] The nanny was called "Nanya" and had a simple, devout Christian faith. (Sounds familiar!) Apparently, this woman to whom the boy was devoted was rather old and ugly; an English governess hired by the family when the boy was four or five referred to the Nanya as a witch. The nanny spoke a Slavic language (not Moravian Czech, but Russian), while the boy and apparently the parents (like the Freuds) spoke German. The boy was sexually seduced, by his older sister, at age three and a quarter. The boy's parents appear to have been nonreligious, although the mother did teach the boy Bible stories. For some years, the family lived on a country estate. Then the parents sold the estate and moved into a large town (like Vienna). In short, the basic family situation of the boy has a truly uncanny similarity to Freud's own early situation. (Most of this information was given by Freud under the section title "The Seduction and Its Immediate Consequences.") There were, of course, differences from Freud's own life: It was the boy's slightly older sister who sexually seduced him (a servant-girl figure?); there were both a nanny *and* a grandmother; and, after the age of six or seven, the patient's life diverged from Freud's. Thus, I am not suggesting that this was an example of disguised autobiography, but rather that Freud was drawn to and perhaps even chose to write up patients whose past life and psychological traumas were similar to his own.

Besides the objective similarity to Freud's life, there is also in this case clear evidence that Freud projected his own preoccupations onto the patient and introduced his own concerns as though they were the patient's. The psychoanalyst Donald Spence shows in a recent book that the Wolf-Man case was heavily contaminated by Freud's own psychology or "countertransference."[58] Spence, in particular, shows how in Freud's report of a crucial memory of the Wolf-Man, he added important details and subsequently treated them as part of the original report of the patient, even though Freud's own written record shows that this was not the case. In a most illuminating example, Spence documents how Freud himself introduced a castration threat into the report, and then a page or so later assumed that this threat was a major part of the Wolf-Man's own psychological problem.[59]

Now the nanny in the Wolf-Man case was not involved in any sexual seduction of the boy, although she was a source of castration anxiety. After being involved in masturbation with the older girl, the Wolf-Man was rejected by her. The boy, motivated by a passive sexual desire to be touched, then turned to the Nanya and played with his member in her presence. The Nanya scolded him for this and threatened castration. So he turned away from her in fear, and his later sexual attachments involved servant girls.

The Wolf-Man got his name from a frightening anxiety dream he first had at about age four. This was a repeating dream of white wolves sitting in a tree, wolves that he was afraid would eat him. The wolves came in part from his knowledge of fairy tales, but the deeper themes involved castration anxiety and fear of his father, for Freud interpreted the wolves as father-symbols. Freud gave a long discussion of the significance of the boy's probable witnessing of a primal scene involving his parents (Amalia and Philipp?). He then turned to an explanation of obsessional neuroses, from which the boy suffered from the ages of about four and a half to ten; his obsessions were associated with his mother's reading New

Testament stories to him. (One is reminded of Sigmund's Bible-reading period starting at about the same age; in Freud's case, however, the Bible stories were from the Old Testament and were read to him by his father.)

The boy's neurosis centered around his identification with Christ, followed by his religious doubts and rejection of Christ. (Such an identification with Jesus also probably occurred when Freud was with his nanny. It certainly showed up in his response to Christian paintings of the Madonna and Child.) The Wolf-Man's doubts were such as these: How could God be the father of Jesus? In what sense was Mary's husband, Joseph, a father? (the theme of ambiguous paternity). Why was Christ so passive in response to God's harsh treatment? He then began to connect God to blasphemous ideas (e.g., "shit," "swine.") The guilt caused by these blasphemies and doubts was atoned for and controlled by various actions, such as making repeated signs of the cross and holding his breath to keep in the Holy Spirit. Most of these obsessive acts came to an end through the influence of a skeptical and rationalistic German tutor, who came on the scene when the patient was about ten.

We now turn briefly to the autobiographical element in Freud's other two major cases dealing with male subjects: the Rat-Man and Little Hans.

The Rat-Man, in his early 20s, was plagued by an obsessive fantasy in which a pot containing rats was put on the buttocks of someone.[60] The rats then bored or ate into the anus of the person. (The victim of the fantasy was a lady whom the Rat-Man admired.) The patient reported a sexually stimulating experience when he was three or four years old, involving a pretty young governess; he was eroticized by touching her genitals. Later, with another such governess (servant girl), Fraulein Lina, he remembered being criticized as sexually "too clumsy."[61] The Rat-Man had an early problem with masturbation between the ages of three and four or five, and it arose again later when his neurosis expressed itself through the symptom of masturbation in adolescence. The Rat-Man had a severe castration fear associated with his father, who had strongly opposed his son's prematurely developed erotic life. Also part of this early castration complex was a nanny who was especially important for the Rat-Man during the ages of three and four.

The Little Hans case[62] involved only one session with Freud; the rest of the material was provided in written form by Hans's father, a friend of Freud's.[63] Nevertheless, several of its themes were similar to those of the preceding three cases. The Little Hans case, like the others, was based on the boy's castration anxiety and the fear of his father—again, all beginning at the age of three and a half. (It was this article that contained Freud's reference to the common practice of parents' or caretakers' caressing a child's genitals.[64]) Hans had a little sister Hannah (like Freud's sister Anna), whom Hans associated with a box, his mother, and travel (to Gmunden). Associating a sister with a box is reminiscent of Freud's memory (see Chapter One) in which he recalled his half-brother Philipp's opening a cupboard for him and his own thoughts of his nanny as "boxed up"; young Freud then connected the cupboard or box to his mother's now being thin after having given birth to his new baby sister. (There were also other but less relevant autobiographical elements.)

From all the preceding material, I conclude again that Freud as a child was eroticized by his nanny or by some other female servant, and that his half-nephew John also probably contributed to this; the seductions set up a kind of compulsive masturbation combined with sexual fantasies. The childhood erotic behavior was also severely challenged by a strong castration threat, reinforced by the nanny but ultimately traceable to Freud's father. All of this was enough to make Sigmund preoccupied, fearful, and obsessively fascinated with the effects of such sexual experiences, and it was enough to make him "disturbed" in other ways as well.

Freud's Personality: Splitting

Before I take up Freud's personality, some preliminary remarks are called for. Although I propose here that Freud suffered from moderate degrees of various psychological pathologies, such as splitting and aspects of borderline personality disorder, such diagnoses should not be misinterpreted to mean that I suggest that Freud was seriously disturbed. Instead, I believe that such conditions, present in a limited degree, gave Freud an essential first-hand understanding of such pathology. That is, his own mental states were the primary sources of his psychological observations and insights. The remarkable fact about Freud, however, was not that he suffered from such conditions, but that he refused to succumb to them like countless others, and that he went on to understand them and finally to conceptualize them in such a way as to create not only his own particular theories but to establish a major new conceptualization of psychology.

In 1919, Freud published a rather well-known essay, The 'Uncanny,' in which he analyzed the nature and origin of this feeling. In the first part, he surveyed the various dictionary definitions and historical origins of the words for "uncanny" in German and other languages. He noted that in German Heimlich ("homelike or familiar") and Unheimlich ("uncanny") are not simple oposites, but often similar[65]; he observed that often the unfamiliar turns out to be a special or odd form of the familiar.[66] He also commented that the Hebrew word for "uncanny" means "demonic."[67]

Freud then went on to comment on a fantastic tale by Hoffmann, called "The Sand-Man."[68] The story begins, not unlike that of the Wolf-

Man, with the childhood recollections of a student, Nathaniel. The Sand-Man is described by Nathaniel's mother as just a figure of speech, not a real person. But Nathaniel's nurse (nanny) gives much more detailed information. She reports that the Sand-Man is a wicked old man who punishes children who won't go to bed by tearing their eyes out. He often does this by first throwing hot coals into the child's eyes; later he takes the eyes out and feeds them to his bird-beaked children. Hoffmann's strange story is not easily summarized, but certain themes were singled out for special emphasis by Freud. Having one's eyes torn out was interpreted as a disguised expression of castration, and, not surprisingly, the Sand-Man was seen as representing both a demonic figure and the boy's familiar father.[69] In the story, the Sand-Man's presence is fear-inducing; his hypnotizing stare can bring his victim to suicide.[70] Such uncanny figures carry malign, secret power, of a kind that Freud mentioned as present in Mephistopheles and intuitively sensed by Margaret.[71] (At this point Freud made the interesting suggestion that psychoanalysis might easily be judged as uncanny by many.[72] One wonders whether Freud ever thought of himself as the Sand-Man. As a young doctor he practiced hypnotism, and throughout his adult life his powerful, arresting gaze was commented upon by many.) As for what creates an uncanny effect, Freud claimed that it is often brought about by conditions that remove the distinction between imagination and reality.[73] Such conditions make a thing one thought of as only imaginary now appear as real. That is, the uncanny experience occurs when a past fantasy unexpectedly seems to become a present reality—a condition common in the experience of neurotics.

Freud's interpretation of the Sand-Man further reinforces the picture of his father as the primary source of castration fear, and of the nanny as a secondary source of this fear.[74] The crucial theoretical concept in Freud's essay, however, was that the demonic, uncanny Sand-Man is a kind of alter-father, or image split from the father, who is dreaded because he threatens castration and death through his stare.

"Splitting," as a psychopathological phenomenon, refers to the tendency found in some people for consciousness to break into two or more distinct centers, each more or less separated from and ignorant or ill-informed about the other. Extreme forms of this condition are found in people suffering from "character disorders" (in particular, the "borderline character disorder")[75] and the "multiple personality syndrome."[76] The latter condition is rare, although in recent years it has received considerable documentation and even public attention. Those who are familiar with multiple personalities have discovered several factors that appear to be the commonest causes of this condition.[77] The first is sexual seduction or sexual abuse in childhood, the most frequent victims being young girls abused by their fathers or stepfathers. An abused child struggles with the experience of sexual trauma, and in order to escape the meaning or identity given to him or her by the perpetrator of the sexual abuse, the child attempts to create a new, ideal identity. This new center of personal identity and consciousness allows escape from the traumatic past, but only if the new center is separated or dissociated from the rest of the personality. Multiple new centers of consciousness occur because the original fantasized new identity often needs to be changed as the child's circumstances change, e.g., as he or she gets older and needs a more sophisticated new identity. Dissociation is also a characteristic experience of patients suffering from splitting. In mild cases such as that proposed here for Freud, the experiences of being "cut off" or dissociated from one's normal consciousness are of short duration; in the rare, extreme cases, such states might last for days. Other quite reliable characteristics of this syndrome include an extensive fantasy life and frequent use of repression; in addition, involvement in the occult characterizes about 20% of those diagnosed as "multiples."

Now Freud did not come close to suffering from the true multiple personality syndrome. But Freud's own early diagnosis of himself as an hysteric means that he suffered from a mild form of splitting or "fracturing,"[78] and that his understanding of splitting was in large part due to a sensitive observation of his own psychology. Freud was in fact one of the first psychologists to give the notion of splitting serious theoretical attention.

The claim that Freud analyzed his own splitting is not unique: The psychoanalyst Gedo has already proposed that it is reasonable to infer that Freud first became aware of splitting within his own personality.[79] Gedo also subscribes to the position of Sadow and his collaborators[80] that "a successful piece of *self-analytic* work had been the source of clinical evidence on which Freud . . . erected each portion of his theory."[81] We have already seen ample evidence of the presence of autobiographical elements in Freud's case histories and other theorizing.

Although Freud referred to splitting at various times throughout his subsequent years of work, he did not explicitly return to the topic in a paper until many years later in one of his final contributions: *Splitting of the Ego in the Defensive Process*. In this unfinished article, Freud introduced a summary of an earlier case history. He did not explicitly reference the case, but it was either the Wolf-Man or a very similar case.[82] Here is the case history:

A little boy while he was between the ages of three and four years of age, had become acquainted with the female genitals through being seduced by an older girl. After these relations had been broken off, he carried on the sexual stimulation which had been set going in his way by zealously practicing manual masturbation; but he was soon caught at it by his energetic nurse and was threatened with castration, the carrying out of which was, as usual, ascribed to his father. There were thus present in this case conditions calculated to produce a tremendous effect of fright.[83]

Freud went on to say that although often a boy can avoid the trauma of castration anxiety, this was not possible in this particular instance, because for the boy in question the extreme threat of castration was tied to the memory of the girl's genitals: That is, she had been castrated; hence the fear was confirmed. Given the conflict, what did this particular boy do? The usual response would be to give up masturbation, but this patient did not. The boy continued with his masturbation as though it implied no danger to his penis, but at the same time

. . . he developed an intense fear of his father punishing him, which required the whole force of his masculinity to master. . . . The boy produced yet another symptom, though it was a slight one which he has retained to this day. This was an anxious susceptibility against either of his little toes being touched, as though, in all the to and fro between denial and acknowledgement, it was nevertheless castration that was finding the clearer expression. . . .[84]

This interesting discussion contains evidence that points to its autobiographical nature. The psychoanalyst Spence, as mentioned earlier, has shown that in the original Wolf-Man case it was not the patient who introduced the nurse's threat of castration, but Freud himself. Freud subsequently treated the threat as part of the patient's report. This same (presumably projected) threat of castration loomed large in the case at hand, which was apparently a summary of the Wolf-Man case.

But let us return to splitting. In Freud's discussion, the sexual conflict between the drive to masturbate (caused by the earlier seduction) collided with the fear of castration to cause splitting; that is, there was a "conflict between the demand of an instinct and the command of reality."[85] The boy chose to allow both drives to be satisfied, but at a real price:

[T]his success is achieved at the price of a rift in the ego which never heals but increases as time goes on. The whole process seems so strange to us because we take for granted the synthetic nature of the workings of the ego.[86]

And, as Freud pointed out, this synthetic function is subject to many serious disturbances.

In summary, then, because of Freud's life-long tendency to focus theoretically on psychological conditions from which he himself suffered; because of the evidence that Freud was sexually seduced; and, finally, because of the autobiographical aspects of his writings on splitting, it is reasonable to assume that Freud suffered from occasional splitting of his ego (i.e., splitting sometimes consciously experienced). (A specific example of this is provided in Chapter Six.)

Freud's Personality: Borderline Personality Disorder and the Devil

I now turn to a more detailed investigation of Freud's multiple identifications, and to the evidence that he suffered from reduced (but still noticeable) aspects of borderline character disorder with narcissistic elements. I have already mentioned Freud's habitual tendency to identify with certain kinds of positive male models—heroes who often took on the function of alter-egos for Freud. This tendency can be interpreted as a seeking of idealized identities, with each hero serving to help focus and define one aspect of Freud's fractured ego (really, an integrated ego with a number of serious fault lines). Each part of his ego somewhat anxiously sought to provide a new identity better than his father could provide. This search for new identities often was also an expression of Freud's narcissistic grandiosity—for example, his comparing himself to Moses.

Here is a list of figures Freud is known to have identified with at some time of his life. Some were simply strong military heroes: Alexander the Great; William the Conqueror[87]; Napoleon and his general Massena. Others were part of his anti-Rome ego: Hannibal, Hutten, Oliver Cromwell, Garibaldi.[88] Still others were part of his complex Jewish identity: Moses, who, according to Freud, wasn't a Jew; Jacob,[89] who wrestled with the angel; Joseph,[90] the interpreter of dreams. Others were part of his pro-Christian or ambivalent Christian self: Jesus, Scipio, St. Paul, and Brentano and Romain Rolland[91] (both ex-Catholics). Some were part of his anti-Christian identity: Satan or the Devil, Oedipus, the Anti-Christ, Faust, Frollo, and perhaps Leonardo[92] and Goethe[93] belong here. Others were scientific, professional, or artistic models whom Freud greatly admired: Brücke, Charcot, Fleischl,[94] Fliess,[95] and Schnitzler.[96] These different models all captured different parts of Freud's ego—different spirits (or demons) of Freud's personality. These identities and the motivation behind them can help account for the multicentered ambivalence of Freud, as well as his intense, often overriding fantasy life. The strength of Freud's fantasies, especially those fantasies connected to castration anxiety, was described by Jung as so strong that they could cause Freud to faint.[97] (One is also reminded here of Freud's involvement in the occult, his hearing of voices in Paris, the effects of cocaine, his belief in "revenants," and the like—all related to splitting.)

The symptoms of Freud described here are similar to those of various character disorders. The character disorder syndromes often have hysterical elements as well, and the various forms of character disorder are related to one another also. Specifically, I would like to propose that the previously mentioned "borderline character disorder" is probably the condition most relevant to an understanding of Freud's own abnormal psychology. Again, no claim is made that Freud was suffering from a typical "borderline character disorder," but only that aspects of this condition appear to have been present in him. Among them are the following conditions, all identified in the official DSM-III psychiatric diagnostic description:

1. Considerable uncertainty about identity; great concerns with the issue "Who am I?"[98]
2. Very emotionally changeable evaluations of others, moving from complete idealization to extreme rejection.[99] Freud's extreme idealizations and intense rejections of Breuer, Fliess, Jung, and others have already been noted.
3. Some substance abuse.[100] Freud's cocaine use is of course applicable here, as well as his excessive and compulsive cigar smoking (i.e., serious nicotine addiction).[101]
4. Marked affective changes.[102] Here, for example, can be considered Freud's depressions of some duration.

The presence of this number and degree of the borderline character disorder diagnostic categories is the basis for my claim that Freud suffered from the problems of an attenuated "borderline character."

We can now turn at long last to Freud's explanation of the Devil, who, he said, is the result of splitting.[103] Here are his major theoretical comments on the psychological origin of the Devil. The first interpretation was proposed by Breuer and Freud in *Studies on Hysteria*:

The split-off mind is the devil with which the unsophisticated observation of early superstitious times believed that these patients were possessed. It is true that a spirit alien to the patient's waking consciousness holds sway in him; but the spirit is not in fact an alien one, but a part of his own.[104]

As for the origin of this splitting, Freud proposed later that splitting "creates" the Devil by breaking the original father-image into two figures with opposite attributes. Indeed, for Freud, God and the Devil were once one, and were later split into two figures.[105] He proposed that a similar splitting happens in each individual to account for the psychological representation of God and the Devil: They are the representation of the good and bad father. Elsewhere, Freud suggested that the Devil is caused by a splitting of the *self* into good and bad representations.[106]

On the basis of the preceding Freudian analysis, one can, I believe, conclude that Freud's psyche was to some extent fractured into separate centers, and that at least one significant part of him was identified with the Devil. For example, in January and in August 1884—the year of the proposed April 30 cocaine-*Walpurgisnacht* pact—Freud referred to himself as a "miserable devil"[107] and a "poor little devil."[108] One is also reminded of Freud's description of the Rat-Man, a description that seems apt for Freud himself: "[H]e had, as it were, disintegrated into three personalities."[109] Presumably that part of Freud that identified with the Devil was mostly unconscious, was associated with his early sexual abuse, and represented the frightening aspects of his father-image initiated by the threat of castration.

That Freud's involvement with the demonic was something like this allows me to agree wholeheartedly with Shengold, a psychoanalyst, who, after summarizing Freud's struggle with Jung, proposes: "Freud discovered that he was Mephistopheles as well as Faust; the devils were not without but within."[110]

Freud's Personality: Splitting and Object Relations Theory

In recent years, Freud's early theory on the nature of splitting has been augmented, and to some extent replaced, by a different interpretation based on object relations theory.[111] This theory of splitting is really a set of related interpretations proposed by such psychoanalysts as Mahler, Winnicott, Fairbairn,[112] Kernberg,[113] and others. A common assumption by these writers is that splitting derives from the mother, rather than the father, and that it is a consequence of inadequate or traumatic mothering in the pre-Oedipal period (i.e., prior to the age of three). In this earlier period, especially from one and a half or two years of age to three, the child is involved in separating from the mother and developing an individual identity. If the mother is seriously inadequate, if she is absent for a prolonged period, or if she otherwise traumatizes or abuses the child, then splitting of the child's ego will often occur, and the process of separation and individuation will be incomplete. The child's internalized representation of the mother is split into "good mother" and "bad mother" components. Since this internalized image is an important part of the child's own ego, the child therefore suffers from splitting.

Some object relations theorists, especially Melanie Klein, claim that the mother's behavior is only a secondary source of the bad mother.[114] She proposes that the child is born with large amounts of innate rage and anger (a kind of death instinct theory), and that this is projected onto the mother by the child. Although I lean toward the more environmentally determined origin of Freud's pre-Oedipal object relations problems, a Kleinian interpretation can also account for Freud's early psychology. For present purposes, since both theories can be used to interpret Freud's pre-Oedipal problems, there is no need to choose between them.

In the case of Freud, an object relations interpretation predicts that the negative aspects of his functional mother, the nanny, would have split or partially split to form a separate part of his ego. This "bad mother" or "bad nanny" component would be a kind of "witch image," and because the nanny told Freud about Hell and presumably about the Devil, this internalized bad mother would be closely linked to demonic themes. Freud's letters and other writings certainly do show a significant preoccupation with witches. Here it should be noted that witches are central figures in Goethe's *Faust*, especially at the *Walpurgisnacht* orgy. We may recall that Freud's important letter to Fliess of January 24, 1897 was all about witchhcraft: He mentioned the *Malleus Maleficarum*, referred to a patient's nurse as a witch, and so forth.[115] His theory of hysteria as analogous to possession implied that all female hysterics are witches; his description of the patient's nanny as ugly and elderly made her out as witch-like.

Peter Swales has very powerfully documented the witch theme in Freud's thought in three of his papers on Freud.[116] For an understanding of the depth of Freud's personal "witch psychology," the reader should read them. But some of this involvement is captured in two quotes of Freud. In *Analysis Terminable and Interminable*, using a line from Goethe's *Faust*, Freud wrote: "We can only say, 'So after all we must bring in the witch'—the witch Meta psychology."[117] Here he connected the witch to all higher speculation (i.e., "Meta psychology," and, by implication, theology). And in a letter to Lou Andreas-Salomé, Freud wrote, "we must have recourse to the witch prehistory or phylogenesis."[118] In the context of the letter, Freud was implicitly connecting the witch to his own prehistory—his origins in early childhood.

The actual trauma precipitating the split could have been the nanny's abandoning Freud (when she was dismissed), as well as possible sexual abuse. Any tendency of Freud's own mother, Amalia, to reject young Sigmund (e.g., to stop nursing him, or to nurse a younger sibling, or even to leave him with the nanny much of the time) could also have contributed to the "bad mother" image. Otto Kernberg notes the close association of the internalized "bad object" to the tendency to use the mechanism of projection.[119] In addition, he points out that grandiosity and omnipotent thoughts and feelings, aspects of which often characterized Freud's personality, are common features of people suffering from splitting.[120] Kernberg also links experiences of the internalized "bad" object to feelings of the uncanny[121]—an emotion already documented as being of significant interest for Freud.

The previous evidence, discussed above, is that Freud had some degree of serious identification with the Devil or with matters demonic. The "witch" or "bad mother" or "bad nanny" interpretation has been brought in as an example of Freud's involvement with a closely related theme. It should be noted, however, that there is no evidence that Freud actually identified with the witch, but only that this subject was for Freud closely linked to the Devil.

This association is well captured in a passage from the Witch's Kitchen scene in *Faust*, quoted by Freud to Lou Andreas-Salomé in a letter discussing masturbation: "You are on familiar terms with the devil, and yet you shrink back from the flame."[122] These words are addressed by Mephistopheles to Faust, who is taken aback by a potion that emits a flame. A moment later, Faust drinks the potion to seal his *Walpurgisnacht* pact.

Freud's Pact: Part Two

We return now to Freud's pact as understood by Bakan: namely, that for Freud the Devil was a kind of metaphor derived from his experience of the powerful sexual and aggressive forces in the unconscious. Bakan argues that Freud perceived the impulses from the unconscious (or the id) as a kind of Hell, which his own self-analysis allowed him to be the first to explore.[123] Thus, Bakan explains the "pact" with the Devil as a kind of psychological strategy, by which Freud decided to suspend his super-ego—his moral or higher judgmental capacities—in order to explore the lower, hellish world of the unconscious. This explanation, of course, means that Freud had no pact with the Devil as a supernatural figure or even as a personal figure in any psychologically real sense, but instead that he reached a special kind of internal agreement: He had to be willing to go to Hell, to delve into psychological "Hell," in order to understand his own instinctual passions. (It should be pointed out that neither Aeneas nor Dante, whose voyages to the nether regions Freud referred to, was obliged to enter into such a pact in order to descend into Hell.)

Before returning to Bakan and the issue of a pact, let us take up Freud's psychological explanation of the Devil, given in his 1923 paper *A Neurosis of Demoniacal Possession in the Seventeenth Century*. There Freud explicitly claimed:

What in those days were thought to be evil spirits to us are base and evil wishes, the derivatives of impulses which have been rejected and repressed. In one respect only do we *not* subscribe to the explanation of these phenomena current in medieval times; we have abandoned the projection of them into the outer world, attributing their origin instead to the inner life of the patient. . . .[124]

The paper itself was a detailed discussion of a case history from the 17th century in Austria, in which it was reported that a painter, one Christoph Haitzmann, had twice made a pact with the Devil and had been redeemed through the Virgin Mary. A noteworthy thing about Freud's treatment of the case was the set of reasons why the artist made the pact, reasons to which Freud gave considerable prominence. The man was motivated to sign up with the Devil not for money, power, or women, but rather because (1) his father had recently died; (2) he was depressed (suffered from melancholia); and (3) he was unable to work and thus was anxious about the future.[125]

Now Bakan shows very persuasively that all three of these reasons were clearly present in Freud's life in the decade of the 1890s.[126] During these years Freud was often very depressed, and as a consequence unable to work. As a further consequence, he was concerned about his livelihood; about just meeting the daily expenses of his rather large household. Freud's depression was also in many respects the result of his lack of advancement and success—for example, his failure to get promoted to the rank of professor while others around him were being promoted. And, of course, Freud's father died in 1896, and he described this as a deep and troubling loss. Cocaine use and withdrawal symptoms would constitute another major source of depression. As a result, Bakan's case for the remarkable similarities between the situation of the painter Haitzmann in the 17th century and that of Freud in the 1890s is in many respects quite convincing.

But there are sound reasons to believe that there was much more to Freud's dealings with the Devil than Bakan's purely "psychological" interpretation would suggest—that they started earlier, and had deeper, more complex, and less rationalistic roots. First, as pointed out above, what about Swales's discovery of Freud's *Walpurgisnacht* cocaine, procured from Merck and taken 12 years before the death of his father? (The cocaine was taken, we should note, at a period when Freud's psychological preoccupations—his separation anxiety and the depressions triggered by his fiancée's move away from Vienna—were even more conducive to a pact than later.) And what of his early 1886–1888 articles, in which he referred to hysterical symptoms as being like those of witches and other people described as possessed?[127] (The connection of cocaine use with the occult and black witchcraft has been rediscovered in recent years.)

If we look again and more carefully at Freud's fascination with the Devil and demonic pacts, it is not hard to come to an interpretation of Freud's pact that is more specific and more extreme than Bakan's thesis, but an interpretation that is generally consistent with Bakan's position. In order to develop this proposed more explicit notion of a pact, it is important to remember Bakan's essential argument. Bakan claims that the Haitzmann article, whatever it might show about Haitzmann, definitely expressed Freud's own psychological state; that it was filled with Freud's own projected concerns; and hence that it implicates Freud in some kind of pact. This understanding is accepted here, and it gives the basis for looking for additional important autobiographical elements in this case.

First, the similarities of the Haitzmann case to Goethe's *Faust* clearly underline the special psychological attraction of the story for Freud. Besides involving a demonic pact, the Haitzmann case begins with the

Devil, as a merchant with a black dog, much like the start of *Faust* (see Figure 5-1). The story ends with the pact being broken and Haitzmann saved through the intervention of a beautiful young woman—in this case, the Virgin Mary (see Figure 5-2).

There is also now new evidence provided by Vandendriessche that supports Freud's tendency to project his own psychology onto the Haitzmann case.[128]

In his interpretation of the meaning of the historical documents, Freud first identified the painter's motives for making a pact (already noted above). Freud then focused on the documents' reference to Haitzmann's making *two* pacts with the devil—the first in ink, the second in blood (see Figures 5-3 and 5-4). Since the dates of these two pacts appear to have been a year apart, and because of various ambiguities in other dates and in Haitzmann's response to the supposed two pacts, Freud tried to show

Figure 5-1. Haitzmann, *The Devil as Merchant.* (Österreichische Nationalbibliothek)

Figure 5-2. Haitzmann, detail of *The Virgin Mary with the Infant Jesus* (devotional painting from the town of Mariazell). The painter represents himself at the bottom kneeling in front of four monks. (Österreichische Nationalbibliothek)

Figure 5-3. Haitzmann, *The Devil with the Ink Pact.* (Österreichische National-bibliothek)

that there was only one pact with the Devil—the one in blood. The first pact in ink was presumed by Freud to be a fabrication by Haitzmann, and Freud tried to argue that the painter unconsciously slipped in ways to show that the ink pact never really occurred. This very peculiar concern of Freud—that only the blood pact was real—was the central issue of the paper. One would think that Freud might have attempted to psychoanalytically explain in some detail the neurotic basis behind belief in the Devil; instead, he was preoccupied with showing that Haitzmann made only *one* pact.

Vandendriessche's rebuttal of Freud's evidence that the ink pact was fabricated is extremely thorough. (As already noted, it is important to keep in mind that in this case all the evidence exists in historical documents that are available for anyone to study, unlike a normal case history). Vandendriessche has studied the documents carefully, and his

Figure 5-4. Haitzmann, *The Devil with the Blood Pact.* (Österreichische Nationalbibliothek)

conclusions are simple and firmly supported by objective evidence. He concludes that there were, in fact, two pacts, and that if Freud had known more about history (especially the history of legal documents), he would have been less likely to deny the first pact, the ink pact. Vandendriessche shows that in Austro-German culture at the time of the Haitzmann pact, it was customary to have a legal contract in "two consecutive yet unequal phases, each of which gave rise to the signing of a document."[129] The first of these was a provisional text (in the Haitzmann case, this would be the ink pact), and the second was a more officially binding document (for Haitzmann, the blood pact). Vandendreissche also shows that Freud's attempt to explain away the first pact in ink on psychoanalytic grounds was "insufficiently free from his own preoccupations: it [Freud's interpretation] transmits an historical picture that repeatedly assumes the form of Freud's own problem."[130] That is, Vandendreissche documents that

Freud was insufficiently objective, even with the facts at his disposal.[131] For example, it is not at all clear that Haitzmann's father had recently died; the word used in the document reporting the death just meant a parent or possibly just a member of the family. The basic bias of Freud, however, was to consider important information in the case as having its roots in deception when straightforward historical information could account for the supposed problems.

The arguments against Freud in the Haitzmann interpretation are very analogous to those of Meyer Schapiro and of Jack Spector in their mutually supportive rebuttals of Freud's interpretation of Leonardo's *The Virgin and Child with St. Anne* (already discussed in Chapter One). In that instance, also, Freud projected himself and his preoccupations at the cost of distorting the facts available to him, as well as at the cost of ignoring historical explanations.[132] In other words, the fact that Freud showed a strong tendency to project himself into his interpretations of historical cases supports my intention of looking for additional evidence of his projection.

But if Freud was really putting much of his own psychology into the Haitzmann interpretation, the question arises: What does that imply about Freud's pact with the Devil? I propose that Freud's language describing a pact is an apt description of his own pact. Freud interpreted Haitzmann's pact as a "neurotic fantasy,"[133] and not merely as some kind of metaphor for a suspended superego. Thus I propose that Freud had neurotic fantasies about the Devil and that at some time, while fantasizing, he concluded a pact.

Now one hypothesis is that Freud, as in his interpretation of Haitzmann, made only one pact (not two), and that he made this in blood. That is, he "sealed" his fantasy pact by cutting himself slightly in order to use real blood. When and how might this have taken place? Here, the Swalesian interpretation of Freud's taking cocaine on *Walpurgisnacht* in 1884 strongly suggests a considerably earlier date than Bakan considers. Perhaps shortly after April 30, 1884, or perhaps later, in the 1890s, Freud took cocaine via hypodermic needle and in the process bled slightly, thus "fortuitously" allowing a blood pact to be sealed. (Swales has proposed that Freud might have injected himself with cocaine on occasion. Freud very early suggested in print that the hypodermic needle be used to administer cocaine; he later denied he made such a suggestion, thus showing his anxiety about this method of taking cocaine.[134])

Here, a very strange statement by Freud, made in a letter to Fliess, suggests itself as relevant.[135] The situation involved a patient of Fliess and Freud's named Emma, who had been badly treated by Fliess in an operation on her nose. Another doctor discovered that Fliess had left "at least half a meter of gauze"[136] in her nose by accident. The bungled operation resulted in the patient's bleeding, even to the point of coming close to death. Freud, in trying to cover up for Fliess, went so far as to argue that this hemorrhaging, obviously caused by the botched operation, could be attributed to the patient's neurotic fantasies—that is, to her being an hysteric. Freud wrote; "Emma has a scene [in mind] where the *Diabolus* sticks pins into her finger and puts a piece of candy on each drop of blood."[137] This quote sounds much more like Freud's reminiscences of needles and cocaine—and the occult—than the natural expression of Emma Eckstein, a Jewish woman of 32 and a strong feminist.[138]

It is very possible that Freud's frequent use of cocaine itself induced neurotic fantasies (hallucinations) of a demonic kind, not unlike those in *The Temptation of St. Anthony*. Again, the specifics are hard (and perhaps impossible) to track down, but the evidence certainly points to something more than a metaphoric pact. (This is no criticism of Bakan, whose thesis appeared years before much of the present evidence was available. Indeed, in retrospect, Velikovsky's hypothesis and especially Bakan's thesis of a pact are remarkably prescient.[139])

Another hypothesis concerning Freud's pact is a variation on the preceding. This interpretation, also modeled on the Haitzmann case, is that Freud, like Haitzmann, made two pacts at different times in his life. Presumably, the first would have been in 1884, on April 30 or shortly after; the second would have been not too long after his father's death, during his self-analysis. This would have been some time between 1896 and 1898, when his letters to Fliess were filled with Roman themes and references to the Devil. This was also a time of serious depression and of professional doubt. Indeed, this is when Bakan proposes that Freud made his metaphoric pact,[140] and this is also the time of those dreams that Velikovsky argues show Freud making a Faust pact.[141] It is even possible that Freud's first pact was in writing and the second, at the time of the "Emma" quote above, in blood. (Freud's labored interpretation of the Haitzmann case, according to this second hypothesis, would therefore have been an expression of Freud's denial of his own first pact.)

There is a curious piece of information to support the hypothesis of Freud's two pacts. On April 28, 1885, one year (minus two days) after his 1884 *Walpurgisnacht* cocaine episode, Freud wrote to Martha that the chemist was to pay him for his cocaine research on April 30, a kind of one-year anniversary payment. He then went on to tell Martha that he had almost finished destroying "all my notes of the past fourteen years, as well as letters, scientific excerpts, and the manuscripts of my papers."[142] He would presumably have completed what he called a "worthy funeral" for his papers (a kind of *auto-da-fé*) by April 30, the first anniversary of his *Walpurgisnacht* pact. This destruction of his papers, Freud wrote, would be resented by "a number of yet unborn and unfortunate people—my biographers."[143] (And he was absolutely right about this!) However, let me suggest that at this time, April 28, 1885, as the memory of his pact was revived and as the first severe criticisms of his cocaine work were starting to surface, Freud burned his own written pact along with his other notes and writings. Of course, the memory remained to serve later as the motive for his denial of such a pact in the Haitzmann paper. One other piece of possibly relevant evidence for Freud's making two pacts is that he destroyed his letters and personal writings *two* times in his life—the first in April 1885, the second in 1907.[144] This latter date would have been about nine years after his proposed second pact—a "pact" that others suggest took place near the end of his self-analysis (i.e., circa 1898).

For my part, I find it hard to choose between these two hypotheses. But let us now leave the pact issue to focus on a related issue: Freud's involvement with the occult. It is clear that Freud was far from being a consistent scientific rationalist.

Freud and the Occult

Throughout his life, Freud was strongly attracted to the occult in various forms. Ernest Jones gives a great deal of evidence for Freud's involvement in such phenomena.[145] As to the reality of spirits, telepathy, and the like, Freud vacillated rather sharply between a very skeptical "no" and a believing "yes." His relationship with the occult had certain important similarities to his relationship with religion. In both, there was a tendency to public denial and private acceptance, no doubt expressing Freud's great ambivalence. For example, all of Freud's publications relating to psychical or occult forces provided rationalistic interpretations in terms of psychological processes, mainly unconscious. But in private conversations and in his letters, Freud voiced very different sentiments. And Jones admits that Freud's favorite quotation, when such questions arose, was "There are more things in heaven and earth than are dreamt of in your philosophy."[146]

Freud was often quite superstitious—a fact that he admitted on several occasions. He was, in particular, almost obsessed with numbers, especially with those that he thought foretold the year of his death. (Two of Freud's psychoanalytic colleagues, Jung and Ferenczi, were very involved in the occult and at times had a strong influence on him.[147]) There were moments when Freud expressed great enthusiasm for psychical research, and he once wrote that perhaps if he had his life to live over again he would "devote myself to psychical research rather than to psychoanalysis."[148] Later, he denied that he had in fact written this, thus revealing his ambivalence and repression of the issue.[149] Freud was particularly inclined to believe in telepathy or thought transference, and often referred to its possibility; however, in public—in his scientific writings—only his skeptical position was expressed.

Freud did acknowledge, in an essay written with the express purpose of interpreting rationally and hence "debunking" belief in spirits, that at times he found himself believing in them: "Consider now the fact that belief in spirits, apparitions and returning souls, which finds so much support in the religions to which, at least as children, we [!] have all clung, has by no means entirely vanished among all educated people."[150] Jones, who quotes this, goes on to describe how taken aback Freud was on encountering the sister of a dead patient, whom she closely resembled. Freud said that he thought to himself, "so after all it is true that the dead may return."[151]

If part of Freud could believe in telepathy, poltergeists, and the returning spirits of the dead, then part of him could certainly believe in the Devil.

Freud and the Anti-Christ

Freud's memory slip with respect to the Signorelli frescos has been introduced earlier (see Chapter Three), but it turns out that this incident is rich in connections to Christianity, and I return to it here. Freud's own analysis of his inability to remember the name of this artist was not just a trivial lapse; rather, within psychoanalysis, it is considered to be "the prime specimen of a 'Freudian slip.'"[152] Much of its deeper psychological and some of its important religious significance has been identified by the psychoanalyst Schimek, and in this treatment I draw on his insights. To set the stage, the reader should look at these frescos, found in the exquisite small cathedral (*duomo*) at Orvieto (Figure 5-5); details of the frescos are shown in Figures 5-6 to 5-8.

Now Freud could not remember the artist's name. His closest association was "Botticelli"; he had the last part right but missed the crucial first part, "Signor." Zilboorg,[153] as mentioned above, sees this as evidence of Freud's repression of God's name: "*Signor*" and "*Herr*." Schimek, though unaware of Zilboorg's earlier short discussion, comes to the same conclusion as part of his deeper theoretical analysis.

Freud explained his lapse by associations to the place to which he was traveling, Herzogovina.[154] "Herzogovina" he connected to "*Herr Doktor*"—that is, the "Lord Doctor," but not the "Lord God." He also associated this country with the Turks, and with an anecdote about the alleged great importance attached to sexuality by these people (exemplified by the belief that it is better to die than to lose one's capacity for sex). All this reminded Freud of a recent unpleasant message from one of his

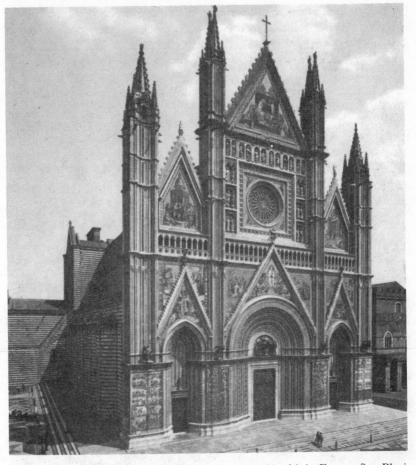

Figure 5-5. The Cathedral (Duomo) at Orvieto. (Archivio Fotografico Pluri-graf Narni-Terni-Italia)

patients, with whom he had taken a great deal of trouble. This patient had just committed suicide on account of his depression over an incurable sexual disorder. Freud concluded that these associations accounted for his own repression of the name "Signorelli."

It is curious that Freud began the investigation of his slip by the categorical (and unsupported) statement: "The reason why the name Signorelli was lost is not to be found in anything special about the name itself or in any psychological characteristics of the context in which it was introduced."[155] As Schimek so aptly puts it, Freud's denial was an example of what Freud himself described as the defense of negation: "You ask who this person in the dream can be. It's *not* my mother."[156]

Figure 5-6. Signorelli, *Hell* (detail). (Archivio Fotografico Plurigraf Narni-Terni-Italia)

Figure 5-7. Signorelli, *Preaching of the Anti-Christ* (detail showing the two artists who worked on the fresco, Lucas Signorelli and Fra Angelico). (Archivio Fotografico Plurigraf Narni-Terni-Italia)

Figure 5-8. Signorelli, *Preaching of the Anti-Christ* (detail showing the Devil speaking to the Anti-Christ). (Archivio Fotografico Plurigraf Narni-Terni-Italia)

Somewhat later, Freud did hint that there may be some connection between the painting and the themes of death and sexuality, but he did not follow it up; he left the reader with the slip "explained" on the basis of the external surface associations mentioned above. Schimek's primary point is that Freud's deep, underlying anxiety about death, sexuality, and religion was a far more probable basis for the memory failure. Schimek rejects Freud's explanation as superficial; I summarize his interesting remarks here.

Schimek notes that once one has seen the paintings in question, one need not seek far to find a connection to the topics of death and sexuality: These frescos of Heaven and Hell consist in large part "of an apocalyptic vision of hundreds of naked bodies in various postures of lust and torment"[157] (see Figure 5-6). Schimek then goes on to underline the theme of the "guilty therapist" (or the "bad doctor") as it involves the paintings and Freud's associations to them. One of the events that Freud connected to his slip was, as mentioned, the recent suicide of one of his patients. This raised the issue of his therapeutic competence in a most painful way. Freud had often been plagued by doubts about his therapeutic competence. Schimek mentions the Irma (Emma) dream as having a heavy preoccupation with what Freud termed "professional conscientiousness."[158] The dream is regularly interpreted as containing evidence of Freud's guilt over the bad treatment of Emma (the woman with the nasal hemorrhage).[159] Schimek also identifies the relevance of Freud's nanny to the religious themes of the paintings—Heaven and Hell—and also to sexuality. In Freud's recollection of his early years, he wrote in his letters to Fliess:

[T]he whole dream was full of the most wounding references to my present uselessness as a therapist . . . she [presumably the nanny] encouraged me to steal (coins) to give her. . . . The dream can be summed up as bad treatment. Just as the old woman got money from me for her bad treatment of me, so do I get money for the bad treatment of my patients.[160]

All of this highlights the complex links between and among the anxiety over his patient's recent suicide, the topics of the frescos, his old nanny, his identification with her and her bad treatment, and the themes of death and sexuality.

There are still other connections here that are not developed by Schimek, but that are well worth our attention. Details of the fresco that Freud remembered the most clearly, a fresco devoted to the Anti-Christ, are shown in Figures 5-7 and 5-8. We know that Freud saw and remembered this particular fresco, because he explicitly said, "I saw before my eyes, with special sharpness, the artist's self-portrait—with a serious face and folded hands"[161]; this self-portrait is shown in Figure 5-7.

Now there are several reasons to think that Freud may have associated himself with the Anti-Chirst. This figure, like Faust, is portrayed here as carrying out false miracles (in particular, false cures); also like Faust, he is shown with the Devil whispering in his ear. Freud early in his career used hypnotism for psychological "cures," but later dropped the technique as being seriously inadequate. Yet he wrote that while using hypnotism he enjoyed "the reputation of a miracle worker."[162] It was at about the same time that Freud often visited the Anna von Lieben household to treat Anna; here he was known by the children as "The Magician."[163] (We may recall also that in Goethe's work, Faust makes a point of describing his medical cures as accidents, as fakes.) Such a Faust-and-Mephistopheles pair as is portrayed in the fresco (see Figure 5-8) would certainly have attracted Freud. Swales, who first brought these connections to my attention, has also pointed out that there is even a certain physical similarity between the face of the Signorelli Anti-Christ and that of Freud. See also the iconographic and thematic similarity of this Signorelli portrayal to two other paintings of significance for Freud: Titian's *Maundy Money* (Figure 3-4) and Dürer's *The Kiss of Judas* (Figure 6-4).

Finally, while it is clear that the theme of the "bad doctor" was implicit in the recent suicide of Freud's patient, Freud's sense of guilt as a false healer would also probably have come from his earlier advocacy of cocaine—a drug that brings temporary relief at the frequent price of long-term destruction. And his approach to the cure of hysterics may well have posed the same questions: Am I really curing my patients? Are they really getting better, and if so, is it my therapy that is healing them? (Evidence of the curative character of psychoanalysis was always rather weak, and in fact still is; Freud took to expressing a lack of interest in the whole issue of whether psychoanalysis cures patients.)

The idea of the Anti-Christ is an interesting one, and since it bears so directly on Freud, it needs a brief introduction. The Anti-Christ is a figure referred to in a few of the prophetic passages of the Old and New Testaments. The idea of the Anti-Christ has been elaborated by writers over the centuries. As a result, the Anti-Christ has become a complex figure with many literary and legendary features, which surround and sometimes overlie its scriptural origin. Certain characteristics are usually agreed upon, however.[164] The Anti-Christ is most commonly understood to be an actual human being, possessed by the Devil, who will come during a time of world wide troubles. These troubles will involve great disasters and are interpreted as the Last Days. During this time, Rome will be destroyed, and Christians will be hunted out and killed in large numbers. The Anti-Christ is supposed to reign for a period of three and a half years. He is supposed to be of Jewish origin and will be a false Messiah for many Jews, and for many others as well throughout the world. Often it is assumed that he will rebuild the temple in Jerusalem. This period, the reign of the Anti-Christ, will end with his destruction and with the Second Coming of Christ.

For our purposes, only a few aspects of the Anti-Christ legend are relevant. These are that he will be an enemy of Christ, a true Anti-Christ; that he will be Jewish in origin; and that he will be a real person who will, as St. Jerome put it, be possessed of all of Satan's energy.[165] He will be associated with the destruction of Rome, and may be a pseudo-Messiah for the Jews (perhaps even destroying their true Messiah). A powerful figure, he will be known for his false miracles and false cures.

It should be kept in mind that in the later part of the 19th century, the notion of the Anti-Christ was, to a considerable degree, in the intellectual atmosphere. I think it can hardly be doubted that Freud knew Nietzsche's *Anti-Christ* (1895/1931). Some years earlier, Renan, a favorite of Breuer, had published his *Anti-Christ* (1873/1899). Editions of both these Anti-Christ books are listed in Freud's personal library: the Renan in French (no date); Nietzsche's in two forms (as part of Nietzsche's complete works, and in an English translation dated 1928).[166] In early 1900, Freud wrote to Fliess that he had "just acquired Nietzsche, in whom I hope to find words for much that remains mute in me. . . ."[167] Wilhelm Boussett's *The Anti-Christ Legend* (1895/1896) is also a possible influence on Freud—not to mention the *Malleus Maleficarum*, which, as noted in Chapter Four, refers to the Anti-Christ. It should also be kept in mind that Faust is in many respects an Anti-Christ figure and that the Anti-Christ concept contributed to the origins of the Faust legend.[168]

One further piece of evidence suggests itself. In 1910, prior to writing his essay on Leonardo da Vinci, Freud read *The Romance of Leonardo da Vinci* by the Russian writer Dmitri Merejkowski. Freud certainly knew this work well, since he cited it often in his essay,[169] and Freud's portrayal of Leonardo was similar to that of the Russian writer. Merejkowski's historical romance is part of a trilogy called *Christ and Anti-Christ*, and without doubt the author represents Leonardo as a kind of Renaissance Faust or Anti-Christ figure. The story comes complete with a dramatic *Walpurgisnacht* scene,[170] as well as regular references to Leonardo as impious and sometimes perhaps as the Anti-Christ.[171] Like Faust, Leonardo in the novel is haunted by a woman of great beauty; also like Faust, in spite of his life of religious skepticism (even apostasy), Leonardo is portrayed as receiving the last rites and dying as a faithful son of the Church.[172] The atmosphere of this lengthy novel is much like that of C. F. Meyer's works set in Italy. That is, it is a somber, complex, Italian Catholic environment, in which great historical figures interact in ways rich with irony, sophistication, ambiguity, and ambivalence. At the center stands Leonardo–Faust–Anti-Christ.

In short, the possibility that Freud saw himself, at least in certain aspects, as the Anti-Christ must be taken seriously. And, indeed, it is only in this light that Velikovsky's hypothesis of a diabolical pact involving baptism might make sense. That is, Freud's notion of himself as the Anti-Christ might have required his conversion—his entry into the Church. Some of Bakan's Sabbatian evidence can also be viewed as part of an Anti-Christ identification; that is, the Anti-Christ is part of a

Jewish tradition of a false Messiah (though Bakan does not introduce this idea).

One other important characteristic of early psychoanalysis seems relevant here. In 1913, Freud established a special committee of loyal followers of his thought. This inner sanctum, at its start, consisted of Otto Rank, Sandor Ferenczi, Karl Abraham, Ernest Jones, and Hanns Sachs. This committee's existence and actions were to be "strictly secret." Each member, to signify his membership, was given an antique Greek intaglio to be mounted on a gold ring. Roazen comments that these rings "marked the recipients as specially chosen bearers of his [Freud's] message."[173]

Sachs, a lawyer by training, soon became an important training analyst, one who devoted himself to analyzing future psychoanalysts. Roazen notes that Sachs wrote about his training period in a way that shows his view of psychoanalysis as a religion, not as a science:

Religions have always demanded a trial period, a novitiate, of those among their devotees who desired to give their entire life into the service of the supermundane and the supernatural, those, in other words, who were to become monks or priests. . . . It can be seen that analysis needs something corresponding to the novitiate of the Church.[174]

The possibility that important aspects of Freud's thought represent a systematic critique of and rival to Christianity requires that we now take up a major new topic.

Jesus as the Anti-Oedipus

The central concept in Freud's work, aside from the unconscious, is the now well-known Oedipus complex. In the case of male personality development, the essential features of this complex are the following: Roughly during the age period from three to six, the boy develops a craving for power, hatred of his father, and a strong sexual desire for his mother. At the same time, the boy develops an intense fear of the father and a desire to supplant him. The hatred is based on the boy's knowledge that the father, with his greater size and strength, stands in the way of his desire. The child's fear of the father may explicitly be a fear of castration by the father, but more typically it has a less specific character. The son does not really kill the father, of course, but patricide is assumed to be a common preoccupation of his fantasies and dreams. The "resolution" of the complex is supposed to occur in part through the boy's recognition that he cannot replace his father, and in part through the fear of castration (which eventually leads the boy to identify with the father, the aggressor, and to repress the original frightening components of the complex).

Freud also elaborated a cultural–historical model of this complex, which he described in *Totem and Taboo* (1913). In this book, Freud greatly extended the idea of Oedipal man by hypothesizing an Oedipal origin of religion. Freud put his ideas very pithily, and I quote him here at some length. He began by postulating that the earliest stage of society consisted of "a violent and jealous father who keeps all the females for himself and drives away his sons as they grow up." However,

one day the brothers who had been driven out came together, killed and devoured their father and so made an end to the patriarchal horde. United, they had the courage to do and succeeded in doing what would have been impossible for them individually.[175]

Freud explained the eating of the murdered father by declaring that

in the act of devouring him they accomplished their identification with him and each one of them acquired a portion of his strength. The totem meal, which is perhaps mankind's earliest festival, would thus be a repetition and commemoration of this memorable and criminal deed, which was the beginning of so many things—of social organization, of moral restrictions and of religion.[176]

Freud concluded his interpretation with a reference to motivation of an Oedipal type:

After they had got rid of him, had satisfied their hatred and had put into effect their wish to identify themselves with him, the affection which had all this time been pushed under was bound to make itself felt. It did so in the form of remorse. A sense of guilt made its appearance, which in this instance coincided with the remorse felt by the whole group. The dead father became stronger than the living one had been. . . . They revoked their deed by forbidding the killing of the totem, the substitute for their father; and they renounced its fruits by resigning their claim to the women who had now been set free.[177]

This development in *Totem and Taboo* closely parallels Freud's presentation of the Oedipus complex elsewhere—for example, in *The Ego and the Id* (1923a)—with, however, one interesting difference. In Freud's discussion of the origin of religion in *Totem and Taboo*, there was relatively more concern with violence (i.e., the sons' hatred of and rebellion against the father) than in his other Oedipal writings, where Freud placed heavier emphasis on the sexual link to the mother (the incest theme).

Now central to Christian theology is the doctrine of original sin, the essential nature of which is rebellion against God. As we have seen, this theme of rebellion against God was an obsessive preoccupation of Freud's; it is central in much of the literature in which he immersed himself. Intrinsic to such rebellion is the attempt to replace God in his role as ruler over human life. Lucifer leads an army of angels against God, hoping to take His place on the throne of Heaven. Adam and Eve disobey the Creator, after having been tempted with the promise, "You will be like God."[178] Freud's concept of the Oedipus complex is obviously interpretable as a powerful psychological representation of the universal desire to be like God: to sin by rebellion, by disobedience, by striving to become the autonomous ruler over one's own and others' lives.

Now, in a Christian framework, Jesus provides the model for the negation—in fact, for the canceling out or removal—of the Oedipal structure. In contrast to Oedipal man, Jesus shows not intense hatred but perfect love for God the Father. This love is expressed in what has been called "radical obedience"—that is, total identification with the Father's will (whereas Oedipal man shows radical disobedience). Throughout the Gospels, Jesus consistently speaks of doing his Father's will and not his own: "I seek not my own will, but the will of him who sent me"[179]; "not my will, but thine, be done."[180] The result of this radical obedience is the death of the Son. He is not killed by the Father, but by a group of conflict-filled, frightened, and hateful men. That is, the group of brothers kills not the Father but the Son. It is then the Son's death that occurs, and not the Father's, as was the case for Oedipal man. The results of this death are not the guilt and remorse that follow the Oedipal murder, but atonement, resurrection, and joy. There is a "rebirth," in which the Father and Son are now together and not estranged. The followers of Jesus—the new group of brothers (brothers in Christ)—are called to become sons of God by modeling their lives on that of Jesus. One important way in which this is done is through Holy Communion, in which the followers are commanded to eat the body and drink the blood of the Son in the bread and wine; this "totemic" meal is the opposite of Freud's postulated ancient father-focused Oedipal meal.

To round out the Anti-Oedipal pattern, Jesus shows no sign of sexual desire for his mother; in fact, by choosing celibate life, he explicitly puts sexuality completely aside as a determining motivation. In short, the life of Jesus is the life of *Anti*-Oedipus (see Table 5-1).

Now the extraordinary fact is that Freud was, in many important respects, aware of this logic, which is at the very center of the Christian view of man. He commented in an important, apparently almost completely overlooked, passage near the end of *Totem and Taboo*:

There can be no doubt that in the Christian myth the *original sin* was one against God the Father. If, however, Christ redeemed mankind from the burden of *original sin* by the sacrifice of his own life, we are driven to conclude that the sin was a murder. The law of talion, which is so deeply rooted in human feelings, lays it down that a murder can only be expiated by bloodguilt. And if this sacrifice of a life brought about atonement with God the Father, the crime to be expiated can only have been the murder of the father.

In the Christian doctrine, therefore, men were acknowledging in the most undisguised manner the guilty primaeval deed, since they found the fullest atonement for it in the sacrifice of this one son. Atonement with the father was all the more complete

Table 5-1. Jesus as the Anti-Oedipus: A Summary of the Ways in Which the Life of Jesus is the Negation of the Life of Freud's Oedipal Man

Oedipal man: The old man (from Freud)	Jesus: The new man (from Gospels)
1. The son hates the father.	1. The Son loves the Father.
2. The son shows radical disobedience to the father.	2. The Son shows radical obedience to the Father.
3. The son wants sexual possession of the mother (or all women of the group).	3. The Son renounces sexual possession of all women.
4. Radical disobedience results in death of the father, in fantasy or supposedly in fact in the ancient past.	4. Radical obedience results in death of the Son.
5. Death of the father is caused by the son or by a band of brothers (sons) who hate the father.	5. Death of the Son is caused by a band of brothers who hate the Son.
6. Death of the father is followed by failed resurrection in the form of a created father-totem, by emotions of guilt and remorse, and by permanent separation and estrangement of father and son.	6. Death of the Son is followed by resurrection of the Son, by the emotions of joy and happiness, and by the complete reunion and identity of Father and Son.
7. Death of the father leads to the son's identification with the father, now incorporated as superego, or to the band of brothers' identification with the father-totem.	7. Resurrection leads to the sons' identification with the Son, who is the center of morality and of ideals (a new Superego); the new band of brothers identifies with the "totem" Son.
8. The old sons identify with the father in a totemic meal in which the father is eaten.	8. The new sons (or band of Christians) identify with the Son in a "totemic" meal in which the Son is eaten.
9. The new band, feeling guilt partly from their sexual motives, renounces the women and creates the rule of outmarriage (exogamy). Thus, the women take the name of some other group's father.	9. The new band of sons *and daughters* takes the name of the Son (Christians); the women are not excluded from the "tribe," but take the same name.
10. In short: Hatred and disobedience leading to death of the father bring original sin.	10. In short: Love and obedience leading to death of the Son bring redemption.

since *the sacrifice was accompanied by a total renunciation of the women* on whose account the rebellion against the father was started. But at that point the inexorable psychological law of ambivalence stepped in. The very deed in which the son offered the greatest possible atonement to the father brought him at the same time to the attainment of his wishes *against* the father. He himself became God, beside, or more correctly, in place of, the father. A son-religion displaced the father-religion. As a sign of this substitution the ancient totem-meal was revived in the form of communion, in which the company of brothers consumed the flesh and blood of the son—no longer the father—obtained sanctity thereby and identified themselves with him. [Emphasis added in all cases except the last.][181]

In the exposition above, an orthodox Christian would agree with Freud, except when he arrived at his final inaccurate conclusion that Jesus replaced the Father—that Christianity is a "son-religion." Freud appears not to have understood that in Christianity the Son does not replace the Father: "I and the Father are one."[182]

Setting aside Freud's curious interpretation of Jesus as replacing the Father, we can certainly see that he probably did understand much of the essential message of Christianity when he wrote (and this is, after all, a rather astonishing quotation): "He [Christ] sacrificed his own life and so redeemed the company of brothers from *original sin* [emphasis added]."[183] This concept of Jesus as the Anti-Oedipus is a rich one, with ramifications that go deeply into the psychology of atheism.[184] In this book, however, I can only bring out, briefly, the connections between this theme and Freud's identification with the Anti-Christ. Specifically, to the extent that Freud identified with and championed Oedipal man, he also identified with and championed the Anti-Christ, for just as Jesus is the Anti-Oedipus, Oedipus is the Anti-Christ. (Swales, in particular, makes a systematic case that Freud identified with Oedipus.[185]) But insofar as Freud understood Oedipal motivation to be a natural and unfortunate fact that had to be reluctantly accepted, to that extent Freud can be viewed as a brilliant psychologist of fallen human nature, who showed us, with Oedipus, that the Anti-Christ is Everyman. In this sense Freud has provided, in the Oedipus complex, a profound modern interpretation and analysis of the ancient concept of original sin.

Conclusion

The exact nature of Freud's relations with the Devil still remains uncertain, and perhaps must always remain so; the same is true of his identification with the Anti-Christ. In any case, there is much evidence that Freud's personality (or unconscious ego) was to some degree "split," and that an important part of him was involved in a neurotic fantasy pact with the Devil.

I am inclined to think, however, that whatever Freud's diabolical identification may have been, his substantially stronger affinities were with God in Heaven. In this respect, it must be emphasized that Goethe's *Faust*, after all, ends with the salvation of Faust; *The Temptation of St. Anthony* concludes with the ongoing hope of salvation; *Paradise Lost* implies *Paradise Regained*; Virgil's *Aeneid* ends with the founding of Rome; and Dante's *Inferno* is the first part of a journey that ends in Paradise.

The question of Freud's ultimate allegiance is, of course, a very central one. This book argues that Freud's early traumatic experiences, later amplified by cocaine, determined (along with his temperament and abilities) those emotions, problems, and pathologies that would preoccupy him as an adult. Although I assume this degree of psychological determinism, I also assume that Freud's attitude toward his pathological past was open to a free choice. In this respect, it should be emphasized that Freud chose to wrestle directly with his past, intellectually and emotionally, and not to deny or repress it.

Where does he choose to stand with respect to the basic moral issues of good and evil, God and the Devil? Here I am unable to decide what Freud's final psychological commitment was; indeed, such a judgment is always difficult. (And, of course, any ultimate moral judgment about Freud, or anyone else, is outside the proper sphere of human evaluation.) But, as noted above, my estimate is that in his more fundamental aspects Freud chose the side of the angels. The curious state of the entire question of Freud's Christian unconscious is captured in his own words: "Do you not know that I am the Devil? All my life I have had to *play* the Devil, in order that others would be able to build the most beautiful cathedral with the materials that I produced [emphasis added]."[186]

Freud never lost his memory of Notre Dame, with its "entirely new idea of perfection." And though the cathedral to which he referred remains to be built, I believe Freud would consider that he had done his part.

Chapter Six

The Mature and Final Years: 1900–1939

WE NOW TAKE UP the mature years, the last three decades or so of Freud's life—a time in which he was a world-renowned figure. These were the years in which the intense motivations of his earlier years receded, for the most part, into the background. He had been married to Martha for 20 years and more; his religious crisis was, if not resolved, at least stabilized; he was now a full professor, and increasingly acknowledged as an intellectual figure of historic significance. As a consequence, the intensity of his ambition was allayed. This was also the period in which his energies were spent in the intellectual and personal conflicts associated with his psychoanalytic theories. Freud was not often actively concerned with the reactions of those outside of psychoanalysis; instead, it was the defections of his very best students that would emotionally and intellectually preoccupy him. Adler, and then Jung, Rank, and many others, would at first be part of the Freudian theoretical world, then rebel and go off on their own.

The Freud–Pfister Letters

To begin this section, let us consider a correspondence[1] that contrasts markedly with the prior topics—a correspondence that in many respects constituted the noblest set of exchanges of Freud's life. The correspondence was with the Reverend Oskar Pfister, a Swiss Protestant minister, who also became an early psychoanalyst, and, after they met, a life-long friend of Freud and his family.

In presenting material from the Freud–Pfister correspondence, I make only a few comments, and instead generally let the quotations speak for themselves. I do request that, at the end of this section, the reader ask himself whether the Freud who comes through fits the conventional understanding of him as a man for whom God and Christianity had no positive personal significance.

A few preliminary remarks may, however, be helpful. The Freud–Pfister relationship was both a personal friendship and a professional bond. Pfister was an active and outstanding psychoanalyst, whose character and contributions were admired not only by Freud, but by Carl Jung, Alfred Adler, and others who were frequently at serious odds with one another. Pfister remained loyal to Freud's basic psychoanalytic ideas (as well as to Freud himself), although they did have a serious disagreement about the nature of religion. In spite of this disagreement, the mutual respect and affection between the two were never impaired, and their letters remain a tribute to the memory of each man. (The majority of the extant letters are from Freud; most of those from Pfister are missing.)

As the remarks of Freud's daughter Anna make clear, Pfister was not a friend only of Freud, but also of his family:

In the totally non-religious Freud household Pfister, in his clerical garb and with the manners and behavior of a pastor, was like a visitor from another planet. In him there was nothing of the almost passionately impatient enthusiasm for science which caused other pioneers of analysis to regard time spent at the family table only as an unwelcome interruption of their theoretical and clinical discussions. On the contrary, his human warmth and enthusiasm, his capacity for taking a lively part in the minor events of the day, enchanted the children of the household, and made him at all times a most welcome guest, a uniquely human figure in his way.[2]

The happy evaluation was mutual. Pfister wrote Freud in 1923:

It is now nearly fifteen years since I entered your house for the first time and quickly fell in love with your humanitarian character and the free and cheerful spirit of your whole family. . . . I felt as if I were in a divine, Olympian abode, and if I had been asked what was the most agreeable place in the world I would only have replied: 'Find out at Professor Freud's.' . . .[3]

In Freud's second letter to Pfister, he wrote:

In your case they [his patients] are young persons faced with conflicts of recent date, who are personally drawn towards you and are ready for sublimation in its most comfortable form, namely the religious . . . you are in the fortunate position of being able to lead them to God and bringing about what in this one respect was the happy state of earlier times when religious faith stifled the neuroses. For us this way of disposing of the matter does not exist.[4]

Let us just note that Freud spoke here of the nonreligious state as involving not a gain but a loss.

In the same letter, somewhat further on, Freud made what is now a frequently quoted comment about psychoanalysis and religion:

In itself psycho-analysis is neither religious nor non-religious, but an impartial tool which both priest and layman can use in the service of the sufferer. [Pfister was not a priest; Freud's Roman Catholic center of gravity was showing here.] I am very much struck by the fact that it never occurred to me how extraordinarily helpful the psycho-analytic method might be in pastoral work, but that is surely accounted for by the remoteness from me, as a wicked pagan, of the whole system of ideas.[5]

In another letter, Freud wrote:

Our predecessors in psycho-analysis, the Catholic fathers, did not of course work on the principle of paying a mere minimum of attention to sexual matters, but very explicitly asked for full details. . . . Your work should soon yield a typical result, as the general lines of religious thinking are laid down in advance in the family. God is equivalent to father, the Madonna is the mother, and the patient himself is no other than Christ.[6]

Later in the correspondence, we find Freud writing to thank Pfister for sending him a small silver model of the Matterhorn, about which Freud said:

I propose to endow the Matterhorn with yet a third meaning. It reminds me of a remarkable man [Pfister] who came to see me one day, a true servant of God, a man in the very idea of whom I should have had difficulty believing, in that he feels the need to do spiritual good to everyone he meets. You did good in this way even to me.[7]

The whole tone of the letter was one of amazement, but also of genuine delight; almost of wonder. Shortly thereafter, Freud addressed his next letter to Pfister as "Dear Man of God."[8]

I would like to list some of the short expressions—perhaps one might call them slips—that occur throughout the correspondence, and that contribute to the Christian undertone present in these letters, as in so many of the others that I have cited. In a long letter on a case history and on psychoanalytic technique, Freud referred to the problem of transference (i.e., the tendency for the patient to transfer to the therapist strong, typically neurotic emotions—often emotions and ways of relating originally learned in response to the patient's father or mother). Freud wrote: "The transference is indeed a cross."[9] Later he wrote: "How delightful of you to remember me at Easter,"[10] and still later, "I am looking forward to Easter, which I am going to spend in Venice. . . . "[11] He also expressed his envy of Pfister for his recent visit to Rome.[12]

In a like vein, Freud wrote some years later: "The prospect of having you with us here in Vienna at Easter is, so to speak, a consolation . . . Easter is not far off, and until then I send you my heartiest greetings."[13] In

other letters we find phrases such as "Your good shepherd's optimism
. . . "[14]; writing after a recovery from one of his operations for cancer,
Freud gently chided Pfister, "[A]m I to miss the opportunity of seeing
my old, but by God's grace rejuvenated friend here?"[15] In short, the
frequency of such expressions gives these letters a kind of Christian
coloring.

References to the New Testament include the following: "I hope you
will be coming with a children's train again. Let us alter the saying and
say: Suffer me to come with the little children."[16] And a little later: "I
very much liked your St. Paul [an article by Pfister] . . . I have always
had a special sympathy for St. Paul as a genuinely Jewish character. Is he
not the only one who stands completely in the light of history?"[17]

In another interesting passage, Freud said: "A few centuries ago we
should have prescribed days of prayer for the fulfillment of our wishes
[Freud would seem to be referring to the Catholic practice of saying
novenas, or cycles of prayers] but nowadays all we can do is wait."[18]
Here, as above, in Freud's wording there was a sense of resignation to a
loss.

In a mood of greater and more concrete loss, Freud wrote to Pfister
about the death of his daughter Sophie of influenza in January 1920. In
the letter, he referred to her (as he did elsewhere) as his "Sunday child."[19]
This reference to a child as a "Sunday child" comes out of central
European Christian folk culture.[20]

Pfister wrote in 1922 to Freud about a book of his, a copy of which he
was sending to Freud. (The book was *Love in Children and Its Aberra-
tions*.) Freud replied: " . . . I suspect that it will be my favorite among the
great creatures of your mind and, in spite of Jesus Christ and occasional
obeisances to anagogics [i.e., spiritual interpretation of Scripture], the
closest to my own way of thinking."[21] This is an interesting quotation,
for although it was "in spite of Christ," still Freud felt that he would find
it the closest to him of Pfister's works—or rather of Pfister's "creatures,"
a term assimilating the servant of God to God himself.

A few sentences later in the same letter Freud referred to the "grim
heavenly pair logos and ananke," the two nouns being given in Greek.
Logos is not of course an exclusively Christian word, but it does occur
very prominently in John 1:1: "In the beginning was the Word" (*Logos*
in the original Greek).[22]

Freud and Pfister discussed in their letters the relation of psychoanalysis to religion, and this is one of the most compelling aspects of their
correspondence. Freud's letter of October 9, 1918, concluded:

As for the possibility of sublimation to religion, therapeutically I can only envy
you. But the beauty of religion certainly does not belong to psychoanalysis. It is
natural that at this point in therapy our ways should part, and so it can remain.

Incidentally, why was it that none of all the pious ever discovered psychoanalysis? Why did it have to wait for a completely godless Jew?[23]

Pfister's reply was dated October 29, 1918:

Finally you ask why psychoanalysis was not discovered by any of the pious, but by an atheist Jew. The answer obviously is that piety is not the same as genius for discovery. . . . Moreover, in the first place you are no Jew, which to me, in view of my unbounded admiration for Amos, Isaiah, Jeremiah, and the author of Job, and Ecclesiastes, is a matter of profound regret, and in the second place you are not godless, for he who lives in the truth lives in God, and he who strives for the freeing of love "dwelleth in God" (First Epistle of John, iv, 16). If you raised your consciousness and fully felt your place in the great design, which to me is as necessary as the synthesis of the notes is to a Beethoven symphony, I should say of you: A better Christian there never was. . . .[24]

Freud did not respond directly to Pfister's boldness here, although very possibly his letter of February 16, 1929, responded to a similar remark:

That was an excessively friendly thought on your part, and it always reminds me of the monk who insisted on regarding Nathan as a thoroughly good Christian. I am a long way from being Nathan, but of course I cannot help remaining "good" towards you.[25]

Perhaps the most poignant series of communications came in connection with Freud's publication of *The Future of an Illusion*. On October 16, 1927, Freud wrote to Pfister:

In the next few weeks a pamphlet of mine will be appearing which has a great deal to do with you. I had been wanting to write it for a long time, and postponed it out of regard for you, but the impulse became too strong. The subject matter . . . is my completely negative attitude to religion. . . . I feared, and still fear, that such a public profession of my attitude will be painful to you. When you have read it let me know what measure of toleration and understanding you are able to preserve for the hopeless pagan.[26]

Pfister replied on October 21, 1927: "You have always been tolerant towards me, and I am to be intolerant of your atheism? If I frankly air my differences from you, you will certainly not take it amiss. Meanwhile my attitude is one of eager curiosity."[27]

As the discussion developed, Pfister was to publish a reply to *The Future of an Illusion* in the psychoanalytic journal *Imago*. In reference to that forthcoming reply, Freud wrote on October 22, 1927: "Such is your magnanimity that I expected no other answer to my 'declaration of war.' The prospect of your making a public stand against my pamphlet gives me positive pleasure. . . ."[28] And on November 26, 1927:

I attach importance to your publishing your criticism—in *Imago*, if you like—and I hope that in it you will specifically draw attention to our undisturbed friendship and your unshaken loyalty to analysis. . . . Let us be quite clear on the point that the views expressed in my book form no part of analytic theory. They are my personal views . . . but there are certainly many excellent analysts who do not share them.[29]

Pfister wrote on February 20, 1928:

[W]hen I reflect that you are much better and deeper than your disbelief, and that I am much worse and more superficial than my faith, I conclude that the abyss between us cannot yawn so grimly. . . .

One difference derives chiefly from the fact that you grew up in proximity to pathological forms of religion and regard these as "religion," while I had the good fortune of being able to turn to a free form of religion which to you seems to be an emptying of Christianity of its content, while I regard it as the core and substance of evangelism.[30]

Pfister published his reply, *"Die Illusion einer Zukunft"* ("The Illusion of a Future"), in *Imago* in 1928, and the two men continued their debate for at least another year.

Throughout all this, as throughout their long relationship, the two men remained loyal to and respectful of each other. Freud certainly demonstrated respect and deference to Pfister's "calling," and throughout their correspondence Freud appeared as reasonably conversant and familiar with religious language and symbolism. This all testifies to Freud's complexity and magnanimity, but it seems surprising behavior for such a publicly active atheist.

What is interesting, though, is that for all the familiarity shared, over a long period, Freud remained apparently unmoved by Pfister's religious convictions and arguments. He expressed his enthusiasm about Pfister's reply to his *The Future of an Illusion*, but he never seriously commented on the substance of the reply. He never responded at all to Pfister's statement of February 20, 1928: "[Y]ou grew up in proximity to pathological forms of religion and regard them as 'religion.'"[31]

I would argue that Freud was unmoved by Pfister's position because he was simply not deeply interested in Pfister's evangelical (and somewhat liberal) Protestantism (which seemed to him an "emptying of Christianity of its content").[32] Freud's quarrel with, and thus his interest in (and "cathexis" of) Christianity, was, for reasons already documented, with a simple Roman Catholicism.

In retrospect, the Freud–Pfister letters leave an impression not only of the strong character of the correspondents, but also perhaps of a certain double wistfulness. Freud stuck reliably to his anti-Christian position, as articulated most forcefully in public in *The Future of an Illusion*. But his letters reveal somehow more than just tolerance for Pfister's position. They indicate a real admiration for this "true man of God," and an envy, almost a longing, for Pfister's faith. Pfister, for his part, kept his great respect for his intellectual master throughout his life unblemished by jealousy, defensive resistance, and theoretical antagonism—attitudes that characterized so many of Freud's other intellectual relationships. I would like to suggest that one of the reasons for this was Pfister's intuitive sensing that somewhere deep in Freud there was a longing for God and a sympathy for Christianity. How else is one to account for Pfister's bold claim that—if Freud would only look up, as it were—"A better Christian there never was." I very much doubt that he would have dared to use such words if his psychological and, by then, psychoanalytic intuitions hadn't given him some basis for thinking they would strike a responsive chord. Yet Pfister's hope—that Freud would respond to this buried desire—remained unfulfilled.

The Freud–Jung Letters: 1906–1914

Although the letters exchanged by Freud and Jung between 1906 and 1914 were often concerned with technical discussion of cases and theory, plus a good deal of business (e.g., about the various journal publications coming out during this time), there were interesting personal exchanges in them nonetheless. Of course, the personal components centered on the friendship, then the tension, and finally the unpleasant break between these two powerful psychological theorists. The amount of material directly relevant to Freud and religion in these letters is hence limited, but it is still of considerable interest.

To begin with, as in so many of his other letters, Freud referred not infrequently to God, and in ways that were implicitly positive. These references were in casual expressions that might be considered slips of the pen: "How am I going to work on my many, absolutely necessary scientific projects, God only knows"[33]; "My week's work leaves me numb. I would invent the seventh day if the Lord hadn't done so long ago"[34]; and "Why in God's name did I allow myself to follow you into this field?"[35]

Moreover, Freud used a very interesting Latin expression, "*corpora vilia*," in one of his letters. This expression, meaning "vile bodies" comes from the Vulgate Bible and occurs in St. Paul's letter to the Philippians in the following passage: "[W]e shall change our vile body that may be fashioned like unto his [Christ's] glorious body" (3:20-21).[36] Here is the context in which Freud used this expression: He had just acknowledged that Jung "acutely noticed" that Freud had not fully elucidated his own dreams in *The Interpretation of Dreams*. About his dreams, he continued:

In none do I bring out all the elements . . . because they are personal dreams. And as for the *corpora vilia* in whose dreams we may *ruthlessly* disclose everything [emphasis in original], these can only be neurotics, that is patients. . . .[37]

Now it is most curious to find here the New Testament concept of (and Pauline expression for) the fallenness of the flesh, fallen humanity (for which the cure is Jesus Christ). It is all the more surprising to find this term brought in on such a personal issue as Freud's censorship of his dreams, and at such a basic conceptual level; it is basic in that neurotics in their dreams are assumed to be expressing a vileness in need of ruthless exposure and of cure. (Freud was not averse to occasionally calling himself a neurotic.)

Early in the correspondence (1907), Freud pointed out that he attributed much more importance to a particular psychological factor than did Jung. He continued as follows: "[A]s you know, I am referring to ††† sexuality."[38] The use of the three crosses is a simple Catholic form of piety or superstition common among ordinary believers. Later, three crosses also appeared in another letter before the word "unconscious." The editor of *The Freud/Jung Letters* footnotes this: "Three crosses were chalked on the inside of doors in peasant houses to ward off danger."[39] Freud used three crosses in his "dream" book as well, where he put them in front of the word "diptheria" as though the crosses would protect him from the dreaded disease. In the letters to Fliess recently published by Masson, Freud introduced such crosses in three similar instances.[40] Again, this was a peasant and Catholic superstitious usage; in particular, these crosses were put on doors prior to *Walpurgisnacht* to protect against witches![41] The irritating thing is that Strachey, in rendering a similar passage of *The Interpretation of Dreams* into English, omits the crosses altogether by mistranslating their significance as "word of ill omen."[42]

Let us now look at one letter that is of special significance. It was written by Freud rather early in the relationship, while he was in Rome. He described the atmosphere in which he was living there:

Here in Rome I am leading a solitary existence, deep in day dreams. I don't intend to return home until the end of the month. . . . At the beginning of the holidays I put science far away from me, and now I should like to get back to normal and produce something. This incomparable city is the right place for it.[43]

During this visit Freud visited the Catacombs[44] and the Vatican treasures.[45] He wrote to his family: "What a pity one can't live here always! These brief visits leave one with an unappeased longing and with a feeling of insufficiency all the way round."[46] (The sense of the connection of this longing to the nanny is made stronger still by a comment in another letter two days earlier: "The women of Rome, strangely enough, are beautiful even when they are ugly, and not many of them are that."[47])

In the same letter to Jung cited above, Freud quoted from C. F. Meyer's *Huttens Letzte Tage*:

> And now that bell which rings so merrily
> Says: One more Protestant has come to be.[48]

(Shades of Freud's talk with Breuer about becoming a Protestant?) Freud regretted that he couldn't recall the rest of this part of the poem. However, the missing lines are supplied by the editor of *The Freud/Jung Letters*. The part Freud could not recall reads:

> Over the lake an endless sound of bells is carried;
> Many, it seems, are being baptized and buried.

> When human blood is born into new veins
> The sluggish human spirit new life gains.

> The bell which just so mournfully has tolled
> Said: now a papist's buried, parched and old.[49]

The part that Freud couldn't remember raises the theme of baptism and new life, all within the atmosphere of the sound of bells (a common enough one in the Rome of that time, as in Freiberg, much earlier), plus hostility to Rome.

A paragraph later, Freud started off on a new topic, urging Jung to go ahead with their journal. He began with the words, "Now for my *Ceterum censeo*: . . ."[50] What is this Latin expression? The editor of *The Freud/Jung Letters* provides a gloss: The Latin statesman Cato the Elder ended all his speeches to the Roman Senate with the words, "*Ceterum censeo Carthaginem esse delendam*" ("Also, I think that Carthage must be destroyed").[51] Here was Freud daydreaming in Rome, quoting poems about church bells and baptism, and quoting Latin sentences containing anti-Carthaginian exhortations! In short, we see here very clearly both Freud's Christian yearnings and his hostility to the Semitic enemy of Rome, Carthage (the anti-Hannibal part of Freud).

In the Freud–Jung correspondence, there was also something of an Easter concern. Freud referred to Easter 12 times, while the Gentile Jung did so only 7 times, and virtually always in response to an earlier use of the word by Freud.[52] (The correspondence consists of slightly more letters by Jung than by Freud. Thus, Jung had a somewhat greater chance to use any given word.) The word "Easter" was generally brought up by Freud when plans were being laid for a meeting, or with reference to something Freud wanted to do over Easter.[53] In any case, Freud seemed to like using the word "Easter" (e.g., "Happy Easter!"[54]); the expression "spring holiday," used twice by Jung,[55] did not occur in

Freud's letters. Similarly, Freud referred to Pentecost twice in the correspondence; Jung did so but once, and that in response to Freud.[56]

For readers who may have been dubious earlier about the emphasis placed on the sound similarity of the names of Freud's mother and nurse and other important women's names—Amalia, Amme, Anna, Nana, Madonna, Dame—here is a quote exemplifying Freud's own understanding of such associations and meanings. In a letter to Jung, he wrote about one of his cases:

> Just now I had a consultation with one of my patients who has made my head spin so that I can think of nothing else. Her main symptom is that she can't hold a cup of tea if anyone is present. . . . She worked very poorly this morning. "No sooner was I back in the entry hall," she says now, "than I saw it all. Obviously it's innate cowardice! After all *lâcheté* and *Schale Thee* aren't so far apart." [*lâcheté* = "cowardice" in French; *Schale Thee* = "cup of tea" in German. Obviously a sophisticated patient!] She has a habit of inverting words. She spent her childhood between her mother and her nurse, who stayed with her for many years. The mother's name is Emma; turn it around: Amme. The devil take our harebrained critics![57]

Besides the rather strained search for sound similarities with respect to *lâcheté*, we see here Emma and *Amme*, a nurse, a mother, and even the Devil making their appearance. It is relevant also to note that the names for Freud's famous female cases also seemed to come from the same acoustic world: Anna, Irma (Emma), Nora.

The Freud-Abraham Correspondence

One of Freud's most loyal and helpful colleagues was Karl Abraham; the correspondence between them (1907-1926) has been published, and these letters give us still another glimpse of Freud and his psychology.[58] What is intriguing is to find, once again, an Easter-Pentecost theme in *these* letters, even though Freud was writing to a secular Jewish intellectual who had no apparent connection of any kind with Christianity. Early in the correspondence, for instance, Freud wrote, "On this rainy Whitsunday . . ."[59]; in a later letter, he mentioned that he had been "unable to work since Easter."[60] Still later, he expressed the desire to see his daughter and grandson at Easter.[61] These references imply, in each case, some sadness, or some emotional block, or the yearning to see family members. The most striking example is Freud's comment on a visit with Abraham and his family that had fallen through: "I cannot get over the disappointment of Easter. It would have been so delightful to see you all together for once."[62] On yet three other occasions Freud referred to Easter, including a request that Abraham come "be with us, Friday before Easter."[63]

During this correspondence, Abraham wrote substantially more letters than Freud, but he referred to Easter only twice—once in response to Freud,[64] the other in the expression "the Easter holidays"[65]; he never referred to Pentecost. Freud also used, here again, the Latin quotation "*Ceterum censeo*" in one letter.[66] In short, these letters, though written when Freud was primarily concerned with the problems and politics of psychoanalysis—and long after his earlier years of anxiety about career, Martha, and marriage—still show the vestiges of the same unconscious motives.

Heine's *Lazarus*

The other favorite book of Freud's—in addition to *Paradise Lost*, discussed in Chapter Four—was Heine's *Lazarus*, and it is worthwhile to describe this little-known work briefly here.[67] (Let us keep in mind that the author was a converted Jew related through marriage to the Bernays family.[68]) The title of *Lazarus* was given by Heine to a series or cycle of 20 short poems written and published near the end of his life. This was in the 1850s, when Heine was ill—in fact, slowly dying of a long-term, fatal condition. These poems are very autobiographical and refer constantly to the experiences of Heine's life. Thus, in contrast to *Paradise Lost*, with its universal and cosmic themes, Heine's work is personal and particular in many respects. The mood or attitude of *Lazarus* is, however, similar to that of *Paradise Lost*, in that both have strongly melancholic, retrospective themes. Heine's poems are also filled with bitterness and sarcasm, though.

These poems turn out to be of interest to us because they contain, in abundance, emotions, themes and even events remarkably similar to those of Freud's life. The poems therefore reflect, in a sense, Freud's life as well as Heine's, and it is no wonder that they were among Freud's favorite pieces of literature.

The Lazarus in question is primarily the "poor man . . . full of sores" referred to in the gospel of Luke,[69] but some of the poems seem to evoke the other Lazarus as well, the one whom Christ raised from the dead.[70] The fact that the names are the same tends to conflate the two men and their stories.

One important theme of the poems—sometimes treated positively, sometimes bitterly and sarcastically—is resurrection. For example, in "*Der Abgekuhlte*" ("The Cooling Off"), we find these lines:

And if one is dead, one must lie in the grave; I am worried (frightened); yes, I am worried (anxious) that the resurrection will not come soon.

But then, in the next stanza, Heine turns satirical and begins speaking about his need for some love life.

Various poems take up themes of loss, such as *"Verlorne Wunsche"* ("Lost Wishes") and *"Wiedersehen"* ("Reunion"); the latter speaks of the desire to meet someone lost in the past. Also prominent are themes of exile, which would speak to Freud's longings for Freiberg and Rome and to his permanent sense of exile in Vienna.

We followed the corpse, the lovely boy. They have buried him under May flowers. For long years how often, oh little one, I have thought of you with envy and sadness.

These lines could well have triggered Freud's recollections of his response to the death of his little brother Julius, who, not long after his death on April 15 so many years ago, would have laid under May flowers. But Freud could also be mourning himself—his childhood, which died in late May.

One of the later poems, *"Frau Sorge"* ("Woman of Sorrows"), is most intriguing. Heine speaks of her as a guardian who sits next to his bed in the winter night. Described as an "old and ugly woman nodding by his bed," she is very reminiscent of Freud's nanny as he depicted her. In the last section of this poem, Heine writes:

Sometimes I dream that happiness and the new month of May have returned. The noise of the dozing one, whom God pities, breaks the soap bubble; the old woman sneezes.

This figure of an old nanny-like woman sitting by the bed of a child at night, together with dreams of happiness in May and the loss of dreams—all of this would have spoken directly to Freud. It is likely that the reference to Frau Sorge would have been naturally associated in Freud's mind both with his nanny and with the character by the same name who is a major figure at the end of *Faust*: It is she who brings Faust blindness, and who informs him that death is imminent.

The next poems all represent religious or Freudian themes. They are: *"An die Engel"* ("To the Angel"); *"Im Oktober 1849"* about exile; *"Boses Geträume"* ("Evil Dreaming"); *"Sie erlischt"* ("My Soul Dies"); and *"Vermächtnis"* ("Testament"). The last poem is *"Enfant perdu"* ("Lost Child"), which ends with a death scene:

The wounds are open—my blood streams out. . . . Yet, I am unconquered when I die and my weapons are not broken—only my heart is broken.

Many aspects of these poems could have drawn Freud: The ambiguous Christian themes, and Heine's situation as a converted Jew; the blend of hope with bitter irony and satire against his "Christian brothers"; and indeed the whole ambivalence of the poems about Christianity and

Christians would all certainly have appealed to him. But, perhaps most importantly, many of Heine's themes of mourning and sorrow must have spoken to Freud: loss, exile, the long-gone month of May, the dead child, the Woman of Sorrows, and the lost, heartbroken child.[71]

Other Examples of Christian Art

Aside from religious paintings already discussed that drew explicit responses from Freud, there were others that he liked. Again, Spector's *The Aesthetics of Freud* is helpful; Spector identifies two paintings with relevant content, reproductions of which hung for years on the wall near Freud's desk in Vienna.[72] One of these was *The Healing of Aeneas and the Raising of Tabitha* by Masaccio and Masolino. (It is reproduced in Figure 6-1, and a photograph of Freud with his copy is shown in Figure 6-2.) This work shows two scenes from the New Testament (Acts 9:32–43) in which St. Peter heals a man with palsy (on the left) and raises the recently deceased Tabitha from the dead (on the right). As Spector notes, Freud very likely interpreted these events as examples of psychological healings of persons suffering from hysteria.[73] Spector specifically comments that Freud considered palsy and cataleptic sleep to be hysterical symptoms, and that the role of St. Peter can be compared to that of Charcot.[74] (See the familiar engraving of Charcot with an hysterical patient in Figure 6-3; this engraving was a favorite of Freud's.) In one of his late works, Charcot concluded that hysterics are among the best subjects for treatment by faith healing.[75] In spite of the theory, however, I have never come across examples of sudden *psychological* cures for either palsy or cataleptic sleep, in Freud's writings or elsewhere in the psychological literature.

The latent meanings for these paintings are not touched on by Spector. Certainly one is tempted to believe that in some respects Freud saw himself as a kind of faith healer, as a kind of competitor to the older Christian tradition. Freud's remark that psychoanalysis is "secular pastoral counseling,"[76] like many other comments cited earlier, supports the secular religious meaning of psychoanalysis rather thoroughly.

These healing scenes also connect with the frescoes by Signorelli, which show the Anti-Christ deceiving people with false healing. To see oneself in competition with St. Peter is surely to invite such an interpretation.

Another work of art mentioned by Spector[77] but not discussed by him is *The Kiss of Judas* (1508) by Albrecht Dürer (see Figure 6-4). Kept in reproduction near Freud's desk,[78] this is a most unusual image for him to have among the art he presumably liked. What could it mean? The attraction of Freud to the scene of the betrayal of Christ first became

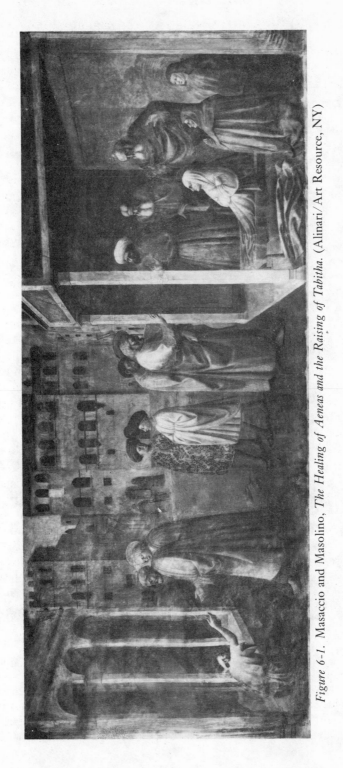

Figure 6-1. Masaccio and Masolino, *The Healing of Aeneas and the Raising of Tabitha.* (Alinari/Art Resource, NY)

Figure 6-2. Sigmund Freud, about 1912; photograph taken by one of his sons on the verandah of his home, Berggasse 19, Vienna. (Mary Evans/Sigmund Freud Copyrights)

Figure 6-3. Charcot demonstrating a case of hysteria; engraving by Docht of a painting by André Brouillet that hung in Freud's consulting room in Vienna. (Mary Evans Picture Library)

Figure 6-4. Dürer, *The Kiss of Judas.* (From W. Kurth (Ed.) *The Complete Woodcuts of Albrecht Dürer.* New York: Dover, 1963)

evident in his deep emotional response to *Maundy Money* by Titian (Figure 3-4). Here a positive identification with Jesus seemed to underlie his response. But in view of Freud's later attraction to the Anti-Christ (as in Signorelli's frescoes; see Figures 5-7 and 5-8), and especially in view of his later identification with Oedipus, one must raise the possibility that the Dürer also appealed to Freud's fondness for the coupling of opposites. No matter what interpretation is offered, for a Jew to have had such a picture in his office is strange indeed.

Another peculiar favorite image of Freud's is mentioned in a 1926 letter to Havelock Ellis (the well-known early English investigator of sex). Freud, who had a modest amount of contact with Ellis over the years, wrote to Ellis in response to receiving a book from him:

Although I cannot imagine being you—I just don't possess your goodness . . . —I nevertheless could not help looking for similarities and was glad to find one in the first chapter. The etching of St. Hieronymus [St. Jerome] in his study is also a favorite of mine and has been hanging in front of me in my room for years and perhaps some of the ideals you have realized in life have also been mine.[79]

The Dürer etching of St. Jerome is shown in Figure 6-5. It reminds one that Freud, not long after his strong response to *The Temptation of St. Anthony*, referred to himself as a monk in his study,[80] and it again reinforces our picture of the religious metaphors that Freud used in speaking of himself.

"Der Liebe Gott"

Some very interesting details about Freud emerge from Jones's reminiscences of their conversations together in the years before World War I. In one of them, he relates:

Freud was fond, especially after midnight, of regaling me with strange or uncanny experiences with patients. . . . He had a particular relish for such stories and was evidently impressed by their more mysterious aspects. When I would protest at some of the taller stories Freud was wont to reply with his favorite quotation from Shakespeare: "There are more things in heaven and earth than are dreamed of in your philosophy." . . . When they were concerned with clairvoyant visions of episodes at a distance, or visitations from departed spirits I ventured to reprove him. . . . I then asked him where such beliefs could halt: if one could believe in mental processes floating in the air, one could go on to a belief in angels. He closed the discussion at this point (about three in the morning) with the remark: "Quite so, even *der lieba Gott*" (the loving God). This was said in a jocular tone as if agreeing with my *reductio ad absurdum* and with a quizzical look as if he were pleased at shocking me. But there was something searching also in the glance, and I went away not entirely happy lest there be some more serious undertone as well.[81]

Figure 6-5. Dürer, *St. Jerome in His Study.* (From W. Kurth (Ed.) *The Complete Woodcuts of Albrecht Dürer.* New York: Dover, 1963)

As was the case in so many of the instances in which Freud expressed interest in and attraction to religion (Christianity), the circumstances for its expression were here informal and private, rather than formal and public: Freud was indeed a *public* atheist. Aside from occurring in dreams, these religious revelations occurred in letters—and there often in the "unimportant" things, such as casual references to its being Pentecost, or to anticipated meetings at Easter, or to his favorite books. Or else (as here), they occurred in informal talks. It is, as one would expect, in such settings that the unconscious does its work.

Even in some of Freud's public anti-religious writings, he occasionally sounded a positive note about God. In *Civilization and Its Discontents* (1930), he made this quite remarkable statement:

One would like to mix among the ranks of the believers, in order to meet these philosophers, who think they can rescue the God of religion by replacing Him by an impersonal, shadowy, and abstract principle, and to address them with the warning words: "Thou shalt not take the name of the Lord, thy God, in vain."[82]

(This comment by Freud reminds me of an indignant remark made by a lapsed Catholic friend of mine, concerning the modern, "liberal" image of God: "*That's* not the God I don't believe in." To be indignant is to reveal one's lack of indifference.)

The Virgin Mary

Freud's nanny, being rather old, would not have made a good psychological symbol for the Virgin Mary. It is not therefore surprising that Freud had relatively little to say about Mary, and when he did comment on her—for instance, in connection with Leonardo's *The Virgin and Child with St. Anne*—it was often in a context in which an older second mother was present or was somehow associated with the Virgin. Nevertheless, it is interesting to look at Freud's explicit comments on the subject.

His most "official" discussion of Mary occurred in a three-page paper written in 1911, titled *"Great Is Diana of the Ephesians."* This article (it had the same title as a poem by Goethe) summarized historical information so as to make a psychological point.[83] Apparently Freud had just read an art-historical treatise on the subject of Diana's worship in the ancient world.[84] Freud's first point was that there had been a cult of a goddess, in particular Diana, at Ephesus in Turkey for many hundreds of years. This cult, besides its religious significance, had been a major source of economic livelihood for the people of Ephesus. Freud noted that, very early in the Christian era, St. Paul created a great tumult at Ephesus because he would have nothing to do with the Diana cult. Somewhat later, however, St. John (author of the fourth gospel) brought the mother of Jesus, who had been entrusted to him, to Ephesus; she took up residence there. About 300 years later, a basilica was built in honor of Mary at Ephesus. Freud interpreted all of this as a revival of the cult of Diana, now baptized as Mary. Some centuries later, the area was conquered by Islam, and all fell into ruin and obscurity. At the end of the article, Freud commented that in "our own days" the Virgin Mary had reappeared to Katherina Emmerich, "a pious German girl" of peasant background. This woman (her full name was Anna Katherina Emmerich) had religious visions that she described, including visions of Mary's journey to Ephesus and of the house (with its furnishings) in which she lived. Both the house and her bed were found by Austrian archeologists "exactly as the Virgin had described them [to Emmerich], and they are once more the goal of the pilgrimages of the faithful."[85]

Various comments are in order here. First, Ellenberger has interpreted this article as showing Freud's identification with St. Paul—someone like Freud, who founded a new "religion"—having serious trouble with a disciple (St. John–Jung).[86] This interpretation is endorsed and further supported by Spector.[87] Second, Freud's interpretation of the origin of the Christian importance of Mary fits his theory that important people are apt to be "revenants" of still earlier figures. In fact, Freud's concern with this topic can itself be interpreted as a "revenant" of (return to) his childhood study of the Philippson Bible. Pfrimmer[88] has shown that the expression "Great is Diana of The Ephesians" and a treatment of her cult were to be found in this Bible, and that the discussion was illustrated by Philippson.

Third, when at the end of the article Freud referred to the visions of Katherina Emmerich, who died in 1824, as being in "our own days,"[89] he uncharacteristically showed no skepticism about her predictions as to the location of Mary's house. Apparently an Austrian archeological expedition in the 1850s to the site of ancient Ephesus found what was reported to be Mary's house.[90]

One wonders whether Freud ever read any of Emmerich's reports of her visions or had contact with her story elsewhere. There are certain reasons to suspect so. The visions of this woman—a nun and a stigmatist, somewhat like Louise Lateau—were written down and published by Clemens Brentano.[91] They were very popular in Europe and went through many translations. (They are still available in an American edition.[92]) Clemens Brentano was a famous romantic poet, part of the family connected to Goethe and a relative of Franz Brentano. Clemens spent years at the side of this bedridden peasant woman recording her extraordinary visions, which covered many aspects of ancient Jewish and Christian religious history. Her story would have been especially familiar to those in the pious Austro-German Catholic culture, such as Freud's nanny.

Another comment of Freud about the Virgin was made a year earlier, in 1910, and probably referred to women like Anna Katherina Emmerich:

Think how common hallucinations of the Virgin Mary were in peasant-girls in former times. So long as such a phenomenon brought a flock of believers and resulted perhaps in a chapel being built on the sacred spot, the visionary states of these maidens were inaccessible to influence. Today even the priesthood has changed its attitude to such things; it allows police and medical men to visit the seer, and since then the Virgin appears very seldom.[93]

Here Freud was in typical antireligious form.[94] But his unconscious mind had entirely different attitudes toward the Virgin. One hint of this came out later in his life, when he wrote, "I do not think our cures can compete with those at Lourdes. There are so many more people who believe in the miracle of the Blessed Virgin than in the existence of the unconscious."[95] In such a remark, Freud was presumably assuming belief in the unconscious as a kind of faith, or perhaps was asserting that both the unconscious and the miracle of the Blessed Virgin are true. At the very least, he was assuming the efficacy of miraculous cures.

A quite casual setting provided the context of one of the most startling revelations of Freud's strange involvement with Christianity. Lou Andreas-Salomé wrote a journal in which she recorded (among other things) her visit to the Freud home in November–December 1921. She told at one point about various conversations with Anna Freud, who very much enjoyed her company:

Listening to Anna talking about her father; picking mushrooms when they were children. When they went collecting mushrooms he always told them to go into the wood quietly and he still does this; there must be no chattering and they must roll up the bags they have brought under their arms, so that the mushrooms shall not notice; when their father found one he would cover it quickly with his hat, as though it were a butterfly. The little children—and now his grandchildren—used to believe what he said, while the bigger ones smiled at his credulity; *even Anna did this, when he told her to put fresh flowers every day at the shrine of the Virgin which was near the wood, so that it might help them in their search* [emphasis added].[96]

That such a very Catholic activity—in this case, more a superstitious than a devotional act—should have occurred at all, much less that it should have been a regular custom, is extraordinary. This was, after all, a family in which even the lighting of candles to mark the Jewish Sabbath was forbidden by Freud, to his wife's displeasure, because Freud said he was opposed to all religious superstition!

While on the subject of family outings, we should mention a report of Martin Freud's about the family summers at Koeningsee. Here occasionally Freud would put his writing aside and take the family on an excursion. The place he liked best "was the small peninsula of St. Bartholomae . . . a truly lovely spot . . . given humanity by a very old inn and an equally old, if not older, chapel or church." Here, his son continues, "The place had the happiest effect on him, allowing him to abandon his usual reserve and even to become a little playful."[97] They all liked especially to pick strawberries in the grove behind the church. Again, we find a positive attraction to an environment with a mild but marked religious atmosphere.

Mysticism, Music, and the Acropolis

In 1926 Freud struck up a correspondence with the French novelist Romain Rolland, a writer with whom Freud identified. Rolland was one of Freud's many secondary alter-egos.[98] In his first letter to Rolland (whom he had admired for some time), Freud used extremely curious and in many ways obviously Christian language. (Rolland, like Franz Brentano, was an ex-Roman Catholic, one of his better-known books being *The Revolt of the Angels*.)

Unforgettable man, to have soared to such heights of humanity through so much hardship and suffering! I have revered you as an artist and apostle of love for mankind many years before I saw you.[99]

Three years later, in another letter, the topic of mysticism having apparently arisen, Freud responded by saying:

How remote from me are the worlds in which you move! To me mysticism is just as closed a book as music. I cannot imagine reading all the literature which, according to your letter, you have studied. And yet it is easier for you than for us to read the human soul![100]

We do not have the letter from Rolland, but nevertheless, from Freud's response, a few assumptions seem safe. It should be noted that in this letter Freud coupled mysticism to music, thus reinforcing the earlier proposal that Freud's rejection of music was rooted in his first experience of music in church with his "Anna." Music always threatened to bring back his Moravian childhood of religious love and trust, followed by the anxiety and depression of being abandoned. And, of course, there would have been erotic associations to music triggered by his nanny as well. Such powerful emotions could best be controlled by avoiding music as much as possible. Freud said that he found mysticism (like all religious experience) foreign, but at least in this instance he was far from expressing hostility to it. Indeed, he implied that those who do know it can more easily "read the soul" than could he and his fellow psychoanalysts. In a later letter to Rolland (January 1930), Freud reverted to his standard (public) attitude by arguing that mystical experience is "highly valuable for an embryology of the soul when correctly interpreted, but worthless for orientation in the alien, external world."[101] Yet even after this return to form, he backed off in the next and final paragraph, with these rather unexpected words: "Just one more thing: I am not an out-and-out skeptic. Of one thing I am absolutely positive: there are certain things we cannot know now."[102]

The topic of mystical experience also came up in a letter written to Romain Rolland in 1936. The letter (really a short article) was composed in honor of Rolland's 70th birthday and was titled *A Disturbance of Memory on the Acropolis*.[103] The letter provided a description and explanation of a peculiar experience that Freud had in 1904, when for the first (and only) time he visited the Acropolis in Athens. (The memory of the visit had kept recurring, and he became determined to analyze it.) For a variety of reasons, the trip to Athens had been decided upon suddenly, and thus with little advanced psychological preparation Freud found himself on the Acropolis. As he cast his eyes around at the landscape, he became aware of his strange psychological state. (Note the evidence in this quote that this state involved a splitting of his consciousness.)

[A] remarkable thought suddenly entered my mind: "So all this really *does* exist, just as we learnt at school!" To describe the situation more accurately, the *person who gave expression to the remark was divided, far more sharply than was usually observable, from another person* [emphasis added] who took cognizance of the remark; and both were astonished, though not by the same thing. The first behaved as though he were obliged, under the impact of an unequivocal observation, to believe in something the reality of which had hitherto seemed doubtful. . . . "So it really *does* exist . . ." The second person, on the other hand, was justifiably astonished, because he had been unaware that the real existence of Athens, the Acropolis, and the landscape around it had ever been objects of doubt. What he had expected was rather some expression of delight or admiration.[104]

Freud emphasized that part of him thought it was all "too good to be true," that the visit was like "when a girl learns that the man whom she secretly loved has asked her parents for permission to marry her."[105] In short, Freud described it as though something he had thought was an illusion had come true.

Freud also described the experience as one of not quite believing that what he saw was real—an experience of "derealization." He went on to characterize derealization as a process of splitting that defends the ego by denying reality. Then Freud provided an interesting historical example of this process. When the Moorish King Boabdil received news that his city Alhama (Alhambra) had fallen, he would not "let it be true."[106] This defense was demonstrated by his killing the messenger and burning the letters. The example is most interesting, because the historical event in question occurred when Boabdil received word that his city had fallen to Spanish Catholics—an event he knew also meant the complete triumph of Catholicism in Spain. Thus, this was another expression of Freud's Hannibal–Scipio complex. From this example, we can interpret Freud's rejection of Catholicism as requiring the psychological defense of derealization, analogous to that of the Moorish king. Freud went on to claim that derealization depends on earlier memories and painful experiences that have probably fallen victim to repression. Although some of Freud's repressed memories would have gone back to Freiberg, others would have involved Freud's Philippson Bible days, for that Bible had a picture of the Acropolis and a section on Athens.[107]

Continuing his discussion, Freud referred to his schooldays, in which he thought the "limitations and poverty" of his condition would preclude travel to such a remarkable and distant place as Athens.[108] His early longing for travel, rooted in dissatisfaction with father, home, and family, was unexpectedly satisfied. It was too good—too much of a wish—to have been fulfilled. He commented that to have reached the Acropolis meant that he really had gone a long way. Freud concluded this point with the following:

So, too, if I may compare such a small event with a greater one, Napoleon, during his coronation as Emperor in Notre Dame, turned to one of his brothers and remarked: What would Monsieur notre Père have said to this, if he could have been here today?[109]

Here was Freud, the intellectual "conquistador," comparing himself to Napoleon being crowned in Notre Dame (and Notre Dame, of course, had religious and "nana" associations for him, e.g., Slochower). He used such a scene to explain his mystical feeling on the Acropolis—feelings tinged with guilt over going further than his father.

Bettelheim (1982) has identified still more of the religious significance in Freud's Acropolis experience. It is Bettelheim's thesis that the English translations of Freud's German commonly distort the original, rich, personal quality of his words by rendering them into abstract, technical, or implicitly scientific English. As an example of this tendency, Bettelheim notes what is missing when the word *heimsucht* is translated into English as "visited." That is, Freud wrote that he was frequently "visited" by the memory of his experience on the Acropolis. However, Bettelheim points out that the word translated as "visited," *heimsucht*, "is fraught with special meaning, because in Catholic Vienna the *Maria Heimsuchung* was (and still is) an important religious holiday, celebrating the visit of the Virgin Mary to Elizabeth, an event depicted in many famous paintings and sculptures with which Freud had become well acquainted . . ." Freud, in referring to his recurring memory, "uses a word that alludes to a profoundly revealing event, the Visitation."[110]

Again, we find evidence of the unconscious Catholic and Marian nature of Freud's mentality.[111]

Pater (Father) Schmidt and the Catholic Church

Near the end of his life, Freud referred a number of times in his correspondence to a certain "Pater Schmidt." The most striking reference was in a letter to Jones in June 1936:

That my chief enemy P. Schmidt has just been given the Austrian Award of Honor for Art and Science for his pious lies in ethnology I claim as *my* credit. Evidently he had to be consoled for Providence having let me reach the age of eighty. Fate has its own ways of making one altruistic. When my Master Ernst Brücke received this award I became aware of a wish that I myself might sometime attain it. Today I contentedly resign myself to having indirectly helped someone else to do so.[112]

From Freud's remarks, I originally assumed that this Schmidt must have been some local Catholic priest of minor intellectual significance who had made a small reputation, perhaps by criticizing Freudian theory. This assumption was reinforced further when I read Jones, and also Schur, who denigrates Schmidt "as a monk with an interest in ethnology."[113]

By chance, I stumbled across a reference to Schmidt in another context and soon discovered that the facts are very different. Father Wilhelm Schmidt (1868-1954), besides being, like Freud, a professor at the University of Vienna, was a scientist of world renown. Historically, he was one of the great ethnologists (cultural anthropologists), and a great linguist of primitive cultures; indeed, he was a founding father of both disciplines.[114] (Among his other accomplishments, he founded the international institute Anthropos and the world-renowned journal *Anthropos*.[115]) His first love was linguistics, and perhaps his greatest contribution was in the field of comparative language.[116] Very early he immersed himself in the languages of Australia and the South Seas, and his studies of these tongues, primarily published between 1900 and 1920, led him to discover the inner connections between the languages of the peoples in Southeast Asia and those of the South Seas. A biographer has described his contribution:

This, the discovery of a genius, is one of the major accomplishments in the field of linguistics, which ranks in importance with the proof of the relationship among all of the Indo-European languages. . . . [T]he language group proposed by Father Schmidt as the "austric linguistic stock" embraces almost two-thirds of the inhabited area of the earth."[117]

He continued publishing important articles on languages of the South Seas until shortly before his death. In Schmidt's over 600 publications, references to topics close to those of concern to Freud appear to be very uncommon.[118]

Schmidt's other contribution, his research on the nature of primitive religion, did lead him occasionally to cross swords with Freud. But for Freud to call him his "chief enemy" was certainly a curious overstatement, and the notion that Schmidt needed to be consoled for Freud's reaching 80 is ludicrous.

Schmidt's greatest work *Der Ursprung der Gottesidee* (*The Origin of the Idea of God*), consists of 12 volumes; the first volume came out in 1912, and the last was published after his death.[119] This massive work is a complete encyclopedia of the religious and ethical beliefs of the world's primitive societies. In addition, Schmidt published shorter books on the nature of primitive religions (some of which came out in English—e.g., the still very interesting *The High Gods in North America*[120]). Schmidt was especially interested in and respectful of the most primitive cultures: for instance, the Semang, the Central African Pygmies, the Bushmen, the Feugians, and the most primitive Indians of North America.[121] His major and well-documented point was that most (sometimes Schmidt argued *all*) of these primitives had a simple monotheism with a concept of a personal god, and that this provided the foundation of their morality.[122] These findings led Schmidt to a direct, strong rebuttal on empirical grounds of Freud's theory of the totemic origin of religion. That is, none of these primitive cultures had yet realized anything as advanced as totemism; yet they had religion, and it was a kind of simple monotheism. Schmidt also made it clear that many other cultures, much more advanced than the most primitive, never passed through a stage of totemism at all.[123] Hence their religion as well could not be accounted for by any totemic theory, much less by Freud's particular totemic theory. No wonder Freud didn't care for Father Schmidt![124]

But the story of Pater Schmidt has another side as well. A year or so before the letter to Jones cited above, in October 1934, Freud reported that after a few issues the publication of the *Italian Review of Psychoanalysis* was stopped. The ban was "said to come straight from the Vatican," as a consequence of Father Schmidt's intervention.[125] I have been unable to verify this conjecture, which Jones reports as a fact.[126] It seems unlikely, but if it was true, Freud had grounds for genuine anger with Schmidt.

In order to circumvent the ban, the editor had recourse to Mussolini, who promised to rescind the ban.[127] However, "even his authority was not great enough for the purpose," according to Jones.[128] Freud himself certainly had some pro-Mussolini sentiments; such sentiments were fed by the fact that Mussolini was an intense enemy of the Catholic Church and attacked it persistently. As late as March 1937, Freud could refer to Mussolini as having been a protector.[129] Il Duce was a political heir to Garibaldi, and he can be seen as another Hannibal figure for Freud. In addition, Freud had a patient whose father was a close friend of Mussolini.[130] At the father's request, Freud sent the Fascist leader a copy of his book *Why War?*, inscribed "From an old man who greets in the Ruler the Hero of Culture."[131]

Meanwhile, back in Vienna, the political situation continued to get worse. Freud said he was worried about offending Catholic authority in Austria with his forthcoming *Moses and Monotheism*,[132] although in all the years Freud lived in Vienna, no official complaint or harassment was ever reported. (The ban in Italy, if Catholic in origin, was probably due to the small number of Catholic families that controlled much of publishing. Some influential Church official might only have had to make a critical comment to a member of his publishing family, and "somehow" the journal would not get published.[133]) Certainly, for Freud to have appealed for help from a Fascist leader has a certain irony to it. After all, in 1936, Mussolini signed a pact with Hitler.[134]

Freud may have said he did not wish to offend the Church in Austria, but there is no evidence that he ever deviated from writing and publishing exactly what he wished. Certain deep parts of Freud (his Oedipal and Anti-Christ psychology) by this time were bitterly hostile to Catholicism—much more so than to Hitler and the Nazis. In 1937, Freud remarked to a visitor, "The Nazis? I'm not afraid of them. Help me rather to combat my true enemy . . . Religion, the Roman Catholic Church."[135] (This was Freud's first expression of such intense hatred of Catholicism; however, we have seen enough evidence of this attitude to expect other expressions of this kind to turn up as more of his correspondence becomes available.)

His occasionally expressed hatred of the Catholic Church contrasted with his understanding that the Church was the only power that stood between the Nazi's and control of Austria. As he said in January 1935, "only this Catholicism protects us against Naziism."[136]

Perhaps Freud was aware that in the same year, 1935, only two years after Hitler came to power in Germany, Pater Schmidt published the second edition of his *Rasse und Volk (Race and People)*, one of the first strong attacks on the Nazi doctrine of race from a scientific point of view.[137] But books never stopped Hitler. The situation got worse until, in February 1938, Freud remarked, "Will it be possible to find safety in the shelter of the Catholic Church?"[138] There was no shelter anywhere, however. In March, Hitler and his forces came in and took over Austria. Before the Nazis were able to control things completely, Freud and his immediate family, with active help from friends, were able to leave very hurriedly; Freud got out on June 3.[139]

There was no shelter for Freud's adversary either: "In June 1938, literally at the last hour, Father Schmidt escaped arrest by the Nazi police and was accorded a friendly reception in Switzerland as a refugee."[140]

Last Letters and *Moses and Monotheism*: 1925-1939

In Freud's final correspondence, we still find the recurrence of the by now familiar theme of Pentecost. For example, he quoted from Goethe—"the pleasant feast of Whitsuntide"—in one of his letters to the secular Jewish writer Arnold Zweig[141]; he referred to Pentecost in a letter to Max Eitingon, who was also Jewish.[142] There were no references to this distinctly Christian feast in any of the letters sent back to Freud by his corresponders.

As for Easter, it appeared in only one instance in the last years—at least in the correspondence currently available. Jones reports on a letter from Freud to Suzanne Bernfeld on April 12, 1936, in which Freud wrote, "Easter Sunday signifies to me the fiftieth anniversary of taking up my medical practice."[143] Jones notes that it was suggested (by persons unreferenced) that Easter had an emotional significance dating from the Catholic nanny, but he thinks that for Freud to have begun work on such a day would seem "like an act of defiance."[144] Of course, Jones provides no evidence to show that Freud *was* disturbed by Easter, or felt "defiant." Once again, Jones's anxiety over this devout old nanny has blinded him to a key to the understanding of his subject. After all, Easter in this instance (as elsewhere) means rebirth, a new beginning.

During the last decade or so of his life (from 1929 to 1939), Freud, like Jews everywhere, was made more and more painfully aware of the rising tide of anti-Semitism. He responded to it both by affirming his identity as a Jew and by conducting a variety of analyses of anti-Semitism and anti-Semites. But the affirmation of his Jewishness almost always took a rather peculiar form, especially as concerns Judaism as a religion. For example, in a letter to the members of the B'nai B'rith Lodge on May 6, 1926, Freud wrote as follows in a letter laced with ambivalence:

That you are Jews could only be welcome to me, for I was myself a Jew, and it has always appeared to me not only undignified but outright foolish to deny it. What tied me to Jewry was—I have to admit it—not the faith, not even the national pride, for I was always an unbeliever. . . . But there remained enough to make the attraction of Judaism and the Jews irresistible [sic], many dark emotional powers all the stronger the less they could be expressed in words, as well as the clear consciousness of an inner identity, the familiarity of the same psychological structure. And before long there followed the realization that it was only to my Jewish nature that I owed the two qualities that have become indispensable to me throughout my difficult life. Because I was a Jew I found myself free of many prejudices which restrict others in the use of the intellect: as a Jew I was prepared to be in the opposition and to renounce agreement with the "compact majority."

So I became one of you, took part in your humanitarian and national interests.
. . .[145]

Aside from Freud's clear lack of any religious allegiance to Judaism, there was in Freud's whole definition of himself as a Jew a distancing: For example, he used past tenses ("I was," "I became," etc.). He never affirmed, "I *am* a Jew."

This strange distancing was also present in a letter written four days later to Marie Bonaparte, when he noted that "the Jews . . . have celebrated me like a national hero, although my service to the Jewish cause is confined to the single point that I have never denied my Jewishness."[146] Why the references, in both of these letters, to the fact that he never renounced his Judaism (it was "foolish to deny it"), unless Freud had been tempted to do precisely that?

During this period, Freud often remained critical of Christianity, as when he commented to Pfister: "My judgment of human nature, above all of the Christian–Aryan variety, has little reason to change."[147] And yet there were pro-Christian comments as well, such as his remarks about the Church protecting him from the Nazis and his description of Christianity in *Moses and Monotheism* (discussed below).

Pentecost also came up one last time. It was in the late spring of 1938; Freud and his family had just escaped from Austria after the National Socialist takeover. He wrote to Max Eitingon on June 6:

[W]e didn't all leave at the same time. Dorothy was the first, Minna on May 5, Martin on the 14th, Mathilde and Robert on the 24th, ourselves incidentally not until the Saturday before Pentecost, June 3.[148]

This last train trip would have redintegrated (in fact, would have been a "reincarnation" of) that traumatic childhood train ride almost 80 years earlier, when at or shortly after Pentecost he had left his home in Freiberg—the ride when he thought about the souls burning in Hell. Here, at the same time of year, he was for the second time leaving his home in a dramatic train trip; this time, however, his Anna (his daughter) went with him.

Both the themes of demonic possession and of the Anti-Christ came up one final time in these last years. Jones mentions that the last book Freud was able to read in the summer of 1939 was Balzac's *La Peau de Chagrin* (*The Skin of Chagrin*).[149] This early story by Balzac features a young man, an orphaned marquis, who is poor and struggling for success. He desires to write a great work, a "theory of the will," which he knows will be involved with hypnotism and the occult. Overwhelmed by the magnitude of the task, he believes he won't be able to succeed and thus considers suicide. While contemplating suicide, he meets a strange character, a sorcerer (shades of Faust!). The sorcerer gives the young man a skin (of a wild ass) that has the power to satisfy all wishes; however, each time the skin is used it shrinks, as does the length of the life of the person using the skin. The marquis very quickly becomes rich and successful, as he is unable to resist using the skin often—and he dies one year later. Although there are no significant Christian elements in the story, apparently the theme of some kind of pact with a Devil-figure still fascinates Freud even in his last weeks, when his life was shrinking like the skin in the novel.[150]

During Freud's last 10-12 years, he had a rather extensive correspondence with Arnold Zweig, as mentioned above. This writer and intellectual knew Freud and his thought rather well by the time when, in 1930, he wrote Freud that "analysis has reversed all values, it has conquered Christianity, disclosed the Antichrist, and liberated the spirit of resurgent life from the ascetic ideal."[151] At least part of Freud apparently accepted Zweig's interpretation; he certainly is not on record as rejecting it, something he presumably would have done if he had felt Zweig's remarks were seriously off the mark. Roazen, to whose book I owe the preceding observation, also points out that Freud specifically criticized Christianity because for him "not all men are worthy of love."[152]

It was, however, in Freud's last major (and very controversial) work, *Moses and Monotheism* (1939), that he produced some of his most unequivocally pro-Christian remarks. The main thesis of the book was that Moses was not a Jew but an Egyptian. Not only was Moses not a Jew, but, according to Freud, the Jews murdered Moses. Now Freud knew very well that this claim would be deeply disturbing to religious Jews: "[I]t is only Jewry and not Christianity which has reason to be offended by its conclusions."[153] This interpretation of Moses constituted, therefore, an attack on the Jewish religion.[154] We are, of course, setting aside the whole issue of whether Freud was correct in his views. The best authorities on the subject, then as now, have generally agreed that the objective evidence for Freud's position is rather weak and at times downright flimsy. Freud himself initially called this book a "novel."[155] At any rate, what we are interested in here is Freud's psychology.

One of the interesting pro-Christian aspects of *Moses and Monotheism* is Freud's interpretation of anti-Semitism. It might be expected that this elderly Jew—supposedly a total skeptic, thrown out of his homeland during an unprecedented period of hatred expressed against the Jews, dying painfully of cancer—would express bitter criticism of the "Christian" culture that had produced the monstrous phenomenon of Naziism. On the contrary, Freud interpreted anti-Semitism as the expression of a culture that has never really been Christianized:

[W]e must not forget that all those peoples who excel today in their hatred of Jews became Christians only in late historic times, often driven to it by bloody coercion. It might be said that they are all "misbaptized." They have been left, under a thin veneer of Christianity, what their ancestors were, who worshipped a barbarous polytheism. They have not got over the grudge against the new religion which was imposed on them; but they have displaced the grudge on the source from which Christianity reached them. The fact that the Gospels tell a story which is set among Jews, and in fact deals only with Jews, has made this displacement easy for them. Their hatred of Jews is at bottom a hatred of Christians, and we need not be surprised that in the German National Socialist revolution this intimate relation between the two monotheistic religions finds such a clear expression in the hostile treatment of both of them.[156]

Freud's writing here was uncannily like that of the great Catholic philosopher Jacques Maritain, who was writing on the same subject at the same time. In his 1939 book *A Christian Looks at the Jewish Question*, Maritain wrote that "hatred of the Jews and hatred of Christians spring from a common source."[157] Maritain's book can still be read with much profit,[158] for it has remained fresh and amazingly insightful. But the interesting point is that Freud said on the "Jewish question" exactly what Maritain said: It is as if he were speaking, like Maritain, from within the logic of the Christian position, and not as a Jewish "outsider."

Throughout *Moses and Monotheism*, for all its exasperating hypotheses and for all its fiction-like characters, Freud's treatment of Christianity was often sympathetic.[159] And these were Freud's provocative closing words:

Only a portion of the Jewish people accepted the new doctrine [Christianity]. Those who refused to are still called Jews today. . . . They were obliged to hear the new religious community . . . reproach them with having murdered God. In full, this reproach would run as follows: "They will not accept it as true that they murdered God, whereas we admit it and have been cleansed of that guilt." . . . A special enquiry would be called for to discover why it has been impossible for the Jews to join in this forward step. . . .[160]

That his analysis led him to the conclusion that Christianity constituted an advance over Judaism is hardly what one would have expected, given Freud's personal situation, the historical context, and the standard version of Freud's beliefs.[161]

Conclusion

It is now time to put particular examples of evidence for this book's thesis aside, and reflect on the general structure of what has been presented in the preceding chapters. First, I would like to officially propose the hypothesis—or, in formal, psychoanalytic terms, a "construction"—that Freud's relation to Christianity was one of intense, often unconscious ambivalence. Now this term "construction," initially introduced by Freud in 1937,[162] refers to a hypothesis or proposition about a person's behavior that attempts to capture both the broad structure and many of the details of a person's past and present.[163] The successful construction is based on data that increasingly demand a particular hypothesis.

Freud's own elucidation of a construction is extremely relevant to the one under consideration—namely, that Freud's intense ambivalence about religion involved a strong pro-Christian component. Early in his discussion of the nature of a construction, Freud made the important point that a patient's "No" is "not as a rule enough to make us abandon an interpretation as incorrect."[164] In turn, I do not accept Freud's proposed, "No, I have no attraction to Christianity with its 'lie of salvation.'"[165] Indeed, with respect to Freud and Christianity, the old saw usually applied to diplomats and politicians appears to be quite applicable: "Nothing is officially confirmed until officially denied." Freud himself encouraged us to put aside his own "No" when he wrote about the person being analyzed that he must be brought "to recollect certain experiences and the emotions called up by them which he has at the moment forgotten. We know that his present symptoms and inhibitions are the consequences of repressions of this kind. . . ."[166] A construction, which Freud claimed gives "a picture of the patient's forgotten years,"[167] is based on

All kinds of things. He [the patient] gives us fragments of memories in his dreams . . . he produces ideas, if he gives himself up to "free associations," in which we can discover allusions to the repressed experiences and derivatives of the suppressed affective impulses, as well as the reactions against them.[168]

Let us look back over this quotation and apply the definitions provided by Freud the great psychoanalyst to the dreams and remarks of Freud the neurotic and Freud the ambivalent:

- "All kinds of things. He gives us fragments of memories in his dreams . . .": "I am at last in Rome . . . it consists of a little stream of dark water"; "gave them to a father who was not myself"; etc., etc.
- ". . . he produces ideas, if he gives himself up to 'free associations' . . .": "the promised land from afar"; "*via dolorosa*"; Winckelmann; etc., etc.
- ". . . in which we can discover allusions to the repressed experiences . . .": "I was crying my heart out"; "he had two mothers"; "Next Easter in Rome"; etc., etc.
- ". . . and derivatives of the suppressed affective impulses . . .": "Pentecost . . . memories . . . precious, lovely . . . some bitter"; "I feel strengthened and relieved by the air and impressions of this divine town"; "see how the old liking breaks through"; "I went away with a full heart"; "Roman women are, strange to say, even beautiful when they are ugly, but not many of them are that"; etc., etc.

• ". . . as well as the reactions against them": "the lie of salvation"; "I am the Devil"; "I am a completely godless Jew"; etc.

A final piece of evidence for our construction about Freud comes in the "hints of repetitions of the affects found in actions . . . some important [e.g., "I became a constant pilgrim," flowers for the Virgin Mary], and some trivial ["I shall be closer to you geographically during the Pentecost weekend]."[169]

It is curious that in his ambivalence Freud strongly resembled his patient the Wolf-Man. In discussing this case, Freud wrote, "The two opposing currents of feeling which were to rule the whole of his later life, met here in the ambivalent struggle over the question of religion."[170] Or, as Freud put it somewhat differently in a letter to Jung: "My paper on Taboo [Totem and Taboo] is coming along slowly. The conclusion has long been known to me. The source of taboo and hence also of conscience is ambivalence."[171] Freud, so obviously driven to debunk, expose, and denigrate the sacred, was equally—and in his unconscious perhaps more than equally—drawn to religion. Hence, in relation to Christian "taboos," he gave "simultaneous expression to both currents."[172]

Freud's ambivalence, as we have seen, had a repetitive (indeed, an obsessive) quality. This obsessiveness is an important part of the construction being proposed. Freud's literary preferences, from Faust to La Peau de Chagrin, were obsessive in their preoccupation with religion and demonic themes. His case histories (such as that of the Wolf-Man) and his essays (such as the ones on Leonardo, Hoffman's "Sand-Man," and Haitzmann) were also obsessive, since he returned over and over to the same set of religious issues and continually reworked them. Obsessiveness was expressed in behavioral terms by his repeated visits to Rome. Freud himself clearly connected obsessiveness with involvement in religion, thus confirming this part of our construction about him: "The predilection felt by obsessional neurotics for uncertainty and doubt leads them to turn their thoughts by preference to those subjects upon which all mankind are uncertain and upon which knowledge and judgments must necessarily remain open to doubt."[173] And we are instructed by Freud in his self-diagnosis contained in a letter to Jung: ". . . I must claim for myself the class 'obsessive'. . . ."[174] Thus it was no accident that Freud, who described himself as an obsessive, also interpreted religion, in one of his major critiques, as a "universal obsessional neurosis."[175] Indeed, whatever the truth about religion may be, one thing is certain: Freud himself had a life-long and neurotic obsession about religion.

One final interpretation of Freud's relationship with religion strongly suggests itself. There was such an overwhelmingly personal quality in Freud's involvement with religion that one may be compelled to understand his critical interpretations of it as being direct expressions of his own psychology. The nature of Freud's relation to religion most emphatically does not suggest that his theories on this subject were cool descriptions of what he just happened to observe in the lives of his patients.

Also extremely common in Freud's reactions to religion was that most widespread, interesting, and probably most powerful of neurotic defenses (and one of Freud's great discoveries): repression. Repression can so frequently be seen in Freud with respect to religion (as shown in many of the preceding pages—e.g., in the memory slips) that I hope that the claim that he defended himself by using this psychological mechanism is established beyond doubt.

There is, however, one particular example of a common consequence of repression not previously discussed—namely, displacement—that will help us to bring this retrospective view of Freud into a final focus. Displacement involves the shift of energy from an original desired object to another object often similar or related to the original. The shift is required because of the anxiety associated with the original goal, an anxiety having its roots in a repressed experience. In spite of the shift, the true source and aim of the first desire remain the same; only what it is directed at has been changed.

Another way of describing this is to remind ourselves that Freud was one of the greatest theorists of metonymy—of the motivations behind and psychological processes involved in shifts in meanings of words and actions. But what was Freud's whole attitude toward Rome if not revelatory of a metonymic process of great importance to his life? To "go to Rome" means to become a Catholic, or to fulfill one's life as a Catholic by going to visit the Seat of St. Peter. But Freud couldn't stand consciously to think about wanting to become a Christian, for the very idea was unacceptable, most especially after his self-analysis and subsequent success. This desire was thus transformed (displaced) into another desire that *was* possible to realize: to go to the *city* of Rome, to visit Rome. Yet the remnants of the original, repressed desire were made evident in many details; his desire to go to Rome was repetitive. He wanted to go to Rome on Easter—not at any old time, but at the quintessentially Christian season. He referred to his visits as making him into a pilgrim. While in Rome, he spent much of his time in Christian edifices admiring Christian art. He spoke of Rome with great fondness (indeed, as this "divine town"); he said he never felt himself to be a stranger in Rome; he told of its constant capacity to renew his zest for life. Even when not in Rome, Freud found himself drawn to churches. He was always "going to church": to the wonderful cathedral and chapel-like museum in Dresden; to Notre Dame de Paris, which he haunted; to the peninsula of St. Bartholomae, with its old church; to the shrine of the Virgin on the way to the mushroom hunt; to all the churches and chapels of his lovely Italy.

Chapter Seven

Epilogue: A Biographical Critique of Freud's Atheism

IN SPITE OF Freud's repeated expressions of attraction to Christianity, the fact remains, of course, that he did not convert or assimilate. Instead, after the crisis period of self-analysis (roughly 1895 to 1900), Freud emerged as a founder of modern psychology and as one of history's greatest critics of religion. As we have seen, the underlying pro-Christian motivation never left him, but it appears to have dropped off, for there is less significant material relating to Christianity from the last three decades of his life than from any earlier period of the same duration.

Certainly one of the more important reasons behind the reduction of Freud's pro-Christian (or pro-assimilation) feelings was the decline in the intensity of his unsatisfied ambition: That is, he was increasingly acknowledged throughout the world as a major thinker, and this recognition appears to have slaked the fires of this need. I am also inclined to think that part of Freud's somewhat greater peace of mind—and hence his reduced attraction to assimilation—came from his finally finding the field of intellectual life that was, in fact, most natural to him: psychology. In discovering that he was a psychologist and a philosopher of culture, not a natural or biological scientist, Freud was freed of some of the sense of failure and frustration that had troubled him for so long, and that would have remained with him had he remained oriented toward scientific medicine as the field in which he must excel.

Another significant factor was that his self-analysis brought to consciousness the buried material about his nanny. This bringing to the surface of previously unconscious material could easily have reduced the extent of Freud's unconscious attraction to his nanny—and to Catholic elements associated with her.

A fourth important factor would have had to do with the changing political climate. Starting at about the same time Freud turned from medical science to psychology (i.e., from the 1880s on), there was an increase in anti-Semitism in Austria. By 1895–1897, the election of Karl Lueger as the mayor of Vienna signaled the end of much of the old liberal political system—and the end of the old Catholic liberalism, with its tolerant, positive support for Jewish assimilation.[1] Hostility to the Jews had grown so strong that the liberal political climate favoring assimilation was clearly over; this political and social environment brought out Freud's tough, obdurate ethnic (though not religious) Jewish resistance. Furthermore, the fact that Freud had moved out of the university world (where Gentiles and assimilated Jews like Gomperz dominated)—first into the essentially Jewish world of private practice (with primarily well-to-do Jewish patients), and then in time into the very Jewish world of psychoanalysis—all meant that assimilation became increasingly irrelevant. In fact, for Freud and many others, assimilation became repugnant as Jews responded to anti-Semitism by increasing their identification with their Jewishness and emphasizing Jewish intellectual and moral superiority.[2]

As a result, Freud's attacks on religion, most of which came in this last period, can be viewed not only as motivated by his political sympathies with the old liberal Austrian program of secularism, but also as a way of fighting anti-Semitism, a great deal of which was associated with Catholic political parties. Thus, there is support for the contention of Thomas Szasz that "One of Freud's most powerful motives in life was the desire to inflict vengeance on Christianity for its traditional anti-Semitism."[3]

In a more psychological vein, Freud's critiques of religion are interpretable as reactions (even "reaction formations") against his earlier and persistent temptations to assimilate, as well as against his remaining unconscious motives. His "loathing" for such Jews as Adler, and for his student Tausk, both of whom assimilated by becoming Christians, can be seen in this light.[4]

However, from the previous chapters, we have seen that political and social motives were not the real forces that drove Freud, especially with respect to religious issues. It is now, finally, time to reflect on this knowledge of Freud's personal relationship to religion, in order to clarify how it sheds a new light on his critique of religious belief. We need to begin by briefly reviewing the major features of Freud's anti-religious position.

Religion as Illusion

Freud's most powerful and influential attack on religion came in 1927, in his work *The Future of an Illusion*. The illusion was, of course, religion, and Freud's conclusion was that it didn't have any future. The essay dealt with three major subjects, religion, science, and culture; we are concerned here almost entirely with his treatment of religion.

First, a few comments on what Freud was *not* writing about are in order. The findings and logic of psychoanalysis were not relevant to his discussion of religion here. He explicitly said in a letter to Oskar Pfister: "Let us be quite clear on the point that *the views expressed in my book* [*The Future of an Illusion*] *form no part of analytic theory* [emphasis added]. They are my personal views, which coincide with those of many non-analysts and pre-analysts, but there are certainly many excellent analysts who do not share them."[5] This was, however, Freud's private message to Pfister; the public impression given by *The Future of an Illusion* then, as now, is that psychoanalysis somehow supports the atheistic thesis.

The Future of an Illusion is not a book in which theology is debated and rationally evaluated. Freud again made this clear: "To assess the truth-value of religious doctrines does not lie in the scope of the present enquiry."[6] Instead, Freud's concern was with a general psychological interpretation of the motives or wishes that lie behind religious beliefs. Given these two important qualifications, what did Freud say about the underlying psychology of religion?

Freud claimed that religious ideas derive from our desires, that they are "born from man's need to make his helplessness tolerable and built up from the material of memories of the helplessness of his own childhood and the childhood of the human race."[7] Religion thus protects us from our greatest anxieties: from the fear of natural forces, from the threat of injury or injustice inflicted by other men, from the terror of death. Religion provides a higher purpose in life and makes us feel that all is well. In the end, we believe that justice triumphs, because in life after death all evil is punished and good rewarded. The sufferings of this life are thus compensated for. Freud claimed that these ideas are convenient illusions, that these religious "truths" just happen to be exactly what we would *want* there to be.[8] These beliefs,

which are given out as teachings, are not precipitates of experience or end-results of thinking: they are illusions, fulfillments of the oldest, strongest and most urgent wishes of mankind. The secret of their strength lies in the strength of those wishes. As we already know, the terrifying impression of helplessness in childhood aroused the need for protection—protection through love. . . .[9]

Freud went on to note, however, that an illusion is not necessarily an error. It is conceivable that an illusion might be true; it is possible that a girl who dreams of a handsome prince may actually meet one, get married, and live happily ever after. (For Freud, we may recall, the Acropolis *did* turn out to exist!) But as Freud saw it, *any* idea or belief is an illusion "when a wish-fulfillment is a prominent factor in its motiva-tion."[10]

A fact that is not widely appreciated today is that the central point of Freud's analysis—namely, that religion is a projection of human needs, and thus an illusion—was widely known decades before Freud's essay. Ludwig Feuerbach, in his historic attack on Christianity, *The Essence of Christianity*,[11] first expressed the projection theory in its modern form. Feuerbach's interpretation had become an intellectual commonplace, especially in German cultural circles. For example, both Karl Marx and Friedrich Engels were familiar with Feuerbach's ideas and spent some time expanding (and refining on) his position, about which they were clearly enthusiastic.[12] Freud in his late teens already mentioned having read Feuerbach on this issue.[13] Even more interesting is that Freud's personal library contained Feuerbach's book expounding this view. The copy in his library had a 1923 copyright date, just a few years before *The Future of an Illusion* came out.[14] It is plausible that Freud reread it at that time to refresh his memory on Feuerbach. Among Feuerbach's more pertinent remarks are these:

Man projects his nature into the world outside of himself before he finds it in himself. In the beginning, his own nature confronts him as being distinct from himself. Religion is the child-like condition of humanity. . . . Hence the historical progress of religion consists of this: that which during an earlier stage of religion was regarded as something objective is now recognized as something subjective, so that which was formerly viewed and worshipped as God is now recognized as something human.[15]

Every bit as "Freudian" are such comments as "God is . . . a personification of man's moral conscience."[16] And as for wish-fulfillment, Feuerbach wrote: "What man misses—whether this be an articulate and therefore conscious, *or an unconscious* [emphasis added], need—that is his God."[17]

Freud's Lack of Experience with Religious Patients

In view of the essentially derivative character of Freud's thesis in *The Future of an Illusion*, how is one to account for the widespread power and influence that this essay had (and still has)? The effectiveness of the work has no doubt derived to some degree from Freud's consummate style, and from his ability to weave together in an interesting fashion his understanding of science with his discussion of the origin of culture and his critique of religion. Moreover, Feuerbach had been to a degree forgotten by this time, and his writings were also generally longer and less elegantly expressed than Freud's. Finally, by 1927 (when Freud's work appeared), there was a much larger audience of unbelievers eager to hear such a message. But certainly one of the greatest reasons for this essay's impact was that it was written by a famous psychologist. That is, by implication, readers have understood that they are reading a man who time after time observed the unconscious needs behind the religious beliefs of his patients. It is implied that somehow Freud was an expert in the psychology of religion not only because he was an expert in psychology (which he was), but because he was an expert in religion, and even more, an expert on the psychology of believers. But here the situation was not what most readers have assumed, for Freud's contacts with religion when he was an adult and a practicing psychoanalyst were few, and limited in the extreme.

For example, not one of Freud's major published cases dealt with a patient who was a believing Christian or Jew. The only case of Freud's, besides the Wolf-Man case, in which I could find any significant reference to the Christianity of the patient was a minor reference to one of his very early patients, reported in his book with Breuer, *Studies on Hysteria* (1893–1895). Here Freud referred to his attempts to relieve the anxiety attacks of an elderly woman who had become extremely religious. Freud commented that she "always received me as if I were the Devil, she was always armed with a small ivory crucifix which she hid in her hand."[18] Freud's diagnosis was that her anxiety attacks derived from a sensual attraction to a young man that she had experienced in her youth, years earlier; she had resisted (repressed) her sensual feelings, and her anxiety was the result. The diagnosis is not especially convincing, but in any case Freud mentioned nothing about any possible connection between her religious beliefs and wish-fulfillment.

A majority of Freud's patients were Jewish; they were typically secular, well-to-do, and educated. However, I have not found one case where Freud analyzed a practicing, devout Jew (e.g., Orthodox). Freud would of course have been moderately familiar with religious Jews from his family and his in-laws, but social familiarity—most of which occurred during his prepsychoanalytic years as a youth and a young man—was not the same thing as psychoanalytic knowledge. In any case, I have not been able to find any case histories involving Freud's secular Jewish patients in which Freud identified childish wishes lying behind an adult's religious belief or religious practice.

One testimony to the absence of religious Judaism in Freud's life comes from Ernest Jones, one of the few Gentiles who was regularly at the center of Freud's circle of friends. Jones, an atheist (from a Protestant background) married to a secularized Jewess, was a close associate of Freud from about 1908 on—thus, for all but the early years of psychoanalysis. He reports: "It has never been my fortune to know a Jew possessing religious belief, let alone an orthodox one."[19] This is a remarkable statement, and can only mean that Freud's world, the world of psychoanalysis, was extremely secularized with respect to Jewish religious life. Freud's own description of himself as "an infidel Jew"[20] captures this absence of religion pretty well. Hence, the conclusion must be that Freud was not a psychoanalyst experienced in the treatment of believing Jews (and still less in that of Christians).

Where, then, did Freud get his knowledge of religion? What made him such an authority on the underlying psychology of religion, especially the religion of the masses of ordinary believers (for this was the only religion he attempted to explain)? By now, the reader should be well prepared for the nanny as the answer to this question. Nevertheless, it is useful to systematically take up and reject other possible sources of religious influence. Doing this makes it even clearer how important the nanny always remained for Freud's "religious" life.

Perhaps Freud was strongly affected through his *friendship* with serious Christians or Jews? But the only Christian believer that Freud appears to have known was Pfister. The impact of Pfister's personal faith and warmth on Freud was considerable, but the letters between them show an ongoing, very basic disagreement about the nature of religious belief. In particular, Pfister wrote: "Our disagreement [with respect to religion] derives chiefly from the fact that you grew up in proximity to pathological forms of religion and regard these as 'religion' . . ."[21] In part, Pfister, as a liberal evangelical Protestant, was criticizing Freud for being overly Roman Catholic in his concept of religion, but one also suspects that Pfister was to some extent aware of Freud's nanny and her traumatic meaning for Freud and religion.

There is no evidence that, after his childhood, Freud was in any sort of close contact with *any* believing Christian other than Pfister. A remote possibility remains that the youthful contact with Brentano might qualify; he was an adult who believed in God and in Christ. From the passages of Freud's youthful letters already quoted in Chapter Two, it is clear that Freud talked over the issue of the existence of God with Brentano. However, it is not at all plausible that the young Freud, decades before psychoanalysis, would have found in Brentano's philosophically oriented discussions evidence for his future position: that religious belief is derived from childhood wishes. Instead, the famous, intelligent, and personally impressive Brentano, who believed in God, seems to have made Freud more favorably disposed toward such belief— at least temporarily.[22]

No doubt, Freud observed religious Jews while growing up. His own father, in his later years, took to frequent reading of Jewish religious texts (such as the Talmud) and became involved in religious discussions.[23] But the point is that even if Freud's father, and his teacher Hammerschlag as well, were deeply devout Jews during the period when Freud was growing up (in fact, there is no reason to think that his father was devout), and even if Freud had felt that behind their beliefs lay childish needs (and this seems extremely far-fetched), still these contacts and impressions would *not* constitute good psychoanalytic evidence.

Perhaps Freud got his knowledge of religion from reading theology? Again the evidence is negative, especially with respect to orthodox (whether Christian or Jewish) religious thought—the only kind of belief he was interested in. With the exception of Feuerbach and similarly secularized writers such as Renan, who were functioning as critics of traditional belief (a position Freud would adopt as his own), there is no evidence that he ever read religious writers at all, and still less evidence that he read any who defined and defended the traditional Christian faith.

Instead, Freud's many references to things Christian and Jewish, which have been cited so often in earlier chapters, came from two major sources: his own youthful reading of the Philippson Bible (Old Testament), and his immersion in a kind of ambivalent "Christianized" literature, such as *Faust, Paradise Lost*, and Merejkowski's *The Romance of Leonardo da Vinci*. His quotations from the New Testament could easily have been picked up from these latter sources and from the widespread use of such phrases in the culture at large during this period. There is no evidence that he actually read the New Testament itself. Freud often took quotations from secondary sources. For example, his quotations from the *Aeneid* as in the motto of *The Interpretation of Dreams*, and in his famous analysis of the *aliquis* slip, both very likely came from a secondary source.[24]

Freud's report that he couldn't read Hebrew—along with the considerable evidence already cited of Freud's antipathy to the Jewish religion—means that he was never seriously involved in the reading of Jewish scripture or of the commentaries, which would have presented to him a mature, intelligent basis for evaluating traditional Judaism.

It might seem conceivable that Freud's insights into religion came from his own personal religious experiences. The answer is negative: Neither I nor any other biographer has found evidence supporting the possibility of any obvious and significant religious experience in Freud's life. On the contrary, in *The Future of an Illusion*, Freud explicitly complained: "If the truth of religious doctrines is dependent on inner experience which bears witness to that truth, what is one to do about the many people who do not have this rare experience?[25] Freud was including himself in this category.

In fact, the evidence supports the notion that Freud was in many respects afraid of religious experience, and to some extent took steps to avoid it. It has been mentioned more than once in this book that Freud did not like music—an almost unheard-of attitude for an educated and sophisticated man in Vienna, a city that was in important respects the very center of Western musical achievement. It was a great Mozart center; the birthplace of Schubert; and the home of non-Viennese imports like Beethoven and Brahms, and later Mahler, Schoenberg, and Berg. We may recall that Freud claimed he didn't like music because he did not wish to be emotionally moved by something he didn't understand rationally.[26] Where rational understanding wasn't possible, he wanted no part of it—even if it meant a life more or less without music, except for *Don Giovanni*! Now in its "irrational" quality, the experience of music is indeed often close to religious experience, and for many listeners it brings on religious experience. For Freud, such experiences were too disturbing, even threatening. Music would trigger Moravian memories of music at the Freiberg church with his nanny, and their associated emotions. These unconscious, religiously tinged memories could only bring on a painful unease.

Freud's word for religious experience was somewhat unusual, and betrayed his desire to avoid such experience. He referred to it as "the oceanic feeling."[27] Such terminology—in contrast, for example, to "the peak experience"—shows that Freud viewed religious experience as something primitive, archaic, lower than the experience of daily life (people live *above* sea level); moreover, he saw it as something dangerous, in which one might drown. In this wateriness, it may also have been associated with baptism, and with feminine principles. By contrast, the term "peak experience" suggests something higher than the experiences of daily life; something elevated and requiring much effort to reach it; something that, when reached, allows one to see far and to look down on others. No, Freud did not have any conscious desire for religious experience; indeed, he had the conscious desire to have *no* religious experience. And as far as anyone has been able to tell, except for the very troubling experience on the Acropolis, he got his wish.

In the context of this discussion, it should be noted that Freud's complaint that many people do not have religious experiences was clearly disingenuous. Since Freud never sought such experience (he even avoided it), it is not so surprising that he didn't have any! Freud would never have been allowed to get away with setting himself up as a critic of music or as an aesthetician of musical experience, nor would he have attempted such a thing. Why, then, has he been allowed to reject, as an "expert," the existence of something that he studiously avoided experiencing and finding out about?

The Nanny and the Projection of Disillusionment

The question of why Freud's critique has been influential would take us far afield into the psychology and sociology of modern life, and so we return to our investigation of Freud, and in particular to his argument in

The Future of an Illusion. If Freud's "understanding" of religion in this work did not come from his familiarity with religious patients or with knowledgeable adult believers, or from the study of orthodox theologians of his time or of the past, or from his own religious experiences, it must have come from his own childhood contact with religion—which brings us back to his nanny. Thus, like so much of Freudian theory, *The Future of an Illusion* had an important autobiographical origin.

In the book itself, Freud stated that psychoanalysis is not the basis of his arguments; in the letter to Pfister cited above, he made it clear that the ideas set forth in the book were an expression of his personal philosophy. This notion was amplified in his postscript to *An Autobiographical Study* (1935), where he wrote that in the past ten years his writings had shown a significant change: After a detour through medicine and science, he had "returned to the cultural problems which had fascinated me long before, when I was a youth. . . ."[28] Whenever Freud wrote about "cultural problems," religion always figured as a central issue.

But the best evidence that Freud's conception of religion in *The Future of an Illusion* went back to his own childhood is to be found in the peculiar words he used to describe religion. He called it the store of ideas "born from man's need to make his helplessness tolerable and built up from the material of memories of the helplessness of his own childhood. . . ."[29] Thus, religious beliefs are illusions, wishes and not "precipitates of experience or end-results of thinking."[30]

This period—childhood—on which Freud focused, somewhat obsessively, was of course the only period when he himself had any serious contact with religion. And we know that his relationship with the one religious person whom he knew was well suited to produce a strongly neurotic interpretation of religion.

The very notion of illusion, which figured so prominently in Freud's argument, is an interesting one. In Freud's own life, the primal and only real experience of disillusionment was the loss of his nanny. (We may recall that Freud suffered no other loss of love, or even real interpersonal failure, until his father died in 1896 after a lengthy illness. His father's death was deeply moving for Freud, but it was no disillusionment.) His first love, and his first and only deeply painful separation—with its resultant mourning, anxiety, and anger—were attached to this woman who introduced him to basic Christian ideas. And her loss would have immediately raised a "terrifying impression of helplessness." The theory that separation causes basic anxiety about one's security is one that Freud himself eventually arrived at, and one that Bowlby has subsequently compellingly amplified. Freud's nanny's sudden disappearance would have set in motion the longing for her return (something that would never happen), and would thus have linked this woman and all she stood for with something that had failed him, with an illusion.

This loss would also have aroused great anger, and this anger would have strongly affected Freud's final stage of psychological disengagement from his nanny, through the building of defenses against her and all she symbolized. I propose, then, that Freud's criticism of religion, as in *The Future of an Illusion*, was an expression of his attempt to cope with the lost happiness of his Freiberg days—with a loss that remained mysterious and painful to the end of his life. In his critiques of religion he was consciously turning with bitterness and anger (tempered by resignation) on his nanny, and most especially on the ideas so deeply associated with her: salvation, Christianity, and the Catholic Church. In abandoning him, in letting him down, she had "proven" that the happiness he had known in her religious world was an illusion.

Whatever the deep yearnings Freud continued to feel for his nanny, he would also have had a strong and equally unconscious need to criticize and reject everything for which the nanny stood. For example, if she stood for things that were trivial or stupid or illusory, then Freud would not really have lost very much after all. In particular, if her religion was an illusion, then Freud was in this respect the better off for her having left him. The interpretation of religion as an illusion thus allowed him the pleasure of interpreting religious belief as other people's problem, not his own loss. Furthermore, if Freud's arguments about the illusory nature of religion caused Christians to lose their faith, then Freud would have the extra satisfaction of hurting his unfaithful nanny and all she stood for. (There would also have been the conscious secondary gain of attacking anti-Semitic Christians as well.)

What might other *unconscious* expressions of Freud's childhood religious complex be? One would be the desire to find or recapture his nanny and her religious world, so to speak. We have already seen many manifestations of this unconscious part of Freud—of this love breaking through, from his haunting of churches to his interpretations of paintings. The use of displacement and of other strategies to cope with his Christian complex has already been covered.

Another common neurotic pattern is known as "fixation," and Freud was clearly fixated on an understanding of religion that his critics have often described as primitive and immature. (Fixation is a consequence of repression and of trauma, both of which were present here.) Freud, in his critique of religion, was only interested in and concerned with the "masses" and their simple religion. Of course this is just a relatively small part of religion, Christianity in particular. Yet it was this simple (indeed, simple-minded) religion of the masses, as communicated to Freud by his nanny and as forever emotionally associated with her, that was the only religion that ever mattered to him. He remained fixated at the one level of religion he had directly experienced—a three-year-old's Catholicism.

It was this religion that was so deeply connected to his separation anxiety, and it was to this kind of religion that Freud returned over and over.

Yet another but related way of clearly seeing Freud's rejection of religion as an illusion is to understand this rejection as an expression of "derealization." As noted in Chapter Six, Freud described this psychic mechanism as that way in which the ego defends itself by denying reality. In introducing derealization in the context of his interpretation of his one vaguely religious experience, the one on the Acropolis, Freud directly implied that his ego used exactly such a neurotic defense against religious reality.

The Future of an Illusion was, then, a neurotic derealization of religious reality and a projection of Freud's own past disillusionment with his "unfaithful," religious nanny–mother. His reactions—that is, his intellectual interpretations of religion—were based on his strong, persistent, unconscious, childish needs, connected to his nanny's early abandonment of him and his first experience of helplessness. In short, Freud's religious neurosis was deeply satisfied by his theory that religion is an illusion.

Origins of Freud's Atheism

I now turn to a new but closely related topic—the factors behind Freud's explicit atheism, as distinct from his conceptualization of religion as illusion. I begin by recalling his life-long rejection of Jewish religiousness, which contrasted with his acceptance of the Jewish ethnic and cultural heritage.

As a young man, Freud was so disturbed at the prospect of being married in a Jewish wedding ceremony, which he called "loathsome," that he contemplated assimilating to Christian culture by becoming a Protestant! In spite of the persistent complaints of his wife, who came from a seriously practicing Jewish family, Freud always refused to allow any Jewish religious ceremonies in their family life. As mentioned earlier, Freud does not appear to have had any seriously religious Jews among his friends or intellectual associates (though he did have one good Christian friend and colleague, Oskar Pfister). Freud never spoke positively of Jewish religiousness, as expressed, for example, in Orthodox or Hasidic life of the times. Finally, in his last book, *Moses and Monotheism*, Freud attacked Judaism by claiming that its great hero (and, to a considerable degree, founder), Moses, was not a Jew but an Egyptian, and that the Jews murdered Moses. Thus, Freud deprived the Jews of their claim of being the first monotheists. Not surprisingly, Freud's thesis was experienced by religious Jews as an unexpected and exceedingly painful attack on Judaism at a time when Hitler's rise to power had made support for the Jews a pressing need.[31] Freud himself acknowledged that *Moses and Monotheism* was an attack on the Jews, but he turned a deaf ear to those Jews who wrote him before the book's final publication imploring him not to publish such an attack.

There is little doubt that Freud's rejection of religious Judaism was derived largely from his rejection of his father, Jakob. Freud's various biographers have identified many reasons for this rejection.

Certainly social and ideological factors must have been important. Freud's father was a nice but unsuccessful man; he was essentially a failure in Sigmund's eyes, in that he never achieved any visible social or economic success. Freud's struggle with and resentment of his poverty were, among other things, implicit indictments of his father. And of course, Freud was dramatically better "educated" and socially more "advanced" than his father, who never went to the university or had any status in a profession or as an intellectual. For Freud, his father must have been a constant reminder of the ordinariness of his family origins—and we know how much Freud wished to be free of his poverty, how intensely he desired success. Some of his friends from similarly humble backgrounds could at least point to their fathers' commercial prosperity; Freud could not. In short, Freud had "good" social reasons for rejecting his father and his father's world—for putting all that behind him as he moved, as they say, up the social (and financial and cultural) ladder. (It can hardly be doubted that countless young men of accomplishment in the modern period have rejected their family and their religious origins for precisely the same reasons: social needs for self-esteem.) But it was far from just a social and economic issue, for Freud's whole concept of being a participant in modern intellectual life—and, even more so, his desire to make psychoanalysis a universal science—required that any religious taint or specificity be left behind, if possible. Freud, like almost all of those trying to make a career in the secular world, knew that atheism was simply the best policy.[32] To be religious, especially Jewish, would have been a serious handicap for the acceptance of his ideas, and Freud's ambition demanded as few handicaps as possible.

None of these reasons, however, necessarily accounts for Freud's hostility to and active rejection of Jewish religiousness. After all, he could, like so many other intellectual Jews moving into modernism, have simply let go of his religious origins while maintaining a comfortable ethnic identity. But Freud actively rejected Jewish religiousness, and for the animus behind this we must turn to the psychological reasons for his rejection of his father.

At least three major psychological explanations are available to account for Freud's rejection of his father—and, with him, of Judaism and of God. First, there is the often-cited incident of his father's passive acceptance of anti-Semitism. (We may recall that Jakob told his son, when Sigmund was about ten, of the time when his hat was knocked off by a local anti-Semitic youth; Jakob just picked up his hat and walked away. Sigmund was ashamed of his father upon hearing this story.) Whatever the power of this one incident, it certainly symbolizes the passivity that characterized Jakob as far as his son was concerned. Whatever Freud was, he was most certainly a fighter, who admired strength and despised passivity and weakness in any form. He did not identify with generals for nothing; Freud was, as he himself said, an intellectual "Conquistador."[33] During the Fascist buildup in Germany in the 1930s, there was an anti-Semitic joke going the rounds that Jews were parading in Berlin carrying signs that said, "Throw us out." Freud is reported to have briefly believed it to be true, and to have been very angry about it.[34] His tendency to believe such a tale strikes one as a kind of fear of his father's weakness, and as a deep anger that there even were Jews like Jakob. Thus, Freud's own resistance to anti-Semitism, in contrast to his father's passivity, is perhaps ample reason to account for his rejection of his father.

Then, too, there was the alleged affair between Freud's mother and his half-brother Philipp—which I am very inclined to think actually occurred, on the basis of the evidence. Jakob may have been unaware of this affair (if so, this would have made him look rather a fool); if he was aware of it, he apparently made no strong response. (He certainly didn't react like King David in the Bible or King Sigismund!) Such an insult to his father's authority not only would have undermined Freud's respect for his father, but also would have raised doubts about his own paternity. Who was his father? This is a question he apparently never psychologically resolved.

And finally, there are still other possible reasons for Freud's rejection of his father, noted in Chapter Five.[35] We may recall the statements of Freud in letters to Fliess, suggesting that his father was a cause of hysterical symptoms in his own family[36] and that his own father was "perverse."[37] It was only a year or so prior to these comments that Freud had concluded, in a letter to Fliess on October 15, 1895, that "Hysteria is the consequence of a presexual *sexual shock* [Freud's emphasis]."[38] Later, Freud followed up this remark by writing, "Well then, let us speak plainly. In my analyses the guilty people are close relatives . . . it then turned out that her supposedly otherwise noble and respected father regularly took her to bed when she was from eight to twelve years old. . . .[39] Thus, there is evidence that for Freud his father was linked to some kind of sexual abuse of his own children.[40] In summary, any or all of the reasons given above could have served as an adequate source of Freud's strong rejection of Jakob.

Why would Freud have rejected God as well? There is conclusive evidence throughout Freud's writings that he reliably associated the concepts of father and God. The logic of such a rejection is explicit in such a statement as this:

Psycho-analysis has made us familiar with the intimate connection between the father-complex and belief in God; it has shown us that a personal God is psychologically nothing other than an exalted father, and it brings us evidence every day of how young people lose their religious beliefs as soon as their father's authority breaks down.[41]

Here we have in a nutshell Freud's theory of the psychological basis for loss of belief. And again, as in so many instances, we need only assume that it was true for him and not that it is necessarily true for everyone. Let the father's power, strength, or authority be undermined, and God no longer seems credible—this is hardly a sound *rational* basis for atheism. However, the psychological basis of atheism receives a still clearer expression within the Freudian system.

Atheism and the Oedipus Complex[42]

The most powerful expression of Freud's rejection of his father is to be observed in the concept of the Oedipus complex. In this motivational system, which is at the very heart of psychoanalysis, Freud proposed hatred of the father and the desire to kill him, in fact or in fantasy; he saw this proposed complex as the source of countless dreams, wishes, and illusions. And, certainly, Freud's own neurotic tendencies were intimately bound up with his father.

Now one striking thing about Oedipal motivation is that, in postulating it, Freud was inadvertently proposing a powerful, unconscious, universal, childish, and neurotic wish for the death not only of the father but also of his symbolic surrogate, God. As a consequence, Freud himself has given us the conceptual basis for understanding atheism as Oedipal wish-fulfillment. By Freud's own definition, atheism is an illusion like any other—a belief where "wish-fulfillment is a prominent factor in its motivation."[43] Freud's life is a rich testimony to his theory: He was a man so permeated with Oedipal motivation that his atheism was overdetermined. And from Freud's example, one has reason to suspect that behind many an atheist, agnostic, or skeptic of today lies shame, disappointment, or rage directed at the father. For many people, disbelief in "God the Father" is the closest to revenge that they can get.

In the case of Freud, the childhood suffering that burdened him all his life, and with which he obsessively and tenaciously struggled, arouses our sympathy. Sigmund Freud, like Heinrich Heine in his last *Lazarus* poem, never put down his weapons. Our sympathy for Freud's struggle must not, however, be allowed to blind us to the understanding that his own life gives us of the neurotic, and untrustworthy, origin of his unbelief and the unbelief of many others.

Conclusion

In Chapter One and in this section, I note that Freud powerfully expressed the argument that the psychological needs served by religious beliefs make such beliefs no longer believable. But, as I have shown here, such a thesis is a sword that cuts both ways; indeed, I claim that it cuts more deeply into the roots of atheism than it cuts in the other direction. The case for this claim is based on two final arguments that the reader can now evaluate.

First, I have noted that at no time did Freud psychoanalyze someone who believed in God so as to show in any specific way how belief is a consequence of neurotic childhood experience. But in the preceding pages, we have seen how detailed clinical evidence does show that the rejection of God can be a consequence of unconscious neurotic needs. Furthermore, the unbeliever in question is Freud himself, and the unbelief in question includes his specific critical theories of religion.

Second, the present theoretical understanding ties Freud's atheism—and, by extension, the atheism of many others[44]—much more firmly to the theoretical structure of psychoanalysis than Freud ever tied belief. The interpretation of Freud's unbelief as derived from the effects of separation anxiety is not integral to Freudian psychoanalysis, but its logic is widely found in today's expanded psychoanalytic framework. And of course, the interpretation given here of Freud's atheism as involving derealization, repression, projection, and fixation uses standard Freudian concepts. Finally, the interpretation of atheism as unconscious Oedipal wish-fulfillment is one that comes from the very center of Freudian theory.

The reader may not agree with me that the weight of the psychological evidence now makes atheism a more probable symptom of neurosis than theism. However, at the very least, it should be clear that atheism certainly may often be an expression of a psychological pathology. This conclusion, combined with the preceding rationale, also means that the whole question of God—yes, even *der liebe Gott*—needs a new and much fairer treatment on the part of the "compact majority" that controls contemporary psychology, a majority well known for its persistent criticism of religious belief. In the future, as psychology moves (as I believe it will) toward a more honest approach to the question of the existence of God, I propose that at least two important spirits of Freud would wish such a new venture well: the spirit of his intellectual courage, and the spirit of a three-year-old boy with his nanny.

NOTES

ABBREVIATIONS

C. P.
    Freud, S. (1924-1950). *Collected papers* (5 vols.; J. Riviere, A. Strachey, & J. Strachey, Trans.). London: Hogarth Press and the Institute of Psycho-Analysis. (The original publication date by Freud is the date given in a citation.)

Letters
    Freud, S. (1960). *Letters of Sigmund Freud* (E. L. Freud, Ed.; T. Stern & J. Stern, Trans.). New York: Basic Books.

Origins
    Freud, S. (1954). *The origins of psycho-analysis, letters to Wilhelm Fliess, drafts and notes: 1887-1902.* (E. Kris, introduction; M. Bonaparte, A. Freud, & E. Kris, Eds.; E. Mosbacher & J. Strachey, Trans.) New York: Basic Books.

S. E.
    Freud, S. (1953-1974). *The standard edition of the complete psychological works of Sigmund Freud* (24 vols.; J. Strachey, Ed. and Trans., in collaboration with A. Freud, assisted by A. Strachey & A. Tyson). London: Hogarth Press and the Institute of Psycho-Analysis. (The original publication date by Freud is the date given in a citation.)

CHAPTER ONE

1. S. Freud (1907, *S.E.*, *9*, p. 117).
2. S. Freud (1927a, *S.E.*, *21*, pp. 16-24).
3. Jones (1957, p. 351).
4. A. Freud (1980).
5. Roazen (1975, p. 251).

NOTES

6. See Rubenstein (1968), Cuddihy (1974), Robert (1976), Klein (1981), and Ostow (1982), among others.

7. One exception to the neglect of Freud's involvement with Christianity is noted in the Acknowledgments: Gregory Zilboorg's *Psychoanalysis and Religion* (1962). See also an earlier publication of mine (Vitz, 1983).

Another relevant book, which I came across as this book was going to press, is J. R. Dempsey's *Freud, Psychoanalysis, Catholicism* (1956). Dempsey clearly anticipated aspects of my thesis about Freud's attraction to Catholicism, as represented especially by his desire to visit Rome.

8. S. Freud (1900, *S.E., 4*, p. 247). The nanny's dismissal has been commonly connected with the period when Freud's mother was in bed at the time his younger sister Anna was born on December 31, 1858—Freud would have been two years and eight months old on January 6, 1859.

9. Sajner (1968); Eissler (1978, p. 11).

10. Clark (1980, p. 5).

11. For the extremely strong Marian character of Czech Catholicism and the rationale for the title of "Marian Garden" for Moravia, see Nemec (1981).

12. Nemec (1981, p. 119). There must have been many more prior to the Communist takeover of Czechoslovakia.

13. Markham (1984, p. 1); see Nemec (1981) for additional evidence.

14. For example, see Jones (1953, Ch. 1) or Schur (1972, p. 22).

15. Sajner (1968, pp. 167–180).

16. Sajner (1968). For some time it was thought that the nanny was Monika Zajic, a member of the landlord's family. Because of the Roznau spa registration, this is now know to be incorrect. (See note 19.)

17. For the family living arrangements, see Sajner (1968), Schur (1972), and Eissler (1978).

18. See Jones (1953, Ch. 5).

19. Krüll, (1979, p. 305, note 20); also confirmed by Sajner to Swales (personal communication). Krüll gives her name as "Rosi"; this mistake has been acknowledged by Krüll (personal communication, 1983). The nanny's name was Resi.

20. Krüll (1979, p. 266); my translation.

21. "Theresa" had strong Catholic connotations, primarily because of the Catholic Archduchess of Austria, Queen of Hungary and Bohemia from 1740 to 1780, whose name was Maria Theresa (1717–1780). There are also a number of prominent saints bearing the name Theresa.

22. Jones (1953, p. 15).

23. Jones (1953, p. 6); Krüll (1979, p. 130). Sajner (1968) notes that Monika Zajic was at least some of the time the nanny for John and Pauline Freud.

24. Krüll (1979, pp. 149–161).

25. There was also a second wife, named Rebekka, between the first wife and Freud's mother, Amalia. There is almost no information about her. In spite of one attempt to give her great psychological importance, she does not appear to have been important in Freud's life. See Swales (1983d) for the most extensive summary of the historical information on this topic.

26. Krüll (1979, p. 130).

27. S. Freud (1900, *S.E., 4*, p. 247).

28. Julius seems to have been born in October 1857. See Swales (1983d, p. 12); Krüll (1979, p. 266).

29. Krüll (1979, p. 266).

30. For example, see Jones (1953, pp. 7–8).

31. *Origins* (p. 219).

32. Jones (1953, p. 3).

33. Krüll (1979, p. 134).

34. Swales (1983d, p. 12).

35. Swales (1983d, p. 12).

36. This possibility was suggested to me by Swales as rather likely.

37. Full breast feeding suppresses ovulation, thus acting as a natural mechanism for child spacing. Ratner (1983) writes, "The birth of children every 11 or 12 months or so is abnormal and, with rare exception, is only found in mothers who bottle feed or token breastfeed their infants [or use a wet nurse]" (p. 201).

38. Grigg (1973).

39. Mahony (1977).

40. McGuire (Ed.), in S. Freud & Jung (1974, p. 59).

41. Schur (1972, p. 21).

42. Swales (1983d, p. 12).

43. *Origins* (pp. 219–220).

44. S. Freud (1900, *S.E., 4*, p. 248).

45. *Origins* (p. 222).

46. *Origins* (pp. 221–222). A second church in Freiberg is St. Valentine's. It is baroque and has many statues. See Muk & Šamánková *et al.* (1985, p. 443).

47. The importance of Pentecost for 19th-century Czech Catholic communities has been attested to me by Professors Rutar, Nemec, and Zezula.

48. The musicality of Czechoslovakia, especially in the 18th century, is noted by Burney (1773/1959, Vol. 1, pp. 33 ff.), and Czech musicality was widely recognized throughout the West in the 19th century as well. A common expression was that every Czech was born with a violin in his hands; the term "Bohemian" has its origin in the lifestyle of many Bohemian musicians who roamed about Europe looking for employment in orchestras or bands. Czech music consisted of two strands: one a strong and stable folk or popular music tradition; the other the Catholic Church's long-term cultivation of high or classical music (e.g., in the monasteries, especially Benedictine, and in the courts). In Freud's time, Czechoslovakia produced Smetana (b. 1824) and Dvorak (b. 1841) from Bohemia and Janáček (b. 1854) and Mahler (b. 1860) from Moravia. See also the "Mysticism, Music, and the Acropolis" section in Chapter Six.

49. See Jones (1953, p. 12) for the fame of the Freiberg church chimes; see Rieger (1867, p. 936) for the major renovation in the 1850s of the main church that dated back to the 13th century.

50. Zilboorg (1962, p. 137).

51. Jones (1953, p. 6).

52. Swales (personal communication, 1982), however, notes that there was a

small Jewish prayer room in Freiberg not far from the Freuds. (Original information as personal communication from Sajner to Swales.)

53. Suggested to me by Dr. Henry Elkin (1980), and confirmed by others
knowledgeable about Eastern European Jewry in the mid-19th centrury.

54. Rainey (1975, p. 35) also makes this general point; Falk (1978,
pp. 377–378, 385) has similarly noted some of the Christian significance of the
nanny.

55. The church was called *Mariae Geburt* ("The Nativity of Our Lady").
See E. Freud, Freud, & Grubrich-Simitis (1978, p. 49). It had a gothic Madonna. See Muk & Šamánková *et al.* (1985, p. 443).

56. Swales (personal communication, 1983) has visited Freiberg and has seen
the statue; I have also seen his photo of it. There is also a photo of the statue in
Sajner (1968, facing p. 168).

57. Zezula (personal communication, 1981); also confirmed by Professors
Nemec and Rutar. See also Nemec (1981, e.g., p. 127), for the old Marian
column, Old Town Square, Prague.

58. I was informed of the Czech popularity of St. Anne by Professor Zezula
(personal communication, 1981); see also Nemec (1981). For a brief history of
the Catholic saints of Moravia see Rutar (1983). "Anna" and "Maria" then, even
more than now, were notably Catholic names. (The fact that Emanuel Freud's
wife was called Maria and her children were named John and Pauline, plus the
fact that Sigmund's sister was named Anna, all suggest a strong assimilative
current in the Jakob Freud family, at least in the 1850s.)

59. Jones (1957, pp. 349–350).

60. This point is very clearly made by Drobin (1978, p. 48).

61. Jones's denial of the nanny is so peculiar that it means he is distinctly
threatened by the association of his master with a religiously oriented mother-
figure. Other evidence for this is provided in later sections.

62. Jones (1953, p. 13).

63. Sajner (1968, p. 173); Schur (1972, p. 21).

64. Freud's gift with language and his familiarity with different languages
are attested to by all of his biographers.

65. For Freud's memory of the Czech language, see Jones (1953, p. 7);
S. Freud (1900, *S.E.*, *4*, p. 196).

66. A visit by Freud to Freiberg in his teens is described in his *Screen
Memories* (S. Freud, 1899a, *S.E.*, *3*, pp. 303–322). At that time he visited the
Fluss family, who were German-speaking Jews.

67. Swales (1983d, p. 13). See also Sajner (1968); Gicklhorn (1969); Krüll
(1979, pp. 167–176).

68. Freud's sister Anna wrote as an old woman that the family left Freiberg
six weeks after her birth on December 31, 1858 (Bernays, ca. 1935). This is
obviously incorrect, since documents attest to the Freuds' being in Freiberg 12
weeks after her birth (i.e., March 23). It is likely that her memory was a
corruption of "six months," which would mean that they left at the end of May
or early June 1859. Swales (1983d, p. 13) notes the discrepancy and thinks it is
possible that "six weeks" is a corruption of "six months." Jones (1953, p. 15,
note b) also comments on the mistaken dates of Freud's sister in her memoirs.

69. Swales (1983d, p. 13).

70. Krüll (1979, p. 266).

71. E. Freud *et al.* (1978, pp. 107, 327).

72. S. Freud (1899b, *Gessamelte Werke, 1*, p. 473).

73. Krüll (1979, p. 261).

74. See Harvey (1967, p. 951); all subsequent dates for Easter and Pentecost are from this calendar.

75. *Origins* (pp. 221–222).

76. In 1897, Freud's mother Amalia was 62 years old and Freud was 41. Amalia was born August 18, 1835 (Jones, 1953, p. 2). Freud's father had died the preceding fall, so there was no chance to ask him about the nanny.

77. S. Bernfeld (1946).

78. S. Freud (1899a, *S.E., 3* p. 311).

79. Krüll (1979, p. 266).

80. *Origins* (p. 219).

81. Jones (1953, p. 13).

82. This possibility was suggested to me by Professor Rutar (1983), a native Czech, whose "Nana" did in fact take a prized toy of his when he was a child. Later, the toy was found being used by a child of the "Nana's" family.

83. This possibility was brought to my attention by Professor Robert Holt.

84. For example, see *Catechism of Christian Doctrine* (1885/1977, p. 4).

85. Zezula (personal communication, 1983); also, children who died unbaptized went to limbo, according to Church teaching.

86. Rutar (personal communication, 1983).

87. Baptism was an especially common rite for adults on Holy Saturday, as it still is.

88. M. Freud (1957, p. 35).

89. M. Freud (1957, p. 36). Martin Freud (1957, p. 54) also mentioned that his sister Mathilde was allowed to go to church with a friend during summer vacation; Klein (1981, p. 60) writes that the Freud children apparently never attended synagogue. Thus, the Sigmund Freud family was without any significant Jewish *religious* atmosphere, and at least somewhat benevolently disposed toward the surrounding Catholic culture.

90. Sencourt (1971, p. 17).

91. Sencourt (1971, p. 20). Sencourt comments that Eliot's first 16 years, spent mostly in St. Louis, were the most important in his life for establishing the material (images, emotions, experiences) on which his poetry was based; he also notes an important youthful poem by Eliot, "A Fable for Feasters," set in a very Catholic setting of abbots, holy water, rites, and so on. The hypothesis of a connection between Eliot's Catholic nanny and his later religious conversion was brought to my attention by Professor James Hitchcock.

92. *Origins* (pp. 220–221, emphasis added).

93. Holt (personal communication, 1981).

94. Many Christians mean "Have you been baptized?" when they ask, "Have you been washed in the blood of the Lamb?"

95. Matthew 27:33. In this and subsequent references to the Bible, the Revised Standard Version is used unless otherwise noted.

96. It was after learning of Holt's proposal that I read Suzanne Cassirer Bernfeld's paper (S. C. Bernfeld, 1951), in which she connects this same memory to Freud being "preconsciously occupied with church matters" (p. 123). She writes that "[T]he priest at Easter Mass washes his hands in red wine diluted with water which stands for Christ's blood" (pp. 122–123); she also notes the Latin *experimenta crucis* and assumes that the nanny had major religious meaning for Freud centered around Easter and resurrection.

97. *Origins* (pp. 222–223).

98. Bowlby also thoroughly connects his concept of separation anxiety to the research and theory on animal instinct as understood by the ethologists. Bowlby thus sees his work as a partial answer to Freud's explicit request for a theory of the instincts. In particular, he notes (1969, pp. 185–198) that separation anxiety is a common powerful motivation in the life of many young animals, especially young primates.

99. Bowlby (1969, p. 10).

100. S. Freud (1939, *S.E.*, *23*, p. 74).

101. Bowlby (1969, p. 28; 1973, p. 27).

102. Deutsch, cited by Bowlby (1969, p. 30). The boy is now known to have been Helene Deutsch's son, Martin (Roazen, personal communication, 1985; see Roazen, 1985).

103. Bowlby (1973, p. 375–383).

104. S. Freud (1905, *S.E.*, 7, p. 224).

105. Bowlby (1973, p. 378, note 2), quoting S. Freud (1917b, *S.E.*, *16*, p. 407).

106. S. Freud (1926, *S.E.*, *20*, pp. 136–137).

107. It is most significant that Freud said that the "crying my heart out" scene had occurred to him from time to time over the previous 29 years without his having any understanding of it (*Origins*, p. 222). This memory is obviously very important in conceptualizing Freud's psychology.

108. Jones (1953, p. 13).

109. *Origins* (p. 237).

110. Jones (1953, p. 13).

111. S. C. Bernfeld (1951); Grigg (1973).

112. Bowlby (1973, Ch. 18).

113. Roazen (1975, pp. 27, 553) reports an interview with Edward Bernays in which financial losses by Emanuel and Philipp in South African ostrich feather farms are suggested as the explanation of why the Freud family left Freiberg. This claim is presumably based on the recollection of Edward's mother, Anna (Freud's sister); see also Bernays (ca. 1935, p. 90).

However, Swales (personal communication, 1985) has informed me that the situation may have been quite different. Oliver Freud throws doubt on Edward Bernays's claim in a letter to Siegfried Bernfeld (letter in the Bernfeld Collection, Library of Congress, with two sections dated April 13 and June 25, 1944). Oliver Freud wrote that the ostrich feather farms, destroyed by a bird disease and bringing financial ruin, were in England. Thus, this disaster came *after* departure from Freiberg.

114. See Krüll (1978). For example, the Fluss family stayed in Freiberg and prospered.

115. See S. Bernfeld & S. C. Bernfeld (1944); Sajner (1968); Krüll (1979).

116. Bowlby (1969, Ch. 2; 1973, p. 253; 1980, pp. 28–29).

117. Burnham, cited by Bowlby (1973, p. 251).

118. S. C. Bernfeld (1951, p. 113).

119. This conclusion that Freud would spend a lifetime trying to undo his childhood loss was proposed by Zilboorg (1962, p. 138).

120. Gedo (1968/1976).

121. Spector (1972, p. 61); see also Swan (1974).

122. Sophocles (1939, pp. 21, 22).

123. For example, see Jones (1955, p. 363–367).

124. Exodus 2:10.

125. S. Freud (1910a, S.E., 11, pp. 112–113).

126. Spector (1972, p. 54).

127. Jones (1955, p. 346); Lichtenberg (1978) further enriches our understanding of the projective, autobiographical character of Freud's *Leonardo* essay.

128. Schapiro (1956).

129. Spector (1972, p. 58).

130. Spector (1972, p. 58).

131. Spector (1972, p. 57).

132. It should also be noted that Freud's future relationship with his wife and her sister Minna (who lived in the Freud house beginning in 1896) represented a recreation of the "two mothers" situation, a situation powerfully explicated by Swales (1982a). Roazen (personal communication, 1985) also sees Martha and Minna as an example of two mothers.

133. For example, see *Origins* (p. 245). In this letter Freud used "*Amme*" for his nurse; at other times he used "*Kinderfrau.*" See Grigg (1973, p. 112).

134. Machek (1971, p. 389). It was Professor Zezula (personal communication, 1981) who first informed me of this common Czech expression for a nanny.

135. Machek (1971, p. 389) notes that the term "Nana" is used mainly by children and that it is most prevalent in Moravian dialects.

136. Zezula (personal communication, 1981).

137. Freud's proposal of a psychoanalytic aesthetic—that is, a psychological interpretation of the artist—was so contaminated by his own psychology that, in spite of his claim of analyzing the artist, much of what he discussed is now understood as a projection of his own psychology. That is, what he gave us was a psychoanalytic interpretation of the critic. This "aesthetic of the critic" is interesting, of course, but it tells us little or nothing about Leonardo or his work. The richness of the autobiographical element in Freud's writing is constantly stressed throughout this book. The pervasive tendency of Freud to project his own psychology has led Swales to comment that "taken as a whole, Freud's work represents the longest and strangest autobiography in Western literature" (personal communication, 1982). This overstates the case, but the remark nevertheless contains much truth.

138. This well-known earlier version, the Burlington House Cartoon, is in the

National Gallery, London. Freud did refer to this version in a 1923 footnote to his Leonardo essay. See S. Freud (1910a, *S.E.*, *11*, p. 114).

139. S. Freud (1900, *S.E.*, *5*, p. 487); see also E. Freud *et al.* (1978, p. 167).

CHAPTER TWO

1. Jones (1953, p. 15).

2. Freiberg was much smaller and much more rural than Vienna, but when the Freuds first lived in Vienna there was still a good deal of space in open parks (such as the *Prater*). Only later did the Jewish section become crowded and completely urban (Krüll, 1979, p. 178; Swales, personal communication, 1984; see also Schnitzler, 1970).

3. S. Freud (1899a, *S.E.*, *3*, p. 312).

4. Jones (1953, p. 15).

5. Bowlby (1973, pp. 9–22).

6. S. Freud (1923a, *S.E.*, *19*, p. 29).

7. Bowlby (1973, p. 21).

8. Ricoeur (1970, p. 372).

9. Jones (1957, p. 350).

10. Heller (1956, p. 419).

11. See also Drobin (1978).

12. Rainey (1973, p. 10).

13. Jones (1957, p. 350).

14. Rainey (1975, p. 13).

15. *Letters* (p. 395); Ostow (1982, p. 21). See also the preface of the Hebrew translation of *Totem and Taboo* (e.g., cited in Bergmann, 1976/1982, p. 119). Falk (1978, e.g., pp. 386–387) claims Freud was taught Hebrew by Hammerschlag. Nevertheless, Falk proposes that as an adult Freud was unable to read it, probably in large part because he rejected being associated with such a distinctive form of Jewish religiousness.

16. Jones (1953, p. 19).

17. Bergmann (1976/1982, p. 116).

18. E. Freud *et al.* (1978, p. 57).

19. S. Freud (1925, *S.E.*, *20*, p. 8).

20. Pfrimmer (1982, e.g., pp. 379–380).

21. Jones (1953, p. 163); E. Freud *et al.* (1978, p. 67); Klein (1981, pp. 42–45).

22. *Letters* (pp. 86–87).

23. M. Freud (1957, p. 11).

24. Trosman (1973/1976, p. 63).

25. See Pfrimmer (1982, e.g., pp. 22–23) for the occasional Talmudic comment in the Philippson Bible.

26. That Freud generally rejected the religious aspects of Judaism is well established; for example, see Robert (1976) and Klein (1981). Our focus is on the psychological reasons behind his rejection.

27. Schur (1972, pp. 105, 109).

28. Jones (1953, p. 2).

29. Jones (1953, p. 3).

30. Jones (1953, p. 4).

31. Krüll (1979, p. 265).

32. Martin Freud (1957, pp. 20–21) mentions the lifelong impact of poverty on his father's mentality. In Vienna there is no evidence that Jakob Freud paid taxes; thus he apparently always worked for others. His source of income is not especially clear. Evidently, much of it came from other members of the family. See also Grollman (1965, p. 50).

33. S. Freud (1900, *S.E.*, *4*, p. 197).

34. Krüll (1979, pp. 176–186).

35. Krüll (1978; 1979, pp. 179–186); Gicklhorn (1976).

36. Krüll (1978, e.g., p. 124; also 1979, pp. 176 ff.).

37. See Krüll (1978; 1979, pp. 262–263); see also Gicklhorn (1976).

38. Gicklhorn (1976).

39. S. Freud (1900, *S.E.*, *4*, p. 138).

40. Krüll (1979, pp. 150–155).

41. For example, see Krüll (1979, pp. 140–144); M. Freud (1957, p. 11).

42. Krüll (1979, p. 118).

43. *Origins* (p. 222).

44. S. Freud (1901, *S.E.*, *6*, p. 51, note), quoted by Krüll (1979, p. 151).

45. Jones (1953, p. 10).

46. S. Freud (1900, *S.E.*, *5*, p. 583), quoted by Krüll (1979, pp. 151–152).

47. Jones (1953, p. 27).

48. Grinstein (1980, pp. 447–460).

49. Grinstein (1980, pp. 452–453).

50. Grinstein (1980, p. 454).

51. Grollman (1965, p. 47).

52. In Schaller's Czech Roman Missal (Rimsky missal); see also Thurston & Attwater (1956/1980, Vol. 4, pp. 209–210). St. Sigismund is listed for May 1, or May 2 for those in the diocese of Prague. His relics are in Prague (Rutar, per-personal communication, 1983). One probable reason Freud changed from Sigismund to Sigmund is that "Sigismund" had become a standard name to refer to Jews in anti-Semitic jokes (Klein, 1981, p. 46).

53. For the life of St. Sigismund, see Gregory of Tours (1927, pp. 87–88); Thurston & Attwater (1956/1980, Vol. 4, pp. 209–210).

54. S. Freud (1906, *S.E.*, *9*, p. 105).

55. S. Freud (1913, *S.E.*, *13*, p. 112).

56. Jones (1953, p. 18).

57. Jones (1955, pp. 40, 43).

58. Swales (personal communication, 1983).

59. *Letters* (p. 30).

60. The card is unpublished; it is in the Sigmund Freud Archives, Library of Congress (unrestricted section).

61. Jones (1953, p. 23).

62. Jones (1953, p. 24).

63. S. Freud (1900, *S.E.*, *4*, p. 196).

64. See account by Grinstein (1980, pp. 78–80). For an account of Hannibal's life, see DeBeer (1969).

65. Gedo & Wolf (1973/1976, p. 92); on this question, see also Grinstein (1980, pp. 80–81).

66. *Letters* (pp. 96–97).

67. Gedo & Wolf (1973/1976, p. 98, note 8).

68. Gedo & Wolf (1973/1976, p. 89).

69. Gedo & Wolf (1973/1976, p. 90).

70. Jones (1953, p. 175).

71. Gedo & Wolf (1970/1976).

72. Stanescu (1971).

73. Feuerbach (1841/1957, pp. 11, 65). Freud's library contained 1923 editions of this work by Feuerbach and of *The Essence of Religion*; it is quite possible that he acquired and reviewed them shortly before he wrote *The Future of an Illusion* (1927a). See Trosman & Simmons (1973).

74. See Rieff (1979, p. 266, note.)

75. Gedo & Wolf (1970/1976, pp. 79–80).

76. Philippians 2:12. Its other uses by St. Paul occur at 1 Corinthians 2:3, 2 Corinthians 7:15, and Ephesians 6:5; it also appears in the Gospels at Mark 5:33. In addition, the phrase served as the title for Kierkegaard's *Fear and Trembling* (1843/1941), with which Freud was also familiar.

77. Gedo & Wolf (1970/1976, p. 80).

78. Gedo & Wolf (1970/1976, p. 80).

79. Jones (1953, Ch. 4).

80. Jones (1953, Ch. 4).

81. Jones (1953, e.g., p. 41); for a much more scholarly and sophisticated treatment of this topic, see Sulloway (1979).

82. Holt, *Intellectual Biography of Sigmund Freud* (in preparation); Knoepfmacher (1979, pp. 294, 296) also makes it clear that Freud was strongly influenced by D. F. Strauss, Büchner, Lecky, Feuerbach, and others in his high school days, and that he passed their ideas on to his fellow classmates.

83. For a very positive treatment of Feuerbach, Strauss, Renan, Büchner, Lecky, and others in the same intellectual tradition, see Robertson (1929).

84. S. Freud (1900, *S.E.*, *4*, pp. 212–213).

85. E. Freud *et al.* (1978, p. 84).

86. In my discussion of Freud and Brentano, I would like to acknowledge the helpful thesis of a student of mine, Frederick A. Drobin (1978).

87. E. Freud *et al.* (1978, p. 326, note 43); however, Rancurello (1968, p. 9, note) says that the issue of papal infallibility had no or at best little relevance to Brentano's religious crisis, since his crisis occurred *before* the dogma was made official.

88. Puglisi (1924).

89. See Rancurello (1968, p. 10, and note).

90. Svoboda (1967, p. 786).

91. Drobin (1978, p. 59); Barclay (1960, p. 9); Ellenberger (1970, p. 541).

92. Drobin (1978, p. 59); also Rancurello (1968, pp. 6–7, 11–12).

93. Jones (1953, p. 56); also, "a *glance* at philosophy in Brentano's reading seminar" (1953, p. 37; emphasis added).

94. Merlan (1945). See also Merlan (1949).

95. Merlan (1945).

96. However, the only Brentano work listed in Freud's library was *Neue Räthsel von Aenigmatics*, published in 1879 (Trosman & Simmons, 1973). Only part of Freud's library has been recovered and identified; that is, many books he is known to have owned or read are not in the existing identified parts of his library. See Swales (1982b).

97. Clark (1980, p. 34).

98. Clark (1980, p. 34).

99. Drobin (1978, p. 59).

100. Copleston (1965, Vol. 7, p. 205).

101. Kraus, introduction to Brentano (1930/1966, p. xi).

102. Quoted in Srzednicki (1965, p. 10).

103. Svoboda (1967, p. 365).

104. Chisholm (1967, p. 365).

105. Boring (1950, pp. 316, 439).

106. Barclay (1960, p. 11).

107. Barclay (1960, pp. 11–13).

108. Barclay (1960, p. 25).

109. S. Freud (1900, *S.E.*, *4*, p. 122).

110. Vergote, quoted by Ricoeur (1970, p. 379).

111. *Origins* (pp. 348–445).

112. Fancher (1977, p. 207 [abstract]).

113. Drobin (1978, pp. 61–62); Barclay (1960, pp. 17–18).

114. Brentano (1874/1973, esp. Ch. 2).

115. Brentano (1874/1973, p. 103); see also Fancher (1977, pp. 299 ff.).

116. Drobin (1978, pp. 66–68).

117. For comments on this issue, see Drobin (1978); Zilboorg (1962); Stock (1963).

118. Swales (1982b, pp. 16–17, note). The letter, according to Swales, is in the Sigmund Freud Archives, Library of Congress; it was in the unrestricted portion till 1980, but has been in the restricted portion since 1980. See also Stanescu (1971).

119. Swales (1982b, p. 17).

120. Lateau's wounds, from which issued blood, appeared only on Friday, while she was having visions of Christ's passion. For an extensive treatment of this "Catholic-blood" complex, see Swales (1982a), concerning the *aliquis* slip. See also Graef (1967, p. 403). Again we have a Freudian association to blood within a very special Catholic context.

121. Franz Brentano was the nephew of Clemens Brentano (1778-1842), one of the more notable converts to Catholicism (from skepticism) in the 19th century, and a major German romantic poet. Clemens's sister Bettina d'Arnim (1785-1859) was in close correspondence with Goethe and got to know him well. She learned much about the great man's childhood through her acquaintance with Goethe's mother. In 1835 she published her well-known *Goethes*

Briefwechsel mit einem Kinde, a popular but imaginary correspondence between Goethe and a young child. Clemens and Bettina were two of the many children of Maximiliane Brentano, *née* von La Roche, whom the young Goethe had found delightful many years before Bettina was born. In short, the Brentano family was intimately associated with Goethe. See Rancurello (1968, pp. 1–2).

122. For example, see *Letters* (pp. 269, 303); Gomperz (1974); Swales (1985).

123. Gomperz (1974).

124. *Letters* (p. 303).

125. Merlan (1945).

126. Jones (1953, p. 55).

127. Merlan (1945).

128. Merlan (1945).

129. Brody (1970).

130. *Our Crowd* (Birmingham, 1967) tells the story of the old, wealthy, influential Jewish families of New York City. A fine description of much of Freud's social and political "crowd" can be found in Schorske (1980).

131. Puglisi (1924, p. 417).

132. Schorske (1980, pp. 147, 297).

133. Puglisi (1924, p. 417); Rancurello (1968, p. 9).

134. Sulloway (1979, p. 54).

135. Kraus (1919, p. 82).

136. Swales (1985) has shown that Freud's patient known as Cäcilie M. was in fact Anna Lieben; see also Van Lier (1983) on the close connection between the Lieben and the Gomperz families.

CHAPTER THREE

1. Jones (1953, pp. 98 ff.)

2. Schur (1972, p. 30).

3. Eissler (1971, p. 233).

4. Eissler (1971, pp. 233–234).

5. Eissler (1971, p. 234).

6. *Letters* (p. 7, note).

7. Jones (1953, pp. 101, 116–118, 120).

8. Jones (1953, pp. 100–101).

9. Jones (1953, pp. 100–101).

10. Jones (1953, p. 101).

11. Heine's baptism and subsequent complex attitude toward the German Christianity of his day were well known in Freud's time. See Clark (1980, p. 12); see also Chapter 6 of this volume (note 161).

12. Jones (1953, p. 101).

13. Jones (1953, p. 101).

14. Jones (1953, p. 116).

15. M. Freud (1957, p. 13).

16. Rainey (1975, p. 63).

17. Jones (1953, Ch. 7, e.g., pp. 110, 116, 118–119).

18. Roazen (1975, p. 48).
19. Jones (1953, Ch. 7, e.g., pp. 118–119).
20. Jones (1953, Ch. 14); see also *Letters*.
21. All of the examples in this list are from *Letters*, except where indicated.
22. Jones (1953, p. 171).
23. The German word is *Pfingsten*; hence "Pentecost" is the better translation. "Whitsun(day)" is peculiar to Anglican England.
24. *Letters* (p. 112).
25. Pentecost was an ancient Jewish holiday but there is no evidence that it was celebrated in the Jewish world of 19th-century Eastern Europe. Its Moravian significance was described to me by Rutar (personal communication, 1983); Nemec (personal communication, 1983).
26. August 1882 letter quoted in Jones (1953, p. 169).
27. *Letters* (pp. 146–147).
28. The family reasons may have involved the desire of Martha's mother to distance her daughter from Sigmund. In any case, see Jones (1953, pp. 118–119); Eissler (1971, p. 262).
29. S. Freud (1985, p. 351).
30. *Letters* (p. 12).
31. Jones (1953, p. 119).
32. Jones (1953, p. 119).
33. Jones (1953, p. 140).
34. *Letters* (p. 144).
35. *Letters* (p. 144, note).
36. *Letters* (p. 158).
37. For the Paris trip, see Jones (1953, pp. 183–189).
38. For the fellowship, see Jones (1953, pp. 74–76).
39. *Letters* (pp. 182–183).
40. S. Freud (1900, *S.E.*, 5, p. 469).
41. Jones (1953, p. 184).
42. *Letters* (p. 40).
43. *Letters* (p. 185).
44. *Letters* (p. 175).
45. Jones (1953, p. 152).
46. *Letters* (p. 154).
47. *Letters* (pp. 187–188).
48. *Letters* (p. 208).
49. Jones (1953, p. 66).
50. Jones (1953, p. 66).
51. *Letters* (p. 81).
52. *Letters* (pp. 81–82).
53. *Letters* (p. 82).
54. *Letters* (p.82–83).
55. The only direct way to Dresden by train from Vienna would be through Prague.
56. For an example of Freud's involvement in exactly this kind of sound symbolism, see S. Freud & Jung (1974, p. 59).

57. Schapiro (1956).

58. *Letters* (p. 293).

59. See Jones (1953, pp. 60–62).

60. Freud used the term "monomaniac" to refer to himself (Jones, 1953, p. 269).

61. For a discussion of this period, see Jones (1953); Schur (1972); Eissler (1971, p. 234).

62. See Jones (1953, Chs. 10–13).

63. S. Freud (1925, *S.E.*, *20*, pp. 9–10; see also Jones (1953, p. 45).

64. Schorske (1980, p. 297).

65. For the fact that Meynert was in certain respects a model, see the many index entries for Meynert in Jones (1956, e.g., pp. 56, 65).

66. Jones (1953, p. 152). My friend the late Dr. Henry Elkin has suggested that for Freud to identify as much as he did with Brücke implies that Freud was in important respects hostile to his Jewishness. Brücke, with his brusque manner and piercing blue eyes, was the epitome of the Prussian *goy*.

67. See Jones (1953, p. 44) for Fleischl's social standing; also see Jones (1953, pp. 89–90) for his secular character.

68. Jones (1953, p. 289); Sulloway (1979, Ch. 5).

69. Sulloway (1979, Ch. 6).

70. Jones (1953, p. 290); Sulloway (1979, pp. 147 ff.).

71. An in-depth scholarly treatment of the Fliess–Freud relationship that provides a still more complete understanding of Fliess is now in press (Swales, in press).

72. Jones (1953, p. 289); Sulloway (1979, p. 135).

73. Jones (1953, pp. 314 ff.); S. Freud (1985, pp. 449–458).

74. Sulloway (1979, pp. 222–224).

75. Sulloway (1979, especially Ch. 6).

76. For Darwin, see Sulloway (1979, Ch. 7); for the others, see Sulloway's index entries.

77. The original versions of Freud's letters are in *Origins*; very recently, Masson has published Freud's complete, uncensored letters (S. Freud, 1985).

78. *Origins* (p. 236).

79. *Origins* (pp. 219–221, 221–223).

80. *Origins* (p. 236).

81. *Origins* (p. 269).

82. *Origins* (p. 276).

83. *Origins* (p. 279).

84. *Origins* (p. 294).

85. *Origins* (p. 317).

86. I am informed by Swales (personal communication, 1983) that Fliess had visited Rome at Easter 1887, a time when he spent several months in southern Italy. This was six months before his first meeting with Freud. No doubt at some point Fliess told Freud about the time he spent in Italy and described the experience of Easter in Rome.

87. Zezula (personal communication, 1980); Rutar (personal communication, 1982). Today Czechs are forbidden to make such a trip by their government

although many, I am told, wish to go; the same custom is still strong in Catholic Poland, however.

88. Zezula (personal communication, 1980); Rutar (personal communication, 1982).

89. This is also the conclusion of Grigg (1973).

90. References to Easter in *Origins*: Draft C, Letters 44, 54, 56, 84, 88 (twice), 101, 104 (three times), 106 (twice), 116, 130 (twice), 131 (three times), 132, 133, 141, 142. Additional references to Easter in S. Freud (1985) from 1897 to 1902: 1897, March 7 (twice); 1898, February 9, February 23, March 10, March 15, March 24, April 3, April 27; 1899, March 19, March 27 (twice), April 13. References to Pentecost in *Origins*: Letters 62, 63, 64, 89, 136, and 137. Additional references to Pentecost in S. Freud (1985) from 1897 to 1902: 1898, April 27; 1901, May 1 (twice), May 24, May 25 (twice), and June 9 (twice).

91. *Origins* (p. 292).

92. *Origins* (p. 211). Freud also expressed an interesting attitude toward the father here, to say the least.

93. See Freud's letters referring to his visiting Rome published in *Origins* or *Letters*, all of which mention August or September visits.

94. *Origins* (pp. 335–336).

95. Jones (1955, p. 18).

96. *Origins* (p. 251).

97. In *Origins* (p. 252), it is called "High Mass"; *Letters* (p. 236) notes it as "Easter Mass." This was Freud's closest experience to Easter in Rome.

98. *Origins* (p. 252).

99. Why Freud was finally able to overcome his neurotic restraints and visit Rome is not clear. It is generally suggested that publishing *The Interpretation of Dreams* freed him somehow. This seems too general an explanation, and is not persuasive. After all, that book was published almost two years before his first visit. A dramatic yet scholarly interpretation of how Freud broke the sexual and religious inhibitions that kept him from visiting Rome has been published by Swales (1983b). Swales's interpretation, convincing in most respects, is too long and detailed to summarize here. Swales's case, however, hinges on the symbolic equivalence of Freud's sister-in-law Minna and his old "Nana." One crucial link in Swales's paper is his argument that Freud's analysis of the famous *aliquis* memory lapse was actually an analysis of Freud himself, and not of some stranger riding with him in a train in Italy. This particular claim receives a good deal of support in the present book; throughout, we see that Freud was closely connected to distinctively Catholic experiences and associations involving his nanny, churches, children, and often blood, as discussed in Chapter One. Freud's dreams, as discussed in this chapter, also showed much Catholic preoccupation. In short, the remarkably Catholic associations attributed by Freud to his hypothetical Jewish traveling companion in the *aliquis* case look very much like another example of Freud projecting his own psychology onto another. Swales goes into these associations in great and convincing detail.

100. Jones (1955, p. 16).

101. *Letters* (p. 105).

102. *Letters* (p. 231).

103. Jones (1953, pp. 334–335).

104. *Origins* (pp. 251–252).

105. Zilboorg (1962, p. 167).

106. *Origins* (p. 276).

107. S. Freud (1900, *S.E.*, *4*, p. 205).

108. Jones (1955, p. 38).

109. Jones (1955, p. 95).

110. Jones (1955, p. 95).

111. *Letters* (pp. 261, 267); Jones (1955, p. 19); *Letters* (p. 266).

112. *Letters* (p. 293).

113. Freud wrote in a letter, for example: "[M]y relationship to this work [*Moses*] is something like that to a love child. Every day for three lonely weeks in September 1913 [actually, September 1912] I stood in the church in front of the statue, studying it . . . One of the consequences of my failing health difficult to bear is that I can no longer come to Rome . . ." (*Letters*, p. 416). Elsewhere, Freud wrote, "How often have I mounted the steep steps of the unlovely Corso Cavour to the lonely piazza where the deserted church stands, and have assayed to support the angry scorn of the hero's glance"; see S. Freud (1914a, *S.E.*, *13*, p. 213).

114. *Letters* (p. 302).

115. Jones (1955, p. 37).

116. Bowlby (1980, p. 85).

117. Jones (1953, p. 330).

118. Jones (1955, p. 17).

119. Velikovsky (1941, p. 490).

120. Velikovsky (1941, p. 490).

121. Banks & Mitchell (1980, pp. 505–531).

122. Banks & Mitchell (1980, pp. 505–531).

123. S. Freud, quoted by Velikovsky (1941, p. 490). A "herbarium" is a collection of dried plant specimens, usually mounted and systematically arranged for reference.

124. Velikovsky (1941, p. 490–491).

125. Velikovsky (1941, p. 492).

126. Velikovsky (1941, note 4).

127. Velikovsky (1941, p. 492–493).

128. Velikovsky (1941, p. 493).

129. Velikovsky (1941, p. 493–494).

130. Velikovsky (1941, p. 494).

131. S. Freud (1900, *S.E.*, *4*, p. 194).

132. S. Freud (1900, *S.E.*, *4*, p. 194).

133. Strachey (Ed.), in S. Freud (1900, *S.E.*, *4*, p. 195, note 1).

134. For clear interpretation of Karlsbad as a nanny symbol, see Grigg (1973); not surprisingly, Karlsbad was also strongly linked by Freud to Rome (e.g., S. Freud (1985, pp. 373, 378, 387).

135. S. Freud (1900, *S.E.*, *4*, p. 196).

136. Strachey (Ed.), in S. Freud (1900, *S.E.*, *4*, p. 196, note).

137. See Leppmann (1970) for biographical material on Winckelmann.

138. It is probable that this Herr Zucker was the same as Zuckerkandl, a man whom Freud refers to in a letter to Martha Bernays written September 4, 1883 (*Letters*, p. 53). This man, Emil Zuckerkandl (1840–1910), was mentioned by Freud as able to get him a free railroad ticket for a trip he wanted to make to Budapest. Zuckerkandl was a prominent member of the University of Vienna medical school, Jewish, and widely known in Vienna. Perhaps he, or other members of his family, were associated with baptism.

139. Grigg (1973).

140. Heine, quoted by Clark (1980, p. 12).

141. S. Freud (1900, *S.E.*, *4*, p. 195).

142. Schorske (1980, p. 190).

143. Schorske (1980, p. 190).

144. Oehlschlegel (1943).

145. Schorske (1980, p. 187).

146. S. Freud (1900, *S.E.*, *4*, pp. 137 ff., pp. 191 ff.).

147. S. Freud (1900, *S.E.*, *4*, p. 191).

148. S. Freud (1900, *S.E.*, *4*, p. 193).

149. Jones (1955, p. 17).

150. Eisler (1971, p. 259).

151. Jones (1955, p. 17).

152. Schorske (1980, p. 187).

153. S. Freud (1900, *S.E.*, *4*, p. 194, note).

154. S. Freud, quoted by Velikovsky (1941, p. 501); original in S. Freud (1900, *S.E.*, *4*, pp. 229–230).

155. Velikovsky (1941, p. 501).

156. Velikovsky (1941, p. 502).

157. For Paneth's impatience for further advancement, see Schur (1972, p. 157); for Freud's reluctance to give up science and move to the world of "practice" outside of Brücke's research–university world, see Jones (1953, p. 61). There is no evidence that the Jewish Paneth ever converted to Christianity; when he died on January 4, 1890, his death was recognized in the *Israelitische Kultusgemeinde*, Vienna. Baptized Jews were not noted in this source (Swales, personal communication, 1984).

158. Swales (1982a).

159. S. Freud, quoted by Velikovsky (1941, p. 508); original in S. Freud (1900, *S.E.*, *4*, pp. 441–442).

160. Velikovsky (1941, pp. 508–509). "Easter" in original, S. Freud (1900, *S.E.*, *4*, p. 443); Velikovsky incorrectly uses "Passover."

161. Velikovsky (1941, p. 509).

162. S. Freud (1985, p. 268).

163. Grinstein (1980, p. 322).

164. Grinstein (1980, p. 322).

165. Grinstein (1980, p. 325); Falk (1978, pp. 382–383) also supports the Jewish and Christian ambivalence of this dream in a different but closely related interpretation.

166. S. Freud (1900, *S.E.*, *5*, p. 443).

167. Grinstein (1980, pp. 329–330).

168. Grinstein (1980, p. 329) also asserts that Herod Antipas "is the Herod referred to in the Gospels who was responsible for the death of Jesus Christ." Although it is true that Herod had Jesus mocked, he was only reluctantly involved in the condemnation of Jesus to death; see Luke 23.

169. S. Freud (1900, *S.E.*, *4*, pp. 209–210); Velikovsky (1941, pp. 498 ff.).

170. Velikovsky (1941, p. 499).

171. Velikovsky makes this point (1941, p. 500, note).

172. The primary traditional purple or violet days are most of Lent (40 days) and much of Advent (four weeks).

173. S. Freud (1900, *S.E.*, *4*, p. 212).

174. Strachey (Ed.), in S. Freud (1900, *S.E.*, *4*, p. 212, note 1).

175. S. Freud (1900, *S.E.*, *4*, pp. 212–213).

176. For example, see Grinstein (1980).

177. S. Freud (1900, *S.E.*, *4*, p. 206).

178. Strachey (Ed.), in S. Freud (1900, *S.E.*, *4*, p. 206, note 4).

179. Grigg (1973, pp. 112 ff.).

180. Bowlby (1973, e.g., Chs. 1 and 2).

181. S. Freud (1900, *S.E.*, *5*, pp. 452–453); Velikovsky (1941, pp. 505 ff.).

182. S. Freud (1900, *S.E.*, *4*, p. 206).

183. Velikovsky (1941, p. 507).

184. Velikovsky (1941, pp. 506–507).

185. S. Freud (1900, *S.E.*, *5*, p. 453).

186. Velikovsky (1941, p. 507).

187. Velikovsky (1941, p. 506); S. Freud (1900, *S.E.*, *5*, p. 453).

188. Erikson (1954).

189. Erikson (1954, p. 40).

190. Erikson (1954, p. 39).

191. Jones (1955, p. 17).

192. Jones (1955, p. 35).

193. Jones (1955, p. 17).

194. Klein (1981) documents Freud's temptation to assimilate when he was a young man—a tendency discussed by Klein primarily in terms of social and political factors. Falk (1978) does the same more briefly, but he also notes the nanny as a personal and psychological reason for this temptation.

195. S. Freud (1900, *S.E.*, *4*, p. 206).

196. Jones (1953, pp. 59, 295).

197. Jones (1953, p. 101).

198. Jones (1953, pp. 252–256).

199. Roazen (1975, p. 80).

200. S. Freud (1914b, *S.E.*, *14*, pp. 8–9).

201. *Origins*, (p. 247).

202. Examples of Freud quoting from *Huttens* can be found in S. Freud & Jung (1974, p. 202); S. Freud (1909a, *S.E.*, *10*, p. 113).

203. The summary of *Huttens Letzte Tage* is based in large part on the very helpful recent book *Conrad Ferdinand Meyer* by Marianne Buckhard (1978).

204. *Origins* (pp. 256–257).

205. Summaries of Meyer's short novels are based on Williams (1962) and on Meyer (1976).

206. *Origins* (p. 258).

207. *Origins* (p. 255).

208. *Origins* (p. 270).

209. Burkhard (1978, p. 146).

210. Burkhard (1978, p. 146).

211. *Origins* (p. 270).

CHAPTER FOUR

1. The absence of the Devil from the beliefs of the great majority of "liberal" or "enlightenment" Jews such as Jakob Freud has been confirmed by many of my Jewish sources. In particular, it is attested to by Dr. Philip Miller, librarian at the Hebrew Union College, New York.

2. Ellenberger (1970, p. 544); Ostow (1982, p. 6, note).

3. Trachtenberg (1943/1966) shows how the topics of Faust, the Devil, the wandering Jew, sorcery, the Anti-Christ, and so on were all ingredients in a gruesome anti-Semitic interpretation of the Jews that became a significant social force in the later Middle Ages.

4. Bakan inaccurately describes the Devil as "a Christian legendary figure" (1958, p. 181). However, the Devil's existence and character are scriptural in origin, as a consequence central to much of traditional Christian theology. (As examples, see Matthew 4:1–11; Matthew 12:24–29; Mark 8:33; Luke 10:17–20; John 8:44).

5. See Sulloway (1979).

6. Pfrimmer (1982); the humanistic and literary character of Freud and his writing is also a central point of Bettelheim (1982).

7. Papini (1973, p. 100).

8. Breuer & Freud (1893–1895, *S.E.*, 2, p. 160).

9. D. H. Lawrence was the author of *Psychoanalysis and the Unconscious* (1921), in addition to many novels with psychoanalytic overtones; Freud's significance for André Breton's surrealist writing is well known. I suppose that at least since Lionel Trilling (e.g., 1955), the pervasive significance of Freud for literary theory has been quite generally acknowledged. For a good recent example of Freud's impact on literary theory, see Meisel (1981).

10. S. Freud (1925, *S.E.*, 20, p. 72). Elsewhere, Freud explicitly said that he had no talent for natural science; see Jones (1955, p. 397).

11. One writer of some importance to Freud, but not discussed here, is Emile Zola. Freud read Zola's *Germinal* and *La Terre*, and in *The Interpretation of Dreams* he discussed a memory lapse involving these works: He attributed an association to *Germinal* that actually came from *La Terre*. Both works are similar and are "concerned with such themes as primal scene material, violent aggression against the father figure, castration material, etc. . . . aspects of the polymorphous perverse orientation of the child" (Grinstein, 1980, p. 123). That is, they were works of personal biographical significance for Freud, but without any direct

reference to demonic elements. Grinstein's discussion (1980, pp. 111–150) of the personal relevance of these works to Freud's is quite interesting; he even notes (p. 111) that Freud's slip may have been linked through "dandelions" to his screen memory experience.

12. Jones (1953, pp. 174–175). This was an emotion-laden trip, as it was Freud's experience of the "yellow flowers" here in the Alps that triggered his childhood recollection of the meadow scene with its yellow flowers (dandelions) when he was aged three and still in Freiberg. This memory was the source of *Screen Memories*. See Swales (1983b) for the fascinating details of the context of this trip, and for a discussion of the significance of the screen memory with respect to his relationship with Martha at the time.

13. Jones (1953, p. 175).

14. Jones (1953, p. 175). The summary of the novel that follows is taken from a 1920s edition in the original French (Flaubert, 1874/1924).

15. Jones (1953, p. 175).

16. See Buck (1966, p. 53).

17. Eissler (1978, pp. 28–29).

18. Papini (1973, p. 99).

19. See the many references to Faust throughout Freud's books and letters. One example of the influence of Goethe and especially *Faust* was the tribute to Freud that accompanied the Goethe Prize awarded by the city of Frankfurt in 1930; see E. Freud *et al.* (1978, pp. 251, 334). As another example of many, Freud was critical of Breuer because there was "nothing Faustian in his nature" (E. Freud *et al.*, 1978, p. 139).

20. For example, see Kaufmann (1961, pp. 16 ff.); the major earlier Faust works from which Goethe's version was such a moral departure were Spies's *Faustbuch* (1587) and Marlowe's *The Tragicall History of Dr. Faustus* (1604).

21. Gretchen is a nickname for Margaret commonly used in *Faust*.

22. The summary of *Faust* is taken from the translations by Kaufmann (1961) and Macneice (1951).

23. Kaufmann (1961, pp. 119, 121).

24. For example, see J. G. Frazer's *The Golden Bough* (1911/1966, entries in index under *Walpurgisnacht*).

25. For Freud's conflict with Martha's mother and brother, see Jones (1953, pp. 115 ff.); also Eissler (1971, p. 262).

26. *Cocaine Papers by Sigmund Freud* (Byck, 1974) is the first volume to have focused on the presence of this drug in Freud's life.

27. Jones (1953, Ch. 6). For example, Jones doesn't note the *Walpurgisnacht* April 30 date; he also restricts Freud's use of cocaine to a three-year span, without pointing out that Freud was still using it ten years later.

28. See Swales, (1981, 1983c).

29. See Thornton (1983).

30. Byck (1974, p. xii).

31. See S. Freud (1884/1974, pp. 48–73, e.g., p. 58); see also Thornton (1983).

32. Jones (1953, pp. 81, 91); Merck (1884/1974, pp. 78–79).

33. See Jones (1953, pp. 44, 80–81); Bernfeld (1953/1974, pp. 326, 348).

34. See Jones (1953, pp. 90–92); Bernfeld (1953/1974, p. 342).

35. Jones (1953, p. 80).

36. The doctor was A. Erlenmeyer. See Jones (1953, p. 85) for quote; also see S. Freud (1887/1974, p. 172).

37. Jones (1953, pp. 78–79).

38. Eissler (1971, pp. 258–259) calls Freud's ambition "pathological"—at least up to his early 40s.

39. Also see Jones (1953, p. 84).

40. Jones (1953, p. 85).

41. Jones (1953, p. 84).

42. Jones (1953, p. 94).

43. Jones (1953, p. 94).

44. Jones (1953, pp. 86–88); see also Becker (1963/1974).

45. Swales (1983c, p. 6, note); Gillie with Swales (1981); Swales (1984).

46. The first two have been provided by Velikovsky (1941) and Bakan (1958).

47. Byck (1974, p. xii).

48. Faust drinks the potion at the end of the Witch's Kitchen scene (e.g., Kaufmann, 1961, p. 255).

49. Gillie with Swales (1981).

50. Jones (1953, pp. 78, 88); Merck (1884/1974, p. 78).

51. Eissler (1978, p. 110).

52. Goethe (1831/1949, p. 444).

53. Goethe (1831/1949, pp. 488, 542, 638).

54. S. Freud (1917a, *C.P.*, *4*, p. 360).

55. S. Freud (1917a, *C.P.*, *4*, p. 360). Earlier, in the "Rat-Man" case history, Freud noted in a familiar manner how the patient had read and reacted to an incident in *Dichtung und Wahrheit* (S. Freud, 1909b, *C.P.*, *3*, p. 341).

56. S. Freud (1884/1974, p. 50).

57. Eissler (1971, p. 259).

58. Thornton (1983).

59. Thornton (1983, p. ix; also Chs. 2, 8, etc.).

60. It is quite possible that Freud used cocaine in the intervening years between 1887 and 1892, but at present there is no evidence for this, since most of his letters from that period remain to be published.

61. Thornton (1983, p. 243).

62. S. Freud (1985, p. 201).

63. Thornton (1983, p. xi).

64. Thornton (1983, Ch. 15).

65. Thornton (1983, e.g., p. 199).

66. Thornton (1983, pp. 113, 125, 141, 149–150); for examples of Freud's use of cocaine and of his nasal problems, see S. Freud (1985, pp. 106, 126, 127, 132).

67. Thornton (1983, pp. 125–126, 139, 177–178).

68. *Letters* (p. 28).

69. *Letters* (p. 98).

70. *Letters* (p. 4).

71. Thornton (1983, Ch. 8); Sulloway (1979, Ch. 5).

72. *Letters* (p. 368).

73. Unpublished letter, July 12, 1883; cited in E. Freud *et al.* (1978, p. 96).

74. S. Freud (1931, *S.E.*, *21*, p. 259).

75. S. Freud (1899a, *S.E.*, *3*, p. 312).

76. E. Freud *et al.* (1978, pp. 184, 331).

77. The summary of *Paradise Lost* is taken from the Signet Classic edition of the poem (Milton, 1667/1968).

78. Jones (1953, p. 173); the quotation is from *Paradise Lost*, Book I, line 191 (Milton, 1667/1968, p. 52).

79. One might add that Milton's creative life was apparently influenced strongly by a visit to Italy (Rome in particular) during his youth; see Parker (1968, Vol. 1, pp. 169–182) and Freeman & Low (1984, pp. 87–148). Also, Milton wrote *Paradise Lost* after he had become blind (cf. the fates of Oedipus and of Faust).

80. S. Freud (1914a, *S.E.*, *13*, p. 211). One wonders whether Freud ever read Shakespeare's powerful comment about those who get no pleasure from music:

> The man that hath no music in himself,
> Nor is not moved with concord of sweet sounds,
> Is fit for treasons, stratagems, and spoils;
> The motions of his spirit are dull as night,
> And his affections dark as Erebus.
> Let no such man be trusted.
> *The Merchant of Venice*, Act V, scene i, lines 83–88

81. Jones (1953, p. 178).

82. Jones (1953, p. 178).

83. The summary of *Don Giovanni* is taken from the Dover edition (Mozart, 1787/1964).

84. Mozart (1787/1964, p. 64).

85. Jones (1953, p. 188).

86. Jones (1953, p. 184). The summary of the novel that follows is taken from an 1880s edition in the original French (Hugo, 1831/ca. 1885).

87. *Origins* (p. 172).

88. *Letters* (pp. 193, 195, 201).

89. *Letters* (p. 187).

90. Swales (1983c, pp. 9–10); Thornton (1983, p. 202).

91. *Origins* (p. 172, note 1).

92. *Origins* (p. 172).

93. Kaufmann (1961, p. 31).

94. *Origins* (p. 172).

95. Schorske (1980, p. 200).

96. *Origins* (p. 183).

97. *Origins* (p. 187).

98. *Origins* (pp. 188–191).

99. Kramer & Sprenger (1486/1971).

100. Kramer & Sprenger (1486/1971, p. 99).

101. Kramer & Sprenger (1486/1971, p. 126).

NOTES

102. See Freud's remarks on his visit to Charcot (S. Freud, 1886, *S.E.*, *1*, p. 11) and also *Hysteria* (S. Freud, 1888, *S.E.*, *1*, p. 41).

103. *Origins* (pp. 188, 189).

104. *Origins* (p. 189).

105. A few months later, in May 1897, Freud quoted in a short letter (*Origins*, p. 202) a phrase from *Don Giovanni*; the phrase is from a song by Leporello, in which he humorously lists the many conquests of his master. Freud implied that his intellectual accomplishments, as reflected in his bibliography, were like the list of Don Giovanni's sexual seductions. Some weeks later, in June (*Origins*, p. 211), he referred to the Almighty, and then wrote: " . . . I am in a cocoon, and heaven only knows what sort of creature will emerge from it." Then came the letters in which he discovered his nanny and her great importance for him.

106. *Origins* (p. 225).

107. *Origins* (p. 236).

108. *Origins* (p. 237, note).

109. *Origins* (p. 253).

110. *Origins* (p. 258).

111. *Origins* (p. 279–280).

112. *Origins* (p. 286).

113. *The Interpretation of Dreams* actually came out in late 1899, although its copyright date is 1900; Freud's reference to this work as the "Egyptian dream book" (e.g., *Origins*, p. 294) obviously links it with the Egyptian images he pored over in his childhood in the Philippson Bible. Curiously, Freud also expressed reservations about his major work in the same language. In 1925, in *An Autobiographical Study*, Freud describes his disillusionment over an early electrical cure of neuropathology: "[W]hat I had taken for an epitome of exact observations was merely the construction of phantasy. The realization that the work of the greatest name in German neuropathology had no more relation to reality than some 'Egyptian' dreambook, such as is sold in cheap book-shops, was painful . . ." (S. Freud, 1925, *S.E.*, *20*, p. 16). With this language, he provided an unconscious expression of doubts about the validity of his own ideas.

114. *Origins* (p. 314).

115. *Origins* (p. 318–319).

116. *Origins* (p. 323).

117. Gillie with Swales (1982, p. 27); Wittels (1924, p. 100).

CHAPTER FIVE

1. Krüll (1979) appears to have initiated the scholarly investigation of this question about Freud.

2. *Origins* (pp. 219–220).

3. S. Freud (1896a, *S.E.*, *3*; pp. 191–221; first made public in a lecture of May, 28, 1896); see also S. Freud (1896b, 1896c).

4. See the discussion of this issue in Masson (1984, pp. 195–200). In spite of Masson's argument that Freud completely abandoned the seduction theory, the 1916, 1924, and 1925 quotes from Freud (pp. 195–198) make it clear to me

that Freud always maintained a modest but significant belief in real sexual trauma as a cause of neurosis.

5. Masson (1984, e.g., Ch. 4).

6. See, for example, McGrath (1985).

7. Sulloway (1979, pp. 198, 206–208, 313–314, 512–518).

8. Swales (1983c); Thornton (1983).

9. Swales (1983c, e.g., pp. 10–11).

10. Swales (1982b, 1982c).

11. Swales (1982b, p. 6).

12. *Origins* (pp. 187–188); *Letters* (p. 269).

13. See Swales (1982b) for the extensive evidence.

14. For good recent treatments of the great importance of childhood abuse for the development of later psychopathology, see, as examples, Finkelhor (1979); Herman (1981); Miller (1983, 1984).

15. Masson (1984, Ch. 2).

16. Quoted in Blumenthal (1981, p. C5); see also S. Freud (1985, pp. 230–231).

17. S. Freud (1985, p. 264).

18. S. Freud (1985, p. 266).

19. Krüll (1978, 1979); Balmary (1979/1982).

20. Jones (1953, pp. 8–9). With reference to John, Freud wrote: "An intimate friend and a hated enemy have always been indispensible to my emotional life; I have always been able to create them anew, and not infrequently my childish ideal has been so closely approached that friend and enemy have coincided in the same person; but not simultaneously, of course, as was the case in my early childhood." Swales (1982d) gives a striking and detailed analysis of this mixture of hostility and "homosexuality" in Freud's relationship to Fliess. The Schreber "case" (see S. Freud, 1911a), based on the published comments of Dr. Paul Schreber, fits Freud's "homosexual" pattern well. That is, the homosexual relationship was between two "brother"-figures, Schreber and a Dr. Flechsig; the only "father"-figure in the case was God, who was viewed as castrating, not as a homosexual seducer. One curious autobiographical note in this case is that Schreber suffered from two distinct periods of mental crisis and deterioration: The first lasted from the autumn of 1884 to the end of 1885; the second started in October 1893 and lasted till 1895–1900 (S. Freud, 1911a, *C.P.*, *3*, pp. 390–393). These two periods rather closely correspond to Freud's own periods of maximum psychological disturbance. One can assume in this case that Freud identified with Schreber in his Flechsig relationship, on a pattern set up in Freud's early relationship to John and later shown in Freud's relationships with Fleischl, with Fliess (i.e., Flechsig), and also probably with Jung (i.e., John).

21. Krüll (1978; 1979, pp. 144 ff.).

22. *Origins* (p. 220).

23. Grigg (1973, p. 111) has suggested that it was a fantasy.

24. Krüll (1979, p. 146).

25. Ariès (1962, p. 100).

26. Ariès (1962, p. 100).

27. Ariès (1962, p. 102).

28. Ariès (1962, pp. 103–104).

29. S. Freud (1909a, *S.E.*, *10*, p. 23, note 2).

30. For example, see S. Freud & Jung (1974, pp. 33, 82).

31. S. Freud (1899a, *S.E.*, *3*, pp. 303–304).

32. Bernfeld (1946, p. 16).

33. S. Freud (1899a, *S.E.*, *3*, p. 319).

34. S. Freud (1899a, *S.E.*, *3*, p. 322).

35. S. Freud (1896b, *C.P.*, *1*, p. 149).

36. S. Freud (1896c, *C.P.*, *1*, p. 157).

37. S. Freud (1896c, *C.P.*, *1*, pp. 157–158).

38. S. Freud (1896c, *C.P.*, *1*, p. 158).

39. S. Freud (1896c, *C.P.*, *1*, p. 167).

40. S. Freud (1896a, *S.E.*, *3*, pp. 198, 201).

41. S. Freud (1896a, *S.E.*, *3*, p. 203).

42. S. Freud (1896a, *S.E.*, *3*, p. 204).

43. Krüll (1978).

44. *Origins* (pp. 206–207).

45. S. Freud (1900, *S.E.*, *4*, p. 238).

46. *Origins* (p. 207).

47. Letter from Jones dated February 20, 1952, Bernfeld Collection; cited in Swales (1983b, p. 5).

48. Bernfeld to Jones, letter dated February 13, 1952, Bernfeld Collection; cited in Swales (1983b, p. 5).

49. Swales (1983b, e.g., pp. 17–18).

50. Jones (1953, pp. 8–9).

51. Jones (1953, p. 8).

52. Jones (1953, p. 23).

53. Brody (1970).

54. For example, none of the other cases identified by Brody (1970) have any religiously significant elements.

55. S. Freud (1918, *C.P.*, *3*, pp. 473–605).

56. S. Freud (1918, *C.P.*, *3*, p. 481).

57. S. Freud (1918, *C.P.*, *3*, p. 481).

58. Spence (1982).

59. Spence (1982, pp. 117–122).

60. S. Freud (1909b, *C.P.*, *3*, pp. 304–305).

61. S. Freud (1909b, *C.P.*, *3*, p. 299).

62. S. Freud (1909a, *S.E.*, *10*, pp. 5–147).

63. S. Freud (1909a, *S.E.*, *10*, pp. 5–6).

64. S. Freud (1909a, *S.E.*, *10*, p. 23).

65. S. Freud (1919, *C.P.*, *4*, pp. 370, 375, 399).

66. S. Freud (1919, *C.P.*, *4*, p. 377).

67. S. Freud (1919, *C.P.*, *4*, p. 371).

68. S. Freud (1919, *C.P.*, *4*, p. 379).

69. S. Freud (1919, *C.P.*, *4*, p. 384).

70. S. Freud (1919, *C.P.*, *4*, p. 382).

71. S. Freud (1919, *C.P.*, *4*, pp. 396–397).

72. S. Freud (1919, *C.P.*, *4*, p. 397).

73. S. Freud (1919, *C.P.*, *4*, p. 398).

74. The Sand-Man is also reminiscent of the stone Commendatore at the end of *Don Giovanni* and of the glaring *Moses* of Michelangelo (see Figure 3-5).

75. American Psychiatric Association (1980, pp. 312–323); for a discussion of the borderline disorder in particular, see the same source (pp. 321–323).

76. American Psychiatric Association (1980, pp. 257–259).

77. Personal communications (letters) from the following psychiatrists, all with special knowledge of multiple personality disorders; Ralph B. Allison, M.D.; Philip M. Coons, M.D.; Donald W. Schafer, M.D.; Dale P. Svendsen, M.D.

78. Freud proposed in an early paper (1894, *C.P.*, *1*, p. 60) that "it may be taken as generally acknowledged that the syndrome of hysteria . . . justifies the concept of splitting of consciousness." He continued in the same paper to describe splitting as primarily the result of trying to cope with an intolerable sexual idea—usually a sexual memory.

79. Gedo (1968/1976, p. 289); see also Stamm (1969/1979).

80. Sadow *et al.* (1968/1976, pp. 257–285).

81. Gedo (1968/1976, p. 288).

82. This case history, according to Roazen (personal communication, 1985), refers to Mark Brunswick. Regardless, its close similarity to the Wolf-Man case makes it another example of the autobiographical character of the cases Freud tended to concentrate on. For relevant material on Mark and Ruth Brunswick and the Wolf-Man, see Roazen (1975, pp. 420–426).

83. S. Freud (1940, *C.P.*, *5*, p. 373).

84. S. Freud (1940, *C.P.*, *5*, p. 375).

85. S. Freud (1940, *C.P.*, *5*, p. 372).

86. S. Freud (1940, *C.P.*, *5*, p. 373).

87. For Freud's identification with William the Conqueror, see Jones (1957, p. 228).

88. For Garibaldi, see Roazen (1975, pp. 38–39).

89. For Jacob, see *Origins* (pp. 318–319).

90. For Joseph, see Shengold (1961/1979).

91. For Rolland, see Kanzer (1976/1979).

92. See footnote 169; Leonardo da Vinci (with whom it is clear Freud identified) was associated by Freud to the Anti-Christ. This theme is explicit in an historical novel based on Leonardo's life, *The Romance of Leonardo da Vinci* by Merejkowski (1902/1928; available in German translation from the original Russian in 1908 or earlier), which Freud read before writing his essay on Leonardo and cited in the essay several times.

93. *Faust* obviously contains much of Goethe's character; it is a small jump, really, from Goethe's *Faust* to Nietzsche's *Anti-Christ* (1895/1931).

94. Jones (1953, pp. 89–90).

95. See *Origins*, especially the early letters; see also Jones (1953, Ch. 13) and Schur (1966/1979).

96. See *Letters* (pp. 251, 339–340).

97. Jung (1961, p. 156); see the discussion of Freud's tendency to fainting spells in Shengold (1976/1979, pp. 225-228); see also Rosenberg (1978, Part III).

98. American Psychiatric Association (1980, p. 323).

99. American Psychiatric Association (1980, p. 322).

100. American Psychiatric Association (1980, p. 322).

101. Schur (1972, e.g., pp. 40-62, 91, etc.). Schur proposes that Freud had a heart condition combined with nicotine addiction in the 1890s. Cocaine may also have been a contributing factor, since this drug is now known to cause heart attacks.

102. American Psychiatric Association (1980, p. 323).

103. My discussion here owes a great deal to a paper by Rizzuto (1976).

104. Breuer & Freud (1893/1895, *S.E.*, *2*, p. 250).

105. S. Freud (1923b, *C.P.*, *4*, pp. 446-451).

106. See Rizzuto (1976, pp. 168, 169).

107. *Letters* (p. 85).

108. *Letters* (p. 124).

109. S. Freud (1909b, *C.P.*, *3*, p. 383).

110. Shengold (1976/1979, p. 200).

111. For example, see the recent summary of these theories by Greenberg & Mitchell (1983).

112. See Greenberg & Mitchell (1983, Ch. 9). For Mahler, see also Blanck & Blanck (1974, Ch. 4); Mahler (1971); and Mahler, Pine, & Bergman (1975). For Winnicott and for Fairbairn, see Greenberg & Mitchell (1983, Chs. 6 and 7).

113. Kernberg (1975, 1976); see also Greenberg & Mitchell (1983, Ch. 10).

114. See Greenberg & Mitchell (1983, Ch. 5).

115. *Origins* (pp. 188-190).

116. Swales (1982b, 1982c, 1983a).

117. S. Freud (1937a, *S.E.*, *23*, p. 225).

118. S. Freud & Andreas-Salomé (1972, p. 80).

119. Kernberg (1975, p. 30; 1976, p. 150).

120. Kernberg (1975, p. 33).

121. Kernberg (1975, p. 266; 1976, p. 64).

122. S. Freud & Andreas-Salomé (1972, pp. 72, 225). Freud quotes the same line to Jung in a letter (see S. Freud & Jung, 1974, p. 211).

123. Bakan (1958).

124. S. Freud (1923b, *C.P.*, *4*, p. 437). Apropos of this case, Freud also made the interesting comment: "Despite the somatic ideology of the era of 'exact' science, the demonological theory of the dark ages has in the long run justified itself" (S. Freud, 1923b, *C.P.*, *4*, p. 436).

125. S. Freud (1923b, *C.P.*, *4*, pp. 443 ff.).

126. Bakan (1958).

127. S. Freud (1886, *S.E.*, *1*, p. 11; 1888, *S.E.*, *1*, p. 41).

128. Vandendriessche (1965).

129. Vandendriessche (1965, p. 175).

130. Vandendriessche (1965, p. 167).

131. Vandendriessche (1965, pp. 164–167).

132. The other major Freudian analysis of a historical figure is the well-known Schreber case (S. Freud, 1911a, *C.P.*, *3*, 390–466). Here again, the historical evidence has been looked at by others, and Freud has again been found to be in error and to have grossly distorted things through his own preoccupations. See Schatzman (1976) and also Israëls (1981).

133. S. Freud (1923b, *C.P.*, *4*, p. 448).

134. Freud suggested using a needle in 1885 (S. Freud, 1885/1974, p. 109), and denied it in his discussion of the Irma dream (S. Freud, 1900, *S.E.*, *4*, p. 117).

135. The letter is available in Schur's "Day Residues" paper; see Schur (1966/1979).

136. Schur (1966/1979, p. 96).

137. Schur (1966/1979, p. 114).

138. Swales (1982b, p. 9); Masson (1984).

139. Jones also seems to have some intuition of Freud's "pact" when he writes that Freud "was a man possessed by a daemon—a man vouchsafed an overwhelming relevation that took possession of his soul and never let him go."

140. Bakan (1958); see also Kanzer (1961/1979) for a discussion of Freud's frequent "demonic" references to his own psychology.

141. Velikovsky (1941, p. 490).

142. *Letters* (p. 140).

143. *Letters* (p. 141).

144. Jones (1953, p. xii).

145. Jones (1959, Ch. 14).

146. Jones (1959, p. 381).

147. Jones (1959, pp. 383–407).

148. Jones (1957, pp. 391–392).

149. Jones (1957, pp. 391–392).

150. S. Freud, quoted by Jones (1959, p. 383).

151. Jones (1959, p. 383).

152. Schimek (1974, p. 210).

153. Zilboorg (1962).

154. S. Freud (1901, *S.E.*, *6*, pp. 2–4).

155. S. Freud (1901, *S.E.*, *6*, p. 2); Schimek (1974, pp. 211–212).

156. Schimek (1974, pp. 213–214).

157. Schimek (1974, pp. 213–215).

158. Schimek (1974, pp. 222–223).

159. For example, see Schur (1966/1979).

160. *Origins* (p. 220).

161. S. Freud (1898, *S.E.*, *3*, p. 290).

162. S. Freud (1925, *S.E.*, *20*, p. 17).

163. Swales (1985).

164. See Maas (1907, pp. 559–562); Rodriquez & Dyer (1967, pp. 616–618); Boussett (1895/1896); and Miceli (1981).

165. Boussett (1895/1896, Ch. 10).

166. See Lewis & Landis (1957) for the Renan; see Trosman & Simmons (1973) for the Nietzsche.

167. S. Freud (1985, p. 398).
168. Wegner (1962, pp. 15–16, 125).
169. S. Freud (1910a, *S.E.*, *11*, e.g., pp. 81, 122; footnotes, pp. 73, 102, 103, 104, 111).
170. Merejkowski (1902/1928, pp. 112–119).
171. Merejkowski (1902/1928, pp. 13, 19, 32, 38, 61, etc.).
172. Merejkowski (1902/1928, p. 626).
173. Roazen (1975, p. 323).
174. Sachs, quoted by Roazen (1975, p. 323). The cult-like and religious aspects of Freud and his students are also noted by Fromm (1959).
175. S. Freud (1913, *S.E.*, *13*, p. 141).
176. S. Freud (1913, *S.E.*, *13*, p. 142).
177. S. Freud (1913, *S.E.*, *13*, p. 143).
178. Genesis 3:5.
179. John 5:30.
180. Luke 22:42.
181. S. Freud (1913, *S.E.*, *13*, p. 154).
182. John 10:30.
183. S. Freud (1913, *S.E.*, *13*, p. 153).
184. Vitz & Gartner (1984a, 1984b).
185. Swales (1982a).
186. S. Freud, quoted by Bakan (1958, p. 181). Freud's involvement with the demonic, and the opposition of much of his theory to the life and principles of Jesus, combined with the competition of psychoanalytic practice with the Church, show that in some respects psychoanalysis developed as a kind of anti-Christian gnostic cult—a form of religious sect. These religious elements, presented in the guise of a new, emerging science, probably lie behind much of the widespread appeal of Freud's thought to 20th-century intellectuals. As the scientific pretensions of psychoanalysis are removed through criticism (e.g., Grünbaum, 1984), perhaps its pervasive literary and religious character will be more widely understood and publicly acknowledged. Important parts of this religious character are identified by Roazen (1975, e.g., pp. 322–331). For more on Freud's identity as the Devil being tricked into building a church, see Roazen (1975, pp. 327–328).

CHAPTER SIX

1. S. Freud & Pfister (1963).
2. A. Freud, in S. Freud & Pfister (1963, p. 11).
3. S. Freud & Pfister (1963, pp. 90–91).
4. S. Freud & Pfister (1963, p. 16).
5. S. Freud & Pfister (1963, p. 17). Not too long after, Freud gave an interpretation of a patient's dream presented by Pfister in a Protestant religious journal (*Evangelische Freiheit*). The dream was interpreted by Freud as expressing both the dreamer's belief in and doubts about the Immaculate Conception and the Virgin Birth (S. Freud & Pfister (1963, pp. 20–22). I have been unable to obtain Pfister's original paper, but even if (as seems unlikely) the dreamer was a

Catholic, the interpretation by Freud seems more a projection than an appropriate commentary. (Pfister's response to Freud's interpretation is also missing.)

6. S. Freud & Pfister (1963, pp. 21–22). In view of Freud's frequent response to paintings of the Madonna and Child (with or without St. Anne), this comment further suggests that Freud at times identified with Christ.

7. S. Freud & Pfister (1963, p. 24).

8. S. Freud & Pfister (1963, p. 29).

9. S. Freud & Pfister (1963, p. 39).

10. S. Freud & Pfister (1963, p. 48).

11. S. Freud & Pfister (1963, p. 61).

12. S. Freud & Pfister (1963, p. 76).

13. S. Freud & Pfister (1963, p. 97).

14. S. Freud & Pfister (1963, p. 27).

15. S. Freud & Pfister (1963, p. 137).

16. S. Freud & Pfister (1963, p. 74).

17. S. Freud & Pfister (1963, p. 76).

18. S. Freud & Pfister (1963, p. 56).

19. S. Freud & Pfister (1963, p. 75).

20. Kluge (1960, p. 717).

21. S. Freud & Pfister (1963, p. 86).

22. There is also a reference to this sentence early in *Faust*, Part I.

23. S. Freud & Pfister (1963, p. 63).

24. S. Freud & Pfister (1963, p. 63).

25. S. Freud & Pfister (1963, p. 129).

26. S. Freud & Pfister (1963, pp. 109–110).

27. S. Freud & Pfister (1963, p. 110).

28. S. Freud & Pfister (1963, pp. 112–113).

29. S. Freud & Pfister (1963, p. 117).

30. S. Freud & Pfister (1963, p. 122).

31. S. Freud & Pfister (1963, p. 122). For a recent discussion of Pfister's "The Illusion of a Future," see Meissner (1984, pp. 73–103).

32. S. Freud & Pfister (1963, p. 122).

33. S. Freud & Jung (1974, pp. 248–249).

34. S. Freud & Jung (1974, p. 256).

35. S. Freud & Jung (1974, p. 459).

36. Philippians 3:20–21.

37. S. Freud & Jung (1974, p. 395).

38. S. Freud & Jung (1974, p. 19).

39. McGuire (Ed.), in S. Freud & Jung (1974, p. 79).

40. S. Freud (1985, pp. 382, 441, and 461).

41. For the use of crosses on *Walpurgisnacht*, see Frazer (1911/1966, Vol. 1, Part VI, pp. 158–162; Vol. 1, Part VII, pp. 159–160; Vol. 2, Part VIII, p. 74).

42. Strachey (Ed.), in S. Freud (1900, *S.E.*, 4, p. 114).

43. S. Freud & Jung (1974, pp. 88–89).

44. *Letters* (p. 261).

45. *Letters* (p. 267).

46. *Letters* (p. 266).

47. *Letters* (p. 263).

48. S. Freud & Jung (1974, p. 87).

49. McGuire (Ed.), in S. Freud & Jung (1974, pp. 87–88).

50. S. Freud & Jung (1974, p. 88).

51. McGuire (Ed.), in S. Freud & Jung (1974, p. 88, note 5).

52. S. Freud & Jung (1974, pp. 22, 23, 33, 83, 104, 218, 281 [two times], 282, 413, 415 [Freud]; pp. 24, 97, 111, 205, 215, 217, 280 [Jung]).

53. For example, see S. Freud & Jung (1974, p. 205, note 3).

54. S. Freud & Jung (1974, p. 140).

55. S. Freud & Jung (1974, pp. 20, 117).

56. S. Freud & Jung (1974, pp. 317, 508 [Freud]; p. 319 [Jung]).

57. S. Freud & Jung (1974, p. 59).

58. S. Freud & Abraham (1965).

59. S. Freud & Abraham (1965, p. 39).

60. S. Freud & Abraham (1965, p. 177).

61. S. Freud & Abraham (1965, p. 272).

62. S. Freud & Abraham (1965, p. 306).

63. S. Freud & Abraham (1965, p. 353).

64. S. Freud & Abraham (1965, p. 308).

65. S. Freud & Abraham (1965, p. 335).

66. S. Freud & Abraham (1965, p. 239).

67. The information about Heine's *Lazarus* is taken from the poetry and the notes in Heine (1975). Additional information and help in translation were provided by Professor Doris Guilloton.

68. Jones (1953, pp. 100–101).

69. Luke 16:19–31.

70. John 11.

71. In 1923, Heinele, a grandson of Freud, died. The boy had become very dear to Freud, and while the boy was dying Freud wrote to friends that he was not aware of ever having loved anyone so much, especially a child. He went on to say he never had experienced grief as intense as he had at this loss (*Letters*, p. 344). Jones (1967, p. 92) reports that this was the only time Freud was known to have shed tears.

It is not hard to see that Heinele's death at the age of four and a half redintegrated Freud's own psychological loss of his nanny and of Freiberg when he had been a child. Heinele's name was closely connected with Heine, one of the heroes Freud identified with; the boy died at about the same age as Freud had been when his early loss took place. His expression of intense grief was written on June 11, about the same time of year as the dismissal of the nanny and the departure from Freiberg are hypothesized to have happened—that is, around Pentecost, June 12, in 1859. In 1923, Pentecost was on May 20. In the letter Freud notes that the boy had fallen seriously ill some two weeks earlier and that afterwards he realized that the child was lost. Freud's mourning for Heinele was thus going on around Pentecost time in 1923. Freud's sorrow was further reinforced by the fact that it was in the spring of 1923 that he first became aware of his cancer and its probable fatal consequences for him (Jones, 1957, pp. 89–

95). In his response to Heinele, his little alter ego, Freud was mourning his own coming death as well.

72. Spector (1972, p. 27 [Figure 5]).

73. Spector (1972, pp. 27-28).

74. Spector (1972, pp. 27-28).

75. Spector (1972, pp. 27-28).

76. S. Freud (1927b, *S.E.*, *20*, p. 255).

77. Spector (1972, p. 17).

78. Spector (1972, pp. 16-17).

79. *Letters* (p. 371).

80. "I have to fight against the sensation of being a monk in his cell. . . . Strange creatures are billeted in my mind" (*Letters*, p. 68). See also Swales (1983b, pp. 13-14).

81. Jones (1957, p. 381).

82. S. Freud (1930, *S.E.*, *21*, p. 74).

83. S. Freud (1911b, *S.E.*, *12*, pp. 342-344).

84. Spector (1973, p. 66).

85. S. Freud (1911b, *S.E.*, *12*, p. 344).

86. Ellenberger (1970, p. 816).

87. Spector (1972, p. 66).

88. Pfrimmer (1982, pp. 139-141 and Plate XVI).

89. S. Freud (1911b, *S.E.*, *12*, p. 343).

90. S. Freud (1911b, *S.E.*, *12*, p. 344).

91. See Schmöger (1870/1976 [a reprint of the first English edition of 1885], especially the preface and introduction).

92. Emmerich (1833/1970, 1833/1983).

93. S. Freud (1910b, *C.P.*, *2*, p. 293).

94. His comment, however, about such women and their visions has several intellectual weaknesses. The first is that there is no evidence that Freud ever systematically studied the issue in question. He was operating on secondary sources. This time, oddly enough, he referred to "former times," while in the *Diana* article it was in "our own days." The issue of time is not trivial, since, in fact, the 100 years from 1820 to 1917 were probably richer in such historical visions than any other such period. Besides Lateau (ca. 1868) and Emmerich (1818-1824), there was St. Bernadette of Lourdes (1858); seven years *after* Freud's skeptical comment, the most famous visions of all were reported—those of Fatima in 1917. Anyone familiar with these cases will know that police arrests, medical tests, and rejection, hostility, and skepticism from neighbors and especially the Church were common to all.

95. S. Freud (1933, *S.E.*, *22*, p. 152). Freud may have first heard such a remark from Charcot; see Wortis (1954, p. 138).

96. S. Freud & Andreas-Salomé (1972, p. 231).

97. M. Freud (1957, p. 98).

98. Kanzer (1976/1979, p. 288).

99. *Letters* (p. 364).

100. *Letters* (p. 389).

101. *Letters* (p. 393).

102. *Letters* (p. 393).

103. Important aspects of this work for Freud's religious psychology were brought to my attention by Professor Slochower (see Slochower, 1970).

104. S. Freud (1936, *C.P.*, 5, p. 304).

105. S. Freud (1936, *C.P.*, 5, p. 305).

106. S. Freud (1936, *C.P.*, 5, p. 308).

107. For this connection, see also E. Freud *et al.* (1978, p. 171); Pfrimmer (1982, Plate XV, pp. 180–191).

108. S. Freud (1936, *C.P.*, 5, p. 311).

109. S. Freud (1936, *C.P.*, 5, p. 311).

110. Bettelheim (1982, pp. ix, x).

111. The Visitation of the Virgin Mary to her cousin Elizabeth, who was pregnant with John the Baptist, is well known as one of the five joyful mysteries meditated upon when a person is saying the Rosary. One wonders whether Freud's nanny said the Rosary with him or with him listening. The word *heimsucht* is also close to *heim* (home), *heimlich* (secret), and *unheimlich* (uncanny), thus bringing Mary and the Visitation into Freud's important associative complex centered around the uncanny. The interpretation that Freud sometimes identified with Jesus is further strengthened in this instance by the presence of an older "cousin" named John.

112. Jones (1957, pp. 208–209).

113. Schur (1972, p. 470).

114. Schebesta (1954, pp. 89–90); Gusinde (1954, pp. 868–870).

115. Schebesta (1954, pp. 89–90).

116. Gusinde (1954, pp. 868–870).

117. Gusinde (1954, p. 868).

118. See Henninger (1954/1956) for his complete bibliography.

119. Schebesta (1954, p. 90).

120. Schmidt (1933). See also Schmidt (1935a).

121. Schebesta (1954); Gusinde (1954).

122. Schebesta (1954, p. 90).

123. See Schmidt (1935a, pp. 109–115).

124. As far as I can judge, the reasons for the lack of awareness of Schmidt's contribution even today among social scientists are that, first, Schmidt's main writings have not been translated from the German; second, they are very scholarly, especially with respect to his great knowledge of primitive languages; and, finally, he was a Catholic priest who showed how much evidence supports the general picture of religion as portrayed in Genesis. That is, he was saying on the basis of systematic anthropological evidence something that not only Freud but very few social scientists wanted to hear then—or want to hear now.

125. *Letters* (p. 422).

126. Jones (1957, p. 192).

127. Jones (1957, p. 192).

128. Jones (1957, p. 192).

129. Jones (1957, p. 213).

130. Jones (1957, p. 180).

131. Jones (1957, p. 180).

NOTES

132. *Letters* (p. 422).

133. This suggestion has been made by Msgr. William Smith of St. Joseph's Seminary, Dunwoodie, New York (personal communication, 1983). Father Smith is a Catholic priest and theologian knowledgeable about pre-World War II Italy.

134. For all one knows, Mussolini was responsible for banning the journal in the first place. By 1936 he would probably have accepted Hitler's hostile policy with respect to the "Jewish" science of psychoanalysis.

135. Clark (1980, p. 491).

136. Jones (1957, p. 194).

137. Schmidt (1935b). The first edition, published several years earlier, was prior to any obvious Nazi menace. The second edition contains anti-Nazi material in the introduction and throughout the first six chapters.

138. Jones (1957, p. 217).

139. In the *Letters* (p. 445), Freud said June 3; Jones (1957, p. 226) says June 4.

140. Gusinde (1954, p. 868).

141. *Letters* (p. 430).

142. *Letters* (p. 445).

143. Jones (1953, p. 143).

144. Jones (1953, p. 143).

145. *Letters* (pp. 366–367).

146. *Letters* (p. 368).

147. *Letters* (p. 418).

148. *Letters* (p. 445).

149. Jones (1957, p. 245).

150. Jones (1957, p. 245).

151. S. Freud & Zweig (1970, p. 23). Zweig's letter was dated Dec. 2, 1930; Freud's next letter, July 12, 1931, was not a direct response to Zweig. Apparently there were intervening letters.

152. Roazen (1975, p. 527); original in S. Freud (1930, *S.E.*, *21*, p. 102).

153. *Letters* (p. 453).

154. The Jewish Biblical scholar, Abraham Shalom Yahuda, published a review of *Moses and Monotheism*, in which he described Freud's words as those "of one of the most fanatical Christians in his hatred of Israel" (cited in Jones, 1957, p. 370). For intense Jewish hostility to Freud's publishing of *Moses and Monotheism*, see also Clark (1980, pp. 523–524).

155. Jones (1957, p. 193).

156. S. Freud (1939, *S.E.*, *23*, pp. 91–92).

157. Maritain (1939, p. 30).

158. Maritain quoted a then-recent radio broadcast address of Pope Pius XI, commenting on these words of the Mass: "*sacrificium Patriarchae nostri Abrahame*" ("the sacrifice of our father Abraham"). The Pope said: "Notice that Abraham is called our Patriarch, our ancestor. Anti-Semitism is incompatible with the thought and sublime reality expressed in this text. . . . Anti-Semitism is unacceptable. Spiritually we are Semites" (Maritain, 1939, p. 41). Maritain then (1939,

p. 42) went on to discuss Christians who became anti-Semitic. On this, he concluded: "It is no little matter, however, for a Christian to hate or despise or to wish to treat degradingly the race from which sprung his God and the Immaculate Mother of his God. That is why the bitter zeal of anti-Semitism always turns in the end into a bitter zeal against Christianity itself."

159. This sympathy of Freud's for Christianity in the closing passages of *Moses and Monotheism* has already been observed by Roazen (1975) and Bergmann (1976/1982); also see Lifton (1982, p. 152).

160. S. Freud (1939, *S.E.*, 23, p. 136).

161. In many ways, Freud's attitude toward anti-Semitism can be seen as a consequence of his ambivalence toward Christianity—an ambivalence that characterized Heinrich Heine as well. Here is Heine's remarkably prophetic understanding of the effects of the collapse of Christianity on the German people, written in 1834-1835, a full 100 years before the effects of the collapse were obvious:

The German revolution will not prove any milder or gentler because it was preceded by the "Critique" of Kant, by the "Transcendental Idealism" of Fichte, or even by the "philosophy of nature." These doctrines served to develop revolutionary forces that only await their time to break forth and to fill the world with terror and admiration.

. . . The philosopher of nature will be terrible in this, that he has allied himself with the primitive powers of nature, that he can conjure up the demonical forces of the Old German pantheism; and having done so, there is aroused in him that ancient German eagerness for battle which engaged in combat, not for the sake of destroying, not even for the sake of victory, but merely for the sake of the combat itself. Christianity—and this is its fairest merit—subdued to a certain extent the brutal warrior-ardour of the Germans, but it could not entirely quench it, and when the cross, that restraining talisman, falls to pieces, then will break out again the ferocity of the old combatants, the frantic berserker rage, whereof Northern poets have said and sung so much. The Talisman has become rotten, and the day will come when it will pitifully crumble into dust. The old stone gods will then arise from the forgotten ruins and wipe from their eyes the dust of centuries, and Thor with his giant hammer will rise again, and he will shatter the Gothic cathedrals. When ye hear the trampling of feet and the clashing of arms, ye neighbors' children, ye French, be on your guard. . . . German thunder is true German character: it is not very nimble, and rumbles along somewhat slowly. But come it will, and when ye hear a crashing such as never before has been heard in the world's history, then know that at last the German thunderbolt has fallen. (Quoted by H. R. Trevor-Roper in the introduction to Grunfeld, 1979, p. 15).

162. S. Freud (1937b, *C.P.*, 5, pp. 358-371).
163. See, for example, Kanzer & Blum (1967, pp. 117-118).
164. S. Freud (1937b, *C.P.*, 5, p. 358).
165. *Origins* (p. 336).
166. S. Freud (1937b, *C.P.*, 5, p. 359).
167. S. Freud (1937b, *C.P.*, 5, p. 359).
168. S. Freud (1937b, *C.P.*, 5, p. 359).
169. S. Freud & Jung (1974, p. 508).
170. S. Freud (1918, *C.P.*, 3, p. 541).
171. S. Freud & Jung (1974, p. 495).
172. S. Freud (1913, *S.E.*, 13, p. 36).

NOTES

173. S. Freud (1909b, *C.P.*, *3*, p. 368).
174. *Letters* (p. 256).
175. S. Freud (1907, *S.E.*, *9*, pp. 126–127).

CHAPTER SEVEN

1. Schorske (1980, Ch. 3); Klein (1981, Ch. 1).
2. Klein (1981, Ch. 1).
3. Szasz (1978, p. 139).
4. For Adler's becoming a Christian, see Eissler (1971, p. 376); for Freud's "loathing" of Adler, see S. Freud & Andreas-Salomé (1972, p. 19); for Tausk's baptism, see Eissler (1971, p. 68); for Freud's "lack of enthusiasm" for Tausk, see Eissler (1971) and Roazen (1969). In addition to Adler and Tausk, the list of important figures in Freud's life who converted to Christianity includes Heine; Michael Bernays; a medical professor called "B" (see *Letters*, p. 150); Mahler; V. C. Blum, the surgeon who performed the Steinache operation on Freud in 1923; and no doubt others, especially in the university medical world. (The Steinache operation—ligature of the vas deferens on both sides, a kind of "symbolic castration"—was performed on the basis of the hypothesis, now discredited, that it would rejuvenate the patient. For more on Blum and the operation, see Jones, 1957, pp. 98–99, and the detailed discussion in Romm, 1983.)
5. S. Freud & Pfister (1963, p. 117).
6. S. Freud (1927a, *S.E.*, *21*, p. 33).
7. S. Freud (1927a, *S.E.*, *21*, p. 18).
8. Freud here overlooks the belief in God's personal judgment, and the notion of Hell, which are hardly comforting. If one has a conscious or unconscious fear of judgment, then God's nonexistence is exactly how an atheist would want things to be; and, of course, for those who make "Faustian" bargains in their life, the nonexistence of God must be a truly urgent desire.
9. S. Freud (1927a, *S.E.*, *21*, p. 30).
10. S. Freud (1927a, *S.E.*, *21*, p. 31).
11. Feuerbach (1841/1957).
12. Waring (Ed.), in Feuerbach (1841/1957, pp. iii–ix).
13. Trosman (1973/1976, p. 47).
14. Trosman & Simmons (1973) list recently republished German editions of both *The Essence of Christianity* (1923) and *The Essence of Religion* (1923) in Freud's library. The latter was another book by Feuerbach, very similar to the first in its criticism of religion.
15. Feuerbach (1841/1957, p. 11).
16. Feuerbach (1841/1957, p. 23).
17. Feuerbach (1841/1957, p. 33).
18. Breuer & Freud (1893/1895, *S.E.*, *2*, pp. 273–274).
19. Jones (1959, p. 210).
20. S. Freud (1928, *S.E.*, *21*, p. 170).
21. S. Freud & Pfister (1963, p. 122).
22. Brentano was a teacher who had considerable personal impact on many of his students, and he was known as a kind and profoundly moral man. For

example, Brentano was a pacifist who in the early 1900s lived in Italy, but after the outbreak of World War I, he moved to Switzerland as a protest against Italy's participation in the war. See Boring (1950, p. 358).

23. See Grollman (1965, p. 50), who cites Heller (1956, pp. 418–421).

24. See Schorske (1980, p. 200). Freud very probably took his Virgil quotes from the political writer and socialist Lassalle; for example, see Swales (1982a, p. 5).

25. S. Freud (1927a, *S.E.*, *21*, p. 28).

26. S. Freud (1914a, *S.E.*, *13*, p. 211).

27. For example, see *Letters* (p. 389).

28. S. Freud (1935, *S.E.*, *20*, p. 72).

29. S. Freud (1927a, *S.E.*, *21*, p. 18).

30. S. Freud (1927a, *S.E.*, *21*, p. 30).

31. For example, see Jones (1957, p. 194).

32. See Vitz (1980/1982, 1985).

33. Jones (1953, p. 348).

34. Jones (1957, p. 198).

35. See Krüll (1979).

36. S. Freud (1985, p. 264).

37. S. Freud (1985, p. 264). Also, Jakob was called by Freud "one of these perverts"; for example, see the summary of Masson's position in Blumenthal (1981, p. C5).

38. S. Freud (1985, p. 144).

39. S. Freud (1985, p. 238; also pp. 213, 286).

40. Blumenthal (1981, p. C5); Masson (1984, e.g., pp. 114–115).

41. S. Freud (1910a, *S.E.*, *11*, p. 123).

42. For a more extensive development of the ideas in this section, see Vitz & Gartner (1984a, 1984b).

43. S. Freud (1927a, *S.E.*, *21*, p. 31).

44. Freud was often willing to generalize from his own psychology to that of others—sometimes to *all* others, as in the proposed universality of the Oedipus complex. Hence, to generalize from the psychology of Freud's Oedipally based atheism to "many others" is a very modest conclusion, at least in Freudian terms.

BIBLIOGRAPHY

American Psychiatric Association. (1980). *Diagnostic and statistical manual of mental disorders* (3rd ed.). Washington, DC. American Psychiatric Association.

Ariès, P. (1962). *Centuries of childhood: A social history of family life* (R. Baldick, Trans.). New York: Vintage.

Bakan, D. (1958). *Sigmund Freud and the Jewish mystical tradition.* Princeton, NJ: Van Nostrand.

Balmary, M. (1982). *Psychoanalyzing psychoanalysis: Freud and the hidden fault of the father* (N. Lukacher, Trans.). Baltimore: Johns Hopkins University Press. (First published in French, 1979.)

Banks, P., & Mitchell, D. (1980). Gustav Mahler. In S. Sadie (Ed.), *The new Grove dictionary of music and musicians* (Vol. 11). London: Macmillan.

Barclay, J. R. (1960, September 6). *Franz Brentano and Sigmund Freud: An unexplored influence relationship.* Paper presented at the meeting of the American Psychological Association, Chicago.

Becker, H. K. (1974). "Coca Koller." In R. Byck (Ed.), *Cocaine papers by Sigmund Freud.* New York: New American Library (Meridian). (First published, 1963.)

Bergmann, M. S. (1982). Moses and the evolution of Freud's Jewish identity. In M. Ostow (Ed.), *Judaism and psychoanalysis.* New York: KTAV. (First published, 1976.)

Bernays, A. F. (ca. 1935). *Erlebtes.* Vienna: Kommissionsverlag der Buchhandlung Heller.

Bernfeld, S. (1946). An unknown autobiographical fragment of Freud. *American Imago, 4,* 3–19.

Bernfeld, S. (1974). Freud's studies on cocaine. In R. Byck (Ed.), *Cocaine papers by Sigmund Freud.* New York: New American Library (Meridian). First published, 1953.)

Note. *For full bibliographical information on the* Standard Edition *and* Collected Papers *see explanation of abbreviations in Notes section.*

BIBLIOGRAPHY

Bernfeld, S., & Bernfeld, S. C. (1944). Freud's early childhood. *Bulletin of the Menninger Clinic, 8*, 107–113.

Bernfeld, S. C. (1951). Freud and archeology. *American Imago, 8*, 107–128.

Bettelheim, B. (1982). *Freud and man's soul.* New York: Knopf.

Birmingham, S. (1967). *Our crowd: The great Jewish families of New York.* New York: Harper & Row.

Blanck, G., & Blanck, R. (1974). *Ego psychology: Theory and practice.* New York: Columbia University Press.

Blumenthal, R. (1981, August 25). Did Freud's isolation, peer rejection prompt key theory reversal? *New York Times*, pp. C1, C2, C5.

Boring, E. G. (1950). *A history of experimental psychology* (2nd ed.). New York: Appleton-Century-Crofts.

Boussett, W. (1896). *The Anti-Christ legend* (A. H. Keane, Trans.). London: Hutchinson. (First published, 1895.)

Bowlby, J. (1969). *Attachment and loss* (Vol. 1: *Attachment*). New York: Basic Books.

Bowlby, J. (1973). *Attachment and loss* (Vol. 2: *Separation: Anxiety and anger*). New York: Basic Books.

Bowlby, J. (1980). *Attachment and loss* (Vol. 3: *Loss: Sadness and depression*). New York: Basic Books.

Brentano, F. (1966). *The true and the evident* (O. Kraus, Ed.; R. M. Chisholm, English Ed.; R. M. Chisholm, I. Politzer, & K. R. Fisher, Trans.). New York: Humanities Press. (First published, 1930.)

Brentano, F. (1973). *Psychology from an empirical standpoint* (O. Kraus, Ed.; L. McAlister, English Ed.; A. Rancurello, D. B. Terrell, & L. McAlister, Trans.). New York: Humanities Press. (First published, 1874.)

Breuer, J., & Freud, S. (1893–1895). Studies on hysteria. *Standard Edition, 2*, 1–305.

Brody, B. (1970). Freud's case load. *Psychotherapy, 1*, 8–12.

Büchner, L. (1924). *Force and matter* (L. Büchner, Trans.). New York: Eckler. (First published, 1855.)

Buck, S. (1966). *Gustave Flaubert.* New York: Twayne.

Burkhard, M. (1978). *Conrad Ferdinand Meyer.* Boston: Twayne.

Burney, C. (1959). *Present state of music in Germany, the Netherlands and united provinces* (Vol. 1, P. A Scholes, Ed.). London: Oxford University Press. (First published, 1773.)

Byck, R. (Ed.). (1974). *Cocaine papers by Sigmund Freud.* New York: New American Library (Meridian).

Catechism of Christian Doctrine, No. 1. (1977). Rockford, IL: TAN Books. (First published, 1885.)

Chisholm, R. M. (1967). Franz Brentano. In P. Edwards (Ed.), *The encyclopedia of philosophy* (Vol. 1). New York: Macmillan.

Clark, R. W. (1980). *Freud: The man and the cause.* New York: Random House.

Copelston, F. (1965). *A history of philosophy* (Vols. 1–8). Garden City, NY: Doubleday.

Cuddihy, J. M. (1974). *The ordeal of civility.* New York: Basic Books.

DeBeer, G. (1969). *Hannibal: Challenging Rome's supremacy.* New York: Viking.

BIBLIOGRAPHY

Dempsey, P.J.R. (1956). *Freud, psychoanalysis, Catholicism.* Cork, Ireland: Mercier Press.

Drobin, F. A. (1978). *Freud and religion: A psycho-historical view.* Unpublished master's thesis, New York University.

Eissler, K. R. (1971). *Talent and genius: The fictitious case of Tausk contra Freud.* New York: Quadrangle.

Eissler, K. R. (1978). Biographical sketch. In E. Freud, L. Freud, & I. Grubrich-Simities (Eds.), *Sigmund Freud: His life in pictures and words* (C. Trollope, Trans.). New York: Harcourt Brace Jovanovich.

Ellenberger, H. F. (1970). *The discovery of the unconscious.* New York: Basic Books.

Emmerich, A. C. (1970). *The life of the Blessed Virgin Mary* (M. Palairet, Trans.) Rockford, IL: TAN Books. (First published in German, 1833.)

Emmerich, A. C. (1983). *The dolorous passion of Our Lord Jesus Christ.* Rockford, IL: TAN Books. (First published in German, 1833.)

Erikson, Eric. (1954). The dream specimen of psychoanalysis. *Journal of the American Psychoanalytic Association, 2,* 5–56.

Falk, A. (1978). Freud and Herzl. *Contemporary Psychoanalysis, 14,* 357–387.

Fancher, R. E. (1977). Brentano's *Psychology from an empirical standpoint* and Freud's early metapsychology. *Journal of the History of the Behavioral Sciences, 13,* 207–227.

Feuerbach, L. (1957). *The essence of Christianity* (E. G. Waring & F. W. Strothman, Eds.). New York: Ungar. (First published in German, 1841.)

Feuerbach, L. (1967). *Lectures on the essence of religion.* (R. Manheim, Trans.) New York: Harper & Row. (First published in German.)

Finkelhor, D. (1979). *Sexually victimized children.* New York: Free Press.

Flaubert, G. (1924). *La tentation de Saint Antoine.* Paris: L. Conard. (First published, 1874.)

Frazer, J. G. (1966). *The golden bough* (Vols. 1 & 2). London: Macmillan. (First published, 1911.)

Freeman, J. A., & Low, A. (Eds.). (1984). *Urbane Milton: The Latin poetry.* Pittsburgh: University of Pittsburgh Press.

Freud, A. (1980). Letter to the author.

Freud, E., Freud, L., & Grubrich-Simitis, I. (Eds.). (1978). *Sigmund Freud: His life in pictures and words* (C. Trollope, Trans.). New York: Harcourt Brace Jovanovich.

Freud, M. (1957). *Glory reflected: Sigmund Freud—man and father.* London: Angus & Robertson.

Freud, S. (1886). Report of my studies in Paris and Berlin. *Standard Edition, 1,* 3–17.

Freud, S. (1888). Hysteria. *Standard Edition, 1,* 41–57.

Freud, S. (1894). The defence neuro-psychoses. *Collected Papers, 1,* 59–75.

Freud, S. (1896a). The aetiology of hysteria. *Standard Edition, 3,* 191–221.

Freud, S. (1896b). Heredity and the aetiology of the neuroses. *Collected Papers, 1,* 138–154.

Freud, S. (1896c). Further remarks on the defence neuro-psychoses. *Collected Papers, 1,* 155–182.

BIBLIOGRAPHY

Freud, S. (1898). The psychical mechanism of foregetfulness. *Standard Edition*, *3*, 288-297.

Freud, S. (1899a). Screen memories. *Standard Edition*, *3*, 301-322.

Freud, S. (1899b). Über Deckerinnerungen. *Gessamelte Werke*, *1*, 465-488.

Freud, S. (1900). The interpretation of dreams. *Standard Edition*, *4*, 1-338; *5*, 339-621.

Freud, S. (1901). The psychopathology of everyday life. *Standard Edition*, *6*, 1-289.

Freud, S. (1905). Three essays on the theory of sexuality. *Standard Edition*, *7*, 125-243.

Freud, S. (1906). Psycho-analysis and the ascertaining of truth in courts of law. *Standard Edition*, *9*, 103-114.

Freud, S. (1907). Obsessive actions and religious practices. *Standard Edition*, *9*, 116-127.

Freud, S. (1909a). Analysis of a phobia in a five-year-old boy. *Standard Edition*, 10, 5-147.

Freud, S. (1909b). Notes upon a case of obsessional neurosis. *Collected Papers*, *3*, 293-383.

Freud, S. (1910a). Leonardo da Vinci and a memory of his childhood. *Standard Edition*, *11*, 59-137.

Freud, S. (1910b). The future prospects of psycho-analytic therapy. *Collected Papers*, *2*, 285-296.

Freud, S. (1911a). Psycho-analytic notes upon an autobiographical account of a case of paranoia (dementia paranoides). *Collected Papers*, *3*, 390-466.

Freud, S. (1911b). "Great is Diana of the Ephesians." *Standard Edition*, *12*, 342-344.

Freud, S. (1913). Totem and taboo. *Standard Edition*, *13*, 1-161.

Freud, S. (1914a). The *Moses* of Michelangelo. *Standard Edition*, *13*, 211-236.

Freud, S. (1914b). On the history of the psycho-analytic movement. *Standard Edition*, *14*, 3-66.

Freud, S. (1917a). A childhood recollection from *Dichtung und Wahrheit*. *Collected Papers*, *4*, 357-367.

Freud, S. (1917b). Introductory lectures on psycho-analysis. *Standard Edition*, *15*, 3-239; *16*, 243-463.

Freud, S. (1918). From the history of an infantile neurosis. *Collected Papers*, *3*, 473-605.

Freud, S. (1919). The 'uncanny.' *Collected Papers*, *4*, 368-407.

Freud, S. (1923a). The ego and the id. *Standard Edition*, *19*, 3-66.

Freud, S. (1923b). A neurosis of demoniacal possession in the seventeenth century. *Collected Papers*, *4*, 436-472.

Freud, S. (1925). An autobiographical study. *Standard Edition*, *20*, 3-74.

Freud, S. (1926). Inhibitions, symptoms and anxiety. *Standard Edition*, *20*, 77-172.

Freud, S. (1927a). The future of an illusion. *Standard Edition*, *21*, 3-56.

Freud, S. (1927b). Postscript to *The question of analysis*. *Standard Edition*, *20*, 251-258.

Freud, S. (1928). A religious experience. *Standard Edition*, *21*, 168-172.

Freud, S. (1930). Civilization and its discontents. *Standard Edition, 21,* 59–145.

Freud, S. (1931). Letter to the Burgomaster of Příbor. *Standard Edition, 21,* 259.

Freud, S. (1933). New introductory lectures on psycho-analysis. *Standard Edition, 23,* 211–253.

Freud, S. (1935). Postscript to *An autobiographical study. Standard Edition, 20,* 71–74.

Freud, S. (1936). A disturbance of memory on the Acropolis: An open letter to Romain Rolland on the occasion of his seventieth birthday. *Collected Papers, 5,* 302–312.

Freud, S. (1937a). Analysis terminable and interminable. *Standard Edition, 23,* 211–253.

Freud, S. (1937b). Construction in analysis. *Collected Papers, 5,* 358–371.

Freud, S. (1939). Moses and monothesism: Three essays. *Standard Edition, 23,* 3–137.

Freud, S. (1940). Splitting of the ego in the defensive process. *Collected Papers, 5,* 372–375.

Freud, S. (1954). *The origins of psycho-analysis, letters to Wilhelm Fliess, drafts and notes: 1887–1902* (E. Kris, introduction; M. Bonaparte, A. Freud, & E. Kris, Eds.; E. Mosbacher & J. Strachey, Trans.). New York: Basic Books.

Freud, S. (1960). *Letters of Sigmund Freud* (E. L. Freud, Ed.; T. Stern & J. Stern, Trans.). New York: Basic Books.

Freud, S. (1974). Über coca. In R. Byck (Ed.), *Cocaine papers by Sigmund Freud.* New York: New American Library (Meridian). (First published in German, 1884.)

Freud, S. (1974). Addenda to Über coca. In R. Byck (Ed.), *Cocaine papers by Sigmund Freud.* New York: New American Library (Meridian). (First published in German, 1885.)

Freud, S. (1974). Craving for and fear of cocaine. In R. Byck (Ed.), *Cocaine papers by Sigmund Freud.* New York: New American Library (Meridian). (First published in German, 1887.)

Freud, S. (1985). *The complete letters of Sigmund Freud to Wilhelm Fliess, 1887–1904* (J. M. Masson, Ed. and Trans.). Cambridge, MA: Harvard University Press.

Freud, S., & Abraham, K. (1965). *The letters of Sigmund Freud and Karl Abraham, 1907–1926* (H. C. Abraham & E. L. Freud, Eds.; B. Marsh & H. C. Abraham, Trans.). New York: Basic Books.

Freud, S., & Andreas-Salomé, L. (1972). *Sigmund Freud and Lou Andreas-Salomé: Letters* (E. Pfiefer, Ed.; E. & W. Robson-Scott, Trans.). New York: Harcourt Brace Jovanovich.

Freud, S., & Jung, C. G. (1974). *The Freud/Jung Letters* (W. McGuire, Ed.; R. Manheim & R. F. C. Hull, Trans.). Princeton, NJ: Princeton University Press.

Freud, S., & Pfister, O. (1963). *Psychoanalysis and faith: The letters of Sigmund Freud and Oskar Pfister* (H. Meng & E. L. Freud, Eds.; E. Mosbacher, Trans.). New York: Basic Books.

Freud, S., & Zweig, A. (1970). *The letters of Sigmund Freud and Arnold Zweig*

(E. Freud, Ed.; E. & W. Robson-Scott, Trans.). New York: Harcourt Brace Jovanovich.

Fromm, E. (1959). *Sigmund Freud's mission*. New York: Harper.

Gedo, J. (1976). Freud's self-analysis and his scientific ideas. In J. E. Gedo & G. H. Pollock (Eds.), *Freud: The fusion of science and humanism*. New York: International Universities Press. (First published, 1968.)

Gedo, J., & Wolf, E. S. (1976). The "Ich." letters. In J. E. Gedo & G. H. Pollock (Eds.), *Freud: The fusion of science and humanism*. New York: International Universities Press. (First published, 1970.)

Gedo, J., & Wolf, E. S. (1976). Freud's *Novelas Ejemplares*. In J. E. Gedo & G. H. Pollock (Eds.), *Freud: The fusion of science and humanism*. New York: International Universities Press. (First published, 1973.)

Gicklhorn, R. (1969). The Freiberg period of the Freud family. *Journal of History of Medicine, 24*, 37-43.

Gicklhorn, R. (1976). *Sigmund Freud und der Onkeltraum—Dichtung und Wahrheit*. Horn, Austria: Ferdinand Berger.

Gillie, O., with Swales, P. (1981, December 27). Sex and cocaine: Freud's pact with the devil. *Sunday Times, Weekly Review* (London), pp. 33, 35.

Gillie, O., with Swales, P. (1982, January 3). The secret love life of Sigmund Freud. *Sunday Times, Weekly Review* (London), pp. 25, 27.

Goethe, J. W. (1949). *Goethe's autobiography: Poetry and truth from my own life* [German title: *Dichtung und Wahrheit*] (R. O. Moon, Trans.). Washington, DC: Public Affairs Press. (First published in German, 1831.)

Gomperz, H. (1974). *Theodore Gomperz, Ein Gelehrtenleben*. Vienna: Kann.

Graef, H. (1967). Louise Lateau. In *The New Catholic Encyclopedia* (Vol. 8). New York: McGraw-Hill.

Greenberg, J. R., & Mitchell, S. A. (1983). *Object relations in psychoanalytic theory*. Cambridge, MA: Harvard University Press.

Gregory of Tours. (1927). *The history of the Franks*. Oxford: Clarendon Press.

Grigg, K. A. (1973). "All Roads Lead to Rome": The Role of the Nursemaid in Freud's Dreams. *Journal of the American Psychoanalytic Association, 21*, 108-126.

Grinspoon, L. & Bakalar, J. (1976). *Cocaine: A drug and its social evolution*. New York: Basic Books.

Grinstein, A. (1980). *Sigmund Freud's dreams*. New York: International Universities Press.

Grollman, E. A. (1965). *Judaism in Sigmund Freud's world*. New York: Block.

Grünbaum, A. (1984). *The foundations of psychoanalysis*. Berkeley: University of California Press.

Grunfeld, F. V. (1979). *The Hitler file*. New York: Bonanza.

Gusinde, M. (1954). Wilhelm Schmidt, S.V.D., 1868-1954. *American Anthropologist, 56*, 868-870.

Harvey, P. (Ed.). (1967). *Oxford companion to English literature* (4th ed.). Oxford: Clarendon Press.

Heine, H. (1975). *Heinrich Heine: Samtliche Schriften* (Vol. 6, K. Briegleb, Ed.). Munich: Carl Hanser.

BIBLIOGRAPHY

Heller, J. B. (1956). Freud's mother and father, a memoir. *Commentary, 21*, 418–421.

Henninger, J. (1956). *P. Wilhelm Schmidt, S.V.D. 1868–1954: Eine biographische skizze.* Freiberg, Switzerland: Paulusdrukerei. (First published, 1954.)

Herman, J. (1981). *Father/daughter incest.* Cambridge, MA: Harvard University Press.

Holt, R. (in preparation). *Intellectual biography of Sigmund Freud.*

Hugo, V. (ca. 1885). *Notre Dame de Paris.* Paris: Marpon & Flammarion. (First published, 1831.)

Israëls, H. (1981). *Schreber—father and son* (H. S. Lake, Trans.). Amsterdam: Privately printed.

Jones, E. (1953, 1955, 1957). *The life and work of Sigmund Freud* (Vols. 1–3). New York: Basic Books.

Jones, E. (1959). *Free associations: Memories of a psycho-analyst.* New York: Basic Books.

Jung, C. (1961). *Memories, dreams, reflections.* New York: Random House.

Kanzer, M. (1979). Freud and the demon. In M. Kanzer & J. Glenn (Eds.), *Freud and his self-analysis.* New York: Jason Aronson. (First published, 1961.)

Kanzer, M. (1979). Freud and his literary doubles. In M. Kanzer & J. Glenn (Eds.), *Freud and his self-analysis.* New York: Jason Aronson. (First published, 1976.)

Kanzer, M., & Blum, H. P. (1967). Classical psychoanalysis since 1939. In B. B. Wolman (Ed.), *Psychoanalytic techniques.* New York: Basic Books.

Kanzer, M., & Glenn, J. (Eds.). (1979). *Freud and his self-analysis.* New York: Jason Aronson.

Kaufmann, W. (Ed. and Trans.). (1961). *Goethe's* Faust. Garden City, NY: Doubleday.

Kernberg, O. (1975). *Borderline conditions and pathological narcissism.* New York: Jason Aronson.

Kernberg, O. (1976). *Object-relations theory and clinical psychoanalysis.* New York: Jason Aronson.

Kierkegaard, S. (1941). *Fear and trembling* (W. Lowrie, Trans.). Princeton, NJ: Princeton University Press. (First published in Danish, 1843.)

Klein, D. B. (1981). *Jewish origins of the psychoanalytic movement.* New York: Praeger.

Kluge, F. (1960). *Etymologisihes Wörterbuch der Deutschensprache.* Berlin: De Gruyter.

Knoepfmacher, H. (1979). Sigmund Freud in high school. *American Imago, 36*, 287–300.

Kramer, H., & Sprenger, J. (1971). *Malleus maleficarum* (M. Summers, Trans.). New York: Dover. (First published, 1486.)

Kraus, O. (1919). *Franz Brentano: Zur Kenntnis seines Lebens und seiner Lehre* (with C. Stumpf & E. Husserl). Munich: C. H. Beck.

Krüll, M. (1978). Freud's Absage an die Verführungstheorie im Lichte seiner ligenen Familien-dynamik. *Familiendynamik, 3*, 102–129.

Krüll, M. (1979). *Freud und sein Vater*. Munich: C. H. Beck.

Kurth, W. (Ed.) (1963). *The complete woodcuts of Albrecht Dürer*. New York: Dover.

Lawrence, D. H. (1921). *Psychoanalysis and the unconscious*. New York: Seltzer.

Lecky, W. E. H. (1955). *History of the rise and influence of the spirit of rationalism in Europe*. New York: Braziller. (First published, 1865.)

Leppman, W. (1970). Winckelmann. New York: Knopf.

Lewis, N. D. C., & Landis, C. (1957). Freud's library. *Psychoanalytic Review, 44*, 327–354.

Lichtenberg, J. (1978). Freud's *Leonardo*: Psychobiography and autobiography of genius. *Journal of the American Psychoanalytic Association, 28*, 863–880.

Lifton, J. R. (1982). Discussion of Martin S. Bergmann's paper. In M. Ostow (Ed.), *Judaism and psychoanalysis*. New York: KTAV.

Maas, A. J. (1907). Antichrist. In *The Catholic Encyclopedia* (Vol. 1). New York: Appleton.

Machek, V. (1971). *Etymologický Slovník Jazyka Českého*. Prague: Nakladatelství Československé Akademie Věd.

Macneice, L. (Ed. and Trans.). (1951). *Goethe's* Faust, *Parts I and II* (abridged). New York: Oxford University Press.

Mahler, M. (1971). A study of the separation–individuation process and its possible application to borderline phenomena in the psychoanalytic situation. *Psychoanalytic Study of the Child, 26*, 403–424.

Mahler, M., Pine, F., & Bergman, A. (1975). *The psychological birth of the human infant: Symbiosis and individuation*. New York: Basic Books.

Mahony, P. (1977). Towards a formalist approach to dreams. *International Review of Psychoanalysis, 4*, 83–98.

Maritain, J. (1939). *A Christian looks at the Jewish question*. New York: Longmans, Green.

Markham, J. M. (1984, January 23). Young people in East Europe turn increasingly to church. *New York Times*, pp. 1, A4.

Masson, J. M. (1984). *The assault on truth: Freud's suppression of the seduction theory*. (2nd ed.). New York: Viking Penguin.

McGrath, W. J. (1985, April 28). Rescued from his protectors. [Review of *The Complete Letters of Sigmund Freud to Wilhelm Fliess, 1887–1904* (J. M. Masson, Ed. and Trans.).] *New York Times Book Review*, p. 7.

Meisel, P. (Ed.). (1981). *Freud: A collection of critical essays*. Englewood Cliffs, NJ: Prentice-Hall.

Meissner, W. W. (1984). *Psychoanalysis and religious experience*. New Haven, CT: Yale University Press.

Merck, E. (1974). Cocaine and its salts. In R. Byck (Ed.), *Cocaine papers by Sigmund Freud*. New York: New American Library (Meridian). (First published, 1884.)

Merlan, P. (1945). Brentano and Freud. *Journal of the History of Ideas, 6*, 375–377.

Merlan, P. (1949). Brentano and Freud—a sequel. *Journal of the History of Ideas, 10*, 45.

Merejkowski, D. (1928). *The romance of Leonardo da Vinci* (B. G. Guerney,

Trans.). New York: Random House (Modern Library). (First published in Russian, 1902.)

Meyer, C. F. (1976). *The complete narrative prose of Conrad Ferdinand Meyer* (Vols. 1 and 2, G. F. Folkers, D. B. Dickens, & M. W. Sonnenfeld, Trans.). Lewisburg, PA: Bucknell University Press.

Miceli, V. P. (1981). *The antichrist.* West Hanover, MA: Christopher.

Miller, A. (1983). *For your own good: Hidden cruelty in child rearing and the roots of violence.* New York: Farrar, Straus & Giroux.

Miller, A. (1984). *Thou shalt not be aware: Psychoanalysis and society's betrayal of children.* New York: Farrar, Straus & Giroux.

Milton, J. (1968). *Paradise Lost.* In *Paradise Lost and Paradise Regained* (C. Ricks, Ed.). New York: New American Library (Signet Classic). (First published, 1667.)

Mozart, W. A. (1964). *Don Giovanni* (E. H. Bleiler, Trans.). New York: Dover. (First published, 1787.)

Muk, J., Šamánková, E. *et al.* (Eds.). (1985). *ABC of the cultural monuments of Czechoslovakia.* Prague: Panorama.

Nemec, L. (1981). *Our Lady of Hostyn: Queen of the Marian Garden of the Czech, Moravian, Silesian and Slovak madonnas.* Woodside, NY: RCH Press.

Nietzche, F. W. (1931). *Anti-Christ* (H. L. Mencken, Trans.). New York: Knopf. (First published, 1895.)

Oehlschlegel, L. (1943). Regarding Freud's book on "Moses"—a religio-psychoanalytic study. *Psychoanalytic Review, 30,* 67-76.

Ostow, M. (1982). Judaism and psychoanalysis. In M. Ostow (Ed.), *Judaism and psychoanalysis.* New York: KTAV.

Papini, G. (1973). A visit to Freud. In H. Ruitenbeek (Ed.), *Freud as we knew him.* Detroit, MI: Wayne State University Press.

Parker, W. R. (1968). *Milton: A biography* (Vols. 1 & 2). Oxford: Clarendon Press.

Pfrimmer, T. (1982). *Freud, lecteur de la Bible.* Paris: Presses Universitaires de France.

Puglisi, M. (1924). Franz Brentano: A biographical sketch. *American Journal of Psychology, 35,* 414-419.

Rainey, R. M. (1975). *Freud as a student of religion: Perspectives on the background and development of his thought.* Missoula, MT: Scholars Press.

Rancurello, A. C. (1968). *A study of Franz Brentano.* New York: Academic Press.

Rapaport, D. (1967). Paul Schilder's contribution to the theory of the thought process. In *The Collected Papers of David Rapaport* (M. M. Gill, Ed.). New York: Basic Books.

Ratner, H. (1983). Nature, mother and teacher: Her norms. *Listening, 18,* 185-219.

Renan, E. (1899). *Anti-Christ* (W. G. Hutchinson, Trans.). London: Walter Scott. (First published, 1873.)

Ricoeur, P. (1970). *Freud and philosophy.* New Haven, CT: Yale University Press.

Rieff, P. (1979). *Freud: The mind of a moralist* (3rd ed.). Chicago: University of Chicago Press.

BIBLIOGRAPHY

Rieger, F. L. (Ed.). (1867). *Slovník naučný* (Vol. 6). Prague: I. L. Kober.

Rizzuto, A.-M. (1976). Freud, God, the Devil and the theory of object representation. *International Review of Psychoanalysis, 3* 165–180.

Roazen, P. (1969). *Brother animal: The story of Freud and Tausk*. New York: Knopf.

Roazen, P. (1975). *Freud and his followers*. New York: Knopf.

Roazen, P. (1985). *Helene Deutsch: A psychoanalyst's life*. New York: Simon & Schuster.

Robert, M. (1976). *From Oedipus to Moses: Freud's Jewish identity* (R. Mannheim, Trans.). Garden City, NY: Doubleday/Anchor.

Robertson, J. M. (1929). *A history of free thought in the nineteenth century* (Vols. 1 & 2). London: Watts.

Rodriguez, M., & Dyer, G. J. (1967). Antichrist. In *The New Catholic Encyclopedia* (Vol. 1). New York: McGraw-Hill.

Romm, S. (1983). *The unwelcome intruder: Freud's struggle with cancer*. New York: Praeger.

Rosenberg, S. (1978). *Why Freud fainted*. Indianapolis, IN: Bobbs-Merrill.

Rubenstein, R. L. (1968). *The religious imagination*. New York: Bobbs-Merrill.

Rutar, S. (1983). The Czech heaven: A glorious chronicle of Czech lands. In L. Nemec (Ed.), *The Czech national chapel in the national shrine Washington, D.C.* Marceline, MO.: Walsworth.

Sadow, L., Gedo, J. E., Miller, J. A., Pollock, G. H., Sabshin, M., & Schlessinger, N. (1976). The process of hypothesis change in three early psychoanalytic concepts. In J. E. Gedo & G. H. Pollock (Eds.), *Freud: The fusion of science and humanism*. New York: International Universities Press. (First published, 1968.)

Sajner, J. (1968). Sigmund Freud's Beziehungen zu seinem Geburtsort Freiberg (Pribor) und zu Mähren. *Clio Medica, 3*, 167–180.

Schapiro, M. (1956). Leonardo and Freud: An art historical study. *Journal of the History of Ideas, 17*, 147–178.

Schatzman, M. (1976). *Soul murder: Persecution in the family*. Harmondsworth, England: Penguin Books.

Schebesta, P. (1954). Wilhelm Schmidt: 1868–1954. *Man, 54*, 89–90.

Schimek, J. G. (1974). The parapraxis specimen of psychoanalysis. *Psychoanalysis and Contemporary Science, 3*, 210–219.

Schmidt, W. (1933). *The high gods in North America*. Oxford: Clarendon Press.

Schmidt, W. (1935a). *The origin and growth of religion* (2nd ed., H. J. Rose, Trans.). London: Methuen.

Schmidt, W. (1935b). *Rasse und Volk* (2nd ed.). Salzburg: Anton Pustet.

Schmöger, C. E. (1976). *The life of Anne Catherine Emmerich* (Vols. 1 & 2). Rockford, IL: TAN Books. (First published in German, 1870.)

Schnitzler, A. (1970). *My youth in Vienna* (C. Hutter, Trans.). New York: Holt, Rinehart & Winston.

Schorske, C. E. (1980). *Fin-de-siècle Vienna: Politics and culture*. New York: Knopf.

Schur, M. (1972). *Freud: Living and dying*. New York: International Universities Press.

Schur, M. (1979). Some additional "day residues" of "the specimen dream of psychoanalysis." In M. Kanzer & J. Glenn (Eds.), *Freud and his self-analysis*. New York: Jason Aronson. (First published, 1966.)

Sencourt, R. (1971). *T. S. Eliot, a memoir*. New York: Dodd, Mead.

Shengold, L. (1979). Freud and Joseph. In M. Kanzer & J. Glenn (Eds.), *Freud and his self-analysis*. New York: Jason Aronson. (First published, 1961.)

Shengold, L. (1979). The Freud/Jung letters. In M. Kanzer & J. Glenn (Eds.), *Freud and his self-analysis*. New York: Jason Aronson. (First published, 1976.)

Slochower, H. (1970). Freud's déjà vu on the Acropolis: A symbolic relic of "Mater Nuda." *Psychoanalytic Quarterly, 39*, 90–102.

Sophocles. (1939). *Oedipus Rex*. In *The Oedipus Cycle* (D. Fitts & R. Fitzgerald, Trans.). New York: Harcourt, Brace & World.

Spector, J. J. C. (1972). *The aesthetics of Freud*. New York: Praeger.

Spence, D. P. (1982). *Narrative truth and historical truth: Memory and interpretation in psychoanalysis*. New York: Norton.

Srzendnicki, J. (1965). *Franz Brentano's analysis of truth*. The Hague: Martinus Nijoff.

Stamm, J. (1979). The problems of depersonalization in Freud's "Disturbance of memory on the Acropolis." In M. Kanzer & J. Glenn (Eds.), *Freud and his self-analysis*. New York: Jason Aronson. (First published, 1969.)

Stanescu, H. (1971). Young Freud's letters to his Rumanian friend, Silberstein. *Israel Annals of Psychiatry, 9*, 195–207.

Stock, M. (1963). *Freud: A Thomistic appraisal*. Washington, DC: The Thomist Press.

Sullivan, J. J. (1968). Franz Brentano and the problems of intentionality. In B. B. Wolman (Ed.), *Historical roots of contemporary psychology*. New York: Harper & Row.

Sulloway, F. J. (1979). *Freud, bioloigst of the mind: Beyond the psychoanalytic legend*. New York: Basic Books.

Svoboda, C. P. (1967). Franz Brentano. In *The New Catholic Encyclopedia* (Vol. 2). New York: McGraw-Hill.

Swales, P. J. (1981, April 27). *Freud, Faust, and cocaine: New light on the origins of psychoanalysis*. Unpublished lecture, New York University.

Swales, P. J. (1982a). Freud, Minna Bernays, and the conquest of Rome: New light on the origins of psychoanalysis. *New American Review, 1*, 1–23.

Swales, P. J. (1982b). *Freud, Johann Weier, and the status of seduction: The role of the witch in the conception of fantasy*. New York: Privately published paper.

Swales, P. J. (1982c). A fascination with witches: Medieval tales of torture altered the course of psychoanalysis. *The Sciences, 22*, 21–25.

Swales, P. J. (1982d). *Freud, Fliess and fratricide: The role of Fliess in Freud's conception of paranoia*. New York: Privately published paper.

Swales, P. J. (1983a). *Freud, Krafft-Ebing, and the witches: The role of Krafft-Ebing in Freud's flight into fantasy*. New York: Privately published paper.

Swales, P. J. (1983b). *Freud, Martha Bernays, and the language of flowers: Masturbation, cocaine, and the inflation of fantasy*. New York: Privately published paper.

BIBLIOGRAPHY

Swales, P. J. (1983c). *Freud, cocaine, and sexual chemistry: The role of cocaine in Freud's conception of the libido.* New York: Privately published paper.

Swales, P. J. (1983d). *On Freud's origins and infancy.* Unpublished manuscript.

Swales, P. J. (1984). Ce que Freud n'a pas dit. In A. Verdiglione (Ed.), *La sexualité d'ouvient l'Orient? Ou val' Occident?* Paris: Belfond.

Swales, P. J. (1985). Freud, his teacher and the birth of psychoanalysis. In P. E. Stepansky (Ed.), *Freud: Appraisals and re-appraisals—contributions to Freud studies.* Hillsdale, NJ: Analytic Press.

Swales, P. J. (in press). *Wilhelm Fliess: Freud's other.* New York: Random House.

Swan, J. (1974). *Mater* and nannie: Freud's two mothers and the discovery of the Oedipus complex. *American Imago, 31,* 1–64.

Szasz, T. (1978). *The myth of psychotherapy.* Garden City, NY: Doubleday/ Anchor.

Thornton, E. M. (1983). *The Freudian fallacy.* Garden City, NY: Doubleday/ Dial.

Thurston, H., & Attwater, D. (Eds.). (1980). *Butler's lives of the saints* (Vols. 1–4). Westminster, MD: Christian Classics. (Frist published, 1956.)

Trachtenberg, J. (1966). *The devil and the Jews: The medieval conception of the Jew and its relation to modern antisemitism.* New York: Harper & Row. (First published, 1943.)

Trilling, L. (1955). *Freud and the crisis of our culture.* Boston: Beacon Press.

Trosman, H. (1976). Freud's cultural background. In J. E. Gedo & G. H. Pollock (Eds.), *Freud: The fusion of science and humanism.* New York: International Universities Press. (First published, 1973.)

Trosman, H., & Simmons, R. D. (1973). The Freud library. *Journal of the American Psychoanalytic Association, 21,* 646–687.

Vandendriessche, G. (1965). *The parapraxis in the Haizmann case of Sigmund Freud.* Louvain, Belgium: Publications Universitaires.

Van Lier, R. (1983). *The discovery of transference.* Unpublished paper, part of PhD dissertation in preparation, Amsterdam.

Velikovsky, E. (1941). The dreams Freud dreamed. *Psychoanalytic Review, 30,* 487–511.

Vitz, P. C. (1982). A response to Hogan and Schroeder. In E. Wynne (Ed.), *Character policy: An emerging issue.* Washington, DC: University Press of America. (First published, 1980.)

Vitz, P. C. (1983). Sigmund Freud's attraction to Christianity: Biographical evidence. *Psychoanalysis and Contemporary Thought, 6,* 73–183.

Vitz, P. C. (1985). The psychology of atheism. *Truth, 1,* 29–36.

Vitz, P. C., & Gartner, J. (1984a). Christianity and psychoanalysis, Part 1: Jesus as the Anti-Oedipus. *Journal of Psychology and Theology, 12,* 4–14.

Vitz, P. C., & Gartner, J. (1984b). Christianity and psychoanalysis, Part 2: Jesus as transformer of the super-ego. *Journal of Psychology and Theology, 12,* 82–90.

Wegner, W. (1962). *Die Faustdarstellung Vom. 16: Jahrhundert bis zur Gegenwart.* Amsterdam: Erasmus Buchhandlung.

Wittels, F. (1924). *Sigmund Freud: His personality, his teaching and his school* (E. Paul & C. Paul, trans.). New York: Dodd, Mead.

BIBLIOGRAPHY

Williams, W. D. (1962). *The stories of C. F. Meyer*. Oxford: Clarendon Press.
Wortis, J. (1954). *Fragments of an analysis with Freud*. New York: Simon & Schuster.
Zilboorg, G. (1962). *Psychoanalysis and religion*. New York: Farrar, Straus & Cudahy.

INDEX

INDEX

INDEX

INDEX

INDEX

INDEX

INDEX

Pietro, S. (Verona), 77
Pietro in Vincoli (Chapel of St. Peter in Chains), 78, 79
Pine, Fred, 249
Poland, 3, 42, 237
Polybos, 26
Ponte Sant Angelo, 84
Pope, 11, 69, 78, 94, 98
Pope Julius II, 78
Pope Pius XI, 256
Porto Romano, 90
Prague, 72, 83, 85, 125, 226, 231, 235
Prater (Vienna), 230
Project for a Scientific Psychology (Freud), 53
Protestant, 3, 95, 97, 98, 100, 102, 172, 177, 180, 211, 212, 217, 251
Providence, 197
Prussia (Prussian), 236
Psalm 137, 91
Psychoanalysis and the Unconscious (Lawrence), 241
Psychology from an Empirical Standpoint (Brentano), 52, 54
Psychopathology of Everyday Life, The (Freud), 77, 127
Puglisi, Mario, 56, 232, 234
Punic, 83, 84
Purgatorio (Dante), 128
Purim, 32
Puritan, 115
Pygmies, Central African, 198

Q

Quasimodo, 120, 122
Quixote, Don, 47

R

Rainey, Reuben, 32, 226, 230, 234
Rancurello, Anto C., 56, 232, 234
Rank, Otto, 165, 172
Raphael, 65, 67
Rasse und Volk (*Race and People*) (Schmidt), 199
Rat-Man, 140, 147, 243
Ratner, Herbert, 225
Ravenna, 83
Reformation, 97, 100
Remus, 137

Renaissance, 97, 99, 100
Renan, Ernst, 49, 165, 213, 232, 250
Resurrection, 74
Revolt of the Angels, The (Rolland), 194
Richterin, Die (Meyer), 98
Ricoeur, Paul, 32, 53, 230, 233
"Riding to a Chapel" (dream), 88–89
Rieff, Philip, 232
Rieger, F. L., 225
Ritter, Tod and Teufel (Dürer), 98
Rizzuto, Ana-Maria, 249
Roazen, Paul, 2, 50, 60, 166, 202, 223, 228, 229, 235, 240, 248, 251, 257, 258
Robert, Marthe, 224, 230
Robertson, J. M., 232
Rodriguez, M., 250
Rolland Romain, 145, 194, 195, 248
Romance of Leonardo da Vinci, The (Merejkowski), 165, 213, 248
Romanes, George John, 72
Rome (Roman), 46, 54, 62, 69, 72–80, 83–88, 90, 93–95, 97, 98, 100, 116, 123, 125–128, 145, 156, 164, 165, 171, 174, 179, 180, 183, 204–206, 224, 236–238, 244
Romm, Sharon, 258
Romulus, 137
Rosary, 255
Rosenberg, Samuel, 249
Rosh Hashona, 32
Roznau, 5, 6, 224
Rubenstein, R. L., 224
Rubicon, 84
Ruler, 199
Russia (Russian), 18, 38, 138, 248
Rutar, Sidney, 225, 226, 227, 231, 235, 236

S

Sabbath, 11, 59, 64, 108, 193
Sabbatian, 101, 165
Sachs, Hanns, 166, 251
Sadow, Leo, 143, 248
Saint Mark's (in Venice), 76
Saint Peter's (in Rome), 62
Saint Peter's Square, 74
Sajner, Josef, 7, 12, 224, 226, 229
Samánková, Eva, 225, 226
Samuel 2 (OT), 40, 41
Sand-Man, 142, 205, 248
Sand-Man, The, 141

INDEX

Santa Claus, 74
Satan (*see* Devil)
Schafer, Donald W., 248
Schaller, Rev., 231
Schapiro, Meyer, 29, 69, 155, 229, 236
Schatzman, Morton, 250
Schebesta, Paul, 255
Schiller, Friedrich v., 124
Schimek, Jean, 158, 159, 161, 163, 250
Schlomo, 42
Schmidt, Pater (Father) Wilhelm, 197–199, 255
Schmöger, C. E., 254
Schnitzler, Arthur, 145, 230
Schoenberg, Arnold, 214
Schorske, Carl E., 87, 88, 125, 234, 236, 238, 244, 258, 259
Schreber, Daniel Paul, 246, 250
Schubert, Franz Peter, 213
Schur, Max, 7, 57, 197, 224, 225, 226, 230, 234, 236, 239, 249, 250, 255
Scipio (Africanus), 46, 56, 72, 145, 195
Screen Memories (Freud), 133, 136, 138, 226, 242
Scuola San Rocco, 76
Seat of St. Peter, 206
Second Coming, 164
Seder, 32
Semang, 198
Semite(s), 84, 256
Sencourt, Robert, 20, 227
Seville, 118
Shakespeare, William, 77, 78, 107, 115, 189, 244
Sheba, Queen of, 106
Shengold, Leonard, 147, 249
Sie erlischt (Heine), 183
Siena, 89, 90
Sigeric, 42
Sigismund, 42, 44, 231
Sigismund, St., 42, 231
Sigismund I, King, 42, 219
Signorelli, Lucas, 77, 158–162, 164, 184, 189
Silberstein, Edward, 46, 47, 52, 54, 114
Silesia, 76
Simmons, Roger Dennis, 232, 250, 258
Sistine Chapel, 78
Sistine Madonna, The (Raphael), 67, 69
Slavic, 138
Slochower, H., 255
Smetana, Bedrich, 225
Smith, Msgr. William, 256

Sophocles, 115, 229
South Africa, 25, 228
South Seas, 197
Spain (Spanish), 12, 25, 99, 113, 118, 195
Spector, Jack J., 26, 29, 155, 184, 192, 229, 254
Spence, Donald, 139, 144, 247
Sphinx, 106
Spies, J., 242
Splitting of the Ego in the Defensive Process (Freud), 143
Sprenger, James, 244
Srzednicki, Jan, 52, 233
St. Louis (Missouri), 20, 227
Stamm, Julian, 248
Stanescu, Heinz, 232, 233
Stauding (Studenka), 13
Stock, M., 233
Strachey, James, 85, 93, 179, 238, 240, 252
Strauss, David Friedrich, 49, 232
Studies on Hysteria (Breuer and Freud), 96, 104, 146, 211, 245
Stumpf, Carl, 50
Sulloway, Frank, 56, 71, 72, 103, 130, 232, 234, 236, 241, 243, 246
Sunday Child, 175
Svendson, Dale R., 248
Svoboda, C. P., 232, 233
Swales, Peter J., 43, 54, 89, 110, 112, 123, 130, 137, 148, 150, 155, 164, 169, 224–231, 234, 236, 237, 239, 242–247, 250–251, 254, 259
Swan, Jim, 229
Swinburne, Algernon Charles, 91
Switzerland (Swiss), 97, 172, 199, 259
Szasz, Thomas, 208, 258

T

Tabitha, 184, 185
Talisman, 257
Talmud (Talmudic), 35, 212, 230
Tamar, 41
Tausk, Victor, 208, 258
Temple of Minerva, 75
Temptation of St. Anthony, The (Flaubert), 105, 106, 109, 114, 128, 156, 171, 189
Tepe (river), 83
Terre, La (Zola), 241
Thornton, E. M., 110, 113–115, 123, 130, 242–244, 246

INDEX

INDEX